MODERN ISLAM

MODERN ISLAM

The Search for Cultural Identity

•

G. E. VON GRUNEBAUM

VINTAGE BOOKS
A Division of Random House
NEW YORK

To Tessa and Claudia

FIRST VINTAGE EDITION, *March, 1964*

VINTAGE BOOKS

are published by ALFRED A. KNOPF, INC.

and RANDOM HOUSE, INC.

Reprinted by arrangement with the University of California Press. Original publication by the University of California Press under the auspices of The Near Eastern Center, University of California, Los Angeles.

The author is grateful to the University of California Press for permission to quote lines from "In Memoriam" by Giuseppe Ungaretti, translated by Lowry Nelson, Jr., which appeared in *Contemporary Italian Poetry* by C. L. Galino.

MANUFACTURED IN THE UNITED STATES OF AMERICA

Design by Jeanette Young

PREFACE

THE PAPERS brought together in this volume owe their origin to a sustained concern with the structure of the Islamic community and its reaction to the intense contact with the West which, in various forms, has directed its development for the past hundred years. It is the trials as much as, if not more than, the triumphs of each subsequent period which offer a cultural community its chance to realize aspects of its potential which hitherto remained submerged. To uncover such possibilities, tie them to the traditional experience, and attune them to the stimuli, both freeing and threatening, of the West, is the wearisome and intoxicating task of contemporary Islam.

Its pitch cannot be understood unless the peculiar cohesiveness of the Muslim community and the dominant attitudes of the West, itself subject to continuous self-review, are appreciated. The process is most clearly grasped through the self-images that the Muslim peoples have been drawing and redrawing. The better part of the discussion is based on Arabic materials; yet it may be claimed that the attempted characterizations bear on every advanced segment of the Muslim world, and in some respects, on the "developing" nationalities outside Islam as well.

The following chapters have been published previously and appear here by permission of the publishers.

I. "Islam: Its Inherent Power of Expansion and Adaptation," in *City Invincible. A Symposium on Urbanization and Cultural Development in the Ancient Near East, ed.* C. H. Kraeling and R. M. Adams (Chicago: University of Chicago Press, 1960), pp. 437-448.

II. "The Problem of Cultural Influence," in *Charisteria orientalia praecipue ad Persiam pertinentia* (*Rypka Volume*) (Prague: Czechoslovakian Academy of Sciences, 1956), pp. 86-99.

IV. "Von Begriff und Bedeutung eines Kulturklassizismus," in *Klassizismus und Kulturverfall*, ed. G. E. von Grunebaum and W. Hartner (Frankfurt-am-Main: Vittorio Klostermann, 1960), pp. 5-38.

V. "Self-Image and Approach to History," in *Historians of*

the Middle East (University of London, School of Oriental and African Studies, 1962), pp. 457-483.

VI. "Das geistige Problem der Verwestlichung in der Selbstsicht der arabischen Welt," *Saeculum*, X (1959), 289-327.

VII. "Fall and Rise of Islam: A Self-View," in *Studi Orientalistici in onore di Giorgio Levi Della Vida* (Rome: Istituto per l'Oriente, 1956), I, 420-433.

VIII. "Die politische Rolle der Universität im Nahen Osten, am Beispiel Aegyptens beleuchtet," in *Universität und moderne Gesellschaft*, ed. C. D. Harris and M. Horkheimer (Frankfurt-am-Main: Universität Frankfurt a/M, 1959), pp. 88-98.

IX. "Problems of Muslim Nationalism," in *Islam and the West*, ed. R. N. Frye (The Hague: Mouton & Co., 1957), pp. 7-29.

X. "Nationalism and Cultural Trends in the Arab Near East," *Studia Islamica*, XIV (1961), 121-153.

XI. "Acculturation as a Problem in Contemporary Arab Literature," in process of publication in French translation under the title "L'acculturation, thème de la littérature arabe contemporaine," *Diogène* (Paris), no. 39 (1962).

In being republished the papers have undergone certain changes; there have been additions to the text of chapter ii and to the documentation of chapters iv, vi, x, and xi. The translation from the German in chapters vi and viii was undertaken by Mr. D. P. Little, Near Eastern Center, University of California, Los Angeles, to whom I wish to express here again my gratitude. The translation of chapter iv is my own. Chapter iii has benefited from the comments of Professor Bernard Lewis, University of London, some of them too general to allow of specific acknowledgment in the text.

G. E. VON GRUNEBAUM

Near Eastern Center, University of California, Los Angeles
January 1, 1962

I have taken advantage of the present reissue to make a certain number of additions to discussion and documentation. Since the book was first published, Chapter III has appeared in a slightly shorter form in the *Actes of the Colloque sur la sociologie musulmane (11-14 Septembre 1961)*, (Brussels, 1962); pp. 21-71.

Los Angeles, October 19, 1963

CONTENTS

MODERN ISLAM

I

Islam: Its Inherent Power of Expansion and Adaptation

THE SPECTACULAR SUCCESS of the Arab Muslims in establishing an empire by means of a small number of campaigns against the great powers of the day has never ceased to stimulate the wonderment and the admiration of the Muslim world and Western scholarship. The survival of Arab-Muslim dominance, or in fact its solidification after the first three or four generations had passed, does not seem to have impressed the observers as requiring an explanation. It is the causes of the political decay of the caliphate which have attracted attention. And yet, when the history of the Muslim state is compared with that of other empires which before or after the coming of Islam controlled the Middle East, it is the persistence of the Muslim political community and the growth of a Muslim civilizational area expanding in the face of political fragmentation which emerge as phenomena peculiar to the Islamic development and as such call for consideration.

The survival of the Muslim state after the explosive *élan* of the origins had spent itself, confronted as the state was by unsympathetic neighbors, supported by nothing more than a militant minority within its borders, and engaged in a constant struggle against the weaknesses and the inefficiencies of its obsolescent organization, cannot be attributed to the scientific or technological superiority of the rulers. What scientific and technological superiority they came to possess was acquired slowly and painfully after the great battles had been won and the community had demonstrated its staying power. It is open to question whether the Muslims ever actually did surpass the military technology of their permanent enemies, the Byzantines.

It could be argued that the power constellation in the decisive centuries during which the Muslim community took root throughout the Middle East was such that the caliphate was never seriously endangered by an outside government bent on conquest or reconquest. This argument may well be sustained and yet ruled inadequate to account for the stabilization of Muslim unity. For it was not, to point to an obvious contrasting instance, an outside force that shattered the two Mongol empires of the thirteenth/fourteenth and fourteenth/fifteenth centuries; they fell apart for lack of numbers, yes, but mostly for want of a cohesiveness that would have been strong enough to outweigh the disintegrative effect of the higher civilization, of the more complex ideologies of their subjects. The Arab Muslims, on the other hand, used the superior achievements of the conquered to debarbarize and amalgamate the alien culture under their leadership.

With more justice it could be claimed that the Muslim victors did not in fact have to contend with an ideology whose appeal was comparable to that of their own message. Zoroastrianism had passed its missionary phase; though it was the official religion of the Sasanians to the end, it had had to fight formidable opposition in its homeland and was besides too intimately identified with a specific culture area to offer effective resistance to the potential universalism of Islam. Judaism, then as later, seemed to its followers and to the outside world restricted to social groups whose stability, not to speak of their history, would lead to their being considered not merely a community but a people apart. Manicheanism proved attractive to an urban intelligentsia that was irritated by the comparative crudeness of Arab-Muslim thinking and resented the assumption of Arab superiority on which much of the contemporary social and political life was based. But, as in an earlier battle in which dualism had succumbed to monism, Islam pushed Manicheanism aside even more decisively than the Christians had defeated the Gnostic separatists and the Manicheans themselves.

Christianity itself, separated from its intellectual centers by political and, increasingly, by linguistic and cultural boundaries, and divided into competing denominations reflecting competing ethnic and cultural aspirations, was in a sense discredited by the subordinate position of the Christian communities in relation to the Muslim rulers. Though retaining recognition as the theologically strongest and, as a matter of fact, the sole dangerous adversary of the Muslim faith, it had been marked by the Koranic revelation as obsolete while the heart-pieces of its doctrine and the concept of man which this doctrine presupposed had been branded in the Koran as errors and fictions far removed from the message and intentions of Jesus. The shunting off of Christianity into the ghettos of denominational isolation effectively prevented any specifically Christian intellectual movement from taking the lead in the spiritual debates of the Muslim world, and gradually imposed on the Christian communities, in the sphere of cultural creativeness, an unmistakable aura of parochial irrelevancy.

The survival and the consolidation of the rule imposed on vast and highly heterogeneous territories by comparatively small Arab armies are inseparable from the fact that those armies were serving a distinctive ideology. It has often been pointed out, and correctly so, that the overwhelming majority of the conquerors were not primarily actuated by religious zeal, or at least that the bulk of the

Arab soldiery had a very poor idea of the nature of the ideology whose paramountcy they were striving to establish. Their lack of commitment to Islam does not, however, invalidate the fact that this ideology constituted the *raison d'être* of the organization they fought to make powerful, just as indifference and even hostility to the Communist ideology on the part of Chinese or Viet-Minh soldiers will not prevent them, by the very fact that they bear arms in its service, from upholding a government whose *raison d'être* is the Communist ideology. It is true, too, that the conquerors tended to look on Islam as an Arab affair and a justification of Arab privilege; but, although the Arabs have maintained a "special position" within Islam, it is no less true—and is perhaps one of the decisive factors when it comes to accounting for the enduring character of the structure—that there was nothing in the fundamentals of the new religion which militated against its interpretation as a universally valid message which could be accepted by all mankind. An ideology provides the hard shell without which no social body can survive for long; the more complex the social body, and the greater the political strains to which it is exposed, the more clearly the function of the ideology as a primary means of cohesiveness, as the fountainhead of any practical measures to ensure it, emerges. An ideology—articulated as creed, law, rules of social conduct—often outlives the political organization that carried it forward, developed and imposed it. To mention but one example, the customary law, codified as the Yasā, long survived the Mongol empire that put it into practice beyond the area of its origin.

The Muslim elite was in many respects distinguished by its openness to foreign cultural influences. In matters of administration and legal practice the following of foreign, that is to say non-Arab and "non-Muslim," models was unavoidable; their adjustment to the maturing pride and the clarified self-vision of the ruling community was a gradual process. In many instances assimilation by means of Arabization of Byzantine or Sasanian governmental procedures and integration in the Muslim system by superimposition of an Islamic emblem or motto on the traditional techniques (as in the early development of caliphal coinage) were found a sufficient method of appropriation. The omnipresence, in the minds of the spokesmen of the community, of the fundamentals of the ideology and, stronger still, of the need to relate to this ideology the total institutional framework within which the community was to live, resulted early in that peculiar "Islamic" patina which any cultural element, however "un-Islamic" its origin, received upon acceptance into the way of life of the *umma Muḥammadiyya.*

Acceptability of an ideology to diverse groups beyond the circle of adherents, as a response to whose existential needs it came into being, has an intellectual as well as a sociological aspect. The new system must prove itself attractive through the intellectual solutions it proposes and through the social order it seems to presuppose or to demand. (It hardly needs to be stressed that what is here called the intellectual appeal of an ideology is inextricably commingled with its appeal to the emotions.) The fundamentals of the Islamic ideology, as they became accessible to non-Arab peoples, demonstrated precisely this double appeal. The nature of this appeal and therewith the causes of its effectiveness are in large measure open to analysis.

A. L. Kroeber has characterized the Islamic message as a reduction and a simplification of the religious concepts of the contemporary faiths, particularly of Christianity. This judgment has its merits when one adopts an ecumenical approach; viewed from the Arabian standpoint, the preaching of Muḥammad unmistakably marked a step forward toward religious maturity and intellectual sophistication. Yet it remains true that the Koranic revelation concentrates on relatively few motifs, all of them clearly of intense concern to the Middle Eastern populations of the seventh century, both inside and outside the Arabian Peninsula. There is revelation through the Chosen Spokesman—in operational terms, the assurance of unimpeachable authority and the security of direct divine guidance of the community; there are monotheism and the Book.

The acknowledgment of these concepts brought the Arabs onto the level of religious thinking which their future subjects had reached many a century before and without which there would not have existed so much as the possibility of discourse or the enjoyment of intellectual repectability by the conquerors. (It must be realized as well that reliance on revelation and a Book tends everywhere to establish the same methods of argumentation, the same criteria of acceptability, and, incidentally, to say the least, similar theological or epistemological problems—one more factor in creating a climate in which shared assumptions can advance a new message.) A Day of Judgment on which sinners would be relegated to the Fire and the pious admitted to Paradise, coupled with the apprehension of the impending end of the world, had long formed a cluster of motifs of unusual emotional effectiveness.

The discarding of the intricacies of Trinitarianism; the harking back to Docetism which had, among Christian sectarians, often been the recourse of a certain primitive rationalism; the elimination of the idea of original sin and the burden of an inevitable inherited corruption which was yet the faithful's personal responsibility; the more optimistic outlook on human nature as needful of guidance rather than of redemption and hence the discouragement of the more extreme forms of asceticism (which has, however, been overstated by interpreters, both Muslim and Western)[1]—in short, Islam's more realistic but also more vulgar adjustment to the world as it is—assisted in presenting the untutored with a system of beliefs that satisfied his primary religious concerns and relieved him of the typically Christian paradox of being in, but not of, the world and, equally comfortingly, of involvement with doctrinal subtleties which he had only too often come to know through the political consequences of their adoption or rejection. With the different concept of man's condition and of his contractual status relation (*ḥukm*) to the

[1] Cf. the interesting discussion by René Brunel, *Le monachisme errant dans l'Islam: Sīdi Heddi et les Heddāwa* (Paris, 1955), pp. 7-15.

Majesty of the Lord, the mysteries of man's redemption by a suffering God-man, God's son and yet not a second deity, mysteries whose articulation had led astray so many, lost their vital significance; the absoluteness of the divine will —for the Islamic God is first and foremost will, apprehensible through the experience of His Majesty—made obedience the gate to rescue, a gate not too difficult to unlock.

The absence of a clerical hierarchy gave the believer relief from fiscal oppression and a certain social discrimination. Whether or not the Islamic message would have been as attractive without its prestige as the faith of the ruling group is an idle question, for without the military victories of the Arabs the message would hardly have had an opportunity to compete in a sufficiently wide area with the existing religious organizations. In any event, it must be stressed that the Islamic message did contain an overwhelming proportion of those religious motifs that appealed to the religious consciousness of the conquered.

Islam's attitude toward conversion must be considered attractive to the outsider on both the ideological and the sociological plane. Ideologically, Islam discourages compulsory conversion. The appeal it hopes to exercise consists, one might say, in its existence, in the availability of ultimate truth made visible through the life of the community in which it is embodied, and of course—and here the sociological aspect comes to the fore—in the possibility, through conversion, of full participation in the activities of the politically and socially leading group. Islam requires control of the body politic for the Muslims; it does not require bringing every subject of the caliph, every human soul, into the fold, and thus eschews the ambiguous successes of persecution. Conversion is desirable from the religious, but not necessarily from a governmental, point of view. In any event, however, it is made easy. There is no period of preparation through which the candidate to community membership must go, no examination that he must pass. His unilateral testimonial to the truth of the basic verities of monotheism and revelation through the historical person of Muḥammad ibn ʿAbdallāh of Mecca, the last and the most perfect of the prophets, suffices as credential. This commitment, once made in due form, is binding on the declarant and, in contradistinction, for instance, to Christian sentiment, on the receiving community as well. Contact with the Holy Book and systematic instruction in the faith are to follow rather than to precede that commitment to the community. Affiliation with the community is expressed primarily in action—in the common performance of the prescribed practices and in the adoption of a way of life. It is orthopraxy that matters most of all, not orthodoxy.[2] The comparative indifference to purity of doctrine and even to accurate conformance with standard practice has made possible, with relatively little strain, the identification with the community of very disparate social bodies. The acceptance into Islam of an individual or a group on the basis of declared intention to belong constitutes the premise of Islamic inclusiveness and hence its amazing cross-cultural absorptiveness. "The abstractness of the identification renders possible a sense of belonging together among peoples that in their actual mentality and way of life have very little in common, and that, on the strictly cultural plane, may regard each other with contempt or incomprehension; it has, in later times, also kept alive a sense of super-national values and obligations which national loyalties are apt to obliterate." [3]

---

[2] To borrow the terminology of W. C. Smith, *Islam in Modern History* (Princeton, 1957), p. 20.

[3] G. E. von Grunebaum, "Reflections on the Community Aspect of the Muslim Identification," in *Proceedings of the International Islamic Colloquium at Lahore, Pakistan, December 28, 1957, to January 8, 1958.* Ibn al-ᶜArabī (d. 1240) considers Islam as one person and the Muslim as its members. Islam has no reality unless it be through the Muslims, even as man has no reality unless it be through his members and his inner and outer faculties; this unitary and, we may add, nominalistic view of Islam reappears in the writings of the Indian Shāh Walī Allāh (d. 1781). It is implied in the concept of the history of Islam as a single process which is at the basis of Pan-Islamic theory as developed, e.g., by Jamāl ad-Dīn al-Afghānī (d. 1897). Cf. M. Asín Palacios, *El Islam cristianizado* (Madrid, 1931), p. 94;

The simplest and most effective mechanism for sociological integration into the community was, in the early period, the institution of clientship (*walāʾ*). To attain full status, not as a believer before God but as an affiliate of the Muslim community, the convert had to win acceptance as client by an Arab tribe or clan. The *maulà* suffered certain social disabilities, but he retained sufficient freedom of action to feel elevated above his earlier status as a protected outsider. Although the system seemed devised to perpetuate Arab supremacy in the religious community, it proved to non-Arabs that admittance into the community was possible—an admittance the more complete the more the *maulà* steered clear of political ambitions and was satisfied with influence on a more specifically religious level. In retrospect, it is easy to see that the system had to break down when the numbers of converts increased sharply with the consolidation of Muslim power and especially when whole groups transferred their allegiance to the new religion, aiming more or less consciously at eliminating the racism of the social structure of the *umma*.

The success of the non-Arab converts in winning equality or near equality with the Arabs, symbolized by the shift from the "Arab" empire of the Umayyads to the "Persian" empire of the Abbasids (A.D. 750), was to set the precedent and the pattern for the absorption of additional populations into the Muslim fold. This divorce from Arab ethnocentrism represented one decisive step toward the implementation of the implied universalism of the Islamic revelation; divorcing the Muslim institution from the tutelage of the Muslim state or states was the next step. It is not that the community ever relinquished the concept of the identity of the religious and the secular; but, under the leadership of the guardians of religious tradition and the exponents of canon law, the *umma* established a purely religious and later also a cultural identity

---

Aziz Ahmad, "Sayyid Aḥmad K͟hān, Jamāl al-Dīn al-Afg͟hānī and Muslim India," *Studia Islamica*, XIII (1960), 55-78, at p. 70; Aziz Ahmad, "El Islam español y la India musulmana moderna," *Foro Internacional*, I (1961), 560-570, at p. 563.

which made its spiritual development, internal continuity, and sense of cohesion very nearly independent of the transitory territorial states under whose rule the sectional communities were to find themselves. Not infrequently, a state advanced the domain of Islam into as yet unbelieving lands; but conversion, although often achieved initially by military pressure, meant affiliation with the timeless far-flung *umma*, of which the particular body politic whose subjects the converts were to become was nothing but an accidentally delimited segment whose existence per se was relevant for the community at large only insofar as it enabled the faithful under its sway to lead the correct life, to safeguard and perhaps to expand the boundaries of the autonomous *umma*.

With the development of Persian as the second culture language in the tenth to the twelfth centuries, the community's catholicity was further strengthened, even though Arabic—the language of revelation and later of its exposition and its unfolding into law and theology—not only maintained a position of prestige but also fulfilled the function of a link, a means of communication, a repository of the traditions and the memories which the community accepted as their shared past. So it could truly be said that "knowledge of Arabic is religion," [4] and it becomes under-

---

[4] Cf., e.g., A. S. Tritton, *Materials on Muslim Education in the Middle Ages* (London, 1957), p. 131 n. 2. Hence experiences like that of the French humanist, Guillaume Postel, who reports of his journey to the Near East (1536-1537) that in Constantinople he wanted to learn Arabic but found it very difficult to obtain a teacher, because "there are few Turks who are able, and fewer still who are willing, to teach, as though they considered Christians profane and unworthy of their language" (quoted from Postel's letter of 1562 to Emperor Ferdinand, in W. J. Bouwsma, *Concordia Mundi: The Career and Thought of Guillaume Postel* (1510-1581) [Cambridge, Mass., 1957], p. 6). As in a nutshell the increasing credulity and the craving for the miraculous, together with the not too effective resistance of the theologians, may be perceived in the *fatwà* in which Ibn Taimiyya (d. 1328) rejects the wondrous deeds which the pious ascribed to ʿAlī as inventions (*Majmūʿat fatāwī* [Cairo, 1326/1907-1329/1910], I, 310-311, no. 227). The competition among

standable that a certain uneasiness persisted as to whether or not a non-Arab *dhimmī* should be taught the holy language and whether or not a *dhimmī* born to Arabic should be permitted to teach his mother tongue.

The gradual drifting away of canon law from operational effectiveness, its character as a moral code, a *Pflichtenlehre* (rather than a regulatory code of community relations), called forth by and calling forth the growing encroachment of local custom and governmental decree as directives in most areas of practical living, again fortified the catholicity of the Muslim institution. It did so in two complementary ways. On the one hand, it facilitated the integration into the community of as yet alien communities by allowing them to carry over into their existence as Muslims much of their traditional way of life; on the other hand, it provided the community with a norm that was all the more readily acceptable because to a large extent there was no insistence on full compliance. So the canon law became one of the strongest cementing factors among disparate communities which continued much of their customary law. At the same time, however, the sense of unity which permeated the *umma* and was sufficiently intense to submerge vast ethnic and cultural differences on the level of the ideal, and was thus an indispensable basis of expansion, required a certain disregard of the realities of life, and, psychologically speaking, an existence on two levels, an existence in a tension that, never completely to be relieved, is still an important element in the inner unrest besetting the crucial parts of the Muslim world.

The ability to absorb alien communities into the *umma* without loss of identity is but the counterpart, as it were, of the ability of functional adaptation of religious belief to

---

different Muslim lands in regard to their religious rank and the function of the *ʿālim* in stressing the basic equality of the community everywhere is reflected in *fatwà* no. 228 (*ibid.*, I, 331) in which Ibn Taimiyya tries to dispel the notion of his Syrian questioners that divine blessing (*baraka*) consists of seventy-one parts, of which only one has been placed in Iraq and the remaining seventy have been placed in Syria.

changing existential needs within the *umma*. This ability, which alone enables a widespread and both ethnically and socially heterogeneous community to outlast historical change, Islam and especially Sunnite Islam have shown to a remarkable degree. That some of the modifications appear not only to the outside observer but to many a learned believer as an abandonment, perhaps even a betrayal, of the blessed origins and the genuine message is only natural. The decisive factor in successful adaptation is, however, not the accuracy of the objective and, so to speak, scholarly terms in which an attempted reinterpretation renders the meaning of founder and sacred text, but the conviction it is able to generate in the minds and the hearts of contemporary believers that it answers to their needs as would the Founder's words were he still in their midst. The maintenance of a sense of community continuity and of undisturbed relatedness to the same authority *in spiritualibus* is in itself a powerful remedy of collective psychological disturbance, for it offers perspective and precedent and through them the guidance of an explanation and a direction regardless of the distortion that the memory of the group may wreak on its past.

The principal means of adapting the changing existential needs to which Islam, like other faiths, has resorted is the integration into "orthodox" belief of religious motifs that the original message had rejected or left to one side. Shiism (which became definitely sectarian only in some of its more "extremist" versions and precisely because of "exaggerated" recourse to the motif) almost immediately reactivated the motif of the God-man, of the leader from the Prophet's line who differed in substance from the rest of mankind and continued that direct contact with Divinity which orthodoxy asserted had ended with Muḥammad's death. The Islamic message was most anxious to reserve creativeness and mastery over nature to God alone; when miracles did occur, they were done by permission or at the behest of the Lord in order to advance his plans for mankind. But no man, however pious and however great, had of himself the power to work miracles; and the reverencing of human beings, which could only too easily shade off into worship of the creature, was both blasphemous and absurd. The Prophet himself was careful to insist on his humanity. But the traditions and the needs of the converts throughout the Middle East demanded otherwise. And after a prolonged theological battle, in which the principal issue would seem to have been to preserve the superiority of the prophetic office over that of the saint, and the secondary, to avoid an imitation of non-Islamic custom, the consensus of the learned yielded to the yearnings of the untaught. Not only was sainthood admitted into Islam, but much thought was subsequently given to its characteristics and to the modality of its operation through a hierarchy of elect. Not only was the extrahuman uniqueness of the Prophet accepted, but he was allowed to become the emotional center of worship.

Only once, perhaps, was Sunnite Islam faced with a serious threat of disintegration from within (in conjunction with the political threat of Shiite domination of the *umma Muḥammadiyya*). That was in the eleventh century, when Sunnite theology was put on the defensive, and indifference and a certain disillusionment with Sunnite religiosity were spreading among the masses. It is quite possible that without the political support extended to the Sunnite caliphate by the Seljuq Turks, internal reform would have had no chance to succeed. At any rate, the orthodox leadership was ready to accept a far-reaching reorientation which secured to mystical piety an increasingly dominant place in the religious life of the community and laid the groundwork for the growth of those religious brotherhoods that were to become the true center and repository of the "living" faith throughout the domain of Islam. To accept the piety of the people and its antirational premises and expectations meant, in the long run, a lowering of the theological level and a withdrawal from those philosophical and scientific pursuits that had been one of the glories of the community. The retrenchment of "official learning" to essentially the Koran, tradition, and the law represents another concession to the needs of the times, which may be interpreted as complementary to the emotional surrender to the more popular currents of piety. It was also in tune with the sentiment that people and times inevitably decline, a process to be reversed only at the onset of the "end time." [5]

Acceptance of a mystical religiosity did not mean removal of conflicts between the representatives of Islam as a religion of legal and theological learning and the representatives of Islam as a means for guiding souls toward the unitary experience, between the *ᶜulamāʾ* and the *mashāʾikh* of the *ṭarīqāt*. Nor did it bridge the chasm between the religious ideas and the mores of rustic and peripheral groups and the norms upheld by the learned who obtained their education overwhelmingly in urban centers. The problem of the admissibility of the untutored marginal populations (which were, as in the instance of the Berbers of southern Morocco, both numerous and politically of great moment) to full Islamic status, so to speak, was common to most parts of the Islamic world, as was the function of saints and brotherhoods in mediating between the conflicting concepts of what constitutes Islam and hence in safeguarding the catholicity of Sunnism. One may perhaps go so far as to say that the ubiquitousness of the contrasts between the Islam of the common man and the Islam of the elite constituted a unifying link among the several Muslim communities, because it created comparable conditions and a kindred outlook among the recognized spokesmen of the *umma* in widely separated lands.

The law itself, however, contains what in theory at least must be considered the most potent means of self-adaptation, by recognizing the consensus of the competent as

---

[5] Cf. Ibn al-ᶜImād, *Shadharāt al-dhahab* (Cairo, 1350/1931-1351/1932), V, 144; Tritton, *op. cit.*, pp. 114, 188. The outlook is typified in the remark of ᶜUmar ibn Khalda, judge in Medina (82-87/701-706): "I still knew people who acted and did not talk whereas nowadays people talk and do not act" (cf. Wakīᶜ [d. 918], *Akhbār al-Quḍāt*, ed. ᶜA. M. al-Marāghī [Cairo, 1366/1947], I, 132).

one of its foundations. This *ijmāʿ* of the local learned is neither postulative nor normative; it is merely verifying, taking note that an agreement on a certain point actually does exist and by doing so making the material content of the agreement binding on the community. It is true that the *ijmāʿ* has assumed a self-limiting character in that the creative initiative of the jurisprudent has increasingly been viewed as restricted by the previously accepted opinions of the leading authority of the school or *madhhab* with which he is identified. Yet to make the *ijmāʿ* an active instrument of adjustment or even a tool of planned change, nothing is needed but a shift in public opinion sufficiently marked to compel its formal recognition by the learned in terms of a restatement of the nature of the consensus (which, were it to come, would unquestionably be experienced and presented as the discovery of its true and original character).

A community's law is, in the last analysis, precisely as elastic and as adaptive as the community would have it, and its criteria of admission are as catholic or exclusive as its identification implies. In Sunnite Islam, the community at large has, for many a century, been more cautious in putting the dissenter (who in the Muslin environment is often more significantly recognized by his practice than by his creed) outside the pale than the lawyer-theologians who act as its spokesmen and, in a sense, its executives. In the general consciousness, the intention to be and to remain a Muslim counts for more than the failings that are observable in its implementation. The concern for the grandeur of Islam, which is inseparable from its unity, overrides the concern for uniformity in detail of practice and doctrine. The adaptability of Islam to changing and especially to "moral" conditions has become a prominent element in the believers' outlook on their faith and a painful problem to those Muslims who are troubled by the actual history of their community since the high Middle Ages. To some extent it can be held that the belief in the adaptability of the community guarantees this adaptability even though the "natural" tendency in a community as tradition-conscious as the Islamic is toward limiting the actual adjustment to the ineluctable minimum. Here, as everywhere in societal life, the primacy of the collective aspiration must be realized and, with it, the superiority of a religious culture to a merely ethnic or political affiliation as the foundation of a social structure which is capable of expansion and of continued existence in history.[6]

[6] Extent and limitation of the adaptability of Islam to a basically alien setting are well set forth by R. Jaulin, "Sur l'Islam noir," *La Table Ronde,* no. 126 (June, 1958), pp. 102-111; cf. esp. the table, pp. 108-109, where the irreducible elements in the Muslim and the African structure are confronted with those amenable to fusion or adjustment. J. Henniger, "Über den Beitrag der Laien bei der Ausbreitung des Islams," in *Das Laienapostolat in den Missionen. Festschrift J. Beckmann* (Schöneck-Beckenried, 1961), pp. 345-371, notes on page 365, with special reference to Indonesia, the profound identification with Islam of the superficially converted.

II

The Problem of Cultural Influence

I

FOR THE PURPOSES of this investigation culture may be described as a "closed" system of questions and answers concerning the universe and man's behavior in it which has been accepted as authoritative by a human society. A scale of values decides the relative position and importance of the individual "questions and answers." In other words, it is a value judgment that will convey coherence to, and regulate interaction of, the various "answers" that are accepted by the particular culture and by which the lives of individual and group are lived. To describe culture as a "closed" system does not, of course, imply limitation in the number of admissible questions; the term merely suggests that those questions reach out into every section of the universe which, at any given moment, is relevant to the experience of the community. By the same token the answers, especially those that appear as rules of conduct, will have to cover virtually every contingency arising in the life of the community.

As the experience of the community changes, the power to formulate and answer new questions in terms of the traditional values and the decisions previously arrived at will indicate a culture's ability to continue. Once internal or external experience creates intellectual, emotional, or organizational needs that cannot be met by the insights or the hypotheses evolved within the particular closed system, this system, its basic values as well as its doctrinal, ethical, artistic, and intellectual solutions, will command less and less unquestioning adherence. The door will be opened for its transformation, or even displacement.

This transformation may be brought about by acceptance of a new aspiration (and the value scale it implies) which is developed within the community itself. More typically, perhaps, it will begin within a group that is somewhat marginal but by no means alien to the community before the transformation sets in and which assumes a central position in the community by virtue of the very transformation that it induced. In both these situations the change will be felt to be orthogenetic, that is, a legitimate growth from native presuppositions.

On the other hand, change and, in more extreme instances, actual transformation of culture may be stimulated (or imposed) from the outside. The change will be ascribable to foreign influence and therefore heterogenetic. It is a characteristic tendency on the part of a receiving community to interpret heterogenetic change (usually experienced as achievement or advance) as orthogenetic. As a rule, the psychological difficulties inherent in the acceptance of change are lessened the more readily such change is understood as orthogenetic. Consequently, a borrowed element may be said to be most securely assimilated when its foreign origin is no longer remembered (or when, at least, it has in some other way become a matter of pride).

Although no exclusively heterogenetic or orthogenetic change is likely to occur in the complex cultural situations we meet in historical civilizations, the difference between a predominantly orthogenetic and a predominantly heterogenetic transformation can hardly be missed. The complexity of civilization, itself the result of previous changes, facilitates further, and especially orthogenetic, change which may consist in a shift of the relative position of the several coexisting but genetically not contemporary layers of a given cultural order. One of those layers may ultimately be eliminated except for "survivals," elements that continue to be adhered to but no longer can be accounted for in terms of the prevailing "system."

In this context, then, "influence" is noted when (*a*) a solution to a cultural problem, (*b*) a problem, or (*c*) both are introduced from outside into a system to which problem and/or solution are not germane. Foreign influence does not, of course, necessarily include, but is apt to provoke or speed, that change in basic values which is transformation.[1]

The rise of Islam with its transformation of contemporary Arab civilization would seem to offer a striking example of the predominantly orthogenetic transformation; the Westernization of Islamic civilization in the last 150 years offers an equally striking example of the predominantly heterogenetic transformation. The Hellenization of Islamic thinking in the ninth and tenth centuries A.D., which neither intended nor resulted in a full transformation of Islamic thought, may allow an operational analysis of influence with a view to establishing a criterion enabling us to measure the depth of influence sustained.

II

The power of a religious movement to effect a transformation of culture is due to its tendency to revise and even to

[1] Cf., for part of the argument, my *Islam: Essays in the Nature and Growth of a Cultural Tradition* (2d ed.; London, 1961), pp. 243-244. The happy formulation by the Senegalese Muslim, Cheikh Hamidou Kane, *L'aventure ambiguë* (Paris, 1961), p. 88, of civilization as "une architecture de réponses" deserves mention. Legitimate use of the word "influence" has also been argued in cases where an outside impulse affects the intensity, or the quality, of the manifestation of an essentially native trait.

replace the basic value judgments that constitute the organizing principle of the cultural system which the new religious aspiration endeavors to conquer, whereas almost any other set of newly introduced ideas will, by definition, remain limited to a restricted field, such as politics, the arts, or economics.

In the rise of Islam from Arab paganism, primarily these three value changes were introduced into contemporary culture:

1) The goal of life is seen to be otherworldly. Life in this world is no longer any more than an opportunity to gain access to Paradise. Any worldly achievement remains valuable only inasmuch as it will be subservient to the organizational structure of the new life.

2) As the whole of a man's life is to be examined on Judgment Day, the relevance of every individual act increases substantially. The heathen Arab appears to have viewed life as a series of more or less disconnected episodes, with blank spaces between the high points. The new faith not only insists on legal and moral individuation by stressing man's personal responsibility to his Creator; it conceives of man's existence here and hereafter as an indivisible unit.

3) Although Islam emphasizes personal over collective responsibility, it makes the community the guardian of the road to salvation. By accentuating the indispensability of the community to the fulfillment of some of the minimum obligations of the individual Muslim, Islam lays stress on political organization. The pagan Arab thought in terms of clans and tribes, with the ephemeral confederation of tribal units the most ambitious political configuration. The Muslim thinks in terms of a state, coextensive with the area of the faith, and therefore ultimately destined to dominate the world. Mankind no longer divides into members of different tribes; it splits into believers and unbelievers and this cleavage is to continue beyond the grave.

By imposing these basic value judgments Islam (A) introduced at least three new fundamental questions:

1) *How to live correctly.* The pagan Arab had to con-

form to a social code that included regulation of his relations to a number of divinities, but problems of religious or ceremonial etiquette were of very minor concern. It was only through Islam that the problem arose as to which one of two or more possible ways of performing an erstwhile irrelevant (routine) action was more pleasing, or possibly the only one acceptable, in the eyes of the Lord. Thus the level of consciousness on which life was being lived was raised considerably. Altogether, correctness as a norm deriving from an extrahuman power and therefore as an absolute was a new psychological concept to adjust one's existence to.

2) *How to think correctly.* The pagan's conclusions on transcendental problems did not affect his metaphysical standing. For the Muslim, on the other hand, the correct understanding of the tenets of his faith became essential. Islam compelled the Arabs to widen their intellectual range: it unlocked the world of metaphysics and it confronted the faithful with questions regarding the nature of God, the universe, and man, the rules governing man's relations to the supernatural and the like, all of which had become relevant only in the framework of the new religion.

3) *How to organize correctly.* The limited success of the few pre-Islamic attempts at establishing a major state in Arabia would seem to have been due to the lack of devotion, on the part of the proposed state, to any purpose of an order higher than expediency. On the other hand, the community of the believers, or rather the new faith itself, could survive only if protected by a body politic erected in its name and destined to defend and spread its message. Its constitution had to implement the precepts of the faith, to guarantee their punctual performance; its policy had to be formulated in terms of religious considerations.

In virtue of its value judgments, however, Islam also (B) indicated novel solutions for at least three recognized problems:

1) *The correct education of the individual.* To make a man a useful member of the Muslim community required more than the physical and soldierly training the pagan

Arab was accustomed to. Membership in the Muslim commonwealth required knowledge: knowledge of the revelation, the impositions of the law, and to some extent of the method by which authoritative decisions could be reached from the Koran and sacred precedent. Ideally, each Muslim was to be equipped to be a defender as well as a missionary of the faith.

2) *The relative rating of human activities.* With the establishment of the Muslim community the mere warrior ceases to be the ideal type. The fighter for the faith ranks high, but does not for his religious prowess become the leader. Islam is city-centered, the merchant the representative profession. The pen holds precedence over the sword, the scholar over the soldier, the merchant over the peasant. The religious athlete, who lives almost exclusively for his devotional duties, becomes an accepted type. Only under Islam does the introvert find a place in society; only in Islam is the thinker felt to be closer to God than the doer. The aimless virtues of the pagan chieftain survive but have to be atoned for by deference to the learned and the saintly.

3) *The purpose and scope of political power.* To the pagan Arab power is an end in itself and is subject only to practical limitations. One might almost go so far as to say that in the times before Islam no ruler could properly be spoken of as good or bad, for there was no standard by which to judge either his ends or his means. The Muslim ruler, on the other hand, finds himself hemmed in by the purpose of his appointment, which is the protection of the faith and the faithful. His power is solely executive. He has no right to legislate. He administers a sacred law in whose interpretation he has no part. In the interest of the community the Muslims are urged to obey the unjust ruler; but he will stand condemned by his own acts.

In consequence of the changes outlined under (A) and (B), Islam (C):

1) *Imposes new, or modifies old, duties and confers new rights on the individual.* In contrast to heathenism, Islam affected the believer's life at every hour. While establish-

ing for him a claim to Paradise, it made the validity of his claim contingent on his obedience to a complex set of rules. These rules required complete remodeling of his daily life: prayer, fasting, pilgrimage, and taxes were exacted; gambling, drinking, and sexual license were restrained. The believer's responsibilities were extended from his kin to his commonwealth. In compensation he was allowed to look upon himself as one of the elect. Not only was Paradise waiting for him, but this world, too, was given over to him to rule and exploit. The state guaranteed the Muslim's superior status.

2) *Causes the revaluation of all experience, external and internal.* The reactions of the heart to the call of the Lord of necessity became a field of intense study. Wide areas of psychological experience were disclosed or rendered articulate. The rediscovery of himself which Islam offered the believer by making him share in the rule of an immense cosmopolitan empire, by giving him the key to the next world, by pointing the way to the intellectual conquest of the universe, and, most important of all, by justifying a wider and more varied emotional experience in a richer and more comprehensive pattern, compensated for the hardship of adjustment, the romantic sense of loss, and even the abandonment of the unlimited freedom of the past. Islam's gift to the pagan convert was more than salvation; it gave him the soul that was to be saved.

We know that Islam, measured by other transformation movements, carried the day against very little opposition, owing to some extent to the intellectual poverty of Bedouin paganism and also to the power configuration in the Arabian Peninsula. But the most important factor in facilitating its acceptance was this: once the necessity of conversion had been realized, identification with the new faith and its objectives, cultural and political, was not impeded by a feeling that it was of foreign growth. Islam was an advance over paganism, an orthogenetic advance, that is, an advance likely to increase the self-respect both of the individual and of the community. It is true that foreign, that is, genetically non-Arab, ideas and aspirations motivated Muḥammad's message to a large extent; but the actual presentation of the message as well as the personality of the Messenger removed from the believers' minds any suspicion of having bestowed their allegiance to an alien gospel.[2]

III

The influence of one system of thought upon another may affect the vantage point or objective, the method, or the content of the receiving system, either jointly or severally. Influence goes deepest when it affects vantage point, or objective; it is least deep when it is confined to the material content on or with which the receiving system operates.

The vantage point of a system of thought is difficult to distinguish from the presuppositions that are implicit in its objective. The existential and therefore primarily affective character of the aspiration of any thought system is fairly obvious. For the investigation of a given system of thought at a given moment in history it may be accepted as a fact and requires no further analysis.

Thus, in Islam, from a human point of view, the goal of life and hence the vantage point of any thinking about life and the world is to attain to eternal felicity through obeying the Lord's commands, which include belief in certain revealed truths that are not necessarily controllable by reason. Interest in the universe is limited to its role within an anthropocentric design of salvation. There cannot be an autonomous nature, as it would imply a restriction of the Lord's omnipotence. Through his prophets

[2] The transformation wrought by the rise of Islam has been studied in somewhat greater detail in my paper, "Transformation of Culture as Illustrated by the Rise of Islam," in *Conflict of Power in Modern Culture,* Proceedings of the Seventh Conference on Science, Philosophy, and Religion (New York, 1947), pp. 218-224. The last rulers of the Ghassanid dynasty (deposed by the Byzantines in 582) seem to have been inspired to some extent by the dream of all (Syriac-speaking) Monophysites under their sway.

God has communicated to man the essential truths, that is, the truths he needs to know to qualify for Paradise. So human reason is charged not so much with discovering unknown areas of facts as with uncovering the insights and the directions implied in divine or prophetic announcements. It is less important to enlarge the stores of knowledge than to make explicit the meaning of available knowledge. So the true task of thought is comment and interpretation.

This fundamental structure of Islamic thinking has been left untouched by Hellenistic influence.

Under *method* two sets of phenomena may be subsumed: on the one hand, the procedures commonly designated as such, and on the other, the intellectual and psychological conditions that render possible the application of any given procedure. Apart from a willingness to learn, these conditions include intellectual discipline, that is, the readiness to subordinate emotional to rationally oriented insights as well as the span of attention which the observer commands and his ability (or need) to integrate his observations in the form of an ordered system, that is, in linguistic terms, in the form of hypotactic periods. It is especially the variability of the span of attention which exercises a great though little regarded influence on the consistency and the composition of scientific and artistic efforts. It is hard to deny that the attention of the Arabic reading public down to the great centuries of Abbasid civilization would flag much sooner than that of the contemporaries of Plato, Demosthenes, or Cicero; this psychological fact is largely responsible for that aversion to coherent composition, and that excessive enjoyment of digression in response to the almost unbridled play of associations, which on occasion have been given the dignity of a literary program. The striving after an efficient hypotactic period which permeates the history of medieval Arabic reflects the gradual expansion of the span of attention.

Method, as the term is usually understood, is constituted by the current procedures of conceptualization and of reaching results that are experienced as satisfactory and conclusive; it reflects the extent to which thought has remained word-bound and submissive to associative progress. The treatment accorded the anthropomorphism of the Koran by Muslin theology requires consideration under this head. Almost everywhere scientific thinking has had to pass through a stage in which the word, its etymology, that is, is expected to disclose the nature of the object designated. The validity conceded to formal logic as a heuristic technique and, again, the range allowed critical sifting of internal and external data enter into the description of the methodological procedure of any given period. Fundamentally, man is inclined to consider trustworthy what he needs to believe, with the collective always more credulous than the individual. The criteria of acceptability not only determine the scientific solidity of the world view but also the range of what may be experienced as reality.

As it was soon realized that neither the text of the Koran nor that of the prophetic traditions would in itself suffice to regulate every detail of the community's life, recourse was had to analogy (*qiyās*), which was to be the typical procedure of the Arab-Muslim deduction as it had already been that of Talmudic Judaism. The acquaintance with Greek thought, which had begun under the Syrian Umayyads but became effective only around 800 in Abbasid Iraq, brings into Islamic thinking the true tripartite syllogism as another instrument of theological and philosophical construction. For analogy illustrates and assigns position, but the syllogism leads ahead. In the style of the vulgarized Gnostic myth and of the Talmud the prophetic tradition preferred to present abstract insights by visualizing them in brief scenes or narratives. When at first certain ideas are communicated through a dialogue between God and the Soul, Man and an Angel, the impact of Greek abstractive ability will make it possible (and even desirable) to omit the frame tale and formulate abstractly. The Aristotelian categories are received with enthusiasm; full use is made of the possibilities for new questions which were implicit in concepts such as substance and accident.

The uncovering of analogies loses out to the logical derivation of truths. This development implies a greater distance from what is merely accidental in the historical situation, for the conclusiveness of the analogy depends largely on participation in the concrete cultural reality, whereas the conclusiveness of the newly adopted logical procedures is fairly independent from participation in identical environmental experiences.

It goes almost without saying that only such elements of the Greek legacy would become effective as were needed in and could be integrated into the framework of the Muslim concern with the world without too much perplexity. At bottom Greek thinking was viewed as merely a formal pattern of organization; at least only such methodological features were accepted as would serve to elaborate an Islamic pattern of intellectual organization. Thus the progressive rationalization in the organization of available materials was admitted from the Greek model, that approach to the subject matter which would suggest, for example, the alphabetic arrangement of biographies, the arrangement by topics of prophetic traditions. But it is precisely in the application of formal principles of organization that the strength of prerational considerations is revealed: thus al-Khaṭīb al-Baghdādī (d. 1071) arranged the biographies of famous Baghdadians according to alphabet yet placed the bearers of the name Muḥammad at the beginning. Muslim theology owes a great deal to Greek methodology in terms of the number of problems that have been opened to discussion and in terms of the clarity of its formulations. But already the contemporaries realized that the more precise articulation of problems due to rationalization would quite often do violence to the emotional or existential content of revelation. Thus it is the rationalization in a system of the intellectual content of certain Koranic verses concerned with human freedom and predestination, where the *condition humaine* is accurately described in logically contradictory statements, which made the data of revelation a stumbling block and created a theological problem of what had been a religious verity.

The rationalization does not, however, affect either vantage point or end of Muslim thinking. Greek ideas of causality were known, as were those of a self-directed nature operating under timeless laws, but they did not penetrate; the miracle as a break of God's habitual manner of acting remains an uncontested and often perceived possibility. Rationalization makes itself felt only when the theologians classify the miracle and gradually work out its varieties and their respective properties in searching detail.

The content of thinking, the material with the aid and for the sake of which the process of thinking is undertaken and which again is identical with the material available for exemplification, is determined by the historical situation and is therefore, in a sense, accidental. Vantage point and method create a disposition to perceive primarily materials of a certain kind; they also generate the need to receive a definite type of materials which may be used to justify and illustrate. Yet, in the last analysis, it is the result of outward circumstances, often political in nature, which determines what materials come within the purview of a given cultural community. That element in religion which ties it to a historical situation, and is therefore accidental in contrast to the timeless truths it propounds, is usually of the greatest emotive significance for the naïve believer but creates the greatest difficulties for the theologian attempting the dogmatic formulation of his doctrine. It suffices to consider the lives of the founders of the great religions from this angle.

Mediated in part through the Harranians, a community only superficially Islamized, the Greek sciences have immeasurably enriched the thinking material at the disposal of the Muslims. In the consciousness of the Muslims the division between the native sciences of theology (and law) and philology (with their many subdivisions), and the foreign sciences such as philosophy and the natural sciences, has never been abandoned. The Arabic or native sciences represented those branches of learning which were indispensable to the completion or perfection of the religious life, collectively as well as individually. Philology was ancillary to the explanation of the Holy Book; history was *Heilsgeschichte* and the source of precedent for concrete legal decisions; geography offered orientation in the Islamic world and assistance to the administrator. In contrast, the natural sciences could be dispensed with as they were not required for the realization of the kind of life the Lord had ordained; they could readily be pushed to the side lines, therefore, when the consolidation of orthodoxy suggested some restriction of the intellectual outreach in the later Middle Ages. This was feasible even though the natural sciences had been received with unexampled enthusiasm in the great period of the Abbasid age, and Muslim scholars had made highly significant additions to the classical legacy.

To recapitulate: vantage point or objective of a thought system determines the problems to be treated and the types of solution felt to be acceptable; method determines the form of the treatment and its factual controls; the content, finally, motivates the actualization of some of the problems implicit in vantage point or objective, and furnishes the requisite evidence and the material elements of education. Thus, for instance, it is implicit in the nature of Muslim religion that clarity will have to be sought with respect to the essence of God; the type of solution that will be experienced as satisfactory is equally implicit in the fundamental orientation of Islam. The method, here a modification of that familiar to us from Christian scholasticism, directs and confines the argumentation. The content that is available for concretization, such as certain verses of the Koran and certain dicta of the Prophet, are merely historical facts that will advance as well as impede the reasoning; they will, in any event, inject a fortuitous element into a search that aspires to findings of timeless validity.

In the terms of this operational analysis the depth of the Hellenization which Islamic thinking has undergone may be described rather simply and accurately. Hellenic thinking in no way affected vantage point or objective of Islamic thinking; by contrast, it greatly affected method:

the discipline of thought tightened, that is, the freedom granted associative and purely emotional impulses lessened. Greek categories and individual concepts assisted in the rationalization of experiential data and made possible the uncovering of hitherto unnoted or at least inarticulable layers of the religious experience. The enrichment of content from Greek sources provided a wider range of argumentation and illustration which at the same time the transfer of Greek forms of presentation assisted in putting into effective use.

IV

Seen from the standpoint of the receiving community, the most important variable in the transmission of influence (leaving aside its concrete content) is the power relationship between itself and the community from which it borrows. The more obvious the power differential between the two culture areas, the stronger will be the psychological difficulties accompanying the urge to adapt. The intelligentsia of the early Abbasid period steeped itself in Hellenistic ways of thinking, took over Indian methods of medicine, adopted Iranian principles of administration, and in general delighted in widening its horizon and gratifying its curiosity about the world without feeling any (but occasional religious) hesitations about taking over elements of non-Arab or non-Muslim origin. The traditions from which influence would emanate were either politically dead, like Hellenism; or subjugated, like Iran; or, like India, irrelevant for the destiny of the empire. The Muslims' sense of being masters in their own house was in no way weakened by the knowledge that they were taking over the best the others had to offer; on the contrary, it merely strengthened their belief in the potentialities of their aspirations. Under those circumstances, when borrowing would sap neither their freedom of action nor their self-assurance, the heterogenetic character of much of the advance caused no emotional hardship.

The complexion of Westernization during the last 150

years is totally different. It was the inadequacy of their power which first induced in some of the Muslim elite a readiness to reform. The objective of the admission of Western influence was not to perfect potential or heritage, but to remove what was felt to be an inferiority; and this inferiority was most smarting in the political area. The question was not, what to adopt, whence to select, but rather, what to retain, or perhaps even, was there, in the traditional culture, anything worth retaining? This question could be asked from a more or less pragmatic viewpoint: Can we ever become the political equals of the West unless we Westernize completely? or from a more or less theoretical viewpoint: What is there in our tradition which is worth keeping in the light of the Western cultural experience? In any possible answer a radical heterogenetic transformation was implied.

To be effective, the transformation had to be total or nearly so. It was not a matter of allowing Western technology or natural science or military art to be grafted onto the traditional intellectual structure. New content would not be enough, nor would new methods. The change had to be admitted down to the very roots, that is, the vantage point of the civilization and its objective. One may say, incidentally, that the greatest difficulty encountered by the Muslim world in its struggle with Westernization is the contradiction between its success in adopting the foreign aspiration and its failure (or unwillingness) to relinquish its traditional vantage point. In practical terms, the transformation imposed by the mere existence of Occidental civilization as the spiritual equipment of a supreme power organization affected mores as well as institutions, economic and social structure as well as the reading of Holy Writ. The Western concept of the nation-state did away with the traditional concept of the Muslim as a citizen of the Muslim world. Western ideas of literature and art effected a transvaluation of traditional forms and norms of self-expression: the despised folk art came to be prized; the age-old canons of poetry were discarded; foreign patterns supplanted rather than supplemented inherited ones; the representational arts long felt to be in opposition to religious injunctions were taken up. Even as parliamentary institutions had to be introduced, as much to suit a novel situation as to demonstrate modernity and progressiveness, so in every sphere of life a new kind of completeness had to be reached to match the accomplishments of Western precedent and to allow for self-respect through equality of achievement, however rudimentary. The individual found himself playing to two galleries at the same time. The world of tradition was as real as ever although submerged and out of fashion; its emotional hold had been broken only in relatively rare instances; the Westernized world held the stage; the future of the nation depended on progressive assimilation and so for countless hearts did their self-respect. But the community, too, had to become (and continues to be) double-faced, tending to overplay Westernization achieved before the comity of nations, and tending to draw strength from underplaying it before the more backward or the more traditional-minded in their own ranks.

Westernization made uncertain not only the present but the past as well. Muslim history needed to be rewritten. In part, Occidental methods had to be applied to the unearthing and the sifting of objective facts. In the main, however, it had to be decided upon whom to place the guilt for the predicament of the present. Was it the theologians of the Middle Ages, whose distortion of the prophetic message caused Islamic inspiration to dry up? Was it the Mamluks, whose ruthless rule sapped the strength of Egypt beyond recovery? Or was it Muḥammad ʿAlī, whose precipitate steps toward Europeanization did more harm than good by creating the psychological confusion that still lies at the bottom of the incessant political unrest of the country? There is no end to questions of this order, and they become more burning as it is less possible to brush them aside by pointing to colonialism as the root of all evil. And, even if colonialism is impugned, the problem is pushed back only one step, for it would be difficult not to ask further: What was it that weakened the Muslim world to such an extent that it no longer could or would resist the intruder? But history has to be consulted not only to ascertain the villain. It has to be consulted even more closely to yield the glories of the Muslim past which may be taken as a warranty of a glorious future. As has happened typically, if perhaps less obviously, in European nationalistic movements, the past is made into the supreme metaphysical justification of the aspirations for the future. The Muslim world has been revising its history for the last hundred years; but a satisfactory integration of adequate self-interpretation, Western methodological technique, and the psychological demands of the times has not yet been achieved. With all this, the lack of certainty about one's place in the universal development remains painful as well as politically unsettling.[3]

The all too obvious heterogenetic character of Western influence and the major borrowings due to it mar to a large extent the satisfaction that would otherwise be inherent in the very substantial and very real progress accomplished in the process of Westernization. Both consciously and unconsciously, the tendency has been to let the heterogenetic appear as orthogenetic whenever possible. The borrowed element is envisaged as something bestowed on the West many a century ago and now come home, as it were, modified, perhaps, yet of Muslim origin. Or it is found adumbrated or even enjoined in the Holy Book. Or it is accounted for as a legitimate, a logical development from Muslim presuppositions correctly interpreted. Parliament and monogamy are intimated in the Koran; equality was practiced during the early period of the empire; the devotion to science, as well as tolerance to minorities and concern over social ills, is characteristic of the Muslim legacy. The tendency to appropriate as many of the results of Westernization as possible by mak-

[3] Among the "modernists" Muḥammad Rashīd Riḍā, *Tafsīr al-Manār* (Cairo, 1927-1934), I, 309-313, esp. p. 311, shows his awareness of the educational importance of history. Cf. also J. Jomier, *Le Commentaire coranique du Manār* (Paris, 1954), p. 110.

ing them into orthogenetic developments will, of course, at times conflict with that scholarly conscience which has been made more delicate in consequence of contact with Western ideas of scientific effort. But in the long run there can be no doubt where popular consciousness will seek its orientation.

With all these psychological impediments Westernization continues to proceed apace. Fundamentally the power relation between Europe and the Near East has not been altered; it may be, though, that more of a semblance of autonomous choice has been restored to the countries concerned. Theirs is now the belief that they are catching up with the West; they overlook not only the distance that still separates them from the technological status that marks the first stage of equality attained, but also the undeniable fact that the West is still moving ahead at a substantial rate, especially on the technological level where Westernization can most easily be measured by the public. The international political organization which the West has imposed on the world fosters the illusion of Westernization attained and thus, by indirection, renders the gains of Westernization more secure. On the other hand, the idealistic or fictitious assumptions under which international bodies are apt to operate may in the long run endanger Westernization by whittling away at the political prestige of the West. The impulse to Westernization through an increased belief in its value represents an orthogenetic development which is counteracted by the decrease in the psychological impulse to allow oneself to be influenced.

As a last resort one may prognosticate the future of Westernization somewhat on the analogy of another eastward wave of cultural influence, the expansion of Hellenism in the centuries after Alexander the Great.

At this point the uneven permeability to influence of the several layers into which a civilization may be dissected comes into play. Analysis will bear out the general statement that the less self-directed a sphere of cultural action, the more readily do its mechanics yield to influence.

The transfer of technology or of techniques of business organization meets with slight obstacles compared with the transfer of an economic outlook or a restructuring of the social system; the approach to artistic creation, the concept of scientific truth, and, above all, the basic ethical, and even more so the basic religious, assumptions and expectations appear to be of quite limited transferability, which is another way of saying that disposition and ability to receive elements of those value levels are for the most part rather slight, perhaps because such reception too manifestly entails the abandonment of identification, personal as well as cultural.

The influence of Hellenism was in its beginnings as much carried forward by the attraction of political power as is Westernization in our day. But, as time passed, the political shifts resulting in the unification of the Near East under the Romans lessened the pressure. One is fond of speaking of the Eastern cultural resurgence in the first centuries of our era and of its pushing back the Hellenistic influence. The facts are indeed well observed. Yet it was not so much a strengthening of Eastern spirituality which regained the area for a (profoundly modified and permanently Hellenized) native tradition; it was, rather, the weakening of Hellenism, whose political and aspirational bases were wearing away, which brought about the ebbing of the ancient tradition so characteristic of the centuries before Islam. And, similarly, I am inclined to believe that the resurgence of a Muslim-dominated political area, which is no longer oriented to the West in terms of arriving at Westernization, however orthogenetically interpreted, is contingent primarily upon a recession of Western civilization, a drying-up of its aspiration, rather than upon any startling developments within Muslim civilization viewed as an isolated cultural unit.

V

Influence presupposes the situation in which a community voluntarily or under compulsion endeavors to diminish a disturbing differential in (cultural, economic, political, etc.) potential or achievement which separates it from potential or achievement of another community that usually is, but need not necessarily be, its contemporary. (This differential does not as a rule concern the full spectrum of cultural endeavor, but only certain areas whose revival through "alien" influence is expected to restore the integrity and the effectiveness of the recipient civilization as a whole. You need only think of the venerable cliché of the materialist West and the spiritualist East which, whatever its accuracy, circumscribes rather neatly the areas within which the East is willing to make open acknowledgment of backwardness and dependence, clearly with a view to restoring the autonomy of its "spirituality" by means of taking over some of the material accomplishments of the West.) A self-view implicit in the attitude that seeks resurgence through the admission of influence, and the realities of the uneven distribution of power which most often accompany and fortify it, almost exclude the possibility that an influence of comparable significance may reach the "exporting" culture unit from the receiving one. We cannot therefore speak of cultural interchange when it comes to the description of processes such as the effect in our time of the West on the Middle East, or of the Middle East on the West some six or seven centuries ago. For interchange, which in our view may constitute the ideal relationship of mature civilizations, represents the borderline case of cultural influence. It occurs when the influences exerted and received by two (or more) communicating culture units are of comparable intensity, effectiveness, and significance (in terms of the scale suggested in the preceding analysis of "influence").

What a prolonged and sufficiently intense radiation and admission of influence may bring about, and have actually done so in a number of instances, is a *rapprochement* of the culture units involved, which leads to a more or less complete integration of the recipient in the orbit of the expanding. This integration need not necessarily be cultural only; it may be the result of political unification as well. But it must be borne in mind that unification is not to be equated with the establishment of a unitary state. Genuine cultural interchange will be possible, therefore, only within a cultural unit already established as such or within a geographical area under the same political organization. Ancient Greece and the modern West, from perhaps the eastern border of western Germany to the Pacific coast of the United States, may be considered areas allowing of genuine interchange.

Interchange thus presents itself as the consummation of cultural unification already attained (and, one may add, attained largely through the processes of one-sided influence or else through the spread in space of culturally homogeneous groups). Within the interchange area, the exchange moves not only horizontally across national and political borders, but also vertically between dominant and dominated groups. Such groups may, for example, interchange the mores of the dominated for the religious notions of the dominant, the forms of organization of the dominant for the techniques of the dominated, and so on. The interchange is directed, or dictated, by the existential and political needs of the dominant group as they relate to the existential and survival needs of the dominated. It must of course be understood that throughout this discussion cultural superiority and inferiority are measured solely in terms of the values which the societies affected by the assimilative process desire to realize and which, incidentally, provide for the contemporary involved in the development the only standard to determine success or failure of his efforts. Let me repeat, interchange is a *cas limite* of influence. Both may be subsumed under the concept of acculturation, which they enable us to render more precise and more concrete in the descriptive apprehension of intricate cultural processes.

III

An Analysis of Islamic Civilization and Cultural Anthropology

I

HISTORICITY IS THE ESSENCE of the human existence. It is man's directedness toward the future which in his consciousness transforms undifferentiated time into historical time. Historical time alone can be experienced as meaningful, and the meaning it has for those immersed in any particular *hic et nunc* is directed by the anticipated realization of present aspirations in a future. The aspirations themselves will in large measure be accountable in terms of causality, but action and self-view are purpose-inspired; the starting point is as dependent on the goal as the goal is on the starting point. Effective history is variously selected from total experience, factual or fictional, and the selection itself is guided by the aspiration, that future self-realization to which the past is to give aid.

The purpose-directedness of human existence—in subjective terms, the primacy of the will—pervades every sphere of man's activity, the technological or the economic as well as the political or the interpretative. The *why* is secondary to the *what for*. Because of this fundamental structure of the human mind, man is not a prey to whim and is not dependent on coincidences of his aspirations with intractable outside reality. Man is permitted, however, to strive for ends that lack an objectively valid orientation and consequently expose him to failure, even though the limitations of his insight into reality may bar him from understanding this failure or his dominant concern may prevent him from realizing the very fact of his failure.

Objectivity means object-orientedness. Thoughts, observations, interpretations receive their objectivity from the ends toward which they are oriented. The end determines the rationality of the means; such rationality is inseparable from the objective validity of the means. As ends are means to higher ends, it is only the ultimate end—the dominant aspiration—whose objectivity (i.e., whose appropriateness to the data to which it is intended to relate) can be in doubt. And it is from the clash of this aspiration with reality that the collapse of a given hierarchy of ends and means—in other words, the collapse of a cultural structure—may result.

Man's capability of mastering the problems of his existence through a multitude of coherent cultural forms unfolds his intellectual and emotional potentialities, not fully and simultaneously in an existence that is typically repeated by contemporaries and descendants, as is true of animal species, but through a sequence (or juxtaposition) in time of cultural forms. His self-revelation, if one may use such a term, is progressive in history; his cultural differentiability is infinite. Any characterization of man is therefore derivable only from as comprehensive a survey of his cultural manifestations as is possible, and, by the very nature of the process of unfolding, is bound to remain incomplete. Man's *Kulturenfähigkeit* (as contrasted with the "*Kulturfähigkeit*" of the animal) limits his capacity for exhaustive self-understanding. Thus, insight into the essential structure of his being emerges as a task from which he can never free himself, as of a problem solved, and any subsequent solution may claim to be nothing more than closer, yet forever asymptotic, approximation to the ontological reality which it proposes to circumscribe. Yet it is an integral element of his nature that man, individually and collectively, does not mature unless he has become a problem unto himself.[1] For a society this means disintegration, unless it possesses a self-image that is, at least pragmatically, satisfactory, or, in other words, operationally effective.

Scientific insights are not conceivable as isolates. No insight becomes scientific unless it is part of a context and unless this context is structured in accordance with a rational principle of organization. Variations in what seems to be rational in different cultural settings are actually not so much variations in logical process as reflections of the major concerns that assign levels of relevance to the individual facts. An increase in credulity proportionately with an increase in physical or temporal distance of the object considered is to be ascribed to the absence of a context within which the critical evaluation of remote data is experienced as necessary. If the criteria of evaluation themselves are lacking in rationality, in terms of their logical stringency and their attunement to observable facts, such credulity is more often than not attributable to the range of experience admitted and sought by the particular society; in other words, it is the hierarchy of aspirations through which the society seeks to relate itself to a

---

[1] H. E. Hengstenberg, *Philosophische Anthropologie* (Stuttgart, 1957), p. 1. For the contrast between *Kulturfähigkeit* and *Kulturenfähigkeit*, cf. W. E. Mühlmann, "Umrisse und Probleme einer Kulturanthropologie," *Homo*, VII (1955), 153-171, at p. 155.

selectively delimited universe which determines what is experienced as conclusive evidence or argumentation. The point never to lose sight of is that the context determines both relevance of data and acceptability of constructive or interpretative argument.

A heightened concern with the human condition, resulting in a rethinking of anthropological ideas, has been typical in periods of social and sociological regrouping. A self-understanding of man as a culturally conditioned being has, however, only fairly recently become an explicit end of intellectual endeavor; a self-understanding based on analyzing and assessing one's own civilization against, ideally, all other civilizations is an end confined to the most modern West.[2]

[2] This tendency to utilize the "other" civilizations in order to understand one's own is clearly to be distinguished from mere recognition of another civilization as an entity of some value; it animates a passage by the Turkish scholar Kātib Chelebi (d. 1657) which, because of the rareness of the sentiment in a classical Islamic setting, may be quoted at some length: "It must also be known that mankind, ever since the time of Adam, has been divided. Every division has its own tenets and its own mode of behavior, which seem at variance with those of other divisions. As God Almighty says, 'Every party rejoices in its own' (Koran 23:55): they all like their own ways and prefer them to any others. But, after all, some men are intelligent; they ponder and observe the inner purpose of this divergence and find that many advantages underlie it, and they will not interfere with or attack anybody's tenets or code. If these seem wrong in the light of their own religion, they content themselves with disapproving of them silently in their own hearts. . . . Now the purpose of civilization and society, which is essential for mortals, demands that men of vision should acquire knowledge and become acquainted with the division of mankind into various sorts, and with the state and condition of every part" (*The Balance of Truth*, trans. G. L. Lewis [London and New York, 1957], pp. 29-30). Even less than the attitude of Kātib Chelebi (who, incidentally, as B. Lewis has informed me, collaborated with a French renegade in translating European history) must mere curiosity or the readiness to listen to a discussion of the essential positions of the "other" civilization be confused with the use the modern West feels constrained to make of the alien experience. The Baghdad Muslims who welcomed Fra Ricoldo da Montecroce (d. 1320) to their homes and invited him to

It may well be that the recurrent intellectual and social crises characteristic of the West for at least the last four or five centuries, with their perpetual shifts in the human self-image, have provided us with an almost permanent

---

discuss God and the Christ with them, and Fra Francesco Suriano who, in the middle of the fifteenth century, compiled contrasting lists of a large number of peculiarities in the behavior of Arab Muslims and Italian Christians, were interested in the unfamiliar, and were probably edified by not being like the others (cf. A. Malvezzi, *L'Islamismo e la cultura europea* [Florence, 1956], pp. 116-117, 125), but there is no indication whatever that the information was gathered as a means of access to themselves. W. Jaeger, "Platos Stellung im Aufbau der griechischen Bildung," *Die Antike,* IV (1928), 1-13, 89-98, 161-176, at p. 3, has observed, without, however, describing the modern Western urge toward autodiagnosis by means of comparative analysis of cultures, that "gerade die intensive Versenkung in die fremden aussereuropäischen Kulturen und ihre Vergleichung mit den Völkern des hellenozentrischen Kulturkreises . . . muss uns als einen grundwesentlichen Unterschied die Tatsache aufdrängen, dass jene von den Ausstrahlungen des Griechentums weniger oder nicht getroffenen Kulturen etwas nicht besitzen, was für unsere von der Antike übernommene Kultur und Bildung das eigentlich Entscheidende und für unser ganzes Lebensgefühl Bestimmende ist, nämlich das Kulturbewusstsein, die bewusste Idee der Kultur als höchster und zentraler Wert in der Sphäre allen irdischen Daseins." Nadjm oud-Dine Bammate, in a discussion incorporated in *Tradition et innovation. La querelle des Anciens et des Modernes dans le monde actuel. Rencontres Internationales de Genève,* XI (1956), 354, has touched upon our conception but, to my mind, has missed the true aspect of the Occidental position by viewing it as a syncretistic tendency. His views are, however, sufficiently relevant to be quoted in this context. He asks whether "syncretism" is legitimate as a "mode de connaissance des autres civilisations. Est-ce qu'un eclecticisme culturel nous permet d'atteindre à l'humanisme véritable, d'élargir notre propre humanisme?" André Gide is recalled as saying that "les littératures étrangères l'intéressaient surtout dans la mesure où elles lui servaient à situer sa propre littérature. Je dois vous dire qu'il ne s'agit pas là d'une approche occidentale, et je citerai en souvenir une commission internationale de traduction qui s'était adressée à tous les pays en leur demandant ce qui, des littératures étrangères, les intéressait au premier chef. Voici la réponse persane. Qu'a demandé l'Iran? Il n'a pas demandé Descartes, il n'a pas demandé les auteurs positivistes, il a demandé . . . les Contes d'Andersen! L'Occident l'intéressait

stimulus to expand "anthropology" into "social anthropology," and that the urge to encompass and interpret "all" accessible cultural solutions of the problem of living has had a good deal to do with the recently realized

---

dans la mesure où, à ce pays de fables, il pouvait apporter de nouveaux contes, de nouveaux motifs d'émerveillement, et non pas de nouvelles constructions rationnelles. Je crois qu'en fin de compte l'eclecticisme culturel, l'exotisme, nous sert toujours à nous raffermir dans la conscience des valeurs qui nous sont déjà habituelles." However well taken Bammate's observations may be, the utilization of other forms of cultural organization for a deepening of collective self-interpretation would yet seem to be a fairly new feature of characteristically Western growth. An interesting instance of this novel attitude is provided by the statement made by the Cairene psychologist Yūsuf Murād in 1958 in connection with an *enquête* on Occidental music arranged by Radio Cairo: "Nous avons grand besoin d'une culture mondiale, d'une culture qui nous extraie de nous-mêmes. Nous avons à étudier et à assimiler l'apport de toutes les nations et de toutes les langues." It appears that Murād made this statement in order to counter the opposition of a section of the Egyptian public against anything that would "manquer d'égyptianité" and "verser dans l'internationalisme." Cf. J. Berque, *Les Arabes d'hier à demain* (Paris, 1960), p. 205. The suggestion of W. M. Watt, *Islam and the Integration of Society* (London, 1961), pp. 232 n. 2, 257, that Western study of non-Westerners "rises from the general Western belief that knowledge of things confers power over them," does not seem to assess the phenomenon in all its breadth. Much more subtly does Max Scheler, *Die Wissensformen und die Gesellschaft* (2d ed.; Berne, 1960; first published in 1926), p. 92, determine the relationship between the *Wille zur Herrschaft* (as the prevailing ethos) and the aims and methods of scientific thought. See also his description (pp. 112-116, 125) of the principal characteristics of the modern Western approach to science, in contrast with the attitudes that were pushed aside between the fourteenth and the seventeenth centuries. Relevant for our confrontation with contemporary Muslim civilization are also pages 117-118, with their strict separation of *Wert- und Sollensprobleme* and *Daseins- und Soseinsprobleme*. The classical Muslim social order, with its hierarchic ranking of believers and unbelievers, is a beautiful instance of the derivation of the *Wertsein* from the *Sein* itself, of axiology from ontology.

As an illustration of the fact that the historical study of alien civilizations can be prompted by intellectual contexts other than our own, reference may be made to the importance ascribed to

necessity to adjust to intercultural living and to adapt ourselves to a newly emerging pattern of power distribution—factors that are compelling us to reëvaluate ourselves. In line, however, with the fundamental aspirations of the modern West—the ever-widening control and understanding of the inner and outer world—aspirations whose togetherness is as characteristic of our civilization as is their methodological concomitant, the craving for completeness and universality of information (and application), cultural self-understanding as based on understanding of other cultures, is not so pragmatic, so directly purposive as the intensity of the urge and the crisis atmosphere of our time would lead one to expect.

An element of *Sachlichkeit*[3]—the readiness to open and surrender oneself to an encounter with reality, rather than to surrender reality encountered to arbitrary treatment—allows us to exploit the alien experience in the adjustment of our own. The comparative absence of *Sachlichkeit* in present-day Oriental self-interpretations (which should be understood rather as self-stylizations) may be derivable from the intensity and the pervasiveness of the crisis through which Eastern civilizations have been passing and the consequent urgency with which syntheses of an emotionally effective kind are sought and abandoned, sometimes as a direct reflection of political changes in the West. The relative crudity of the successive self-images adopted for the sake of psychological consolidation (as in Communist China) or to buttress political realignments (as frequently in Islamic countries) facilitates the diagnosis of

---

the examination of all human societies, past and present, by the fifteenth-century Platonist, Georgios Gemistos Plethon (d. 1452). The binding force, in terms of truth finding as well as ethical injunction, of the *koinai ennoiai,* the ideas shared by all of mankind, requires the philosopher to follow up ideas and mores wherever accessible. Within Christianity, the approach was to lead to a historical and philological verification of the dogma, that is to say, to the establishment of the universally held concepts of speculative theology. Cf. F. Masai, *Pléthon et le platonisme de Mistra* (Paris, 1956), pp. 128-130.

[3] To use Hengstenberg's expression, *op. cit.*, p. 4.

the formative function of a society's aspirations and the extent to which its pursuit may for a while overwhelm the natural sense of reality.

Our need to review and reconstruct ourselves against the background of the totality of the cultural achievement of mankind has made cultural anthropology a central concern of our time. The necessity of considering past history as the locus of many cultural developments—some of them, to us, among the most directly relevant to our quest—has helped cultural anthropology to become "historicized," to converge toward history. This becomes more readily evident especially when we take note of the unfolding of a *Kulturlehre* from both traditional historical research and a cultural anthropology that ventures into the analysis of higher and highest civilizations. Speaking only for the Western world, I am inclined to place an even higher value than has already been suggested upon the importance to the existential needs of our time of a cultural anthropology that is understood as a *Kulturlehre* freed from the constructionist simplifications, or complications, to which theorists like Spengler or Toynbee have had to take recourse. Cultural anthropology is, in fact, the humanistic science for us in that it is, among the humanities and the social sciences, the one most precisely coördinated with our fundamental aspiration. Merely to avoid being misunderstood, I will add that the other aspect of our aspiration, which strives to understand and control the physical world, is of course being served primarily by the natural sciences.

By listing the branches of learning cultivated in any one time, one can bring to life, and, as it were, make visible, the range of interests of that period, its intellectual and material preoccupations, its dominant expectations and attitudes, and hence also its primary aspirations. It is, however, the several attempts made in a period to organize the recognized sciences of the time into a system, and the principles of organization employed, which most strikingly reveal the primary concern of the period. The establishment of a hierarchy of values (or, in less subjective terms, the recognition of such a hierarchy) is directly reflected in the hierarchy represented by any classification of the sciences. In all such classifications there has been one science in reference to which the others had to be justified; one science from whose subject matter the others, in the last analysis, obtained their meaningfulness; one science whence all knowledge received its dignity and toward which it was, by intent at least, oriented. The intellectual orientation expressed by a classification of the sciences is an untarnished mirror of the self-view of the society that needs and therefore sustains those sciences.

The position allotted to theology in the system of sciences in the Christian Middle Ages is a persuasive illustration. Regardless of the actual "research interests" of the medieval scholar, he would always determine the rank of his subject within the hierarchy of values by its relatedness to divinity, the capstone of the system of sciences.[4] The hierarchy of being(s) could be accounted for only by reference to its creator, and the study of subjects within it could receive meaning only because of their necessary connection with, or derivation from, the "prime mover" as the efficient and final cause of their existence. As the last link in any causal chain and the ultimate end of any investigation, God provided the only truly fixed point of reference; theology therefore offered the ultimate justification and utilization of any result reached anywhere within or without the scientific domain; in fact, the very justification of the individual science would hinge on its justifiability in terms of theology (or of its own theological implications). It is true, of course, that in the last analysis, then as always, man has been his own supreme concern. But his self-image, his concept of his position and

[4] As if in anticipation of Max Scheler's (d. 1928) familiar train of thought, the Turkish encyclopedist Ṭāshköprüzāde (d. 1560) describes metaphysics/theology as "the science [that] is free as it does not serve any other [science] in any way, and everything else serves it" (cf. his *Miftāḥ as-saʿāda* [Hyderabad, 1328-1356], I, 28; trans. F. Rosenthal, *The Muslim Concept of Freedom* [Leiden, 1960], p. 106 n. 330).

his role in the universe, the transcendental end in which he recognized the final test and the meaning of his existence, imposed on his thinking a principle of organization of all knowledge (and a principle of selection of what was worth knowing) which called for a theology as the "absolute" to inform the contexts of empirical research and of deductive world construction. For the primary aspiration is necessarily articulated through the science that is assigned the key position in the selective intellectual organization of effective experience.

In the same period, the classification of the sciences which, despite variations, has remained typical for the Muslim Middle Ages betrays a tension, never completely overcome, between the two principal areas of concern of the Muslim scholar and thinker. The cleavage between the so-called "Arabic" and the so-called "foreign or ancient" sciences was never bridged by the application of a principle of organization which would have subsumed both as subordinate classes. The uncertain position of logic as a mere method on the one hand, as a full-fledged "foreign" science on the other, reflects some of the effort made to reappraise the mutual relations of the two groups of sciences. But the genetic disparity between, on the one hand, those areas of knowledge that either grew out of the immediate religious need to organize all life under God, or could be justified as auxiliaries in reference to that need, and, on the other, the areas that became concerns of the learned in consequence of their contact with outside and secular traditions, never ceased to make itself felt; and philosophy, which in the Christian world was able to develop, within the limits set by the primary aspiration, as *ancilla theologiae,* continued to be an embarrassment because its basis in non-Islamic aspirations made Muslim theologians hesitate to admit it as an auxiliary means of doctrinal exposition.

In the West theology was followed by philosophy (or perhaps better, by metaphysics and ontology) as the capstone and the orientation point of a synopsis of scientific effort. This does not mean that theology necessarily lost its position in a classificatory diagram; but it does mean that ends and methods of the individual sciences had now to stand the test of philosophical rather than theological justification and delimitation. A construction like Auguste Comte's attempt to make sociology the highest phase of man's rational mastery of experience, rather than the science to which all others were to be oriented, is, from our point of view, interesting mostly as a harbinger of a change in aspiration which was to set in effectively only half a century after Comte's death, if not later.

It is my contention that for our time cultural anthropology, understood as human self-analysis by means of a *Kulturlehre* (*Kulturanalyse*), holds the key position in the organization of sciences. Not, to be sure, as the capstone of a hierarchic grouping, as theology and philosophy have been and, in a formal sense, will continue to be, but as the actual hub of such scientific endeavor as serves our overriding existential urge to understand ourselves through an understanding of our cultural place and to understand that place through an understanding of all the cultural answers to the problem of living which have thus far been devised by man.[5] "All" the answers—this demand alone

[5] Vico argues that self-comprehension rather than the understanding of nature is the real purpose of our quest for knowledge. It is in the succession of Kant that moral control over ourselves (rather than control over nature) may be postulated as the end of our epistemological Odyssey. The demand for the development of a "comprehensive doctrine of man built up from a knowledge of all human phenomena wherever they are found" is raised by W. Stark, *The Sociology of Knowledge* (Glencoe, Ill., 1958), p. 196; see also pp. 197, 199. Stark's objective is the overcoming of relativism, historical and cultural, by means of a "truly ecumenical" knowledge of man. The approach of both Stark and myself has been anticipated, as it were, in Goethe's dictum that "only all mankind together makes the true man" (*Dichtung und Wahrheit* [München: Hanser, n.d.], Book 9, p. 318). Certain philosophical implications have been adumbrated by Scheler (*op. cit.*, pp. 26-27): ". . . to penetrate into the transcendent secrets of the logos is not given to one nation, one cultural circle, one or all cultural ages, but only to all together, including the future ones, in collective coöperation" (cf. Stark, *op. cit.*, pp. 330, 341, 343 n. 1, and Scheler, *op. cit.*, p. 91.

would suffice to establish that connection with history, inevitably required by consideration of the "higher" civilizations, and imposed upon a valid cultural anthropology by the historical sense, the concern with origins, the con-

---

The epistemological basis was laid by M. Scheler, *Vom Ewigen im Menschen* [4th ed.; Bern, 1954; first published in 1920], pp. 198-205). In retrospect the remarkable achievements of Muslim heresiology and what we may call "comparative religion" would appear as bases from which culture analyses might have developed systematically. In fact, however, these studies were inspired by the needs of polemics and spurred by the conviction that the pointing up of divergencies and contradictions among the sects or within major religions would serve as their most effective method of refutation, an idea that has its parallels in the outlook of Christian theologians such as, for instance, St. John of Damascus. On this topic compare the interesting observations of A. Abel, "La polémique damascénienne et son influence sur les origines de la théologie musulmane," in *L'Élaboration de l'Islam,* ed. C. Cahen (Paris, 1961), pp. 61-85, esp. pp. 83-85.

A disinterested concern for the foreign culture, on the other hand, clearly inspired al-Bērūnī's celebrated work on India, as well as the inclusion of China and Europe in the world history of the Ilkhān vizier Rashīd ad-Dīn (d. 1318). For Indian unconcern with other civilizations one may note not only the almost complete passing over of Islam in Hinduistic literature, but, more importantly, the attitude demanded by the Hindu law books vis-à-vis the *mleccha,* defined as the inhabitant of a country in which the system of the four castes is not valid. The passive intolerance that is prescribed so as to isolate the *mleccha* includes the prohibition of human contact. The *mleccha* is not to be talked to, his country is to be visited only on pilgrimage, and his language is not to be studied. (For references, see P. Hacker, "Religiöse Toleranz und Intoleranz im Hinduismus," *Saeculum,* VIII [1957], 167-179, esp. at pp. 171, 172.) Conversely, the Indo-Muslim writers of the fourteenth and fifteenth centuries displayed no interest in the Hindus for their own sake. Amīr Khusrau (d. 1325), for example, in his *Nuh Sipihr,* touches upon the languages, the music, and the sciences of the Hindus solely to depict the interesting environment in which the Muslims of Hindustan were living; an understanding of Hindu civilization as such is none of his concern. (Cf. the analysis of P. Hardy, *Historians of Medieval India* [London, 1960], p. 114.) It may be useful to underline in this context that in a world centered on man as the focal point of man's concerns history and/or (cultural) anthropology must needs become the basis of the scientific organization of the (non-physical) universe. To

sciousness of flux, and the use of development as a concept of organization (which are all characteristic of the recent West), even if we were not obsessed by the methodological imperative of the quest for completeness. Cultural anthropology is the organizational point where the lines connecting philosophy with history, psychology with biology (and linguistics), and economics with sociology—the six areas of research which are most directly subservient to our needs—meet and intersect. This is the meaning I wish to convey in describing cultural anthro-

---

borrow the words of the great Indologist, Sylvain Lévi, *L'Inde et le monde* (Paris, 1926), p. 135, history in the humanist's world becomes more than an experience; it indicates the direction man is to take; it is, in fact, the only waymark of which man disposes. With the necessary modifications the same claim could be made for cultural anthropology.

For the West, the breakthrough to a universalistic self-interpretation, in the making since the Renaissance, came in the last third of the eighteenth century with what might be called the discovery of India. It is at that time that the basis is laid for "ce recensement de tous les hommes, où l'homme moderne cherchera une explication de soi." (The phrase is R. Schwab's; cf. his *La Renaissance Orientale* [Paris, 1950], p. 25.) The Romantics insisted on total inventorizing as precondition of philosophical solutions and more and more has their theoretical demand been accepted—at times, it is true, at the price of a self-destructive loss of stance and focus. The difficulties and perils that beset the achievement of creative acquaintance with another civilization come out very clearly in H. de Lubac, *La Rencontre du Bouddhisme et de l'Occident* (Paris, 1952). The absence of political interests in this "encounter" underscores the purely cultural attractions and impediments.

Direction and limitations of non-Western study and critique of Western civilization become abundantly clear from the materials, mostly from South and East Asia, which Th. Ohm has brought together in his all too brief study, *Asiens Kritik am abendländischen Christentum* (Munich, 1948). What is lacking in the not infrequently highly perceptive statements of foes and friends of the Christian faith—almost always judged as representative of Western mentality and Western aspirations—is any attempt to get beyond the impressionism of the observer and to achieve a systematic insight into Western civilization, past or present, based on a measure of familiarity with sources and an even rudimentary concept of historical and cultural structure.

pology as the hub rather than as the capstone of what is effective in our system of sciences, always bearing in mind the separate function of the natural sciences in terms of the other, though interrelated, existential need of expanding control.

Whatever the ultimate epistemological accuracy of this interpretation of our present aspiration and its implementation through individual sciences converging toward, if not culminating in, a *Kulturlehre* developed through cultural anthropology, it enables us to classify and evaluate cultural analyses in Islamic (as well as other) fields in terms of their serviceableness to our primary aspirations and to the rationality of our methodological requirements. Our conviction that we must be confronted with "objective" (i.e., object-oriented) fact (or factual observation) for the effective fulfillment of our self-interpretative needs guarantees the operative minimum of objectivity. The assumption underlying cultural anthropology, that humanity reveals its potentialities through the pluralism of cultures it has developed, in historical sequence as well as in simultaneous coexistence, suggests the kindred assumption that even within the complexes that cultural anthropology is prepared to analyze as units there exists a more or less concealed pluralism of cultural aspiration or growth. No one aspiration carries through completely in the cultural manifestations of a society, let alone in a civilization that extends significantly in time, space, and areas of self-realization.

The observable regularities of cultural development (from which it is hoped ever and again that "laws" may be abstracted) have the predictive validity of the laws of the *geistige Sein;* that is to say, those regularities are descriptive, or symptomatic, of the structure of the human mind—the perpetual ultimate object of all research and attempts at cognition. In stating this reduction of ultimate insights to insights of a fundamentally psychological nature we must, however, recognize that the transpersonal character of the *geistige Sein,* which constitutes an effective factor in the human collective, generates "psychological" traits of its own which are not producible (or reproducible) by the individual mind considered as an isolate, and are traceable through the individual mind only when it functions, as it were, as a carrier of this collective *geistige Sein*.

It is clear that in terms of this approach cultural analysis is required to elucidate not merely the immediate data complexes (i.e., the civilizations) but also processes of even greater generality such as "cultural influence," "cultural interchange," "self-image and history/historiography," "tolerance for the clash between the ideal and the actual," and the like, allowing ultimately for a classification of observable instances of processes and relationships of this order by kind and, where applicable (as in the instance of cultural influence), by degree.

How useful, in relation to the aspirations of our culture, the pursuit of cultural anthropology as understood in this context will prove to be is, of course, debatable. The choices of problems and methods which we, as individuals, make are as limited as is the patience of our society whose restlessness we are to allay. It may well be that our comprehensive, or universalistic, approach will lose its attraction; what is more, its epistemological validity may be disproved. And, above all, the sustaining aspiration of our cultural community may change; and this change could conceivably be brought about by a sort of disillusionment with the interpretations stemming from the analyses produced by cultural anthropology. Such disillusionment would be due to the failure of cultural anthropology to induce a self-image that both satisfies our criteria of scientific rationality and provides an adequate justification of the cultural role we would want destiny to assign us in the emerging order of tomorrow's world. And yet, so long as we are carried forward by the impetus of this aspiration, our work will have to be judged by the ends and the standards implied and demanded by the realization of our society's aspirations.

This then, is the point of departure for my discussion of

some of the recent major efforts of Western scholarship to interpret the civilization of Islam.

II

It is essential to realize that Muslim civilization is a cultural entity that does not share our primary aspirations. It is not vitally interested in analytical self-understanding, and it is even less interested in the structural study of other cultures, either as an end in itself or as a means toward clearer understanding of its own character and history. If this observation were to be valid merely for contemporary Islam, one might be inclined to connect it with the profoundly disturbed state of Islam, which does not permit it to look beyond itself unless forced to do so. But as it is valid for the past as well, one may perhaps seek to connect it with the basic antihumanism of this civilization, that is, the determined refusal to accept man to any extent whatever as the arbiter or the measure of things, and the tendency to be satisfied with truth as the description of mental structures, or, in other words, with psychological truth.[6]

[6] Only once, perhaps, in classical Islamic times did the conflict between scientific truth as a progressive approximation and the absolute truth of revelation (and unchallengeable authority in general) come dramatically into the open. That was in a discourse between the famous philosopher-physician, Ibn Zakariyyāʾ ar-Rāzī (d. 925 or 934), and the Ismāʿīlī theologian, Abū Hātim ar-Rāzī, from which the latter's argument against scientific (and, a fortiori, psychological) truth may be inserted here: "If the remedies arrived at by the latecomer are at variance with the position of his predecessors, as you are at variance with those who preceded you, then this variance is not an advantage; rather, variance is an evil, an increase in blindness, added support for falsehood, a contradiction, a corruption. Indeed we find that by your many investigations and speculations you philosophers have increased solely the variety and contradictoriness of your opinions. And when you stipulate in your own case that the latecomer will attain to what the predecessor did not, as you have claimed that you have done in offering views at variance with your predecessors, you cannot be sure that there will not come

The absolute is self-contained; absolute truth is self-sufficient; the study of error and imperfection for their own sake does not deserve a supreme collective effort. The non-Muslim world is interesting enough but, in a

---

after you one striving to dissect what you have been trying to do; who will know what you did but add to it and attain through his intelligence and personal effort and reflection what you failed to attain. He will contradict your judgment and oppose your very principles just as you contradicted your predecessors and opposed their very principles when you asserted the five pre-existents and claimed that your predecessors were mistaken where they were at variance with you. It is just as if you were each at variance with the other. On this basis corruption would be established in the world, truth disappear forever, and falsehood become methodically organized. Those who are at variance with you have accomplished only vanity and error; for variance is vain, and a mistake is error. And you too, on this basis, will necessarily accomplish only vanity and error since those that will come after you will have an advantage and hit upon something you missed, just as in your own case" (trans. G. E. von Grunebaum and M. G. S. Hodgson, *Introduction to Islamic Civilization. Course Syllabus and Selected Readings* [Chicago, 1958-59], I, 388). The modernity of Ibn Zakariyyāʾ's outlook becomes all the more striking when one is reminded of the rejection, in 1642, of Descartes' teachings by the University of Utrecht, "first, because it is contrary to the ancient philosophy, which the universities of the whole world have thus far taught with wise deliberation." To Protestants as well as Catholics, Aristotelianism, in its scholastic integration with Christian doctrine, formed part of the "eternal verities." Cf. P. Geyl, *The Netherlands in the Seventeenth Century*, I (London, 1961), 218 and 215. To underline the contrast with the pertinent attitude of the modern West, a passage from E. Cassirer (d. 1945), *Zur Logik der Kulturwissenschaften* (Darmstadt, 1961; first published in 1942), p. 30, may be cited, where the intellectual consequences of the reorientation are discussed, in which man "statt das Wesen der Dinge als ein von Anfang an Feststehendes zu betrachten, in ihm gewissermassen den unendlich-fernen Punkt sieht, auf den alles Erkennen und Verstehen abzielt. Das 'Gegebene' des Objekts wandelt sich in diesem Fall in die 'Aufgabe' der Objektivität." More dramatically, this sentiment is expressed in Lessing's (1729-1781) statement: "If God held in His right hand all the truth and in His left hand the ever active longing for the truth . . . and said to me 'Choose,' humbly should I grasp His left hand and cry: 'Give me this, O Father! the Truth

sense, obsolete, its foundations outmoded ever since the final revelation manifested through the Prophet the changeless norms of individual behavior and social structure, and the grace of God allowed them to be implemented (within limits, it is true) in the Muslim community. It is not that Islamic society did not knowingly undergo change upon change or that the changes in Muslim ideology which time brought had gone unnoticed by the believers. But the change, to the faithful, was more like a leap from one absolute to another, and less like a development, if it was not merely a manifestation of human failing and acceptable only as a temporary and ultimately irrelevant lapse from what ought to be. A certain reluctance to confront the realities of a historical situation, when the confrontation involves the recognition of conflict with the norm that is dealt with and almost perceived as if it were in unimpeded control, has stayed with a majority of the Muslims through the intellectual humiliation and the perpetual crises of the last century. The testimonial to the lasting and universal adaptability of the faith and its unadulterated (though unspecifiable) cultural implementation still takes the place of an analysis of the contemporary scene and Islam in it (or of the nature of Islam in successive periods and different places) which is not merely

---

Itself is only for you alone' " (quoted by Stark, *op. cit.*, p. 210, from *Sämtliche Werke*, ed. K. Lachmann [Stuttgart, 1886-1905], XIII, 24). In a somewhat different manner does the sense of conflicting concepts of truth find expression in *L'aventure ambiguë* by Cheikh Hamidou Kane, governor of Thiès and minister of planning in Senegal. Here a spokesman for the traditional African Muslim culture insists that the world must come to an end, for only at the end will truth, the total truth, come to light. As long as there is a future, any truth must remain partial and unsatisfactory. The West, on the other hand, is satisfied with conquering every day, thanks to science, a bit more of the truth. It does not wait, whereas to the Muslim "la vérité se place à la fin de l'histoire" (p. 96), a viewpoint that may, incidentally, be open to contestation by the orthodox. On this interesting book cf. S. Van Riet, "Visages de l'Islam noir," *Bulletin du Centre National pour l'Étude des Problèmes du Monde Musulman Contemporain* (Brussels), n.s., no. 6 (1961), pp. 26-35.

a device quickly to project tomorrow's program onto the screen in the guise of a past realization.

This attitude leads to an extreme concern with power and success in history, or, more precisely, with success in history as the validation of revelation—an outlook that represents perhaps the sharpest possible contrast with the outlook that governs Christianity's encounter with history. It is from Islam's relation to history that W. C. Smith sets out to diagnose Islam's present situation.[7]

Islam is the community that has come into being to transfer into actual living the imperative that is the eternal word of God. Before revelation, the essential law of Islam, "the elaboration of that imperative, existed as a transcendent pattern." [8] By revelation, the "word has been made incorporate in history," [9] with the Muslim community its keeper. "As a creed or theological system may be the expression in an intellectual form of a personal faith—as is often the case, particularly with Christians—so a social order and its activities are the expression in a practical form of a Muslim's personal faith." "Membership in the community . . . is an aspect of a personal Islam." [10] Christianity is concerned with its orthodoxy, Islam with its "orthopraxy." "A good Muslim is not one whose belief conforms to a given pattern, whose commitment may be expressed in intellectual terms that are congruent with an accepted statement (as is the case generally with Protestant Christianity), but one whose commitment may be expressed in practical terms that conform to an accepted code." "The fundamental religious debates in Islam have been concerned essentially with what shall be the direction in which the on-going historical enterprise is to proceed." [11]

---

[7] W. C. Smith, *Islam in Modern History* (Princeton, 1957).

[8] *Ibid.*, p. 17.

[9] *Ibid.*, p. 18.

[10] *Ibid.*, p. 19.

[11] *Ibid.*, p. 20. One feels reminded of J. G. Droysen's identification in the preface to the second volume of his celebrated *Geschichte des Hellenismus* (1943) of theodicy as the highest task of the historian; this in pronounced contrast to the tendency, wide-

The direct relevance of the community's realization in history of the divine injunctions, to the ultimate success of the individual believer in winning admission to Paradise was emphasized by the actual historical experience of the beginning of the faith and the political glories of the classical period of Islam. The "striking, comprehensive, creative and responsible" success[12] of early Islam was religious. It "was seen as intrinsic to [the Muslim] faith." [13] By contrast, the early experience of Christianity had the effect that worldly success always remained "something extrinsic" to the faith as such.[14] The duality of Western civilization, as composed of two traditions that have never been integrated, one from Greece and Rome and the other from Palestine, has resulted in persistent discrimination between the secular and the religious. This orientation preserves the Christian from experiencing failure in temporal affairs as a religious failure, whereas Islam, "at least for the community, has been characteristically a religion of triumph in success, of salvation through victory and achievement and power." [15] The early Muslims, by taking

---

spread since the Enlightenment, to take issue with the actual course of world history. On this theme cf., e.g., H. E. Stier, Roms Aufstieg zur Vormacht im Mittelmeer, *Die Welt als Geschichte*, VII (1941), 9-51, at p. 12.

[12] *Ibid.*, p. 28.

[13] *Ibid.*, p. 29.

[14] *Ibid.*, p. 30.

[15] *Ibid.*, p. 31. Thanks as much to the attitude expressed in the New Testament as to the historical situation in which Christianity found itself in its formative period, the test of historical success was never crucial for the recognition of the religious success of either community or the individual. The Christian martyr had a feeling of dying against history, whereas the Muslim martyr had the feeling of dying in the direction of history (cf. *ibid.*, p. 30 n. 27). This may be a somewhat overpointed formulation, but there is no doubt that from the very beginning the Muslims felt constrained, for the realization of a "perfect" life, to have their own state, their own government, their own rules based on revelation and tradition, whereas the Christians had to wait three hundred years to develop a state in which some of their principles could be imposed on the recalcitrant "others." By that time the independence of religious success from political success had been

upon themselves the task of creating a new society, a new government, a new culture under God, confirmed by their accomplishment "the soundness" of his plan. "The brilliant success of the enterprise confirmed the validity of the whole conception. History confirmed faith." [16]

---

established. Later, it is true, there arose various movements to bring the political community under the direction of the spiritual community; yet the separateness of the two areas was never forgotten and the question was merely whether the temporal or the spiritual sword should be the more powerful. There never was a feeling that there was only one sword. In Islam, on the other hand, the theoretical distinction between the temporal and the spiritual is of Western origin. It deserves notice that the difference between the Christian and the Muslim concept of a (religious) community is more frequently quoted by Muslims than by Christians, presumably because the division is part of the Christian tradition, whereas to the Muslim it still represents a fearful innovation which many continue to resist. The debates that preceded the adoption of the Pakistan constitution of 1956 (revoked in 1958) are eloquent testimony to this struggle of traditions.

[16] *Ibid.*, p. 32. The sense of history as the proving ground of faith has not been accompanied by an aspiration to understand the structure of the historical process. History was primarily to learn from, not to analyze into component strands of motivations and interconnected levels of happenings or actions. What history was expected to teach was, often enough, moral commonplace appreciated as an illustration of man's ontological weakness and the blindness of his presumption. Isḥāq b. Bishr (d. 821), *Kitāb al-mubtada'*, sees in the story of Adam and Eve (which to him is, of course, history) an *'ibra*, a warning, an example; the objective of historiography is utilitarian in the sense that "historical events" are recorded not only for their own sake, but "to point the way through such understanding" of the past as they would convey "to good and useful conduct in the interest of the individual's welfare in this world and/or the next" (N. Abbott, *Studies in Literary Arabic Papyri, I* [Chicago, 1957], p. 43; for the text and its author, cf. pp. 40, 46). Illustrations from all periods abound; cf., e.g., Baihaqī (d. 1077), *Ta'rīkh*, ed. S. Nafīsī (Teheran, 1940——), I, 36, where from the lengthy description of how the caliph Ma'mūn (813-833) attained to sole rule (pp. 28-36), the lesson is drawn that to achieve high station (and great knowledge) is an arduous task. In this orientation, Muslim historiography is not alone. The great teachers of the tannaitic period of Judaism (*ca.* A.D. 70-200) also viewed history as *Lehrbuch* offering the great examples of the relations between man and God

The disintegration of the Arab phase of the Muslim venture, marked by the Mongol conquest of Baghdad in 1258, constituted the first great crisis of Islamic history. "It could be felt that the great endeavor to realize God's purpose was petering out, if it had not actually failed." [17] But Islam responded creatively to the disaster through a new "and in some ways fuller expression" in its "mediaeval" period, the most important development of which is Sufism. Besides, "Islam converted the conquerors," "finding for itself . . . new peoples and new cultures to carry forward its advance." [18] Nevertheless, this period has not (except, perhaps, in present-day Turkey) been accepted by a majority of Muslims as a fully valid instance of Islamic history. For one thing, the original tends to be seen as the exemplary. For another, "the mediaeval Muslims themselves felt a much less close link than did classical Muslims between the temporal and the eternal, between their own history and true Islam. The historical leaders and the religious leaders came to feel that they were leading two different things." [19] Finally, Sufism, concerned as it is with the purity of the heart rather than with the correctness of one's actions, evinces small interest in the historical process as such. And, moreover, the success of the "mediaeval" period did not last too long. By the eighteenth century Muslim society everywhere, and in every area of endeavor, was in serious decline. "The Muslim world seemed to have lost the capacity to order

---

and man and man as well as the authoritative illustrations for commandments and mores; ethics and history are inseparable; in fact, ethics follows from history. Cf. N. N. Glatzer, *Untersuchungen zur Geschichtslehre der Tannaiten. Ein Beitrag zur Religionsgeschichte* (Berlin, 1933), esp. p. 73. In the West, comparable views are traceable into the eighteenth century when, however, they had long ceased significantly to affect the actual writing of history.

[17] Smith, *op. cit.*, p. 33. Actually, this disintegration had set in rather more than four centuries earlier, and was an accomplished fact by 1100.

[18] *Ibid.*, p. 34.

[19] *Ibid.*, p. 35.

its life effectively." The degeneration of Islam coincided with the rise of Europe, "the greatest upsurge of expansive energy that human history has ever seen." [20] "The fundamental *malaise* of modern Islam is a sense that something has gone wrong with Islamic history. The fundamental problem of modern Muslims is how to rehabilitate that history." [21] And, we may add, to rehabilitate it under a pressure whose very nature was apt to make Muslims question the possibilities of such rehabilitation. Unless, of course, rehabilitation was to mean reinterpretation with the assistance of philosophy and Sufism as liberalizing and liberating forces. Actually, however, resurgence tended toward recaptivating classical Islam and hence toward repudiating the philosophical and the mystical elements of the tradition.[22] The very drifting into secularist reforms, which conservative leaders were unable to prevent, may have been a strong motivation to limit self-examination, wherever possible, to the particular. The additional circumstance that it was the Western scientific impulse that reactivated the scholarly study of the Islamic phenomenon made such study somewhat suspect; whatever the reason, the core of the faith—revelation and the person of the Prophet; the community concept and the historical relationship to other faiths; and, last but not least, the evolution of phase after phase of Islamic thinking, feeling, and practice—is to this day tacitly excluded from indigenous research. Western Orientalism has in some of its results been found useful for apologetics, but on the whole has been taken by all too many Muslims "as in basic tendency disintegrative of Islam in its central formulations." "The attempt to be analytic is regarded as merely destructive." [23]

The tendency of the Arabs to identify "Arabism" and Islam makes it more difficult for them to react in a positive manner to secularist nationalism and to come to terms

---

[20] *Ibid.*, p. 38.
[21] *Ibid.*, p. 41.
[22] *Ibid.*, p. 55.
[23] *Ibid.*, p. 72 and n. 57.

with a West that, in their view, "is out to crush Islam." "The Muslim world in general, and the Arabs in particular, have no grasp of the serious and strenuous efforts that the West has been making to understand Islam. Certainly they have no inkling of how extremely difficult such understanding is. . . . To a Muslim, Islam is completely straightforward, clear-cut, logical, and obvious. Misunderstanding seems to him appalling and perverse. He does not discriminate, and has never formulated, the presuppositions on which the system silently rests, and which he takes for granted. . . . He does not know how divergent these presuppositions are from the fundamental postulates of other civilizations." [24] Although the West has a very great deal to learn (and unlearn) about Islam, the Muslim world has not even begun to interpret Christianity for what it is; by and large, the Muslims are not even aware that they do not understand it. Moreover, acceptance of historical Christianity as real Christianity would seem to them to run counter to the Koranic rejection of the central Christian doctrines as absurd distortions of actual religious facts.[25]

---

[24] *Ibid.*, pp. 102-103.

[25] Kenneth Cragg, *The Call of the Minaret* (New York, 1956) shares Smith's feeling of the peculiar significance that "success" in history has for the Muslim. Cragg observes correctly the "deep sense of vindication" which the recent rise of Islamic power gives to the Muslim community. "For the community of the final and ultimate religious faith for mankind must necessarily also provide the truest political order and demonstrate how human existence should be organized and controlled" (p. 6). Cragg is keenly aware of the role of the past in the inner life of the contemporary Muslim, and of the "painful problem" this awareness constitutes. "For that sense of history includes the knowledge that somehow it has not always gone aright" (p. 204). When the Muslim world fell on evil days "it seemed that God in general history had half forsaken Islam" (p. 205). The diagnosis of the nature and the cause of decadence exercises present-day Islam, but no consensus has yet been reached. More gently than Smith, but no less convincingly, Cragg points to the unwillingness of the Muslim to view the problem in the total context of revelation and mundane experience and to avail himself of the tools provided by Western methods and concepts of historical and cultural

Semideliberate ignorance of the West, and of other major culture areas such as India or China, coupled with apprehension about facing the Muslim past without the certainty of arriving at a reassuring interpretation, have deprived the process of fortifying a precarious present by frequent recourse to history of stability and much of its potential conviction. Collective daydreaming carries its own penalties. It is at this point, in my opinion, that the Muslim, and especially the Arab Muslim, comes into deadly conflict with the historical role implied by his concept of his religion and culture. If history is the test, the test must be met. To trick oneself through emotionally satisfying but intellectually irresponsible historiography still leaves one with the inevitable task undone. This is why the same recurrent anxiety needs to be quieted again and again by (in principle) the same recurrent compensatory assertions about the past. The scrutiny of modern Muslim self-interpretation, as much as the acquaintance with medieval Islamic theology, suggests some doubt concerning the extent to which Islam is prepared to accept history as a binding experience. Basically, Islam is as Islam

---

analysis (pp. 206-208). Cragg's remarkable and insightful book bears out our contention of the primacy of the aspiration. It is written toward the renewal of the Christian mission to Islam on a higher, that is to say, a better-informed and less pragmatic (and hence, more effective) level than that which is apparently maintained at the moment. The purpose of the book is clearly stated in the preface: "The call of the minaret is perhaps the best single epitome of Muslim belief and action. To seek in it the clue to Islam, and from that clue to learn the form and dimension of Christian relation to what it tells, is the purpose of this book." The key problem for Cragg is contained in the question: "Can we so become aware of Islam as to enter into all its implications for the Christian?" (pp. vii-viii, xi). The purpose of the work removes it somewhat from our concern, but the artistic skill with which the presentation of the essential doctrines and sentiments of Islam is "spun out" of the words of the prayer call should not go without an expression of admiration. M. D. Rahbar, in *The Muslim World,* XLVIII (1958), 40-51, has provided an illuminating discussion of Cragg's book from the viewpoint of a very "modernistic" Muslim theologian.

wills; and history need not be much more than a storehouse of precedents for foregone conclusions.[26]

L. Gardet[27] undertakes to explain Islam through an interpretation of the political community. With the statements of medieval and modern Muslim theorists as his basic materials, Gardet confronts them at every major point with the views of Roman, and occasionally of Lutheran, Christianity; of "secular" Western modernism; and, where necessary, of the classical thinkers of Greece. Gardet accepts Massignon's definition of the ideal Muslim community as an egalitarian lay theocracy. "Le magistère législatif [*amr*] appartient au Qor'ān seul; le magistère judiciaire [*fiqh*] appartient à tout croyant qui, par la lecture assidue et fervente du Qor'ān, acquiert, avec la mémoire des définitions et l'intelligence des sanctions qu'il édicte, le droit de les appliquer. Reste le pouvoir exécutif [*ḥukm*] à la fois civil et canonique; il n'appartient qu'à Dieu seul comme le répéteront les Khārijites,—et il ne peut être exercé que par un intermédiaire, un chef unique. La communauté des croyants prête serment d'obéir à Dieu [*bayʿa*] entre les mains de ce délégué, tuteur que Dieu se subroge pour elle, dépourvu d'initiative législative et d'autorité judiciaire." [28]

The pursuit of an ideal political life (early projected into the reality of the first forty years of the *hijra* when the community was ruled by the Prophet himself and the four "Righty-Guided Caliphs" after him) in disregard of the actual situation has become the permanent drama of Islam. The primary cause for this unresolvable tension between norm and fact is the Muslim identification of the temporal and the spiritual planes. The faith (or faith per se) is a political value; in fact, it is the only political value and

---

[26] The important analyses of Arab, Turkish, Pakistani, and Indo-Muslim Islam in our time in Smith, *op. cit.*, which furnish the bulk of his work, are not here considered as they are tangential to the present discussion.

[27] L. Gardet, *La Cité musulmane* (Paris, 1954).

[28] L. Massignon, *La Passion d'al-Hallāj* (Paris, 1922), p. 719, is quoted by Gardet, *op. cit.*, p. 23.

decidedly the only value that gives the *civitas Islamica* its *raison d'être*. As late as 1939 al-Marāghī, then *shaikh al-Azhar*, expressly rejected as un-Islamic Jesus' command to separate the duty to the political community and the duty to God. The Muslim community is at the same time the Muslim commonwealth. The *umma* is a body politic as well as the body of true believers; it may not have been activated as a unified political organization for many a century, yet it remains the only true "nation" in which a Muslim has membership, a supernational entity without an organization, whose distribution among a number of states is, in the last analysis, accidental and irrelevant.

The basic concepts with which the political philosophy of Islam has had to contend have been those of authority and the hierarchy of power on the one hand, and that of the fundamental equality of the believers qua believers on the other. The balancing of the demands of authority and equality has been easier for Shiite than for Sunnite thinking, because the *Shīʿa* has tended to allow autocratic powers to the *imām* as the infallible perpetuator of prophetic authority. By contrast, the Sunnite caliph is merely the vicegerent (*remplaçant*)[29] of the Prophet. Obedience is to God directly; the human intermediary is but a sign. Nevertheless, the executive power of the intermediary is absolute; he cannot be held to account for it except to God whose omnipotence is its sole source. In principle, authority and power are not separated. The principle of authority and the resultant power are personified in the caliph (or the supreme *imām*).[30] But God has not delegated any of his power to man. God alone governs even though he will do so through a human ruler. Whether this ruler has been appointed or elected, or has merely usurped his position by force, his authority results from direct investiture by God, for God's authority is the only true authority even *in temporalibus*. In Christian doctrine,

[29] Gardet, *op. cit.*, p. 33. One may ask if the concept of hierarchy was not rather a contribution of the Persian, or the Turko-Persian, phase.

[30] *Ibid.*, p. 32.

on the other hand, God has communicated some of his power to man as a rational, free, responsible being. In the spiritual order, administered by the Church, the conditions of the exercise of power are positively established by God; in the temporal order, however, it is left to man to build the organization suitable to actual conditions on the basis of the general principles that the divine will has made known regarding the exercise of power.

The Muslim concept has resulted in what to us seem ill-attuned, not to say contradictory, phenomena: the possibility that the leader may indulge in arbitrary action contrary to the Muslim ideal (operationally, the absence of any mechanism to check such arbitrary action or to correct or depose the ruler guilty of it); the unwillingness of the public to acquiesce in individual actions of a power to which one does not take exception, and, hence, the frequency of riots and revolts; and a remarkable readiness to accept *de facto* government. The possession of authority seems to be like a status (*ḥukm*) with which God has endowed a certain individual. When God leaves the choice of a leader to the community it is incumbent upon the community to look for the morally and intellectually most suitable personality. But God is not bound to operate through "regular channels," and the success of an usurpation is, in the final analysis, nothing but the indication of his will. The corrective to an anarchy that lurks in this conception as a permanent threat is the duty of obedience to God's earthly leaders so long as they exercise their power in accordance with the Koranic law. For in his Book God has defined, once and for all, his own rights and the rights of his creatures as he wishes them observed on earth.[31]

The framework within which these rights come to life is the community. Islam is a religion, but it is no less essentially a community whose religious tie fixes for each member and for all members together the conditions and the rules of life. The unifying link is not an organization *in*

---

[31] *Ibid.*, p. 40.

spiritualibus, nor is it the caliph, who is charged at the same time with "the defense of the religion and the government of the world," but the Book by whose text every Muslim may and must judge the conformity or nonconformity of any given act with the laws promulgated by revelation.[32] Thus the *umma* has the double character of constituting the sole spiritual community for the believers, and yet of becoming fully effective only on a societal level and, as it were, from the outside. The individuals, discrete atoms of the same whole that envelops and absorbs them as well as giving them significance, yet retain and assert the discreteness that establishes their individuality—a concept comparable to Ashʿarite atomistic occasionalism where the discrete atoms are in every moment re-created by the Lord.[33] The *umma* then attempts merely to integrate the existing particularisms without destroying them. It unifies but does not transcend the "cités terrestres"[34]—tribal, ethnic, national, economic organizations. And, tacitly, Gardet seems to imply that this wide-meshed universalism of the *umma* renders possible any social and political adjustment of its individual components to changing conditions, provided (we may add) that the individual component desires to remain identified with that loosely woven solidarity unit. Within the individual component, the actual community of living contact, cohesion is maintained through social relations rather than through an identical ideology; but it is the determination to be regarded and to interact as Muslims which maintains cohesion among "cités terrestres" which may be without contacts, in competition, or even on different sides of a political battle line.

Not unlike Smith, but perhaps in a less "haunted" way, Gardet is aware of the need for a mutual comprehension of civilizations, for mutual respect and for self-respect in matters cultural, for an interaction that preserves the authentic and the unique on both sides. It is in this con-

---

[32] *Ibid.*, p. 194.
[33] *Ibid.*, p. 207.
[34] *Ibid.*, p. 208.

text that Gardet raises the question whether or not it is legitimate to speak of a Muslim humanism. He brushes aside the argument that the absence of an Arabic term for humanism—for *insāniyya* ("humanity") is in this sense a neologism that is far from being generally understood—means the absence of the concept. Avoiding the error of identifying humanism with the classical and classically inspired humanism, or humanisms, of our tradition, Gardet accepts the definition proposed by P. Mesnard, who applies the term to "toute conception théorique, toute attitude pratique, qui affirment la valeur exceptionelle de l'homme." [35] He elaborates this view by quoting J. Maritain to the effect that humanism "tend essentiellement à rendre l'homme plus vraiment humain, et à manifester sa grandeur originelle en le faisant participer à tout ce qui peut l'enrichir dans la nature et dans l'histoire . . . ; il demande toute à la fois que l'homme développe les virtualités contenues en lui, ses forces créatrices et la vie de la raison, et travaille à faire des forces du monde physique des instruments de sa liberté." [36]

It is fairly obvious that these descriptions of the humanistic attitude (rather than of any concrete humanism) were not developed from consideration of Islamic materials. The Koran does indeed assert the "exceptional value of man" as the most noble creature (and passages glorifying him are frequent in Muslim writings), but it would be difficult to claim that the Koranic revelation tends to render man more truly human and encourages him to use the forces of the physical universe as instruments of self-liberation (a term I prefer to the more static conception of "liberty"), even though such a tendency has been found by some Muslim modernists in the sacred text. Gardet insists on the distinction between a humanism that finds both man's *raison d'être* and his ultimate pur-

---

[35] P. Mesnard, "L'Humanisme chrétien," *Bulletin J. Lotte* (June, 1939), p. 7, as quoted by Gardet, *op. cit.*, p. 274.

[36] J. Maritain, *Humanisme intégral* (Paris, 1939), p. 10, as quoted by Gardet, *op. cit.*, p. 274. Maritain's book, comprising lectures given in 1934, was copyrighted in 1936.

pose in himself—essentially a humanism without God—and a humanism that recognizes man's creatureliness and knows him to be destined for a transcendent life of eternal felicity whose attainment, however, presupposes an earthly existence lived on the highest possible level—a humanism with God.

The believer in a monotheistic faith will always have to overcome the (apparent) antinomy of the infinite grandeur of his destiny and his creaturely misery. In Christianity, the incarnation of God in Christ points the way to reconciliation as it affirms the absoluteness of man's value even in this world. Islam, too, assigns each individual a personal end that relates him to eternity; it opens to every man the perspective of an eternal destiny. And it calls on him to organize the *civitas terrena* for the service of man as a believer. This position would render possible a humanistic development. But the sense of the transitoriness of the creature as against the Lord who alone remains, dominates all. The ultimate meaninglessness of this world—whose attraction is, however, realized—is never overcome. And yet the actual manifestations of the Islamic cultures belie this intrinsic limitation. The question, however, remains whether such humanisms as are traceable within the Muslim orbit are incidental to the Muslim message, tolerated as passing and irrelevant phenomena, or whether they are germane, if not necessary, articulations of its fundamental aspiration. The fact that, in spite of their profound attraction, the alien character of the specifically humanistic gifts of the older civilizations with which Islam came in contact was never forgotten may suggest the answer.

It would be wrong, however, to read into the rigidity with which Islam has sustained its basic concepts and attitudes a permanent inability to bring forth a political organization that would be effective in the modern world. There never was complete "Islamization" of the great power complexes. And it should be no more impossible to constitute a modern state as an authentic lay theocracy than it was to preserve it under the autocracy of the great caliphs or the military despotism of Mongols and Turks. But, like Gardet,[37] I feel that it is not through a wider diffusion of the scientific approach or, more particularly, through the growth of a historical sense that a new religious-political integration will be achieved, if it will be achieved at all in an effective, that is to say, in an enduring manner. The peculiar paradox of Muslim civilization—the attribution of absolute importance to the political community which yet is nothing but a means and whose actual organization and cultural achievement are therefore of merely secondary and "relative" value—is too deeply bound up with that experience of nature and relation of God and man to be discarded or resolved by forms of thought whose attraction to the Muslims at large lies in their presumed pragmatic utility rather than in their power to reshape the basic aspiration. One may, of course, always fall back on Hegel and the "ruse of reason." [38]

Smith and Gardet are primarily concerned, respectively, with the Muslim response to history and with essential principle as it shapes political structure and adjusts to history. H. A. R. Gibb[39] derives his vision of Islam from tracing its course in history. Smith and Gardet are, above all, interested in the present and its effect on the traditional structure, and in the potentialities of that traditional structure for the mastery of contemporary problems, but Gibb deals with the unfolding of the traditional structure and refrains from relating it explicitly to the crises of our time. His picture stands as a powerful prologue to the drama in whose uncertain outcome Smith and Gardet seem to have become almost passionately involved.

---

[37] *Op. cit.*, p. 327. Cf. H. A. R. Gibb, *Modern Trends in Islam* (Chicago, 1947), pp. 124-125.

[38] H. A. R. Gibb's *Trends* is not discussed here because, with all its wealth of observations and analyses, it does not attempt a "total" interpretation of Islam of the kind Gardet, *op. cit.*, has undertaken.

[39] H. A. R. Gibb, "Interpretation of Islamic History," *Cahiers d'histoire mondiale*, I (1953-54), 39-62 (reprinted in *The Muslim World*, XLV [1955], 4-15, 121-133).

Gibb's vision of Islamic development is succinctly, and indeed splendidly, stated in one brief paragraph:

> The whole of mediaeval Islamic history is dominated by the effort on the part of the Sunni or "orthodox" religious institution, firstly, to maintain its universalism against internal and external challenges, and secondly, to realize the widest possible measure of religious, social and cultural unity throughout the Islamic world. The second of these objects was not achieved until the political unity of Islam had been disrupted, partially recreated, and disrupted again; but in the effort to achieve it a vast area of interaction was created between peoples of diverse stocks and traditions, and in this process—almost, indeed, as a by-product of it—the mediaeval Islamic culture was brought into existence.[40]

The pursuit of unity as the leitmotif of Islamic development reflects something of the expressed aspiration of the Sunni community itself; it also accounts in our view for the willingness of this community to sacrifice the quest for good government and the urge to expand scientific exploration to the need for legal continuity and the safeguarding of religious experience as its unifying base. The pursuit of unity could become as effective as it ultimately did only because the "religious institution," on freeing itself first from "any domination of its ideals of faith and order by Arab social traditions," and later from "the Persian interpretation of Islam as a state-religion and the dominance of Persian social traditions," yet admitted the discordant cultural elements of the "Arabic humanities" and a measure of the Sasanian heritage "in relation to the principles of government." [41]

The "combination of (1) a God-given and unchallengeable sacred book, interpreted and supplemented by (2) an artificial creation of Prophetic tradition, itself canonized by (3) the doctrine of consensus [*ijmāʿ*], and thereby excluded from any but formal study by predetermined methods and rules, . . . established the basic character and

[40] *Ibid.*, p. 40.
[41] *Ibid.*, p. 47.

attitudes of Muslim theological studies,"[42] and beyond them, one may add, a style of thinking which found satisfaction in ordered transmission to the increasing exclusion of the uncovering and the assimilating into existing systems of previously unknown data. The correlation of Shiite dominance and the intellectual flowering in the fourth and fifth centuries of the Muslim era—explainable, to some extent, by the individualism of sectarian tendencies and their openness to foreign thought, as well as by the political instability of the orthodox institution and its consequent inability to curb or discipline the dissenters—is perhaps not entirely new as an observation, but Gibb has stated it with an admirable and convincing clarity. Similarly clear is his analysis of the weaknesses of that so-called "Islamic Renaissance," whose divorcement from the countryside and whose dependence on unstable and "inorganic" political institutions may have been the aspects most injurious to its survival.

The political stabilization attempted by the Seljuqs was accompanied by an atempt at intellectual stabilization through the Niẓāmiyya madrasas, which must be seen primarily as "training colleges in the Arabic humanities for a new class of administrators, the 'orthodox bureaucracy.'"[43] Simultaneously, "the functional division between

---

[42] *Ibid.*, p. 50.

[43] *Ibid.*, p. 56. Before the Seljuqs, the civil servants were, so to speak, humanistically trained. Their education centered on language and literature; they were the typical representatives of *adab*, a style of education and life, on which I have said more in *Medieval Islam* (2d ed.; Chicago, 1953), pp. 250-257. (The section will be enlarged in the German translation of the book, scheduled for publication in 1963.) Under and after the Seljuqs, the primary training of officials was in law, religious doctrine, and administrative technique, though the art of writing was not neglected. The formalism of their training is to be coördinated with the need of the period for a certain cultural retrenchment —consolidation of the religious heritage in defense against political and cultural disintegration. The structure and the function of the madrasa in the Seljuq age, and, more specifically, of the various colleges founded by Niẓām al-Mulk, have recently been thoroughly reëxamined by G. Makdisi, "Muslim Institutions of

the ruling and religious institutions was more sharply defined than ever by the formal constitution of the Sultanate, as the organ of political and military administration, alongside (though ideally subordinate to) the Caliphate, as the head of the religious institution." [44] As higher education came to be concentrated more and more in the madrasas, the range of intellectual activity narrowed gradually until it embraced only religious and philological sciences; this development was promoted by the decline of urban culture, the unavailability of an outside stimulant comparable to the Hellenistic tradition (parts of which had been "assimilated into the Arabic humanities"), and the standardization of subject matter, and teaching in the authoritarian manner inherent in the structure of the religious sciences.[45] The restrictive effects of the process, however, were not everywhere immediately apparent; the efflorescence of scholarship in Syria and Egypt under the impact of the Sunni revival, under Saladin and his successors, and the relative ease with which the newly formulated orthodox dogmatics pushed back Shiism, testify to the stimulating influence of consolidation in its earlier phases.

When the resurgent nomads (Turkish, Arab, Berber) in the eleventh and twelfth centuries encroached on the territory securely held by the Muslim institution, orthodox leaders realized the "value of the revivalist missions led by *Ṣūfī* preachers among the urban proletariat and in the countryside, which they had hitherto regarded with some suspicion and hostility." [46] Gradually organized Sufism "drained the orthodox institution of most of its vigour and vitality, and, finally, . . . found itself the champion of spiritual independence against both the rulers and the official ʿulamāʾ." From the thirteenth century the func-

---

Learning in Eleventh-Century Baghdad," *Bulletin of the School of Oriental and African Studies,* University of London, XXIV (1961), 1-56.

[44] Gibb, "Interpretation of Islamic History," p. 56.

[45] Cf. *ibid.,* pp. 56-57.

[46] *Ibid.,* p. 58.

tion, once performed by orthodoxy, "of maintaining the unity of the Community . . . passed to the Ṣūfī movement" [47] whose strength lay in its popular appeal. The Ṣūfī orders through their "lay members" reached out into "the guild organizations of artisans and other professions, . . . and extended also to village and tribal areas." [48]

The antirationalism of a religious movement that emphasized intuitive experience at first retarded the fixation of Ṣūfī ideas. When institutionalization compelled doctrinal formulations, "the general trend was toward pantheism," whether illuminationist, in the tradition of Asiatic Gnosticism, or monist, "deriving from popular Hellenistic philosophy." [49] "The intellectual consequences" of this development "were extremely grave. Instead of revitalizing . . . scholastic instruction in the madrasas, it drew intellectual energies off into subjective and anti-rational speculation, leaving the former more inert than ever and supplying no rigorous intellectual discipline in its place." In partial compensation, mysticism informed a new poetical literature which utilized popular forms "transposing their imagery into religious symbolism." [50] The disruption of political institutions in regions such as Anatolia and Persia not infrequently left the Ṣūfī brotherhood "the only form of social organization" intact. Thus it tended to become, in those areas, "the basis of association for self-defence" and, under favorable conditions, the core of a state; in all likelihood the Ottoman Empire and, without question, the Safavid Kingdom of Persia provide the most striking instances.[51]

Whereas Gibb's contribution consists in a broad interpretation of the growth of Muslim civilization through history, R. Brunschvig has enriched the conceptual means of cultural analysis and points toward new ways of investi-

---

[47] *Ibid.*, p. 59.
[48] *Ibid.*, p. 60.
[49] *Ibid.*, p. 61.
[50] *Ibid.*
[51] *Ibid.*, pp. 61-62.

gating source materials.[52] Brunschvig realizes that Muslim faith need not be accompanied by Muslim civilization. Consequently, when concerned with civilization, "we ought to base our studies essentially not on the quality of belief or the degree of religious observations, as some have a tendency to do, but on the effects this belief exerts in many cultural sectors, from humble material usages all the way to the most complex or most exalted psychocultural manifestations." We thus come to consider " 'degrees' in the idea of 'Muslim civilization'—to picture a sort of series of levels, a gradation going from a hard central historiogeographical core toward the more moderated forms, and from these to the peripheral regions subject to frank copartnership of cultures." One may wonder whether or not a modernized and Westernized Muslim state will continue to be a part of Muslim civilization. The answer will be affirmative only if Islam, despite all changes, can again become "a common primordial factor." Otherwise, "the preservation of Islam as a real faith, as a moral attitude, would not exclude the passing-away of 'Muslim civilization,' absorbed as it would be in a possible type of ecumenical civilization the major criterion of which would no longer be religious at all." [53]

From Brunschvig's concept of "degrees" of Muslim civilization, there results the "important task for the Islamologist to base this" thus far "quite . . . impressionistic classification on definite, rank-ordered criteria . . . and to let the general study of civilizations, as well as the very concept of 'civilization,' benefit from the method of research and the results obtained." [54] It is at this point that Brunschvig explicitly joins the effort inspired by what is to us the central motivation of Western interpretative

[52] R. Brunschvig, "Perspectives," *Studia Islamica*, I (1953), 5-21 (I have cited the English translation in *Unity and Variety in Muslim Civilization*, ed. G. E. von Grunebaum [Chicago, 1955], pp. 47-62); and "Problème de la décadence," in *Classicisme et déclin culturel dans l'histoire de l'Islam*, ed. R. Brunschvig and G. E. von Grunebaum (Paris, 1957), pp. 29-51.

[53] Brunschvig, "Perspectives," pp. 48-50.

[54] *Ibid.*, p. 51.

research, and of that *Kulturlehre* in which it finds its rational methodology and the existentially satisfying articulation of its results.

In his search for adequate taxonomic criteria for the identification of Muslim (as of any) civilization, Brunschvig responds to the complexity of the actual situation within the Muslim (as within any culture area by the idea of

> an expectation of varied associations of characteristics, of overlappings, from one group to the other (as in the same group, at different periods). . . . [It] cannot be anticipated that the boundaries for the diverse cultural elements [e.g., political order, language, religion] will exactly coincide among the provinces of Islam. . . . Associated characteristics, commonly reacting one upon another, contribute by the very variety of their combinations to the cultural differentiation of groups, to their peculiar *tonality*, which itself must find a place in the classificatory criteria.[55]

This reflection leads to a "methodological problem of the first magnitude: that of 'correlations.' Nothing could be more fruitful for the general knowledge of civilizations than the study of correlations, . . . and pre-eminently, of correlations between great cultural categories which are the principal sectors of human activity." Correlation, of course, is not to be equated with causal relation. If it be defined as "a non-accidental [Brunschvig is aware of the difficulty inherent in the demonstration of "non-accidental" because of the general impossibility for the historian to draw up "correlation tables"] concomitance of variation between two neighboring and related phenomena, it will express their at least partial interdependence, without prejudging the intimate nature of their relationships." [56]

It is in line with this approach that Brunschvig advocates, in lieu of the search for "common characteristics" in individual cultural elements throughout Muslim history, the study of its significant "*common cultural problems.*" [57]

[55] *Ibid.*, p. 55.
[56] *Ibid.*
[57] *Ibid.*, p. 57.

And when he brings out the complexity of the phenomenon of decline he puts his own methodological precepts to a successful test. Of first importance is the dissociation of cultural from political decay. The disintegration of a state is far from implying in itself a debasement of the cultural level. Muslim history is especially rich in illustrations of the absence of a definite correlation between these two types of decadence,[58] even though this same history would seem to suggest that political decline is apt to lower the cultural level after it has persisted for an extended period. Besides, the different areas of cultural activity (such as the arts, literature, or the physical sciences) neither unfold nor wither necessarily at the same time. Brunschvig insists on one further refinement of the analysis: the question must be faced whether observable facts indicate a regression, or merely a lag in advancement relative to another civilization with which the first is in (perhaps involuntary) competition. Also, the creativeness of a civilization is not to be judged by "lags" or "regressions" that affect limited sectors, especially those that "le jeu de l'évolution" has made to recede into secondary significance for the body cultural.[59]

What we may gain from the finesse of Brunschvig's methodological demands is, above all, the realization that at every point descriptive precision—a detailed phenomenology of the actual cultural situation in every sector—must precede a diagnosis of decline (or, for that matter, of stability or progress). For such a diagnosis may all too often be inspired by a focusing of attention on selectively explored facts where the selection is likely to have been guided by the interests inherent in our own aspirations, or in those reflected in the materials and the judgments left us by the contemporaries of the process which we are trying to investigate and utilize in our quest for total cultural introspection.

---

[58] Brunschvig, "Problème de la décadence," p. 41.
[59] *Ibid.*, p. 42.

III

The study of "correlations," as, for instance, between "economic life and ethics, law, social and political structure," in the way advocated by Brunschvig, will no doubt advance our insight into what may be called the "mechanics" of any civilization; it will prove useful preëminently as a method of tracing the transmission of impulses originating in one cultural sector to other sectors; of identifying the form (or the formulation) they take on in those other sectors; and of assessing the resistance they may meet, which in turn may modify the impulse and the sphere from which it sprang. The transfer from the ethical to the legal and economic sectors of the Muslim disapproval of *ribā* (interest, usury) comes to mind as a simple instance; the loosening of the coördination of secular and religious leadership as implied in the Muslim tradition, owing to the transfer of executive power to non-Arab military groups in the later Middle Ages, provides another obvious example of the heuristic value of research into "correlations" of political, social, and religious phenomena.

Its value must not, however, be allowed to obscure the fact that there are distinct limitations to the search for correlations. Correlation is confined to content; it does not bear on structure. The fact of coördinated developments can be established, but both their nature and their causal and final determination are beyond the reach of this method. Whatever coherence and logical or emotional consistency there may be in the life of a participant in a given civilization, the establishment of correlations cannot circumscribe; and even less can it identify the directing aims or motivations that make living within that civilization meaningful, or at least bearable. To ascertain the transformations of ends in the several sectors of cultural realization, the nature of the ends must first be known. To follow their transformations does, however, provide an efficient test as to whether or not the various drives and ends, which on the evidence of the sources seem to be decisive to the bearers of the civilization in question, have been correctly diagnosed, and whether or not their effectiveness has been correctly assessed.[60]

1

One must start from the fact that cultural achievements develop from definite existential situations or were undertaken as responses to them. For we comprehend a fact to the extent that we comprehend the context within which it happened or existed and from which, when we observe it, it is apt to appear severed or removed. Complete grasp of an individual fact is a function of the full grasp of the totality of its constitutive contexts. This realization determines the aim and the method of historical and cultural research. The interaction between the causal and the teleological—(i.e., the ultimate inseparability of vantage point and end) in the genesis of a historical fact, as of any psychological datum, must be noted as another characteristic of methodological importance. The general direction of interest in a culture or in a given society at a given time, and its feeling for the meaning of life and the true aim of human endeavor, decisively affect the formation of "secondary" fundamental concepts such as education (*Bildung*), scholarship, and artistic beauty. Conversely, the historically characteristic properties of such concepts are unintelligible, or at least cannot be syste-

[60] The material in this section is largely drawn from the following works by this writer: "Islamic Studies and Cultural Research," in *Studies in Islamic Cultural History*, ed. G. E. von Grunebaum, (Comparative Studies in Cultures and Civilizations), no. 2, American Anthropological Association, Memoir 76 (Menasha, Wis., 1954), pp. 1-22; *Islam: Essays in the Nature and Growth of a Cultural Tradition* (2d ed.; London, 1961); "The Problem: Unity in Diversity," in *Unity and Variety in Muslim Civilization*, ed. G. E. von Grunebaum (Chicago, 1955), pp. 17-37; "The Problem of Cultural Interchange," in *Études d'Orientalisme dédiées à la mémoire de É. Lévi-Provençal* (Paris, 1962), I, pp. 141-151. "Reflections on the Community Aspect of the Muslim Identification," *International Islamic Colloquium, December 29, 1957-January 8, 1958* (Lahore, 1963), pp. 39-42 (abridged).

matically organized, without an understanding of the aims and the life of the period. The primary aspiration restricts the freedom of development of the secondary concepts and their materialization, through which alone they become perceptible, while its ability to overcome psychological difficulties, both individual and social, largely depends on the multiple interpretability, the potential richness of the basic experience, as, for example, the religious axiomatics or the experience of the self.

How much, for example, the experience of piety, sprung from the original God-consciousness in a cultural community, may help to alleviate the despair of the soul that feels alone and lost in the cosmic or social universe, depends ultimately on the character of that God-consciousness and of the concept of man in which the community recognizes its ideal (i.e., normative) image. The comparison of self-testimony from representatives of different cultures often allows definite judgment on the varying degrees of existential satisfaction available to the individual and the community as a result of the character of the primary cultural decisions. The necessity of using comparison, open or implied, in any cultural investigation imposes itself, whatever the starting point of methodological reflection may be, just as much as a physician's examination of a patient presupposes comparison.

As pointed out earlier, the identification of a primary aspiration dominating a given society or civilization is not to be understood as denying the competitive or coördinated coexistence of other aspirations, nor as disregarding the fact that the primary aspiration does not affect all areas of cultural endeavor with equal strength. To present the society's cultural structure and achievement in terms of their relatedness to the primary aspiration yet remains perhaps the only effective way of attaining to a synopsis of data by means of a principle of organization which is inherent in the data themselves and which allows the evaluation of their relevance as this appeared to (and motivated) the members of the particular social unit.

For a society whose stated aim is the attainment of

felicity in the next world, the principal requirement of life in this world must be its appositeness to securing admission to Paradise. Life in this world must be so ordered as to conform to the instructions conveyed by the Lord himself through his messengers, and more particularly through his last Messenger, the Prophet Muḥammad; obedience to these instructions gives the faithful a reasonable guarantee that they will escape eternal punishment and attain eternal bliss. By a free act of grace the Lord has communicated to mankind the information from which it can derive the principles and the details of the correct life, including the holding of correct beliefs. The minimal beliefs are simple enough: God is one, and Muḥammad, through whom the last revelation has reached mankind, is indeed his Messenger. Thus the second part of the *shahāda,* the testimonial required of the believer, provides the indispensable authentication of the sole authority on whom mankind has to rely in identifying the divine precepts, their rewards and sanctions.

The service (*ʿibāda*) that God requires of the faithful is impossible without an organized community of believers. Such a community cannot exist without government, and hence the primary purpose of government is to render possible the correct and complete *ʿibāda.* In other words, the state is conceived of as, above all, a moral institution. Political theory derives its powers from the individual believer's obligation "to command the good and prohibit the bad." The government is charged with protecting the Muslim community from possible encroachments by the non-Muslim world, safeguarding it from schism and heresy, and enforcing the stipulations of the good life as set forth in canon law. The canon law (*sharīʿa*) is based on revelation and prophetic tradition; the government can neither add nor abrogate one iota. The transmission of the law is in the hands of lawyer-theologians, who develop it by interpretation and systematization. Thus the very survival of Islam as an organized community under God depends on the existence of an adequate body of *ʿulamāʾ*. Also, integration in that community is indispensable if the individual believer desires to lead the correct life as enjoined by Scripture and defined by the consensus of the learned.

2

Science, as the endeavor to collect and systematize what information the community requires to realize its values, is directed toward two areas of investigation, for, contrary to the prevailing attitude in the West, research per se, as an effort to widen man's insight into the mysterious ways of the Creator, is not a means of glorifying God. Its ethical value depends entirely on the area to which the investigation is to be directed and on the intention (*niyya*) of the scholar who undertakes it. To be fully relevant and fully justifiable, therefore, science must inquire into the data of revelation and of the prophetic tradition, on which every phase of the correct life must be based; and it must orientate the believer systematically to this world, insofar as such orientation is needed for him to understand and organize the world as the appropriate stage of the correct life. So the classification of scientific effort which is meaningful in terms of the Muslim's ultimate objective is a division into two areas of inquiry: (*a*) he may inquire into revelation (*Offenbarungserkundung*), and (*b*) he may inquire into the world around him (*Welterkundung*). This dichotomy agrees in its result, although not in its rationale, with the fundamental division of the sciences into Arabic and "ancient," which is generally proposed by Muslim scholars themselves.

The preference shown by the Muslims for a classification on historical (or genetic) grounds as against a classification consistent with their dominant concern—only rarely are the sciences classed as "religious" or "nonreligious"—is symptomatic of interference in the unfolding of cultural motivations by extraneous circumstances, such as the "accidental" availability of outside stimulation and the equally "accidental" political situation that turns mere availability into a consciously grasped possibility. But the fascination with the ancient sciences never did obscure their relative remoteness from the essential interests of the community. The strictly religious sciences (interpretation of the Book, the collection of tradition, the development of a law from the data of the Koran and the Sunna), with their auxiliaries of a historical-biographical nature (listing and moral evaluation of the transmitters of tradition; the history of the community as the repository of legal and moral precedent as well as the decisive chapter of *Heilsgeschichte*) and of a philological character (the study of the classical language and hence of poetry as a means of understanding the sacred texts, resulting in an intense devotion to grammar and lexicology), and finally of their methodological foundation and procedural justification (the systematic development of the principles of *ḥadīth* criticism and the bases of sacred law), all provided the hard core of the in-intellectual life by whose requirements the concepts of the nature of scholarship and of the nature and function of the scholar were formed. The "foreign" sciences, including all natural sciences, remained marginal in spite of the important contributions made to them by Muslim scholars. The community could continue without cultivating them; they had no roots in its fundamental needs. Consequently it was the foreign sciences that were shunted off when the necessity for consolidation of the Sunni community against the threat of political and intellectual disintegration, under the impact of heterodoxy and philosophical individualism, compelled a cultural retrenchment, or a concentration on education essential to the community's political and religious leaders. The foreign sciences withered away not because of explicit prohibitions but because the community no longer felt it could afford distracting and possibly dangerous luxuries.[61] It is hardly necessary to insist that the type of scholarship encouraged under these circumstances was devoted to ingathering and preserving, reorganizing and adjusting, that is, to didactic exigencies rather than to the initiation of exploration. The-

[61] B. Lewis has called my attention to Judah Halevi's remark likening Greek philosophy to a tree with fine flowers but no fruit.

ological boldness revealed itself in the rejection of parts of the accumulated tradition, and in the setting aside of the contemporary consensus for voices of the early period of the faith.

3

The development of the concept of the *Bildung* that came to be expected of an educated Muslim who was not a religious specialist, and appreciated in him who was, demonstrates more clearly, perhaps, than does the development of the sciences how history bends the fundamental attitudes of the newcomer by exposing them to a *hic et nunc* that is, in a sense, simply accidental, as he had no part in its causation. This kind of accident confronted Islam with the Iranian and the Hellenistic traditions, themselves impregnated by the ancient Oriental heritage, as a possible source of political ideas, perhaps, or of means of rationalization. These traditions, however, were never unequivocally blended with the specifically Islamic outlook, though they transcended it in terms of worldly maturity and helped to make it operative in the different settings in which Muslims were the masters.

The protection of Islam's basic assumptions—revelation, tradition, the methods of their legal-doctrinal utilization—from any but technical criticism entailed a certain formalism in the treatment and the transmission of essential fields of knowledge, which showed a tendency to stray to the less vital areas of learning as well. The feeling for authority; the overwhelming concern with the continuity of the community (leading to an extreme emphasis on the scholar's place in the process of transmission); the idea of knowledge as a fixed body of information, immense but finite, comparable perhaps to an enormous museum; and a sense of form rather than of structure all collaborated with a conviction of the inevitable decline of humankind to introduce an intense concern with patterns of thought and representation, a concern that was not to be matched in intensity by devotion to content. Literary and stylistic training is demanded of the government official, but it is necessarily untouched by any conflict of opinions and equips its recipient to serve any ruler of any persuasion. (The convergence at this point of functional characteristics of a "scribal" class of officials, as traceable, e.g., in China, and the characteristics developing from the particular historical situation of the Muslim Empire deserve close attention. The differences between the pre-Seljuq and the post-Seljuq official are not considered in this overview.) The intellectualistic and, in a certain sense, amoral character of this kind of education, with its strong interest in aesthetically faultless self-representation, becomes solidified through a predilection for form and formalism.

In effect, this means a nearly uncontrollable delight in classification and a consciousness of tradition with a tendency to literal copying; it further implies a certain resistance to inner experience, as well as the treatment of history as a collection of precedents and anecdotes rather than as a creative pattern. In the sphere of human relations the formal perfection of the milieu of the courtier becomes the standard, as does the peculiar neutrality of pure intellectuality and wit in the ethical sphere. In spite of a perceptible admixture of fashionable sentimentality, the cultivation of sentiment lags behind that of intellect; interest is directed, not toward the contents of the inner experience, but toward the re-creation, constantly refined and improved, of the traditional pattern of behavior.

The educated man is schooled in the art of administration but is not brought up as a citizen. The basic difference between the Greek *paideia* and the Islamic educational ideal is that the Greek is ever aware of the state; the Muslim, of the service of God. For this reason, even *adab* (the educational type whose description is here being attempted), with its religious near-neutrality, lacks any element of civic virtue (although there has been citizen participation in certain periods through guilds, militia, "chivalry" organizations, and the like). After all, the individual believer is not responsible for state and society so long and insofar as there exists a government that. in spite of sinful or lawless acts, sustains the framework in which the correct life can be lived. It is left to the religious "heroes," the canon lawyers (*fuqahāʾ*), and the saints to see to it that the government does not deviate too far from the essential demands of the Islamic norm.

4

To sense the manner in which the Muslim outlook affected literature—the only art to be considered in the present context—one may begin by asking: In what manner can a system such as Islam make use of literature? Leaving aside religious and political propaganda, one may reformulate the question: Does Islam actually have any need for literature or for any particular literary genre? The examination of the sciences has already shown us that Islam could not dispense with pre-Islamic poetry, and why it could not. The semireligious function of this poetry guaranteed to both its patterns and its aesthetic presuppositions the same authoritative permanence that was generally conceded to acceptable tradition in the Islamic context. But what beyond the poetry? At what point does the Islamic message offer a natural starting point for the development of one or another of the great literary genres?[62] Do not forget, Islam does not have a liturgy that varies significantly during the "ecclesiastical" year. The Christian liturgy appeals to the imagination; the Muslim inculcates discipline. The Christian liturgy dramatizes a mystery; Islam does not accept this (or a comparable) mystery. Nor does Islam possess a soteriology. As man has not been corrupted by a Fall, his need is not salvation but direction. It is easy to see that the absence of a dialectical tension between the plans of the Lord and the condition of man deprives the Muslim community of a strong motivation for the development of a drama. The literary instrument of

---

[62] See von Grunebaum, *Islam: Essays in the Nature and Growth of a Cultural Tradition*, pp. 104-109, where the interaction of the "Islamic" and the "Arabic" literary traditions has been examined through analysis of the eleventh *Maqāma* of al-Ḥarīrī.

religious pedagogy in Islam is the sermon. With all the desire of Christianity to appeal to the faithful through their imagination and through forcefully represented example, it is doubtful that the Christian Middle Ages, without the availability of the Hellenic tradition, would have resorted to the mystery play as an instrument of religious education. Without a comparable need in its basic outlook, it is no wonder that Islam did not have recourse to the Greek dramatic tradition, with which it had no point of contact. Least of all did Arab Islam entertain a view of man as a *dramatis persona.* In the mind of the orthodox masses, and of their theologians, man lacked the power to make an authentic decision, locked as he was in the cage of predestination, forever guided and never the guide, a prisoner to whom complete acceptance of the rules allowed only the illusion of free movement.[63]

Great Muslim poetry has grown from mysticism and, to a lesser extent, from religious feeling unspecified and

[63] Character in Arabic literature is developed to a point that lies between the pre-Euripidean autonomy of the happening or the action that comes from the outside to the person to whom or through whom it occurs and whose function and fate (rather than whose character) it molds, and the Euripidean primacy of the character, the psychological unity of the individual, the *bios.* Arabic literature is as episodic as the pre-Euripidean tragedy; in fact, it makes a virtue and a program of yielding structure for associative diversion (cf., as one instance among many, at-Tauḥīdī [d. 1023], *al-Baṣāʾir wa'dh-dhakhāʾir,* ed. A. Amīn and A. Ṣaqr [Cairo, 1953], p. 100$^{11-12}$), but it labels the actors as "generous," "brave," and the like, and operates with a typology of function, position, and descent (as partial cause of function and position) which confers a characterlike constancy on the figures that it introduces. Cassirer, *op. cit.,* p. 117, refers to A. Warburg's (d. 1929) demonstration of antiquity creating certain poignant forms of expression for typical and ever-repeating situations: "Gewisse innere Erregungen, gewisse Spannungen und Lösungen sind in ihnen nicht nur festgehalten, sondern sie sind gleichsam in sie gebannt. Ueberall wo ein gleichartiger Affekt anklingt, wird auch das Bild, das die Kunst für ihn geschaffen, wieder lebendig. Es entstehen . . . bestimmte 'Pathosformeln,' die sich dem Gedächtnis der Menschheit unauslöschlich einprägen." The patterns of expression which permeate Arabic literature must be appraised in the same light.

mostly sectarian, and occasionally from skepticism. Beyond this, the great poetry of the Muslim world—of which there is a good deal, almost exclusively in lyrical and epical form—has come out of local historical traditions, primarily Arab and Persian. On the other hand, the theory that underlay poetical production was in harmony with the propensity toward Aristotelianism which, on the whole, left a stronger imprint on medieval Muslim thought than did any other philosophical outlook. In other words, this theory which, except perhaps in certain Persian milieus, imposed definite limitations on literary production, was again in tune with attitudes that were genuinely anchored in Muslim feeling: the distrust of human creativeness (as represented in imagination and invention); and the idea that beauty, like other accidents of form, is a quality added to content as independently as the soul is added to the body of the human but not of the animal embryo.[64] This is hardly the place to analyze the aesthetic structure of the Islamic literatures; the interplay of Islamic and Arabic (or Islamic and Persian, etc.) intellectual and literary traditions in any major work must, however, be noted as characteristic of the interaction everywhere between Muslim civilization and one or another of the local cultures of the Islamized areas.

5

The problem of the relation between coexisting layers of a "universal" and a "provincial" civilization is by no means peculiar to the Islámic scene; it is, in fact, typical of all areas culturally identified with a civilization of a supernational or "universal" outreach. The supernational civilization is characteristically, but not necessarily, associated with and, in its legal aspirations, largely developed from a religious message claiming universal validity; in its be-

---

[64] Cf., for contrast, G. Flaubert's (d. 1880) dictum: "La forme est la chair même de la pensée, est l'âme de la vie" (quoted by W. von Wartburg, *Évolution et structure de la langue française* [5th ed.; Berne, 1958], p. 226).

ginnings it is championed by a distinct ethnic element. The realization of this relational problem presupposes not only the existence of a Muslim identification, but also the separability, in the analysis of outlook and attitudes of a given area at a given time, of elements to which an Islamic origin may be ascribed from others whose presence cannot be connected with Islam. This assumption is sometimes readily substantiated by the historical situation as such, which may be dominated by a clearly felt and openly discussed conflict between two cultural heritages; resolution is attempted within the framework of the universal culture whose essential tenets and values are, consciously at least, not to be compromised.

It must not be assumed, however, that the conflict between the two culture levels, however noticeable it may be to the outsider, always leads to conscious clashes among the people who have to live through it. In fact, awareness of the contradictions between the social forms of their existence and the social forms prescribed by the Koranic revelation, for example, may be almost totally absent; even if a certain self-consciousness about such contradictions does exist, the members of the community do not necessarily feel that their mode of living rules them out of membership in the *umma Muḥammadiyya*. It cannot be emphasized enough that, to the individual believer, it is his own and his group's determination to consider themselves and to be considered Muslims which overrides any hesitation or uneasiness when it comes to an accurate assessment of their beliefs and behavior patterns in terms of the requirements of the "universal" religious culture with which they insist they are affiliated.

One may perhaps generalize this observation to indicate that, in an encounter of disparate civilizations, a subjective criterion as well as a series of objective criteria may be found in order to establish which of the two is the leading civilization, that is, which of them is primarily responsible for the essential cachet of the local integration. This observation ties in well with what Brunschvig proposes to call the different "degrees" of Muslim civilization. The subjective criterion, which may on occasion conflict with the objective and analytically obtained evidence, is best described as the self-identification of the members of the particular culture community. One may go so far as to say that the solidarity feeling of the Muslim *umma,* and especially the solidarity feeling that binds together such alien communities as those of southern Morocco and the Philippines, or as some recently converted Abyssinian tribes and the Muslims of Sinkiang, is based almost entirely on the "personal" decision of the people involved to belong together and to recognize each other as partners. This holds true even when they have no factual knowledge of each other's concrete beliefs and mores, and even though no attempt is made to discover the actual conditions under which Islam exists in those outlying parts. For many a century the articulate Muslim has tended to play down, or rather to underplay, the significance of the local tradition within the religious and social life of his community. The aberrancy of the local believers' behavior patterns from a strictly orthodox viewpoint would be noted, but at the same time it would be excused because of the ignorance of the uneducated. Tolerance for their inadequate comprehension of the nature and the implications of the Prophet's message would be voiced in the expectation that sooner or later the community would slough off those relics of their heathen past and adopt a more truly Islamic way of living. In practice this has always meant that agreement on the minimum demands of Muslim theology and law would ensure acceptance as members in good standing of any community that would wish to be so accepted. In other words, in striking contrast to the Christian attitude, which makes full acceptance contingent on the receiving community's passing on the qualifications of the individual applicant or of the applicant community (through a missionary, a priest, or an otherwise qualified representative), the Muslim *umma* is willing to allow acceptance on the basis of a unilateral declaration of intention to belong to the people of the Prophet. This attitude has greatly facilitated the transcultural effectiveness of the Muslim mission. It has also had the consequence of permitting different patterns of a Muslim life to coexist in different parts of the world, and in different ethnic or social strata of the same political society. None of these patterns actually can be considered the Islamic pattern. In the minds of those who adhere to them, however, all are sufficiently in tune with the ideal represented by Koran and Sunna to qualify as Islamic. Here, in my opinion, is one of the principal factors, if not, in fact, the most important single factor, accounting for the amazingly strong emotional cohesiveness of the Muslim community, a cohesiveness that, after all, is not as a rule buttressed by any kind of formal organization. It is true that those learned in the religious sciences have everywhere tended to form social groupings of a kindred structure, but here again the similarity stems primarily from the determination to continue a mode of living that marks the groups concerned as belonging to the traditional community of Islam.

This "smallest common denominator" of beliefs and practices, which provides the signs of recognition for widely dispersed and often isolated Muslim communities, include belief in the unity of God and in the historical person of Muḥammad as his last Prophet; agreement on the obligatory character of certain practices, such as fasting and prayer (even though in actual fact neither practice may be observed); and the recognition that a certain way of life is most in harmony with religious precept, however imperfectly the precept may be known by the generality of men in a given locality. More important, perhaps, there is agreement on attitudes, that is to say, a consensus as to the method of reaching solutions to practical problems. Largely as a result of shared historical and spiritual experience, there are shared preferences in resolving situations that require choices. And there is, of course, almost everywhere, the non-Muslim to assist in a certain limitation (which may be tantamount to a definition) of what is immediately identified as Islamic. The essential function of such shared knowledge of beliefs and practices, of attitudes and methods of decision-making, is to give the community a sense of structural permanence or continuity even where such continuity has not in fact existed. The recognition that these elements are normative provides the essential link among the subcommunities of the *dār al-Islām,* regardless of the degree to which each community allows its life and thought to be regulated by them.

When it comes to describing conflict, coexistence, and interaction of Islamic and local culture patterns, Redfield's concepts of the great and the little tradition reveal their value. For quite frequently the relationships of those patterns may be characterized as the relationships between the great and the little tradition. One of the two patterns is recognized as the more advanced: it is assumed to have authority; it is almost exclusively represented in the writings as well as in the public actions of the elite; social prestige is dependent on its adoption (or at least on its profession). In the *dār al-Islām* the Islamic pattern is usually in the position of the great tradition. In contrast, the little tradition is the catchment of the popular undercurrent; its effectiveness, though still felt by the intelligentsia, is "officially" denied or deprecated. The hypotheses of the great tradition are considered beliefs; the hypotheses of the little tradition are considered superstitions. (This should not, of course, conceal the fact that the elements of the little tradition often command the allegiance of the whole group.) In fact, the social position of a person may depend on which of the two traditions he determines to live by.

It should perhaps be expressly stated that the two traditions are apt to conflict less on the strictly religious level than on a cultural level more narrowly defined. The bilingual culture of modern Egypt and of certain Berber areas on the one hand, and of the Iranian elite from the ninth through the eleventh centuries on the other, is not the result of opposing religious attitudes toward interpretation of the universal faith of Islam, but rather of unwillingness to sacrifice a cultural aspiration which, though not rooted in the prophetic norm, is yet valued as an adequate means of collective self-expression. And valued above all is the continued universality of the Muslim religious institution, whose maintenance requires at least partial submergence of the local deviation.[65]

[65] The universality of the religious institution is still recognized as binding. Even when contemporary Muslims examine their actual lives, this universality and the aspirations which it upholds, or which uphold it, remain the evaluative standard and the rationale of whatever deviations from the norm are admitted, for these must be defended in terms of the universally valid self-image. This is not to claim that today the world view of Persians, Moroccans, and Javanese is the same. Nor has it, strictly speaking, been the same in the past. But it was and still is one of the characteristics of the Muslim intellectual that he craves to maintain the fiction of the unity of both a Muslim world view and a Muslim behavior pattern, where there is a possibility of some unity of world view but not of behavior. Intellectuals whose personal experience must have taught them to the contrary have been insisting that the Sudanese peasant, for example, leads in all essentials the same religious life as the educated Cairene. Statements of this kind are explicable only when one realizes the strength that the community (and the intellectuals) draw from the acknowledgment of the existence of a universally binding and uniform Muslim world view, and when one takes into account the fear that if this fiction or assumption is relinquished, the solidarity of the Muslims would break up. The element of fiction, the gap between what ought to be and what is, is strong in any civilization, but it seems to be particularly strong in Islam, perhaps as a direct result of the stringency of the demands that the ideal makes in shaping every aspect of the believer's life. When a given community such as that of the Turks is confronted with the tension between the inherited self-image and the modern, Westernizing aspiration, reconciliation is sought by reinterpretation of the heritage and by justifying innovation through the result of such reinterpretation. This has been easier for the Turks, in part because their self-respect is not so tightly bound up with the origins of Islam, as is true of those whose Prophet arose in their midst, in part because in a lay state such as Turkey no direct political danger attaches to the position of the modernizing intellectual. The Turks have managed to identify more strongly, not with the classical, but with the medieval phase of Islam (to use Smith's terminology) as that in which they, as soldiers and later as rulers, reached the first stage of a glorious historical existence. By abstracting the Turkish destiny from the Muslim destiny as a whole, they have been able to steer clear of that peculiar feeling of decay which came to other Muslims from the experience of Arab history between 1100 and 1800. The Turks

The operational concept of culture which underlies the views here presented has been developed and to some extent tested in chapter ii. The concept of the "cultural aspiration" should reveal its heuristic or analytical usefulness by enabling us to develop general concepts of cultural description which allow the identification of comparable cultural traits in civilizations that did not have significant contacts with one another. Certain phenomena may be followed in very different cultural contexts, and analyzed in terms of the function they are called upon to fill in any one of those contexts, and thus their significance as builders or destroyers of cultural growth may be assessed.

The examination of "classicism" has been chosen as a sample of this methodological approach and will be undertaken in chapter iv. We may, however, note at this point that the meaning here attached to this term differs to some extent from the meaning usually associated with it; as a matter of fact, "classicism" is here used to designate a certain cultural phenomenon without exclusive reference to those periods in history with which we commonly identify it.

One further observation may be made in concluding this discussion. The approach to cultural analysis which I have tried to outline and to some extent illustrate would almost seem to demand application to further structural problems of the nature and the growth of civilizations. Concern for

---

put forward various explanations for the decline that overtook them in the seventeenth and eighteenth centuries. But the overpowering influence of religion could not in those days overthrow the more ancient Turkish tradition that their talent has been in administration, soldiering, and ruling. Also, their "national" history has allowed them to ward off inferiority feelings more effectively than some of their Arab contemporaries. A Turkish shoe shiner once said to me, "We all are sons of princes." This feeling makes it easier for the Turks to rejoice in the world as it is, whereas the Arabs have to cope with too long a stretch of unpleasant memories. With all this, to be Muslim is still an indispensable part of being fully a Turk. But this concept of themselves has proven perfectly compatible with the deliberate attempt to restyle themselves as part of the West, not only in their organization, but in their civilization as well.

classicism inevitably focuses attention on the situation that typically induces a period to think of itself as "perfect," that is, as a model for future generations and other civilizations to emulate. I believe the concepts here developed may also shed light upon the psychological response to striking conflicts between the ideal and the actual. The ability to preserve a perpetually reinterpreted ideal or *Wunschbild* as the only valid self-identification, in the face of historical experiences extending over generations which have deprived the living reality of any but the remotest resemblance to the norm, is a problem of peculiar actuality in our own days of cultural transformation.

The problems are many and the workers will always be too few. I sometimes wonder whether it is actually part of our aspiration to answer (rather than register) all the questions of whose discomfiting presence we are aware. We know that history has to be rewritten by each generation to help assuage its own twist of curiosity. What is true of history is, it seems to me, even more true of cultural analysis. All we shall really have time to do is to leave to our successors convincing samples of our kind of perceptiveness and of the kind of truth to which it has led us. Our methodology will not be lost, but many of our results and much of our manner of presentation will imperceptibly but inevitably turn into source material from which those who come after us will recapture our aspirations, as we are now attempting to recapture the aspirations of those before and around us. Provided, of course, that the continuity of Western civilization will not be broken and that they who come after us will still care.[66]

---

[66] The internal rationality extending to all the cultural forms produced by the West may be responsible, as M. Weber (d. 1920) has pointed out, for the "objective preëminence" of Western culture; but this very "universal validity and significance" (*Gesammelte Aufsätze zur Religionssoziologie* [Tübingen, 1947], I, 1-5) has made possible not only its spread over the whole globe but also "the expropriation of a large part of its own principles by peoples outside its historical setting who would push to the limit European abstract rationalism and the mechanical simplification" of the technical aspect of its civilization

(L. Díez del Corral, *The Rape of Europe* [London, 1959], pp. 46-47; first published in Madrid, 1954). J. Austruy, "Vocation économique de l'Islam," *Cahiers de l'I.S.É.A.*, CVI (1960), 151-212, refers (p. 174 n. 60) to the view of F. Dubarle, expressed in 1959, that the "oecuménisme" developing in technology forecasts the denationalization of techniques, their assimilation by all great societies, and their adaptation by all civilizations. What Díez deplores, Dubarle seems to welcome. This universalization of Western history, often accompanied by a *kenosis* of its aspirational meaning and a distinct and aggressive hostility against the area of its origin, decreases in a sense the importance of the cultural dividing line between "East" and "West" with regard to the future; for an analysis of the past and the immediate present the problem of the position of the Islamic world within or without the orbit of the "West" retains of course its urgent significance. This significance extends to the controversy most impressively personified by the great antagonists C. H. Becker (d. 1933), who declared, and E. Troeltsch (d. 1923), who denied, the essential participation of the Islamic *Kulturkreis* in the destiny of the West (contrast, e.g., E. Troeltsch, *Der Historismus und seine Ueberwindung* [Tübingen, 1922], pp. 694-727, and C. H. Becker, "Der Islam im Rahmen einer allgemeinen Kulturgeschichte," *Zeitschrift der deutschen morgenländischen Gesellschaft*, LXXVI [1922], 18-35; republished in *Islamstudien* [Leipzig, 1924-1932], I, 24-39). Recently, J. Kraemer, *Das Problem der islamischen Kulturgeschichte* (Tübingen, 1959) has rallied to Troeltsch's position, mustering new arguments in favor of a viewpoint that, despite its soundness as a historical approach, jars on the leveling universal humanism—inaccurately so called—which to many seems the only ideology capable of justifying the political facts of the contemporary scene.

IV

The Concept of Cultural Classicism

CLASSICISM AS A CULTURAL ASPIRATION may be analyzed as having four constituents: (1) a past (or merely an alien) phase of cultural development is recognized as a complete and perfect realization of human potentialities; (2) this realization is appropriated as a legitimate inheritance or possession; (3) the possibility is admitted that the present may be recast in terms of past (or alien) perfection; and (4) the aspiration of the past (or the alien culture phase) is accepted as exemplary and as binding on the present.

The factual accuracy of any or all of these four judgments is, to some degree at least, irrelevant to the emotional appeal or, better, to the psychological effectiveness of the classicistic aspiration at any given time, even though it may be urged that flagrant misjudgment tends to speed the disenchantment and the frustration which are the characteristic dangers in the way of classicist enthusiasms. It cannot be sufficiently emphasized that the decisive factor in the genesis of a classicistic attitude is not the awareness of the superiority or uniqueness of a given cultural or specifically artistic, political, or religious accomplishment of style, but the attribution to this achievement of a normative character. Classicism discovers in the chosen past an absolute model, and implies that this model must be emulated and recovered, that it may possibly be equaled and—remarkable inconsistency!—perhaps even surpassed. But, whatever the outcome of this process of rivalry and reassimilation, classicism holds that even an imperfect imitation of the model is of greater educational and civilizational value than any attempt at cultural creativeness in the spirit of one's own age. Classicism, if taken seriously, is a supreme effort of the cultural consciousness and cannot simply be equated with decadence and *Epigonentum*,[1] even though, historically speaking, the classicistic aspiration has on occasion been felt with special driving power in periods of disorder and decline.

With an assessment of the cultural productivity of classicism as the objective, skeleton phenomenologies of observable classicistic movements undertaken from different viewpoints result in a number of complementary possibilities of classification, each designed to bring into relief one significant aspect of classicism in the total context of cultural history.

I. The *function* of the particular classicism in its cultural setting calls for consideration. This function may be envisaged as the objective counterpart or the objective manifestation of the aspiration motivating the bearers of the culture at the time when classicism occurs.

A. Viewed, then, from the vantage point of the function it is called upon to fill (and with allowance made for the multiplicity of functions any historical phenomenon

---

[1] Cf. F. Wieacker, "Vulgarismus und Klassizismus im Recht der Spätantike," *Heidelberger Akademie der Wissenschaften, Sitzungsberichte*, phil.-hist. Kl., 1955/3, p. 51. In its essentials this view had already been expressed by Wieacker in his "Vulgarismus und Klassizismus im römischen Recht der ausgehenden Antike," in *Studi in onore di Pietro de Francisci* (Milan, 1954), III, 134.

may assume), classicism may serve in a number of ways.

1. *To stabilize cultural gains.* The classicistic mood whose spread the government encouraged in the second and third centuries of our era in order to deepen the loyalty of its subjects by deepening their identification with the Greco-Roman tradition was animated by a will to maintain, rather than to develop, the Hellenic legacy which had come to be considered one of the benefits bestowed by the emperor's rule. The barbarians could hardly be expected to develop a taste for the Hellenic tradition, and creative assimilation was clearly beyond them; in fact, one might say, the desired educational effect was predicated on the stability of a coherent and inclusive civilization.[2] Again, the so-called renaissance of the twelfth century, with its utilitarian bent and its primary interest in philosophy, medicine, mathematics, and the sciences in general,[3] may be interpreted less as a movement of discontent and radical reform than as an attempt to consolidate, on a safe and respectable basis, certain advances incident to a widening of the horizon of experience which had to be preserved without unsettling the traditional authorities.[4]

2. *To preserve a cultural position that seems to be slipping away.* Within the Hellenic world the classicism of the early centuries of our era seems to have been motivated by precisely this aim—an instructive example of simultaneous functional variation in varying cultural contexts. Spurred perhaps by the reverence of their Roman overlords for the Greek past, and the slight esteem their protectors felt for the present condition of Greece,[5] but motivated primarily by an upsurge of cultural self-con-

[2] Cf. R. R. Bolgar, *The Classical Heritage and Its Beneficiaries* (Cambridge, Eng., 1954), pp. 32, 61.

[3] Cf. P. Koschaker, *Europa und das römische Recht* (Munich and Berlin, 1953), p. 61.

[4] Cf. Bolgar, *op. cit.*, pp. 148-149, 182-183.

[5] Cf. W. Schmid, *Ueber den kulturgeschichtlichen Zusammenhang und die Bedeutung der griechischen Renaissance in der Römerzeit* (Leipzig, 1898), p. 15.

sciousness, the Asian Greeks of the first and especially of the second century strove to revitalize their heritage. They did not, however, strain for an unprecedented cultural manifestation; they merely set themselves the task of reviving, in mores, religious usage, and, above all, in linguistic and literary form, the ways of the model age between the battle of Marathon and the death of Demosthenes.[6] The revival of the form detracted from the failure to revive the reality; the upsurge of an unpolitical, backward-looking Panhellenism sufficed to stabilize the classical heritage; the absence of a competing humanistic civilization of comparable level and complexity secured the movement an almost unparalleled effectiveness. The standards it set were still subscribed if not lived up to when Theodoros Metochites (1260/61-1332) endeavored to make room for contemporary cultural reality in self-expression while maintaining the binding character of the obsolete heritage which still monopolized the intellectual life of Byzantium.[7] Dion of Prusa failed to persuade his contemporaries to "become again like the ancient Greeks," but the Sophistic movement as a whole succeeded in preserving the authority of the formal means and achievements developed by the ancients, and, therewith, the means and achievements themselves for a later and more creative revitalization.

When the Arab poet and literary critic of the golden

[6] Cf. Lucian, *Rhetorum Praeceptor*, c. 18 (ed. Jacobitz, III, 93); reference in A. Boulanger, *Aelius Aristide et la sophistique dans la province d'Asie au IIᵉ siècle de notre ère* (Paris, 1923), p. 52. Pliny the Younger speaks, at the beginning of the second century A.D. of the Greeks as *homines maxime homines*, "men who are in the fullest sense men" (*Epistulae*, viii, 24; trans. Melmoth).

[7] Cf. H.-G. Beck, *Theodoros Metochites. Die Krise des byzantinischen Weltbildes im 14. Jahrhundert* (Munich, 1952), pp. 50-75, esp. pp. 61-62. F. Dölger, "Der Klassizismus der Byzantiner, seine Ursachen und seine Folgen," *Geistige Arbeit*, V/12 (June 20, 1938), 3-5, offers a brief analysis of the function filled by Byzantine cultural classicism; his viewpoint, however, differs considerably from that developed in the present study.

age, and his successor of the subsequent "sick period," [8] strove to uphold the unqualified authority of Bedouin poetry, they found themselves in a more complex psychological situation. For not only was the cultural realization to which they were clinging obsolete in terms of their own cultural milieu, and no longer significantly productive even among the desert tribes, but those very Bedouins whose poetry had at one time been the most potent means of integrating Arabian civilization, yet had never attained to comparable relevance in the Islamic age, were despised and kept at arm's length by the same urban public that insisted on the authoritativeness of their prosodical and thematic conventions. The Periclean Greek could be the human as well as the literary ideal; identification with the Bedouin was out of the question. Yet the very partisan and ambivalent adherence of the littérateurs to the Bedouin tradition won for the pagan literary model a sham permanence almost identical in effective duration with that of the models proclaimed by the Second Sophistic. The insecurity of the later Middle Ages, and the absence of a cultural alternative, may have been factors compensating for the intrinsic deficiencies of the ideal and its creators.

3. *To achieve self-stylization.* In sharp contrast to the urban Arab's outlook on the Bedouin originator of his literary models, the "classical" phase may be adopted as such precisely because of the human identification it permits. When the Romans turned to *humanitas,* they had to turn to the Greeks to give body to their aspiration. When they were in search of a humanistic widening of their traditional self-image, they had to restyle themselves by the Greek ideal as it was presented to them by declining Hellenism.[9] When the Greco-Roman world was no more,

---

[8] To use the verdict of Abū 'l-Fath al-Bustī (971-1010) on his period, *az-zamān al-marīḍ,* in a verse in al-Baihaqī (1105-1169), *Ta'rīkh ḥukamā' al-islām,* ed. M. Kurd ʿAlī (Damascus, 1946), p. 50[9].

[9] Cf., e.g., E. Hoffmann, *Pädagogischer Humanismus* (Zürich and Stuttgart, 1955), pp. 44-45.

Orosius, Gregory of Tours, and Isidore of Seville still saw themselves "as belonging to peoples especially privileged in comparison with 'barbarian' stock." One draws on antiquity for ancestors and begetters. Ethnogenic fables have been devised in France since Merovingian times. Are not the Franks descended from the Trojan Francus? Fiction of this kind "was taken seriously as genealogy and became a veritable form of ethnic consciousness." [10]

In its most uninhibited form we see self-stylization at work in certain documents of modern nationalism, which redefine the collective personality by accepting the precedent and the authority of a pristine civilization. In 1939 an Iraqi educator, Sāmī Shaukat, said to a conference of teachers: "You see how history is made up according to the needs of the moment: this is formative history." In application of this principle he explained that

> Arab history goes back thousands of years; it is by neglect that it has been made to start at the prophetic message. . . . We find that everything makes us lift our heads high when we consider the histories of the Semitic empires formed in the Fertile Crescent—the Chaldean, the Assyrian, the African [*sic!*], the Pharaonic or the Carthaginian; all these things must persuade us that the civilisation of the world at the present time is based on foundations laid by our ancestors. These empires and their dependencies are all our property; they are of us and for us; we have the right to glory in them and honour their exploits, just as we have the right to cherish and exalt the glories of Nebuchadnezzar, Hammurabi, Sargon, Ramses, Tutankhamen, in the same way that we glory and

[10] Jean Seznec, *The Survival of the Pagan Gods* (New York, 1953), pp. 8-20. In different historical contexts the attribution of Trojan origin has, of course, an altogether different motivation and hence an altogether different meaning. In the thirteenth century, for example, it became customary to connect Trojans and French with a view to justifying the Fourth Crusade as a "reconquest." Cf. the interesting discussion in P. Alphandéry and A. Dupront, *La Chrétienté et l'idée de croisade* (Paris, 1954-1959), II, 94-95.

take pride in ʿAbd ar-Rahmān ad-Dākhil, ʿAbd al-Malik b. Marwān, Hārūn ar-Rashīd and al-Maʾmūn.[11]

Differing from Shaukat's outburst, not categorically but merely in subtlety and apolitical intent, is the notion of Wilhelm von Humboldt that the spirit of antiquity had passed to the Germans. It is the Germans who first faithfully understood and experienced the spirit of the Greeks. Humboldt planned to write a history of the decay of the Greek republics because, in his own words, "griechischer Geist auf deutschen geimpft, erst das ergibt, worin die Menschheit ohne Stillstand fortschreiten kann." [12]

4. *To justify change.* As a rule, major cultural changes, whether they affect the basic structure of a civilization as a whole or merely its articulation in a limited area of cultural effort, are accompanied by a feeling of liberation from authority. The contemporary experience of relief from a restraint that has come to seem irrelevant or positively crippling is echoed so insistently in the documents of the period that it is not always easy for a posterity, which perhaps is still profiting spiritually from the dethronement of that particular authority, to realize that the alleged liberation was in fact no more than the re-

[11] *Hādhihi ahdāfu-nā; man āmana bihā fa-huwa minnā* (Baghdad, 1939), pp. 11, 43-44; trans. S. G. Haim, "Islam and the Theory of Arab Nationalism," *Die Welt des Islams,* n.s., IV (1955), 125. The same cultural vision has been articulated in a somewhat more disciplined manner by ʿAbdarraḥmān al-Bazzāz, *al-Islām waʾl-qaumiyya ʾl-ʿarabiyya* (Baghdad, 1952), trans. S. G. Haim, *Die Welt des Islams,* n.s., III (1954), 201-218, esp. pp. 209-210. In 1906, Georges Sorel (d. 1922), spoke of the mythological mode of using the past which makes it "a means of acting on the present." Cf. *Reflections on Violence,* trans. T. E. Hulme and J. Roth (Glencoe, Ill., 1950), pp. 118, 142 and 144; the passage is discussed by J. Goody and I. Watt, The Consequences of Literacy, *Comparative Studies in Society and History,* V (1962-1963), 304-345, at pp. 322-323. In a different context a similar formulation was reached by R. Habachi, *Une philosophie pour notre temps* (Beirut, 1960), p. 25: "L'histoire n'est pas le passé, mais ce que nous faisons avec le passé."

[12] W. Rehm, *Griechentum und Goethezeit* (3d ed.; Bern, 1952), pp. 230-231.

placement of one authority by another. It is obvious that this was true when Renaissance humanism freed itself from the chains of medieval ecclesiasticism to enter into voluntary servitude to antiquity. The humanists of the fifteenth century, not strong enough in the face of traditional opinion to declare the axiomatic or absolute value of their aspirations, had to buttress their argumentation and legitimize their new view of life by an appeal to the classics to whom they knew themselves akin and who rewarded their dedication by allowing themselves to be made into unattainable models. It is instructive to follow the development of antiquity in the minds of the Italian humanists, from an object of imitation to a pervasive standard of scientific, literary, artistic, and philosophical achievement, and, beyond this, a guide of individual and collective existence, and, finally, a lever to elevate the popular civilization of the day to a timeless ideality.[13] When, in the sixteenth century, a number of French scholars and writers claimed full freedom for the individual to follow his own road, this freedom had to be won from the authority of the ancients as well as from the medieval tradition which the Greeks and the Romans had come to supersede.[14]

5. *To provide a stage for experiences, aspirations, and self-views which cannot be satisfactorily accommodated within contemporary reality or its current interpretation.* Man has always felt the need, in Shakespeare's words, "to give to airy nothing / A local habitation and a name";[15] he has never been content to keep his dreams in dreamland, but has always sought to anchor them firmly in space and time so that, endowed with a precarious semblance of reality, they may function as a lever toward the developmental desire symbolized by the dream. With the advancement of geographical and historical knowledge

---

[13] Cf. H. von Srbik, *Geist und Geschichte vom deutschen Humanismus bis zur Gegenwart* (Munich and Salzburg, 1950-1951), I, 47.

[14] Cf. H. Gillot, *La Querelle des anciens et des modernes en France* (Paris, 1914), pp. 33-34.

[15] *A Midsummer Night's Dream,* V, i, 16.

and, more particularly, with the increasing sensitivity of the scientific conscience, it has been more and more difficult for us to locate our fancies, whose extrapolation yet remains intensely important as an unusually powerful means of self-understanding and self-development. History, respectable in method and tone, has in some measure been assigned the role fancy would carry. Willy-nilly the historians "help to elicit or diagnose their country's traditions; or rather, perhaps, . . . they give added leverage or confirmation to the decision which their contemporaries are already making on this point. . . . Over and over again we discover to what a degree, in politics for example, men do their thinking and form their attitudes by reference to some presumed picture of the procession of the centuries." [16]

But the services of history are not enough. We need areas where the factual obstacles to wish assertion are less irksome or less obvious. We mollify the harsh outlines of history in the historical novel; we confront ourselves with a contrasting human ideal to justify our aspirations after we feel chastened by shame. So the early Americans, after the fashion of their European contemporaries, discovered their weaknesses through the image of the good savage; but, in studying him, "in the end they had only studied themselves, strengthened their own civilization, and given those who were coming after them an enlarged certainty of another, even happier destiny. . . ." From cultural primitivism the American gained ultimately "deep affirmation of the role of civilization in America. It turned out, as it had to, that what Indians signified was not what they were, but what Americans should not be. Americans were only talking to themselves about themselves." [17]

[16] H. Butterfield, *Man on His Past. The Study of History and Historical Scholarship* (Cambridge, Eng., 1955), pp. 27, 30.

[17] R. H. Pearce, *The Savages of America. A Study of the Indian and the Idea of Civilization* (Baltimore, 1953), pp. ix, 232. M. Eliade, *Mythes, rêves et mystères* (2d ed.; Paris, 1957), p. 37, quotes the Italian folklorist G. Cocchiara (1948) for the view that the savage was invented before he was discovered. Eliade, *op. cit.*, pp. 37 ff., and other scholars have shown that the ac-

In a comparable manner, the Germans (but not only the Germans) of the late eighteenth century projected their human ideal back into the flowering of Greece, only to feel confirmed in the rightness of their quest when they encountered this ideal in the great centuries of Hellenic civilization. It is, of course, not to deny the reality of the Greek achievement and the unique magic of its legacy when, in this context, the fact is stressed that to the rising post-Renaissance West the Greeks were often but a mirror in which contemporary ideals of beauty and freedom, of *humanitas* and naturalness, were made to shine; their realization at a tangible point in space and time constituted a source of hope and encouragement for the struggling present.[18]

To Wieland the personalities of Greek mythology had been empty "Scheingestalten"; to the poets of the *Sturm und Drang* they became true and tangible incarnations of titanic aspirations, of dominating powers and forces. As the *Lebensgefühl* of these poets was of a tragic hue, they saw the tragic character of the Greek heroic age and took it as a formative and justifying model. The admirers of Ossian discovered a Nordic Hellenism[19] as the authoritative ex-

---

ceptability of projecting the human ideal onto the "noble savage" has its basis in the mythical concept of a "natural man" existing outside historical time and cultural development. The idea of a terrestrial paradise as the initial locus of human existence renders concrete the tendency, apparently inherent in man's unreflected self-view, to look to the original form or phase of a phenomenon for its perfect configuration. At this point an anchoring of classicist movements in group psychology may be indicated as a possible direction for future researches.

[18] Cf. G. Billeter, *Die Anschauungen vom Wesen des Griechentums* (Leipzig and Berlin, 1911), p. 71. Instructive also is the discussion of the variations of the concept of the ideal Greek among the moderns in W. Déonna, *L'Expression des sentiments dans l'art grec* (Paris, 1914), pp. 80-83. The human mind seems to incline toward reinterpreting the life of the great individual as a paradigmatic pattern. That Goethe attempted to realize an exemplary life in the conscious endeavor to create a model has often been noted. Cf., e.g., the discussion in Eliade, *op. cit.*, pp. 29, 30.

[19] "Nordisches Griechentum": cf. Rehm, *op. cit.*, pp. 70-72, 76.

trapolation of their own existential bias. But the next generation of German thinkers and seekers was concerned with the cult of human dignity; it found the absolute measure of man in Greek classical art and in the "soul" it seemed to embody in its impeccably proportioned statuary. Greek classicism was to serve the growth of a German classicism: the Greek was experienced as a possible form of the German, and the reality of the classical Greek was interpreted as assuring the possibility of the realization of a classical German.

Not one of the great German Hellenophiles and classicists had ever been in Greece; some of them deliberately forewent an opportunity to visit the country from which they derived the validity of their dreams. The faith in the Hellenic model assumed religious features, and weakened only when it had become part and parcel of the ideology of educated Germany as well as of German education. With the Greek landscape as his stage, a Hölderlin could seem real to himself; the demarcation line between historical Greece and Elysium was uncertain, but the creative force of the enthusiastic fiction was incalculable. Is it not significant that for the last four hundred years the force most inimical to the cult of the Greco-Roman classics has been, not intellectual disinterest or Philistinism but the pride and the self-reliance of a rising Occidental civilization willing to appreciate and repect the ancestral achievement, but sufficiently self-confident to recognize no authority outside itself?

B. The psychological (*kulturpsychologisch*) aspect of the function of any particular classicism may be interpreted on two different levels.

1. A classicist movement may be understood as the reaction to a feeling of inadequacy. This inadequacy contemporaries may experience as inherent in (*a*) their particular historical situation which is, in their view, incapable of allowing for the display or the development of their potentialities. The French humanists and Hellenophiles of the sixteenth century shared this outlook on their times with the German romantics. Both felt the need for a

thoroughgoing remodeling of the cultural structure of their day so as to make it livable for the kind of existence they aspired to.

But, on the other hand, the inadequacy (*b*) may be found in oneself. Contemporaries may be oppressed by a sense that the world has grown old, as happened in the Greco-Roman world in the early centuries after Christ; or they may suffer from a conviction of the inevitability of human decline, as occurred in the Muslim orbit in the later Middle Ages. In the first instance, the classical model is called upon to serve as a tool for change; the mood of the times is a somewhat irritable and impatient optimism. The more uncompromisingly the authority of the heritage to be shaken off is set against modification, the more joyfully and unconditionally is the authority of the classical age accepted. In the second instance, however, the classical model is called upon to serve as a tool to buttress the crumbling walls of civilization. Reform is backward-looking; not only the spirit but the letter of the past must be recaptured.

Return to the Rightly-Guided Caliphs, to the Islam of the Prophet's lifetime, is longed for. The model is looked to not for relevance to present problems but for the safety and security it is expected to confer on a generation imbued with a sense of its inadequacy and anxious to elude the difficulties that beset it. It is always possible to discern among the causes of an extreme conservatism, or a "classicism" of static intent, a feeling of insufficiency in regard to mastery of the material, social, or intellectual universe, alongside a realization of the increasingly overwhelming complexity of that universe. The object of a "classicism of return" is, in part at least, a decrease in cultural complexity; it is a "rectractile" movement[20] advocating consolidation through shrinkage. A movement of this order characteristically overlooks the fact that the period of apostolic simplicity, which is chosen as authoritative and exemplary, was actually a period of experiential expansion.

[20] To adopt A. L. Kroeber's expression in *The Nature of Culture* (Chicago, 1952), pp. 381-383.

This is strikingly obvious with respect to the period of the *rāshidūn* caliphs, which has so often been "classicized" by Muslim critics dissatisfied with the conditions of their day.

II. Classicism, then, to move on to the second level of psychological interpretation, may be experienced (A) as a dynamic or dynamizing concept. Here the classical model is regarded, not as a given datum to be repeated, but as an ideal whose recapture will transform it into a means of advancement and enrichment of those who succeed in vitalizing it. Not to follow the Greeks but to do as the Greeks did; not to imitate them but to create with as much freedom and self-assurance as they possessed: this is the goal of the French humanist of the sixteenth century and of the German classicist from Winckelmann to Goethe.[21] Here classicism is not an end in itself but, ideally at least, a means, or, one might almost say, a mere tool, the most potent and the most noble, it is true, to serve the contemporary world and, more concretely, to serve one's nation.

By contrast, classicism may be experienced (B) as a static notion of perfection. According to this view, Greece may be nothing less than the home of the golden age. The spirit of the present must be taught to approximate the unattainable where it can be approached, that is to say, where teachable rules can be abstracted, or simply taken over, from the heritage. The impossibility of duplicating the "classical" past is, of course, realized, but the freedom to fall short of the goal is granted and enjoyed somewhat in the spirit in which infringements of moral code and etiquette by the lower classes are condoned—resignedly, wistfully, contemptuously.

Classicism as a static concept, if it is to be culturally

---

[21] Cf. Dionysius of Halikarnassus, *Techne* x.19 (ed. Usener-Radermacher, II, 373): "Not he who speaks the words of Demosthenes, but he who speaks in the manner of Demosthenes, imitates Demosthenes." Rehm, *op. cit.*, p. 18, quotes Humboldt's dictum: "Der Mensch hat nur insoweit einen bestimmten Charakter, als er eine bestimmte Sehnsucht hat," and adds the word of Hölderlin: "Wir sind nichts; was wir suchen, ist alles."

effective at all, must be accompanied by faith in the possibility and the efficacy of "imitation"; in negative terms, it presupposes slight interest in and limited insight into the historical process, or the absence of an effective notion of development. It is incompatible, too, with a cyclical view of history. It is significant that Goethe objected to historicizing the Greek landscape (which he had never seen),[22] and that, when the idea of Greece had become historicized for Bachofen and his generation, classicism as a normative ideal was losing its hold on Germany. May one venture the view that our civilization, as fundamentally history-centered,[23] is by its very structure averse to extended subservience to at least the static version of the classicist ideal? The transition, most readily followed in France, from the dynamic classicism of the sixteenth century to the static classicism of the late seventeenth and early eighteenth centuries, and back to a more dynamic perception of the ancient heritage toward the end of the eighteenth century,[24] deserves close examination in the interest of a deeper understanding not only of classicistic movements but of the fundamental drives of Western civilization as well. The examination of this sequence of classicisms may also shed light on the paradoxical fact, not yet accounted for, that on the whole the great European classicisms shared a belief in "imitation" and a certain weakness of the historical sense, and yet must be interpreted as dynamic phenomena.

III. Classicisms differ in the range allowed them within the archaizing or receptive culture. For classicistic movements vary sharply in regard to the aspects of the model culture which are accorded attention and authority.

A. The "other" culture in its totality may be accorded

---

[22] Cf. Rehm, *op. cit.*, p. 8.

[23] Cf. L. Fèbvre in *Revue de métaphysique et de morale*, LIV (1949), 226.

[24] Cf. the revealing title of L. Bertrand's book: *La Fin du classicisme et le retour à l'antique dans la seconde moitié du XVIIIe siècle et les premières annés du XIXe en France* (Paris, 1897).

the status of the classical model. This seems to have happened at some of the stages of the Japanese adoption of Chinese civilizational standards and accomplishments as well as in the earlier phases of attempted acculturation to the West by Near and Middle Eastern groups. Examples might also be adduced from the periods when Hellenism pervaded the *oikumene* and when the enthusiasms of the Renaissance craved complete identification with antiquity. In all these instances, however, it must be noted that, even though the other culture may have been considered classical in its entirety, in actual fact its recapture and reintegration into contemporary culture were limited to specific areas of intellectual, artistic, or political endeavor.

B. In practice, then, almost all classicisms are movements that elevate a segment (or segments) of the other culture to model rank. In this event, as scrutiny of classicisms past and present will readily indicate, one, or a combination, of the following aspects of the other culture may be considered binding.

1. *Its aspiration may be accorded authoritative value.* This outlook is dominant in most of the Islamic reform movements. Ḥanbalism, Wahhābism, the *salafiyya*, the *Ikhwān al-muslimūn*, however direct a response to contemporary needs their rise may appear to the historian, draw justification and appeal from the resumption of objectives that had been formulated and, allegedly at least, realized by the age acknowledged as authoritative. The view of history which is implied in this attitude bears close resemblance to that of the West from the Renaissance onward, when the Middle Ages were depreciated as an interruption of the true growth of civilization and a direct connection was established between antiquity and the modern era, with the intervening period decried as a regrettable and shameful lapse.

2. *Its formal means may be allowed absolute value.* This desire to recast present achievement in terms satisfactory to another culture appears to have been most frequently effective in law, literature, and the arts. The legists

responsible for the so-called reception of Roman law in the late Middle Ages and in the early phases of the modern period, motivated as they were by the wish to legitimize and solidify the structure of the Holy Roman Empire as well as that of the Italian city-states, had no intention to resurrect ancient art, ancient mores, or even the concrete reality of ancient institutions. They demonstrated the possibility of injecting into a cultural context an essential trait from the outside without developing the psychological or the practical need of permitting the infiltration of additional culture traits.[25] It deserves attention that the classicistic movement between approximately A.D. 400 and 600, to which Roman law owes its continuance throughout the Byzantine period, was perhaps not quite so limited in scope as that leading to the reception of Roman law in Europe; yet it was certainly far from being a "total" classicism, which in that age would have been impossible because of the unavoidable pagan associations, if for no other reason. The overcoming of the vulgarization of the law by "classicistic" means was allowable; the evocation of the classical aspiration, on the other hand, was not to be countenanced.[26]

The ambivalent response of the Justinian age to its pagan heritage reappears, if on a slightly less relevant plane, in the attitude of the urban Muslim who borrowed the Bedouin's literary tools and attempted to identify with

[25] This against A. J. Toynbee. The history of the reception of Roman law, for which cf. Koschaker, *op. cit.*, *passim*, constitutes one more impressive argument against Toynbee's theory that "the carrying power of a culture element is proportional to the degree of its triviality and superficiality in the spiritual hierarchy of cultural values" (*A Study of History* [London and New York, 1934-1954], V, 200; VIII, 514). For the whole problem cf. my "Westernization in Islam and the Theory of Cultural Borrowing," in *Islam: Essays in the Nature and Growth of a Cultural Tradition* (2d ed., London, 1961), pp. 237-246.

[26] For some of the ideas here developed cf. Wieacker, "Vulgarismus und Klassizismus im Recht der Spätantike," pp. 50-51, where, incidentally, the failure of the revival of classical Roman law in the West is instructively discussed.

the nomad's artistic standards while maintaining the *sharīʿa's* discrimination against him.[27] The authoritative appeal of the "other" culture may be even more specialized —has it not been documented that "the literary cult of China and the flowering of *chinoiserie* in the minor arts did not coincide in England" (as they did in France)? [28] This fractional acceptance of an alien model has been well described by A. J. Toynbee:

Artistic flakes of a Far Eastern culture which had similarly been detached from their spiritual core likewise captured a nascent Iranic Muslim society[29] in the 13th and 14th centuries of the Christian Era, and a Modern Western Society from the 18th century onwards, without any simul-

---

[27] For the precedence accorded the *ahl al-ḥāḍira* over the *ahl al-bādiya* in terms of *ʿaṭāʾ* and *faiʾ*, and for the express limitation in the obligation of the community to extend its aid to them, cf., e.g., the *ḥadīth* (with interpretation) collected by Abū ʿUbaid al-Qāsim b. Sallām (773-837), *Kitāb al-amwāl*, ed. Muḥ. Ḥāmid al-Fiqqī (Cairo, 1353/1934), pp. 227-231, nos. 558-563. Cf. also a passage like that inserted by ad-Damīrī (d. 1405) in his *Kitāb al-ḥayawān* (Cairo, 1278/1861), II, 542[17-19], trans. R. Levy, *The Social Structure of Islam* (Cambridge, 1957), pp. 174-175, where, in discussing the question whether or not the *waral* (a large lizard) is lawful food, the author has this observation to make: "The Arabs are the prime authorities in any consideration of this subject, for the reason that the faith is an Arab one, and the prophet was an Arab. But the question can only be referred to the inhabitants of towns and villages and not to uncivilized dwellers in the desert [*sukkān al-bilād wa'l-qurà dūn ajlāf al-bawādī*], who eat without discrimination anything that creeps or crawls."

[28] Cf. W. W. Appleton, A *Cycle of Cathay. The Chinese Vogue in England during the Seventeenth and Eighteenth Centuries* (New York, 1951), p. 62; cf. also, for the minor arts and gardening, R. C. Bald, "Sir William Chambers and the Chinese Garden," *Journal of the History of Ideas*, XI (1950), 288, who speaks of the middle of the eighteenth century. Cf. also the descriptive judgment of G. F. Hudson, *Europe and China* (London, 1931), pp. 273-274.

[29] For criticism of this concept cf. my "Toynbee's Concept of Islamic Civilization," in *The Intent of Toynbee's History*, ed. E. T. Gargan (Chicago, 1961), pp. 97-110.

taneous radiation of a Confucian philosophy[30] and a Mahayanian religion that were the original settings from which these fashionably superficial *chinoiseries* had been detached in order to be made exportable at the price of being made meaningless,[31]

or rather, as we should prefer to say, "to be made exportable and receive meaning in an alien cultural context."

3. *Its psychological experience (or parts thereof) may be considered normative.* This may happen with as diverse elements of experience as types of piety—the transplantation to Byzantium and especially to Mount Athos of the Hesychasm of the Sinai ascetics suggests itself in evidence and the history of religious enthusiasm and of mysticism would easily furnish other instances; types of philosophical argument (the Hellenizing philosophers in Islam come directly to mind) or types of required civic and political attitudes (as when the Augustan age conjured up and bestowed model force on the peculiar patriotism of the early Roman republic).

On the whole, one may surmise, the classicists are unaware that by meeting an immediate existential need through "imitation" they are likely to affect adversely areas of cultural endeavor which are not, at the particular point in time, paramount in their consciousness. Yielding to their thirst for knowledge and possessing themselves of the factual treasures of the ancient heritage, both the Arabs of the Abbasid age and the French of the sixteenth century sacrificed measure and organization for an overflow of diversified content. Conversely, the age of Louis XIII and Louis XIV yielded ornament to order, variety to clarity, and, with a self-consciousness rarely encountered in literary history, enthusiasm to reason, the lyrics of self-expression to the stylization of the great forms.[32]

---

[30] On this point cf. pp. 94-95, below.

[31] *Op. cit.*, VIII, 518.

[32] Cf. St. Evremond (d. 1703), in R. Bray, *La formation de la doctrine classique en France* (Lausanne, 1927), p. 121; for further

IV. Classicisms may be differentiated by the genetic relation between model culture and classicistic culture.[33]

A. Orthogenetic connection (i.e., lineal descendency).

1. A period of one's own bona fide past may be chosen which is not separated from the classicistic movement by an actual cultural break or a thorough shift in the ethnic affiliation of the bearers of the civilization in question. The classicism that seeks orientation to the era of the Rightly-Guided Caliphs provides an especially instructive example; besides illustrating the case in point, it reveals some of the ambiguities inherent in the concept of cultural continuity. Orthogenesis may be claimed by Arab *rāshidūn* classicists regardless of whether their attitude is dictated by a more strictly religious or by a more strictly nationalistic motivation. Quite different, on the other hand, is the position of the Indian or the Pakistani Muslim of the same bent. For him, the orthogenetic affiliation is contingent on the paramountcy of the religious over the national identification, because by no stretch of the imagination can the history of the pre-Umayyad caliphs (apart from a few very marginal incidents) be designated as a part of Indian or Pakistani history. It may not be out of place to observe that what is here called *rāshidūn* classicism is the result of an attitude that, in Islamic societies, goes back to the time of the immediate successors of the first four caliphs. Of Muʿāwiya (661-680) it is reported that he wished to follow in the footsteps of Abū Bakr and

---

detail see my *Kritik und Dichtkunst. Studien zur arabischen Literaturgeschichte* (Wiesbaden, 1955), p. 130 and n. 2. Cf. also D. Mornet, *Histoire de la clarté française* (Paris, 1929), p. 305, on some of the implications of the French striving for clarity in the seventeenth century; by contrast, cf. pp. 18-38 on the disorganization of French literature before the victory of classicism, the craving for miscellaneous erudition, and the fight against the pedant. The absence of antagonism to the pedant on the Muslim scene is symptomatic of, and perhaps responsible for, the unconcern with organization typical of large-scale composition in Arabic literature.

[33] The interesting problem of the conditions under which an age may become convinced of its own model character will not be considered here.

ᶜUmar, but realized his failure to do so.[34] He articulated his feeling that, after those first and greatest of the

---

[34] G. Levi Della Vida and O. Pinto, trans. and annot., *Il califfo Muᶜāwiya I secondo il "Kitāb ansāb al-ašrāf" . . . di Aḥmad ibn Yaḥyā al-Balāḏurī* (Rome, 1938), no. 131, p. 48. The study by L. Veccia Vaglieri, "Sulla origine della denominazione 'Sunniti,'" in *Studi orientalistici in onore di Giorgio Levi Della Vida* (Rome, 1956), II, 573-585, makes possible a certain refinement in our understanding of the "classicism" of the earliest caliphs; we know now that ᶜAlī had already proposed going back to the Sunna of Muḥammad and eliminating the Sunna initiated by the Prophet's three *rāshidūn* successors. The origin of the phrase *sunna māḍiya* in ᶜAlī's reign should also be noted in this context. A decree of the caliph al-Muqtadir (908-932) contains the characteristic phrase: "It is most appropriate for the Prince of Believers to follow the traditions of the predecessors and to be guided by the caliphs of God" (*wa-amīr al-muʾminīna aulà man ittabaᶜa āthār as-salaf wa'qtadà bi-khulafāʾ Allāh*), quoted by Hilāl aṣ-Ṣābī, *Wuzarāʾ*, ed. ᶜA. A. Farrāj (Cairo, 1958), p. 275[8-9] (cf. also the preamble of the decree to abolish the *dīwān al-mawārīth* [Bureau of Inheritance], *ibid.*, pp. 268-269). At the time the superiority of the *salaf* over the *khalaf*, the "ancients" over the "moderns," had been widely accepted and a Ḥanbalite writer like al- Barbahārī (d. 941) advocated emphatically the return to the "old faith" (*dīn ᶜatīq*), the beliefs and practices on which the Companions had been agreed under the three first caliphates. Cf. H. Laoust, *La Profession de foi d'Ibn Baṭṭa* (Damascus, 1958), pp. xxix, 4 n. 1. The sentiment is traceable throughout the Muslim world. For example, the Indo-Muslim historian, al-Baranī (d. after 1357), insists that in all the history of the Muslim community only the *rāshidūn* had been truly Muslim rulers (cf. P. Hardy, *Historians of Medieval India* [London, 1960], p. 26). If we may trust tradition, ᶜUmar had already likened the Islam of his day to an aging camel; cf. Ṭāhā Ḥusain, *ᶜUthmān* (Caire, 1947), p. 79, who follows Ṭabarī, *Annales* (repr. of Leiden ed.; Cairo, 1939), III, 426 (*s.a.* 35). Ṭāhā Ḥusain (*op. cit.*, p. 171) disowns those writers who refuse to give credence to the reports implicating certain Companions of the Prophet in the revolt against ᶜUthmān merely because they hold sacred this first period of Muslim history (*yuqaddisūna dhālika 'l-ᶜaṣr min ᶜuṣūr al-islām*). The conventional romanticization of the period, and more particularly of the years to the death of ᶜUmar, finds a defender in Muḥammad ᶜAbdalqādir al-ᶜAmāwī, who limits the times in which Islam has come up to its ideal to the lifetime of the Prophet and the reigns of Abū Bakr and the two ᶜUmar, and who consequently charges the Umayyads with

rāshidūn, a decline had already set in.[35] The feeling never subsided. For example, we meet it in Ibn Taimiyya (d. 1328),[36] and again a short while later in the writings

---

"falling away" from true Islam (*al-inḥirāf ʿan al-islām*), a process that was to worsen under the dynasties following them (cf. his *Mustaqbal al-islām* [2d ed.; Cairo, 1956], pp. 8, 110). It may be mentioned in this context that the function that E. Dardel, *L'Histoire, science du concret* (Paris, 1946), pp. 115-116, assigns to the image of republican Rome adopted by the imperial period bears an unmistakable resemblance to the role that the stylized image of the early caliphate occupies in the thought world of the *rāshidūn* classicists.

[35] Levi Della Vida and Pinto, *op. cit.*, no. 176, pp. 65-66; the first part is repeated in no. 283, p. 119. Muʿāwiya had some historical sense, realizing as he did the irrevocability of the past; the modern advocates of a reversion to the *rāshidūn* have none. They seem to feel that change in a historical or social situation is a product of a unilateral decision on the part of man and, more particularly, of the men in command; experience teaches that such decisions have usually been sinful in nature, a deliberate falling away from the ways of God, or at times a no less sinful failure of will. The feeling for the uniqueness of the historical moment is absent; or rather, the concrete situation is believed to be timelessly available, like a reel of film which need only be put in the proper projector. This mechanistic attitude toward possible manipulation of time is based on a semideliberate disregard for historical analysis, as well as on an equally semideliberate disdain for self-awareness. Not even a Muḥammad ʿAbduh sensed the contradiction between his acceptance of a law of progress and the conviction that the appearance of Muḥammad marked the acme of history. W. Hartke has been able to bring to life the comparable ahistorical outlook of the last centuries of ancient Rome (especially the fourth century). He sees the life of the times "durch diese akausale Zeitlosigkeit und Identität des eigenen und geschichtlichen Raumes bestimmt," and points out that the *Historia Augusta* (end of fourth century) "will nicht nur Kategorien liefern, sondern auch Gestaltung bewirken. Sie ist Propaganda für eine Ordnung der Weltfragen nach den Masstäben der römischen Kaisergeschichte. Sie will nicht mehr nur geistige Antwort auf Fragen sein, sondern *will reale Lösung der Probleme durch Wiederverwirklichung der geschichtlichen Vergangenheit*" (my italics). See *Römische Kinderkaiser. Eine Strukturanalyse römischen Denkens und Daseins* (Berlin, 1951), pp. 50-51, 59.

[36] *Minhāj as-sunna 'n-nabawiyya fī naqḍ kalām ash-shīʿa wa'l-qadariyya* (Cairo, 1321-1322), II, 112[26-28]; cf. H. Laoust, *Essai sur les doctrines sociales et politiques de Taḳī-d-Dīn Aḥmad b. Taimīya* (Cairo, 1939), p. 281.

of a Persian, ʿAlī b. ash-Shihāb al-Hamadānī (d. 1385), who stated that "since the time of Adam there had only been a limited number of persons such as Joseph, Moses, David, Solomon, Muḥammad and the orthodox caliphs in whose persons the qualities of a righteous ruler had been manifested and who had performed the duties incumbent upon them in a fitting way." [37] In its very beginnings Arab nationalism has had recourse to the authority of the same period. ʿAbd ar-Raḥmān al-Kawākibī (1849-1902) asserts: "Islam brought finally the principles of political freedom which is intermediary between democracy and aristocracy, and put the unity of the godhead on a secure foundation. It brought to the world the rule of the first four caliphs, the like of whom has never been seen by man, before or since. These caliphs understood the meaning of the Qurʾān which is full of teachings against tyranny, and in support of justice and equality." [38] In present-day Pakistan, Muḥammad Iqbāl (1876-1938) is generally followed "in deprecating Muslim imperialism under the *Banū Umayyah* and since. Muʿāwiyah has been denounced as the corrupter of Islām; and social backward-looking is now usually directed to the *Khilāfat ar-Rāshidah*, where alone Islām was 'pure,' 'socialistic,' and simple." The period is held up as "a model of sociological excellence." [39]

---

[37] *Dhakhīrat al-mulūk*, British Museum, Add. MS 1618, fol. 90*a*, *in* Ann K. S. Lambton, "The Theory of Kingship in the Naṣīḥat al-mulūk of Ghazālī," *Islamic Quarterly*, I (1954), 50 n. 5.

[38] *Ṭabāʾiʿ al-istibdād*, summarized in S. G. Haim, "Alfieri and al-Kawākibī," *Oriente Moderno*, XXXIV (1954), 330. In this context belongs the view expressed by the Indian modernist, Sayyid Ameer Ali (1849-1928), that "slavery by purchase was unknown during the reigns of the first four Caliphs" (cf. Levy, *op. cit.*, p. 76 n. 2).

[39] W. C. Smith, *Modern Islam in India and Pakistan* (2d ed.; Lahore, 1947), p. 134. In commenting on the constitution of Pakistan (adopted on Feb. 29, 1956), the Jamaʿat-i-Islami made a statement (on March 18, 1956) to the effect that for the first time since the reign of the fourth caliph "the governmental authority of an Islamic State has passed into the hands of the common people instead of Royal families" (quoted by F. Abbott,

More recently, the presumed ideology of the *rāshidūn* has been made a cornerstone in the Indian Muslim an-Nadwī's (1913——) discussion of the problem, "What has the world lost through the decline of the Muslims?" [40]

"The Jamaᶜat-i-Islami of Pakistan," *Middle East Journal,* XI (1957), 37-51, at p. 47. Contrast with this depreciation of Muᶜawiya the statement of H. Z. Nuseibeh, *The Ideas of Arab Nationalism* (Ithaca, N.Y., 1956), p. 62: "A modern Arab nationalist, if true to his nationalist creed, would have to reassess and reinterpret the historical verdict of his forefathers on the record of the Umayyads. In the light of modern nationalist categories, what was once condemned in the Umayyads as villainous secularism must now be lauded as praiseworthy nationalism, for the foundation of Umayyad policy was the Arab-state principle; and Arab fortunes went down with the demise of the Umayyads." Nuseibeh's self-consciousness about the function of what we would be inclined to call a classicistic construction of the past deserves notice: ". . . historical tradition is a factor contributing to integration provided it is presented in the right way. That is to say, it is not so much a question of creating the present in the image of the past as it is the re-creation of the past in the image of the present" (*ibid.*, p. 79). Another American-educated Arab, N. A. Faris, expressed himself in a comparable manner (*Colloquium on Islamic Culture in Its Relation to the Contemporary World* [Princeton, 1953], pp. 26-27), but not without drawing a rather emphatic reply in defense of Islamic historiography from the Pakistani, H. I. Qureshi (*ibid.*, pp. 27-28). On the other hand, the unnamed author of a tract on the Islamic state (my copy lacks a title page; the pamphlet was circulated in 1957 by the Islamic Literary Research and Educational Institute, Karachi) raises a protest against the view professed by many a Muslim today, as in the past, "that there could be but *one* form of state deserving the adjective 'Islamic' —namely, the form manifested under the four Right-Guided Caliphs—and that, therefore, any deviation from that model must necessarily detract from the 'Islamic' character of the state."

[40] *Mā dhā khasara 'l-ᶜālam bi'nḥiṭāṭ al-muslimīn* (2d ed.; Cairo, 1370/1951), esp. pp. 100-101, 105-109; see chap. vii, pp. 180-190, below. On the *rāshidūn* ideology cf. also W. C. Smith, *Pakistan as an Islamic State* (Lahore, 1951), p. 59, and, for opposition to it, pp. 95-96; see also L. Gardet, *La Cité musulmane* (Paris, 1954), p. 319 n. 2. The following reflections of E. Spranger, "Die Kulturzyklentheorie und das Problem des Kulturverfalls," *Berliner Akademie der Wissenschaften, Sitzungsberichte* (1926), p. liv, should be considered in this context: "Am wenigsten ablösbar von den lebendigen Sinnempfängern und

2. The remote and mediated (orthogenetic) past is made the authoritative model. The Roman idealization of the great age of Greece, and Renaissance and post-Renaissance absolutizations of antiquity, illustrate this cultural situation, which, in the light of what has been said before, hardly requires a detailed analysis. It should, however, be borne in mind that the insight into the existential significance of the connection between the two cultures, which may well lag considerably behind the insight into their actual historical connection and may, indeed, never assert itself as a compelling collective experience, arises perhaps secondarily, in a sense, as the result of a psychological disposition (see I, B, above). It is for this reason, too, that the same model culture may signify different qualities and, therefore, divergent precepts to different classicistic periods. Thus, in the seventeenth century,

> . . . the classical tendency meant harmony, dignity, and purity, not only in words but in sentiments and construction. It meant indeed something much more classical than the classics. To us at the present day the value of the great Greek authors lies in their nearness to realities. We have eyes for their colour and concreteness, and for the warfare in their bosoms between reason and the manifold irration-

---

Sinnträgern sind Gesellschaftsgebilde in weitester Bedeutung: also Staatsformen, Rechtsordnungen, soziale Schichtungen usw. Sie scheinen unwiderruflich mit dem Schicksal ihrer Kulturgeneration verbunden und lösen sich auf, sobald diese sie nicht mehr versteht und nicht mehr bejaht. Wenn auch sie in einigem Masse weiterleben und weiterwirken, so ist dies doch nur so weit der Fall, als sie selbst Gedanke oder Bild geworden sind. Die Idee des römischen Imperiums zeugte weiter, als das Reich selbst längst verfallen war. Das römische Recht, zur Wissenschaft geworden, konnte nicht einmal neue Formen bilden. Aber der Bedeutungswandel, der auch dem Gedanklichen und dem Bildhaften bei seiner Wiederbelebung nicht erspart bleibt, geht dann bis in die Wesenstiefe." The same attitude in respect to the period of the first four caliphs and especially to the personality of ʿUmar may be observed in contemporary Indonesia; cf. G. F. Pijper, *Islam and the Netherlands* (Leiden, 1957), p. 27, and the literature quoted in nn. 47, 48.

alities of human nature. In the seventeenth century . . . they were valued for their remoteness from the Gothic and the barbarous, and . . . their literature . . . seemed to embody an abstract and superhuman regularity.[41]

B. Heterogenetic selection.

In this type of selection a foreign culture serves as the authoritative model. The role of Persian culture in Muslim Turkey and Muslim India, or of Chinese culture in Japan, or of Hindu culture in southeast Asia and Indonesia, parallels to some extent the role of Hellenism in the Middle East in the period after Alexander the Great, and, more recently, the role of the West in most parts of the globe. The inducement to a classicistic approach to a foreign culture may be the religious or the political prestige of the model, if it is not simply a feeling of inferiority and the desire to equalize a given cultural-political situation by more or less limited acculturation. Resistance within the receiving civilization is lessened by orthogenetic reinterpretation of the model; it is weakest when acculturation is experienced as a necessary concomitant of a religious transformation which per se is apt to increase collective self-respect. The degree to which the particular heterogenetic classicism is felt to be a voluntary reaction to the impact of the model deeply affects not only the image formation as such but the directedness of the aspiration that the classicistic movement is intended to serve. One glance at the Muslim countries of today will bear out this generalization through a profusion of illustrations.[42]

---

[41] G. N. Clerk, *The Seventeenth Century* (2d ed.; Oxford, 1947), p. 337. This is, of course, not the whole truth. Did not La Bruyère (and he was not alone) admire ancient sculpture and architecture, not for their stylization, but for their naturalness? Cf. A. Malraux, *Les voix du silence* (Paris, 1951), p. 65. Speaking of the seventeenth century, Malraux observes (p. 97): "L'art contemporain de la littérature classique n'est pas une peinture classique."

[42] The Egyptian historian Aḥmad Amīn (d. 1954) commends the Muslim of the great age for accepting foreign culture elements by relating them to the Prophet through forged traditions. Such procedure bespeaks responsiveness to the needs of the times

V. Classicism, ostensibly always an end but actually never anything but a means, plays its part in a given historical situation as an instrument of cultural manipulation, as a tool to assist in the realization of the aspirations of the age that elects to seek fulfillment on the conjured-up shadow of an authoritative model past.[43] The aspiration of the time, as its true value center, decides whether the classical model is to constitute primarily (1) an authority, or (2) a means of execution (say, to expedite change).

It is well to remember that "the most fundamental changes in outlook, the most remarkable turns in the current of intellectual fashion, may be referable in the last resort to an alteration in men's feeling for things, an alteration at once so subtle and so generally pervasive" that its origins cannot be ascertained with complete accuracy and that it will have to be accepted as an "ultimate." The development of mechanics and astronomy in the seventeenth century remains in some respects unaccountable, unless one fully realizes that "not only was there in some of the intellectual leaders a great aspiration to demonstrate that the universe ran like a piece of clockwork, but that this was itself initially a religious aspiration. It was felt that there would be something defective in Creation itself—something not quite worthy of God—unless the whole system of the universe could be shown to be interlocking, so that it carried the pattern of reasonableness and orderliness."[44] It is in this sense that we insist

---

and to the process of evolution. Amīn's remarks were made between 1933 and 1936. Cf. N. Safran, *Egypt in Search of Political Community* (Cambridge, Mass., 1961), p. 282. The typology of "mimesis" which Toynbee develops (*op. cit.*, VIII, 481-482) is too schematic and too jejune to accommodate the phenomena that it is designed to categorize.

[43] Cf. in this connection the undeservedly neglected book by S. C. Gilfillan, *The Sociology of Invention* (Chicago, 1935); the author advances and documents the idea that the social situation, or, as we should prefer to say, the social aspiration, precedes effective inventive solution of the problems that may present themselves for possible attack.

[44] H. Butterfield, *The Origins of Modern Science, 1300-1800* (London, 1949), pp. 104-106.

on the primacy, in order and in time, of the "aspiration." The objective richness of the ancient heritage, its diversity and multiple interpretability, have made it possible for subsequent ages of contrasting aspirations actually to find in the ancients what they were looking for.[45]

The observable ambivalence of a resort to classicism in terms of its cultural effect is due precisely to its functioning primarily as an authority or as a means of execution. In itself classicism is neutral; its effect depends on the objective, that is, on the psychological circumstances of its adoption. By putting the study of the ancients at the service of patriotism, French humanism of the sixteenth century diminished from the start the dangers of cultural paralysis which are potentially inherent in the acceptance of an overriding authority; by the development of the belief in the perfectibility of the arts and sciences, the danger is even more firmly controlled; and it is completely banned by adoption of the attitude that made Bernard Palissy (d. 1589) say: "Je ne veux aucunement estre imitateur de mes prédécesseurs sinon en ce qu'ils auront fait selon l'ordonnance de Dieu." [46] In a comparable manner, German classicism was later to use the model of the Greeks to inform and legitimize an immense extension of the range of experience. By contrast, consider the motivation of later medieval Muslim "classicisms," which served to make shrinkage of cultural outreach appear as a moral advance and whose "retractile" purposiveness was never mitigated by any of the philosophic axioms that made the French humanist a "modern" and the French classicism of the sixteenth century a force toward the *illustration* and the *décoration* of the fair name of France.

As often as not the cultural model, in some of its aspects at least, is a construct rather than an adequately apprehended historical reality; the inaccuracy of the historical

---

[45] Cf. Friedrich von Schlegel: "Jeder findet in den Alten, was er sucht," *in* Rehm, *op. cit.*, p. 269. For the idea of aspiration cf. the somewhat different concept of E. Rothacker, *Probleme der Kulturanthropologie* (Bonn, 1948), p. 140 (86).

[46] Quoted by Gillot, *op. cit.*, p. 93.

comprehension does not, however, in the beginning at least, impair its effectiveness. The influence of Tacitus was not therefore less beneficial because seventeenth-century readers misconstrued him as an apologist for Tiberius and as the first exponent of *raison d'état*.[47] There are periods in which life tends to be oriented to literary models rather than the literary models to the actual life of those who use them.[48] So to the contemporary mind the question of the factual accuracy of the model may not even arise.

VI. Classicism may be described, then, in terms of its operational effectiveness, as:

A. A value principle; that is to say, as a basis for self-evaluation.

B. A principle of organization (*Ordnungsprinzip*) of the universe insofar as it is relevant to effective experience.[49] It must be noted in this context that the tendency to find absolutes realized in definite historical periods is one of the outstanding characteristics of modern times from the Renaissance onward (but of course not confined to them).

C. A motivation.

To understand the phenomenon of classicism as such, as well as any particular classicistic movement, it is important to realize that these three aspects always appear simultaneously and interdependently. And it is equally if not more important to realize further that the advocates of any classicistic movement whatsoever are invariably interested primarily in their own rather than in the model culture, in themselves rather than in their heroes. This judgment remains true even though it can justly be

---

[47] Cf. D. Ogg, *Europe in the Seventeenth Century* (5th ed.; London, 1948), pp. 519-520.

[48] Cf. W. Rehm, "Kulturverfall und spätmittelalterliche deutsche Didaktik. Ein Beitrag zur Frage der geschichtlichen Alterung," *Zeitschrift für deutsche Philologie*, LII (1927), 301-302, in regard to the German *Hochmittelalter*.

[49] A somewhat weaker formulation of this insight is Rehm's dictum (*Griechentum und Goethezeit*, pp. 54-55): ". . . das Wesen aller Klassik: sie lenkt den Blick auf die Grundordnungen des Daseins."

argued that classicisms may be characterized by the degree of their detached or scientific concern for the "other" culture; for, on closer consideration, it appears that what actually does vary is the degree to which precise apprehension of the other culture (or of some of its segments) is deemed indispensable for the successful attainment of the objective that any particular classicism has set for itself.

From this viewpoint the limited classicism of the Sinophile movement of the eighteenth century may be contrasted with the illimited classicism of the Goethe period. Voltaire did not need a full picture of Chinese institutions in order to play out the authority of China and its religious attitude against the Catholic Church. In fact, he had to suppress certain information on corruption and occasional fanaticism of his idealized Confucian rulers, as well as on their belief in miracles, so as to safeguard the effective stylization of the model.[50] French Sinophilism was entering upon its decline, or, in other words, the authority was beginning to be withdrawn from the alien culture model,

[50] Cf. A. H. Rowbotham, "Voltaire Sinophile," *Publications of the Modern Language Association*, XLVII (1932), 1061-1063. Frederick the Great saw through Voltaire's aims in using the cultural authority of China; cf. his letter to Voltaire, April 8, 1776, quoted by U. Aurich, *China im Spiegel der deutschen Literatur des 18. Jahrhunderts* (Berlin, 1935), p. 68: "Ich sagte ihm [i.e., Abbé Pauw]: Aber sehen Sie denn nicht, dass der Patriarch von Ferney dem Beispiel des Tacitus folgt? Um die Tugend seiner Mitbürger zu fördern, predigte dieser Römer ihnen als Beispiel die Redlichkeit und Mässigkeit unserer germanischen Vorfahren, die doch gewiss nicht verdienen, nachgeahmt zu werden. Ebenso ist Herr von Voltaire unermüdlich, seinen Welschen zu sagen: lernt doch von den Chinesen tugendhaftes Handeln, fördert wie sie den Ackerbau und ihr werdet euer Land von Bordeaux und eure Champagne fruchtbar sehen durch eurer Hände Arbeit und in der Fülle reicher Ernten. Da doch nur ein Gesetz gilt in dem weiten Kaiserreich China, o ihr Welschen, müsst ihr nicht wünschen, es ihnen darin in unserem kleinen Königreiche gleichzutun?" Leibniz, incidentally, made a greater effort than Voltaire to adjust his use of things Chinese to his knowledge (cf. D. F. Lach, "Leibniz and China," *Journal of the History of Ideas*, VI [1945], 436-455).

when an acute French observer analyzed the nature, the goal, and the mechanics of the movement.

The Chinese Empire has become in our time the object of special attention and of special study. The missionaries first fascinated public opinion by rose-colored reports from that distant land, too distant to be able to contradict their falsehoods. Then the philosophers took it up, and drew from it whatever could be of use to them in denouncing and removing the evils they observed in their own country. Thus this country became in a short time the home of wisdom, virtue, and good faith, its government the best possible and the longest established, its morality the loftiest and most beautiful in the known world; its laws, its policy, its art, its industry were likewise such as to serve for a model to all nations of the earth.[51]

---

[51] Baron Grimm, *Correspondance littéraire,* Sept. 15, 1766, in A. Reichwein, *China and Europe. Intellectual and Artistic Contacts in the 18th Century* (New York, 1925), p. 96. For the motivation of English Sinophilism cf. Appleton, *op. cit.*, p. 41: "In England . . . the Confucian legend appealed to both orthodox and heterodox thinkers. Its materialism appealed to the English deists, the humanism and benevolent patriarchy endorsed by Confucius, and the perfected, if mummified, Chinese way of life gratified solid Tories and cautious Whigs. Confucius was the supreme apostle of the orderly *status quo.* It was the temper of the Augustans to find their Elysium not, as their descendants did, in the primitive innocence of the South Seas, but in the glories of a civilized past. With their instinctive Hobbesian distrust of a disorganized society, the classicists, both English and French, preferred the sage to the savage, the static to the dynamic." Cf. further, for the whole question of Sinophilism in Europe and its aims, A. H. Rowbotham, *Missionary and Mandarin. The Jesuits at the Court of China* (Berkeley and Los Angeles, 1942), pp. 247 ff., 278-279, 280-281, 284-285. A comparable psychological constellation gave rise to a similar cluster of ideas in Japan. Cf. D. Keene, *The Japanese Discovery of Europe. Honda Toshiaki and Other Discoverers,* 1720-1798 (London, 1952), pp. 78-79: "For Honda Toshiaki (1744-1821) and some of his contemporaries, Europe was that part of the world whose long years of civilization had taught the nations the folly of war, whose people lived in splendid houses, free alike from the dangers of fire and robbery, and whose rulers devoted themselves entirely to benevolent plans for the welfare of their sub-

Enough is known and enough has been said here of German classicism to make explicit the contrast which—and this must be stated clearly—is by no means a total one: the element of scientific self-consciousness, however strong and however highly valued, did not by any means neutralize the urge to purposive and semifictional styling of the heritage by the German movement.

A classicistic attitude is in itself a symptom neither of rise nor of decline, nor even of a contemporary feeling of living in a time of progress or a time of regression, of expansion or retrenchment. The nature of the model, as historically constituted or as perceived by those in search of authority, is likely to direct and limit the cultural movement that its adoption is intended to render possible. But it is first and foremost the "mood" and the aspiration of the receiving culture, and therewith the functional use to which the borrowing will be put, which allow us to judge, to some degree at least, whether a given classicism is a child of courage or of fear, of senescence or rejuvenation.

---

jects. This portrait of life in eighteenth-century Europe may make us smile . . . but it was not much further removed from reality than contemporary European descriptions of wise Persians and Chinese. The purpose of such fanciful accounts was in both cases the same: to call attention to deficiencies at home by praising the superior ways of little-known foreigners, and thus create a desire for reform and progress."

V

Self-Image and Approach to History

The dream is but one; but diverse are the interpretations.
Ṣā'ib (d. 1670)[1]

I

IN THE *Nekyia,* partaking of the blood of the sacrificial victim readmits the shades to a brief span of relevance to the living. Similarly, the aspiration of the living, through the intermediacy of the searching historian, reinstills life or meaning—its intellectual substitute—into the facts and the fictions of the past. And even as Odysseus fought off the shades so that Teiresias could drink, so the historian, and through him the living generation, must decide whom and what to revive or allow to remain forgotten. One may argue, perhaps, as to how much freedom of decision the historian possesses. The weapon he uses to fight off those

[1] The verse is quoted by V. Monteil, "De la Perse à l'Iran (Itinéraire spirituel)," *Mélanges Louis Massignon,* III (Damascus, 1957), 161-184, at p. 175.

he wishes to keep outside his consciousness is the context or contexts into which he may fit the facts of the past; in a sense these contexts are like lariats of different length and range, or like magnets that can single out or capture responsive data lying buried in the sources, which can be made to betray the past. But the contexts with which the historian is armed, as it were, reflect the aspirations of his time, or possibly merely his own aspirations, and the limitations implicit in these aspirations restrict his freedom and his success before he has even begun his work. Completeness of evidence may be the aspiration of a time, as it is of ours, and yet complete comprehension of bygone events may remain elusive. For the shades are too many, and the hierarchy of relevance among them, which must ultimately determine the selection, will not yield to our methodological demand for the completeness of fact-finding.

Yet it is clear that ours is a historiogenic period, a period that craves contexts of maximum heuristic effectiveness, a period that is trying to adjust its contexts to the shades it expects to encounter. On closer scrutiny, though, it would seem that it does so only in certain areas and intellectual circles of the globe, those that are most simply and most nearly identified by speaking of the West and the Westernized. Outside this geographic and intellectual sphere, the dominant aspiration, and the self-image that parallels it, dictate otherwise. The need to substantiate one's self-view through history, to find the justification of one's future in the past, is almost universal. But the needs of various self-views and aspirations for the future differ in the stylization they impose on known facts and in the stimulus they give to the unearthing of hitherto unknown ones. Western research of recent generations has been fortunate in the coincidence of its driving motivations, first and foremost the will to self-understanding by means of understanding "all" cultural solutions of the problem of living, with the demands of factuality itself. For the unrevived shades are only pushed away from the blood; they are not eliminated as shades.

We may, in a cave, turn a flashlight on this corner or that and note its structure, deliberately overlooking the structure of the sections we choose to leave without illumination. But those sections are still there, and, if we do not pay heed, sooner or later we will suffer from our neglect or be compelled to reorient our lighting. The willful twisting and omitting of historical evidence will fairly soon make the context and its motivating aspiration seem stale and sterile—disillusionment is the emotional counterpart of this kind of intellectual failure. The aspiration compels the point at which the intellectual mastery of the past succeeds or fails. It is in this sense that the self-image of the historian or of his society predetermines, so to speak, not only the results of his endeavors, but the specific cause and mode of their validity or their invalidation.

II

Any historiography is determined, on the one hand, by content (data), function (of data within the context studied), and structure (of the data making them amenable to treatment within that context), and, on the other, by motivation or objective ("use"), and method and style of presentation. The temptation to contrast the two sets of concepts as objective and subjective must be resisted, because the contexts within which the data may be said to fulfill a function[2] do not possess objective reality independent of the human observer; the same must be said of the structure (i.e., the "definable articulation," the "ordered arrangement of parts")[3] which the data exhibit within the context. The researcher's objective, which, at least from a psychological viewpoint, is hardly separable from his motivation, determines the context of the investigation, or, in other words, the principles of data selection and hence the perception or consideration of the

[2] I.e., in the words of S. F. Nadel, *The Theory of Social Structure* (Glencoe, Ill., 1957), p. 7, to show their "adequacy in regard to some stipulated effectiveness."

[3] *Ibid.*

data themselves.[4] The objective and the data, at best, converge like asymptotic curves; only in some instances, such as the description of coins and the like, may full coincidence, to all practical intents and purposes, be claimed as capable of achievement.

The subjective acceptability of research results, is, however, not directly proportional to the closeness reached by those "asymptotic curves"; rather, it is partly by the period's methodological ideas and partly by the strength of the motivation that the immediate conclusiveness of the objective is determined. Method must not be understood simply as the techniques of fact-finding, but the techniques themselves must be defined as accommodating or, rather, as deriving from the criteria of acceptability which the investigator and his society recognize as binding.[5] Credulity (or skepticism for that matter) is often nothing but

---

[4] An especially blunt statement of the aspiration is J. J. Winckelmann's (d. 1768) appeal to the student of classical art: The students "sollen . . . vorher eingenommen sich den Werken der griechischen Kunst nähern: denn in der Versicherung, viel schönes [*sic*] zu finden, werden sie dasselbe suchen, und einiges wird sich ihnen entdecken. Man kehre so oft zurück, bis man es gefunden hat; denn es ist vorhanden" (*Geschichte der Kunst des Alterthums* [first published in 1764], Buch 5, Kap. 6, § 13, in *Winckelmann's Werke*, ed. H. Meyer and J. Schulze [Dresden, 1808-1820], IV, 232). Cf. W. Déonna, *L'Expression des sentiments dans l'art* (Paris, 1914), pp. 80-83, where, at p. 80, Winckelmann's advice is quoted from the 1802 French edition of his works (I, 484), in which the beginning of the passage is formulated more strongly than in the German original: "Approchez-vous d'un esprit prévenu en faveur de l'antiquité." One is reminded of the drastic statement of G. Bachelard, *La Poétique de l'espace* (Paris, 1958), p. 100: "Les valeurs déplacent les faits." Cf. also M. Scheler, *Die Wissensformen und die Gesellschaft* (2d ed.; Bern and München, 1960), pp. 109-110: "Jede Art intellektiver Soseinserfassung [setzt] ein auf diesen Gegenstand bezogenes emotionales Werterlebnis [voraus]. . . . Die Wertnehmung geht stets der Wahrnehmung vorher."

[5] Already J. J. Bachofen (1815-1887), *Das Mutterrecht* (first published in Stuttgart in 1861), in *Gesammelte Werke* (Basel, 1943——), II, 23, observes: "Mit den Zeiten wechseln die Probabilitäten." The dictum is quoted by E. Howald, *Humanismus und Europäertum* (Zürich and Stuttgart, 1957), p. 69.

an expression of a society's disinterest in, or fundamental unconcern with, the area in which it is allowed to prevail, unless it betrays itself as part of the psychological machinery that is required to sustain and further a valued aspiration.

The style of historiographical presentation must be recognized as another instrument for the realization of the research objective. Stylistic patterns such as the annalistic or the declaratory (as in certain royal inscriptions, for instance) are in themselves limitative; their replacement bespeaks a shifting objective as much as does inquiry into, or by means of, new contexts.

Considerations of this order make it obvious that there is a definite link between a society's motivation to support historiography, usually of a clearly defined type, and its self-image. Whether descriptive (*konstatierend*) or normative ("pedagogical"), the self-image is reflected in motivation and objective of research and presentation. The connection becomes painfully evident when the "use" to which history is to be put is the adjustment of the collective self-image to that held by the observer and the minority within the society for which he is the spokesman. The varying judgments on the Greek *polis*, on the relative merits of Sparta and Athens, or on unitary and federative forms of organization in the Hellenistic world, are likely to reflect the author's outlook on his society, his aspirations for its future, and, in any event, the concerns that reflect his society's objectives (generally apprehended as its "problems").

Objectivity, in this context, means primarily self-consciousness about the nature of historical research and an ever-increasing, but obviously a never-complete, willingness to strike historical situations that have been proven unsuited for the purpose by examination of the sources from the dossier of arguments marshaled in support of one's aspirations; one may say, perhaps, that objectivity is an increased independence from history as an instrument of change, an independence that seems to be brought about most readily by having the possession of historical insight incorporated as an important trait in a society's self-image. Besides, it is not merely a statement of fact that some proposed uses of history, and some questions asked of it, are more germane than others; it is in the nature of objectivity, as just characterized, to suggest more questions and uses than can be pursued and consummated without an obviously arbitrary handling of the data consulted. In other words, a self-view that accepts one's historicity protects the historicity of the dead and widens the areas of psychological response; that is, it makes ever-wider segments of the experience of the human past meaningful, or utilizable in the service of currently effective aspirations. In this sense historical objectivity, that is, object-orientedness, if placed in the widest possible judgmental perspective, tends to liberate, or to purge, the self-image from aspirations that are not *richtigkeitsrational*;[6] it assists in a rational adjustment of purposes where otherwise only a purposive rational adjustment of means to nonrationally apprehended ends would have been possible.[7] If this is true, one may well postulate that distortions of a period's historiographic seizure of reality (excluding, of course, simple error, neglectfulness, and defective information) are functions of the peculiarities of the society's self-image,

---

[6] For the concept cf. M. Weber, "Ueber einige Kategorien der verstehenden Soziologie," *Logos*, IV (1913), 253-294, at pp. 254, 257-263; Weber contrasts *subjektive Zweckrationalität* and *objektive Richtigkeitsrationalität*. The idea is taken up by S. F. Nadel, *The Foundations of Social Anthropology* (London, 1953), esp. p. 271 (where, in n. 1, the reference to Weber's study is inexact).

[7] The creative primacy of the self-image has been stated by Goethe in the famous lines of the *West-Östliche Divan:*

> Volk und Knecht und Ueberwinder
> Sie gestehn, zu jeder Zeit:
> Höchstes Glück der Erdenkinder
> Sei nur die Persönlichkeit.
>
> Jedes Leben sei zu führen,
> Wenn man sich nicht selbst vermisst;
> Alles könne man verlieren,
> Wenn man bliebe was man ist.

as these are most easily understood by analysis of its aspirations. The aspiration determines what part of the total heritage that is potentially at a society's disposal activates the emotions.

Ṭāhā Ḥusain (b. 1889) has noted this connection by denying the value of the *qudamāʾ* when they cease to inspire the living generation; he therefore sets himself the goal of re-creating ancient history as an inspiration for his contempories.[8] When the Moroccan M. A. Lahbabi speaks (in a very different context, it is true) of *la vérité des XIXe et XXe siècles,* and then states that "en analysant la vie, en expliquant et en décrivant ce qui *est* et ce qu'on doit *faire,* le philosophe accélère le mouvement d'émancipation de l'homme en lutte contre la matière et contre sa nature," he takes account of the incessant shifts in what the human mind accepts as conclusive, and stresses, as we have done, but from a different vantage point, the liberating force of an "open" self-image oriented to an objectively and not merely affectively valid correctness. For, as Lahbabi states in another passage, man, in contrast to animals, has a transcendent image of himself to realize.[9] This philosophical assertion of the primacy of the self-view is at the same time (and in a sense not intended by the philosopher) a clue to the understanding of the concern for history in the contemporary Arab world.[10]

---

[8] *ʿAlà hāmish as-sīra,* I (Cairo, 1933), Introduction, pp. 8^{16}-9^{2}, 9^{3-9}.

[9] M. A. Lahbabi, *Liberté ou libération? (A partir des libertés bergsoniennes)* (Paris, 1956), pp. 20, 21, 81-82. The nature, the role, and, in some instances, the primacy of the image are examined forcefully if impressionistically by K. E. Boulding, *The Image* (Ann Arbor, Mich., 1956); cf., e.g., the passage on p. 122: "The history of the technological revolution must be written largely in terms of the dynamism of the image—the image of change as a good and desirable thing introduced by the various religious reformations, and the image of an orderly universe whose secret relations might be explored by experiment and observation."

[10] Not with regard to historiography, but with regard to social and political attitudes, the extremely interesting book by A. Memmi, *Portrait du colonisé précédé du Portrait du colonisateur*

If it be asked why the frequently observable discrepancy, not to say contradictoriness, between the ends and the facts of a society's self-view does not result in either their adjustment or their mutual destruction, it must be said that in the long run such an adjustive or destructive process, resulting in a replacement of current aspirations by new ones, does in fact take place. But, more importantly, it must be noted that contradictions and maladjustments of this order are as a rule only faintly perceived; or, to put it more accurately, they will be the less clearly perceived, the stronger the emotional hold of the aspirations.

Periods of self-criticism are periods of aspirational shifts. As a matter of fact, the very aspiration that may, on the level of rational analysis, cause the maladjustments, gives, for the time of its effective dominance, the necessary psychological cohesion to the *disjecta membra* of the self-image, and renders bearable the chasm between the realities of the historical situation and the assumptions of its "creative misinterpretation" of the objectives for which the society believes it lives. It is more than fifty years since Th. Ribot saw that the principle that confers unity within the sphere of "la logique affective" and "régit la logique des sentiments toute entière" is the principle of finality. Psychologically, the coexistence of rationally incompatible affirmations is explainable on the ground that each one of them is experienced as necessary by individual or society.[11] (Logically, of course, the contradiction cannot be concealed.)

III

The nature and the development of the Western attitude toward, and expectation from, research in general, and Oriental studies in particular, as it appears to those Near

(Paris, 1957), which deals with the French and the Muslims of Algeria, provides an illustration of the same truth; an analysis of the roles played by religion, language, and the like in the several self-views adds to the merits of the study.

[11] Th. Ribot, *La Logique des sentiments* (Paris, 1905), pp. 49, 58.

Eastern scholars and leaders who identify with it, have been formulated by Adnan Adivar (d. 1951) in his introduction to the Turkish edition of the *Encyclopaedia of Islam*.[12] He notes a difference of motivation between early and contemporary Oriental scholarship in Europe: "In taking over early Eastern science and philosophy into their own language, the Orientalists were primarily concerned with improving their own knowledge and refinement rather than in making a scientific study of the East, and they were not seeking to discover anything original in Eastern languages and history. In this respect, these early Orientalists were engaged in an endeavor which somewhat resembles our [i.e., modern Turkey's] own activity in translation and adaptation from the West." The Western scholar may hesitate to consider the translators of the thirteenth (and later) centuries as his predecessors in any but a formal sense; yet the parallel drawn with the assimilative tendencies of the contemporary East deserves attention. By the middle of the eighteenth century the framework of modern Orientalism had been established. Adivar finds it in the subtitle of d'Herbelot's (1625-1695) *Bibliothèque Orientale*,[13] which, after the fashion of the age, describes its contents as "everything necessary for an understanding of the Eastern peoples, i.e., their history, their real and legendary traditions, their religions, sects, governments, politics, more recent customs, and the organization and administration of their states." In this "more or less complete definition" of our studies we miss primarily a statement of objective; however, as it is quoted here not for its adequacy, but for its mirroring an Eastern view of our pursuits, a placing of d'Herbelot in the Western development may be dispensed with.[14]

Without trying to analyze Western motivation, Halil

---

[12] *Islâm Ansiklopedisi* (Ankara, 1943——).

[13] Paris, 1697.

[14] Adnan Adivar, "A Turkish Account of Orientalism" (translation of introduction to Turkish edition of *Encyclopaedia of Islam*), *The Muslim World*, XLIII (1953), 266-282, at pp. 264, 266.

Inalcik declares that Occidental scholarship today deals with Islamic history in an "essentially scientific and objective" way. What is decisive is that "there is no other way for any serious student of the Islamic past. There is no need to say more about this. The scientific method is concerned only with discovering historical truth and explaining the causes which brought them forward." This statement is to be read in the light of Inalcik's awareness of "the dangers of requiring history to conform to current political views." Such modern writers, Eastern and Western, "who have a fanatical devotion to traditions are unaware that historical truth is beyond their reach . . . because they are bound to past errors and prejudices." After rejecting the influence that some scholars in Islamic countries have allowed their nationalism to exert on their research, Inalcik asserts that, in his opinion, "historical studies will form a strong foundation for the real cultural movements in Islamic countries today. The objective study of Islamic history with Western methodology will bring about general progress in all Islamic learning." [15]

The epistemological presupposition of this statement, of which Inalcik may not have been fully conscious, as well as the objective of the attitude for which he speaks, had been expressed with his usual merciless precision by Atatürk: "We shall take science and knowledge from wherever they may be, and put them in the mind of every member of the nation. For science and for knowledge, there are no restrictions and no conditions.[16] For a nation that insists on preserving a host of traditions and beliefs that rest on no logical proof, progress is very difficult, perhaps even impossible." [17]

[15] Halil Inalcik, "The Study of History in Islamic Countries," *Middle East Journal*, VII (1953), 451-455, at pp. 454-455.

[16] Here, as so often in our times, science is assuming the leveling and unifying role of the *ḥikma khālida* of the tenth and eleventh centuries.

[17] In a speech made to a meeting of teachers on Oct. 27, 1922, *Atatürk'ün Söyler ve Demeçleri* (Ankara, 1952), II, 44. The passage is quoted in a somewhat free German version by J. Ritter, *Europäisch-asiatischer Dialog* (Düsseldorf, 1956), pp. 20-21.

The self-image of Western man, as it has been recognized in his intellectual history and at work in his present intellectual endeavors, has been described by Edmund Husserl (1859-1938) in terms of

> . . . the very idea that defines and constitutes him as Western man. That idea is no other than the idea of philosophy itself; the idea of a universal knowledge concerning the totality of being, a knowledge which contains within itself whatever special sciences may grow out of it as its ramifications, which rests upon ultimate foundations and proceeds throughout in a completely evident and self-justifying fashion and in full awareness of itself. Closely connected with this idea, whose first inception in Ancient Greece in the VIIth and VIth centuries B.C. marks the historical beginning of Western man, is the idea of a truly human, i.e., philosophical existence, an existence oriented towards the ideas, ideals and norms of autonomous reason, which alone permits Western man to live in conformity and at peace with himself.[18]

From this interpretation of "Western man," Husserl diagnoses his present crisis as caused by his having forsaken "those very philosophical aspirations out of which Western science was born," and proposes to remedy the malaise by leading him back to those aspirations through philosophy reunderstood. In our context, however, it is not the crisis of Western intellectuality that is of concern, but Husserl's and, by his postulate, Western man's orientation toward "the teleological idea of philosophy, that very idea which gives unity and meaning to the historical process as a whole. A teleological idea which, because it displays itself in the medium of history, by necessity undergoes trans-

[18] In my exposition of the relevant ideas of E. Husserl's posthumously published work, *Die Krisis der europäischen Wissenschaften und die transzendentale Phänomenologie,* ed. W. Biemel (The Hague, 1954), I have utilized the excellent analysis by A. Gurwitsch, "The Last Work of Edmund Husserl," *Philosophy and Phenomenological Research,* XVI (1956), 380-399; XVII (1957), 370-398, largely because of Gurwitsch's admirable English formulations of Husserl's statements. The passage quoted is from Gurwitsch, *op. cit.,* XVI, 381-382.

formations and yet preserves its identity, defines an *infinite task*. . . . The historical significance of a philosophical theory consists but in its contribution towards the infinite task." [19]

The infinite task, which Husserl assigns to philosophical theory, Western man has actually assigned to himself in every sphere of life; hence his willingness to recognize his insights as provisional, his anticipation that his lifework will be superseded by subsequent correction and refutation, but also his conviction of the manipulability of the social and economic universe, with the implied duty to strive after this-worldly perfection which he yet knows to be unattainable.

The insight into history which Husserl demands is not to culminate in knowledge of the past for its own sake; it will enable us "to see and understand ourselves," and by such *Selbstverständnis*[20] "to find our specific task within the infinite task." It is true that Husserl confines his demands to the philosopher who in our day is guided by comprehension of his position in history toward assuming the specific task of renewing and transforming the very idea of philosophy through transcendental phenomenology.[21] But this restriction is justifiable solely by the

[19] *Ibid.*, XVI, 384-385. Where the modern Occidental seeks confrontation with alien cultures the medieval Westerner confronted the Bible which, to adopt H. de Lubac's phrase, "fait notre propre exégèse." The concern of the interpreter is less with the text as such but with himself; the scriptural text serves as a lever for self-explication with a view to outgrowing the human condition. Incidentally, Husserl himself once said that no one knows himself unless he knows the Bible. Cf. de Lubac, *Exégèse médiévale*, I (Paris, 1959), 569-570. The unceasing endeavor to approach ever more closely an ultimately unattainable truth is strikingly expressed by the Greek Church Father Gregory of Nyssa (d. *ca.* 395) where he describes the process of the soul's "assimilation to God" as an *epekteinesthai*, a stretching and straining toward the goal, a continual self-surpassing that can never reach its end; cf. W. Jaeger, *Humanistische Reden und Vorträge* (2nd ed.; Berlin, 1960), pp. 279-280.

[20] For his concept of *Selbstverständnis* cf. *Die Krisis* . . . , pp. 275-276.

[21] Gurwitsch, *op. cit.*, XVI, 385.

purpose of Husserl's reflections. Self-understanding, unqualified by orientation to a specific objective, is essentially the purpose of Western man's immersion into history, and, to spell out a significant implication, of the cultural solutions to the problems of societal living which punctuate its flow. We may then accept Husserl's characterization of "Western Man" as a human type who "in der Endlichkeit lebend, auf Pole der Unendlichkeit hinlebt," [22] and whose historicity and "wissenschaftliche Kultur" have the sense of "Entwerden des endlichen Menschentums im Werden zum Menschentum unendlicher Aufgaben." [23] The world that Western man uses as his material and as his stage is, to transfer an idea of Husserl's from epistemology to the philosophy of history, a world "deren Sein Sein

[22] Husserl, *op. cit.*, p. 322; Gurwitsch, *op. cit.*, XVI, 388.

[23] Husserl, *op. cit.*, p. 325; Gurwitsch, *op. cit.*, XVI, 388. The joyful realization of the infinity of the task of the searcher and the implied readiness to see one's lifework rendered obsolete by the efforts of one's successors shines through the analysis of his science which the great classicist August Boeckh was in the habit of presenting to his students in the University of Berlin. In his *Encyclopädie und Metholodogie der philologischen Wissenschaften,* which he offered no less than twenty-six times between 1809 and 1866, he observes in discussing philological interpretation: "Wenn also die fremde Individualität nie vollständig verstanden werden kann, so kann die Aufgabe der Hermeneutik nur durch unendliche Approximation, das heisst durch allmähliche, Punkt für Punkt fortschreitende, aber nie vollendete Annäherung gelöst werden" (quoted by K. Reinhardt, *Von Werken und Formen* [Godesberg, 1948], pp. 429-430). An extreme formulation of the Occidental attitude was proposed by Nietzsche when he said: "Die Grösse des 'Fortschritts' bemisst sich sogar nach dem Masse dessen, was ihm alles geopfert werden musste" (*Genealogie der Moral,* 2d Treatise, Section 12). In the Islamic orbit, this sense of the infinity of the human task, of the eternally provisional of the human achievement, which is yet striven for in gladness and without hesitation or discouragement, is met with only in the quest of the mystic (cf., e.g., the characteristic passage from the writings of Najm ad-Dīn Kubrà [d. 1221] which F. Meier translated on pp. 92-93 of his book *Die Fawā'iḥ al-Ǧamāl wa-Fawātiḥ al-Ǧalāl des Naǧm ad-Dīn al-Kubrā* [Wiesbaden, 1957]). The attitude to scholarship which Muḥammad ar-Rāzī (d. 925) professes, *Opera philosophica,* ed. P. Kraus (Cairo, 1939), I, 300-303, seems to have died with him.

aus subjektiver Leistung ist." [24] This world stands revealed "as a correlate and product of subjective functions, activities, and operations." [25] It is therefore, we may add, a world in which operationally psychological truth takes the place of absolute truth—an outlook that would seem to be made to order for the historian, but at the same time an outlook that it would be extremely difficult for a Muslim historian, not so much to accept, but to utilize toward the critical reshaping of an effective self-image. For it does imply the determination to place man and the structure of his consciousness in the center and to acknowledge the autonomy of reason as an essential property of the idea of man.[26]

The teleological nexus in which man is placed, and which in retrospect appears as a nexus of causation, is, for contemporary Western society, describable in terms of its central aspirations—the ever-widening control and understanding of the inner and outer world. The coexistence of those aspirations is as characteristic of our civilization as are their accompanying methodological requirements of completeness and universality of information (and application). Specialization for control, and generalization for understanding, are, in a slightly oversimplified formulation, the objectives toward which we are pushed by somewhat conflicting internal drives. But generalization in the service of a "self-understanding" that is existentially satisfactory and factually correct, and allows for the development of control over the expanding human (political,

---

[24] Gurwitsch, *op. cit.*, XVI, 398. Cf. Husserl, *op. cit.*, p. 346: ". . . eine absolut eigenständige Geisteswissenschaft . . . , in Form einer konsequenten Selbstverständigung und Verständigung der Welt als geistiger Leistung."

[25] Gurwitsch, *op. cit.*, XVI, 398. For Husserl it falls to phenomenology "to account for the world at large as well as mundane existence in particular, and for that matter, for all objective entities whatsoever, in terms of experiences, acts, operations, and productions ['Leistungen'] of consciousness" (*ibid.*, XVII, 379).

[26] Cf. also Husserl's formulation (*op. cit.*, p. 310): "Umwelt ist relativ auf eine für sie fungierende Subjektivität—die Typik fungierender Subjektivität ist selbst historisch."

social, etc.) and intellectual universe,[27] presupposes specialized knowledge—a fact which ensures the perpetuation of conflicting intellectual valuations and educational systems. The intellectual position of our civilization is, however, incompletely assessed unless we realize one consequence of the peculiar combination of aspirations and epistemological assumptions to which we are dedicated (or, by which we are possessed), namely, that our self-understanding must be based on an understanding of other cultures. We are forced "to review and reconstruct ourselves against the background of the totality of the cultural achievement of mankind," and this concern, connected as it is with our paramount objective and the collective self-extension or self-transcendence it demands, compels us to move toward a convergence of historical and anthropological research which is to culminate in a *Kulturlehre*.[28]

---

[27] What has been called "the mastery of things," a sense that nature need not rule but can be ruled, is precisely one of the attitudes that successful Westernization inculcates—and presupposes. Cf. the remarks of M. Berger, *The Arab World Today* (New York, 1962), p. 159.

[28] For more detail see chap. iii, pp. 30 ff., above. Husserl, *op. cit.*, p. 332, indicates how the pre-Socratic thinker comes to develop the concept of truth from contemplation of the "Mannigfaltigkeit der Nationen." Note in this context the *Bildungsbegriff* developed by W. Schadewaldt, *Die Anforderungen der Technik an die Geisteswissenschaft* (Göttingen, 1957), p. 41: "Auf dem Sich-Auskennen in den einfachsten Dingen, dem Sich-Auskennen in den Sachen und den Sachbereichen, baut sich danach organisch die Bildung auf als ein letztes und höchstes Sich-Auskennen im Ganzen der Welt, eine Orientierung meines gegenwärtigen Orts im Jetzt und Hier, in den grossen Zusammenhängen von Zeit und Raum, Natur und Geschichte." The philosophical (or anthropological) assumption underlying our methodological requirement of "completeness and universality of information" is very clearly brought out in this passage from Claude Lévi-Strauss, *Tristes tropiques* (Paris, 1955), p. 183: "L'ensemble des coutumes d'un peuple est toujours marqué par un style; elles forment des systèmes. Je suis persuadé que ces systèmes n'existent pas en nombre illimité, et que les sociétés humaines, comme les individus—dans leurs jeux, leurs rêves ou leurs délires—ne créent jamais de façon absolue, mais se bornent à choisir certaines combinaisons dans un répertoire idéal qu'il

At this point again we are intellectually and emotionally well located for object-oriented historical research, because the instructiveness in terms of our existential objective, of our conclusions with regard to our own past and the past and present of "other" societies and civilizations, is independent of their material content.

In this sense one may speak of the superior aptitude of the modern West for the analysis of civilizations. One may go further and describe it as the only civilization that has, in its concept of man, fully utilized his *Kulturenfähigkeit,*[29] that is, his potential (and largely actualized) cultural pluralism. By basing its interpretation of man's psychological structure and, more particularly, its self-image on the fact of this human *Kulturenfähigkeit,* the West has developed a secular means of accounting for, of functionalizing, and perhaps of allowing to coexist a number of disparate civilizations without having to deprive them intellectually of their specific properties. From the religious viewpoint this attitude could have been reached through the acknowledgment that such pluralism was suggested, if not demanded, by the very fact of God's having created different peoples realizing themselves in different civilizations. But whereas the great religions accept the fact, the nature of religious truth precludes, or renders superfluous, the utilization of the experience of cultural pluralism as an essential means of collective self-understanding. Religious truth, and especially revealed religious truth, can and should be communicated to all; but the diversity of the societies that may be, or may be made, receptive to it,

---

serait possible de reconstituer. En faisant l'inventaire de toutes les coutumes observées, de toutes celles imaginées dans les mythes, celles aussi évoquées dans les jeux des enfants et des adultes, les rêves des individus sains ou malades et les conduites psycho-pathologiques, on parviendrait à dresser une sorte de tableau périodique comme celui des éléments chimiques, où toutes les coutumes réelles ou simplement possibles apparaîtraient groupées en familles, et où nous n'aurions plus qu'à reconnaître celles que les sociétés ont effectivement adoptées."

[29] Cf. chap. iii, nn. 1 and 2, pp. 31, 32, above.

while illustrating the ways of the Lord, has little to teach the faithful about himself.

The contrast of approaches which is inherent in the contrast of aspirations comes strikingly to the fore in certain contemporary studies of comparative religion, in which the researcher places himself outside his civilization and his own historical moment in order to judge both of them from the perspective of other civilizations and other religions. The motivation for choosing a vantage point of such location is to be found in the problems dealt with, and the choice depends, in turn, on the cultural or existential aspiration scholarship is called upon to serve. In his essay, "Symbolisme religieux et valorisation de l'angoisse," M. Eliade places himself in the position of "un observateur qui participe à une autre civilisation et nous juge à l'échelle de ses propres valeurs." [30] Whether or not such abstraction from one's historical location is possible, the need for it is felt; and it is this need that constitutes the uniqueness of the Western position.

History has often been cultivated for the instruction to be gained from contemplation of the past, especially of its errors and catastrophes. The lesson derived, however, always depends on the question asked. Thus, in the world of Islam, for instance, it is generally found in an asseveration of the transitoriness of everything human and in the advice to adopt a pragmatic pattern of personal and especially political behavior. Let us illustrate the familiar by somewhat unfamiliar examples. After Baihaqī (d. 1077) has told the tragic end of Er-Yaruq and Il-Ghazi, he observes: "And lo, what was the outcome of what the two generals did? All came to an end, one might say, as if it had never been. Time and the turning of the sky by the command of God have often acted thus and will often act thus in the future." The wise man is he who does not allow himself to be deceived by the favors of Time (*zamāna*), and remains on guard and sees to it that he

[30] M. Eliade, *Mythes, rêves et mystères* (2d ed.; Paris, 1957), p. 61.

leaves behind him a good name.[31] Khwāja Ḥasan, the *kadkhudā* of Sultan Muḥammad, joins Sultan Masʿūd after the latter has brought about his master's fall—"not putting himself in the hand of Satan but taking the path of right and truth; for he was a man of perfect insight" who had experienced good and bad turns of fortune, "had read the old books [*wa-kutub-i bāstān khwānda*], and knew the consequences of things [or, the end things will come to, *ʿawāqib-rā bi-dānista*]"; and so he preserves his position.[32] "Insight into the history of man is a mirror in which the onlooker finds the verification of good and bad actions and which instructs the men of perception and natural gifts. Through it God reminds those of his servants whom he finds worthy of such reminder and deserving of his recompense and his reward." [33] Almost six centuries later,

---

[31] *Taʾrīkh*, ed. S. Nafīsī (Tehran, 1319-1332/1940-1953), I, $279^{13ff.}$.

[32] *Ibid.*, I, 96, esp. ll. 8-9. When in 1347 the Marīnid Abū 'l-Ḥasan made himself master of the Ifrīqiya, he admired greatly the buildings and gardens which earlier rulers had constructed. Reaching finally the sea at Mahdiyya, he bethought himself of the Koranic verse (40:22): "Have they not travelled about in the earth and seen of what nature was the end of those before them? They were of greater power and left greater traces in the earth than they; but Allāh took hold of them for their sins, and from Allāh they had no protector." Cf. Ibn Khaldūn, *Histoire des Berbères*, trans. de Slane (2nd ed.; Paris, 1925-1956), IV, 252-253 (where the Koranic passage is, however, not quoted in full). G. Marçais, *La Berbérie musulmane et l'Orient au moyen âge* (Paris, 1946), pp. 302-303, refers to the incident to suggest the new ruler's realization of cultural continuity.

[33] Muḥammad b. ʿAbdalmalik al-Hamadānī (d. 1127), *Takmila Taʾrīkh aṭ-Ṭabarī*, Part I, ed. A. Y. Kanʿān, in *al-Mashriq*, XLIX (1955), 21-42, 149-172, at p. 25^{8-10}. We find a remarkably wide concept of the scope of history in the Moroccan al-Yūsī (d. 1691), but its function remains confined to the intracultural one of legal and ethical illustration. Cf. J. Berque, *Al-Yousi. Problèmes de la culture marocaine au XVIIe siècle* (Paris and The Hague, 1958), p. 26. The relationship between history and religion is defined somewhat differently by another Moroccan, Abū ʿAbdallāh Muḥammad b. aṭ-Ṭayyib al-Qādirī, who died in Fez in 1773, in his *Nashr al-mathānī* (Fez, 1310), II, 143. He allocates all that concerns religion in history, includ-

Kātib Chelebi suggests to the ruler that, "like his mighty ancestors, he should read history, and draw the moral from the story of their illustrious deeds." [34]

In reflecting on the fact that modern Arabic historiographical self-analysis has been satisfied with a somewhat crude psychological approach to its themes, and has besides confined its attention almost totally to the Islamic or, better, to the Arab-Muslim sphere, one wonders whether the absence of the neohumanistic strain (to use E. Spranger's expression) from the Arab nationalist ideology may not have something to do with its intellectual limitations.

The degeneration and obsolescence of European and especially German nationalism in some of its historical manifestations must not induce one to overlook its connection with the humanistic movement that has been, since the Augustan period, if not before, the unfailing companion of national patriotism in Europe. The achievements of a Vergil, a Horace, or an Ovid were motivated by the aspiration to equal the perfection of the Greek models. To introduce a Greek literary genre into Rome was an act of patriotic duty. The ennoblement of his nation was the first obligation of the poet; the pride felt in the great past and in the potentialities of the people needed justification by a supreme creative achievement. In the Western orbit the yardstick of such achievement has always been sought in the Greek past. This was as true for the Scipios and their circle and the Augustans as for the Elizabethans and the age of Louis XIV, and again for the Italian humanists and the Germans from Winckelmann to Spranger and Jaeger. To them the individuality

---

ing for instance the history of coinage, weights, and measures, the description of old mosques, etc., to religion. History itself may deal with any state or states, the foundation of towns, or the life of important people. Although not part of religion it is good as long as it stimulates ethical behavior. The passage is paraphrased in A. S. Tritton, *Materials on Muslim Education in the Middle Ages* (London, 1957), p. 170, without indication of the author, for whom cf. C. Brockelmann, *Geschichte der arabischen Litteratur, Supplement* (Leiden, 1937-1942), II, 687.

[34] *Op. cit.*, p. 147.

of the nation and the individuality of the person were inseparable; the formation of the one not only entails but presupposes the formation of the other. The education of the individual can be accomplished only by his participation in the life of the nation; and conversely, the upward development of the nation is unthinkable without the spiritual and ethical growth of its citizens. Political power does not carry its legitimation in itself; it becomes legitimate when the ruler equals or outreaches the ruled *in spiritualibus*. The nation is the ever-imperfect embodiment of *Deutschtum* or *Franzosentum; Deutschtum* itself is an idea, an unending process, in short, an aspiration.[35] Every

---

[35] For the characterization of "neohumanistic nationalism" see, e.g., E. Spranger, *Der Anteil des Neuhumanismus an der Entstehung des deutschen Nationalbewusstseins* (Berlin, 1923), esp. pp. 4-5, 5-6, 11; Howald, *op. cit.*, esp. pp. 3-7, 23-41. A striking illustration of the contrasting approach of much of Arab nationalism is provided by Michel ʿAflaq, the leading theorist of the Syrian *Baʿth* party. ʿAflaq sees Arab nationalism as an existential rather than a rational fact; it exists independent of any Arab's positive acceptance of it. It is a destiny that binds him who is born into the Arab fold, but it can also be adopted by him who has been associated with the Arabs in history and has become one of them in thinking and feeling. Cf. L. Binder's analysis of ʿAflaq's ideas in "Radical-Reform Nationalism in Syria and Egypt," *The Muslim World*, LIX (1959), pp. 101, 103, 104. Clovis Maqsoud (Maqṣūd; b. 1927), born in the United States of Lebanese parents, and at present the Representative of the League of Arab States in India and Southeast Asia, proclaims Arab nationalism a humanist movement. "Suffice it to state . . . that our concept of nationalism is that it is a movement and not an ideology. As such it is functional, transitional and an authentic humanist involvement. As a movement, it seeks to liberate, as an ideology, it becomes closed and egocentric. As a movement, nationalism is transitional and functional—the removal of foreign control and the unity of a divided nation. As an ideology, nationalism renders the ascertainment of personality a purpose in itself and also a fulfilment. Nationalism as a movement is basically egalitarian and deeply involved in the human situation; as an ideology, self-involvement is total and distinctiveness from the other is a matter to be cherished and glorified. Nationalism as a movement is a human necessity while nationalism as an ideology is a dangerous anachronism. Nationalism in this context is an enrichment of the internationalism mankind

European nation has risen to become a *Kulturnation* by following the example of Rome in attempting to find a spiritual expression of its national aspirations. To follow the example of Rome implies acceptance of the Greeks as the norm and hence that "totale Lebensbeziehung zum Altertum" to which no part and no period of the Muslim development ever could be dedicated.[36] It has been the misfortune of the Arabs that the European sources of their nationalistic ideology (or, in some instances, the Arab transmitters themselves) represented a different strain of Western nationalism.[37]

---

yearns for while nationalism as an ideology is a disruptive factor in a desirable world order.

"This clarification of what is meant by nationalism is not an original definition but one which has characterized the general evolution of contemporary nationalism in Asia and Africa. Of course some of the assertive overtones can be easily discernible in these nationalist movements but these come to the forefront when the imperialist or the colonial power deliberately seeks to depersonalize the national entity it rules or administers. Yet the essence of these functional nationalisms is their egalitarian urge and motives." Cf. *Lebanon and Arab Nationalism*, paper prepared for the Conference on Lebanese Democracy, University of Chicago, May 28-31, 1963, pp. 22-23.

[36] Cf. Howald, *op. cit.*, p. 7. The phrase is Spranger's, as quoted by J. Kraemer, "Die Bildungsideale des Islams und ihre gegenwärtige Problematik," in *Erziehung zur Menschlichkeit. Festschrift für Ed. Spranger* (Tübingen, 1957), pp. 273-289, at p. 278. It is no accident that the European humanists were the first to be troubled by the relationship between past and present; they experienced the relevance of the past to the present and hence the phenomena of change and cultural survivals as problems.

[37] It is useful to remember that Western consciousness of cultural stiucture is of relatively recent growth, and that it was preceded by a rather naïve awareness of what to us are minor contrasts in behavior patterns; the quotation offered by A. Malvezzi, *L'Islamismo e la cultura europea* (Florence, 1956), p. 125, from F. Suriano's *Trattato di Terra Santa* (1450) is a suggestive sample. The interest in things Christian observed by Ricoldo da Montecroce (d. 1320) during his visit to the Holy Land and especially in Baghdad (*ca.* 1300) indicates a remarkable "transcultural openness" among the educated Muslims with whom the Frater had to deal; cf. Malvezzi, *op. cit.*, pp. 116-117

IV

How far removed the objective of contemporary "Islamic research" is from that of Western, or Western-inspired, historical self-interpretation and *Kulturforschung* may be documented from a statement made by Muhammad Rafi-ud-Din, a prominent Pakistani, director of the Iqbal Academy at Karachi, in a lecture given in December, 1956. Defining "Islamic Research" as research that "is centered around the contents of" Koran and *ḥadīth*, or prophetic tradition, Dr. Rafi-ud-Din includes in it

> all that Muslim scholars have written in the past or may write in the future (A) on the sacred books and (B) on books written about the sacred books. It excludes (C) all that Muslim scholars have written in the past or may write in the future on a subject other than Islam, e.g., on Medicine, Physics, Astronomy, Chemistry, Lexicography, History, Art or Literature. It excludes also (D) all research work that we may undertake on books written under (C) above. Moreover, since the contents of the sacred books are not intelligible to non-Muslims, as such, and non-Muslims cannot be expected to make them intelligible to others as sacred contents of the sacred books or even to have the intention to do so, Islamic research will also exclude (E) all research work done by non-Muslim scholars on the sacred books or on books written about the sacred books.[38]

---

and the literature quoted on p. 147. Attention should be drawn to Sāṭiʿ al-Ḥuṣrī's *Muḥāḍarāt fī nushūʾ al-fikra 'l-qaumiyya* (3d ed.; Beirut, 1956) as an interesting survey of the rise of nationalistic thought in western and central Europe, the Balkans, and the Turkish and Arab Near East.

[38] Muhammad Rafi-ud-Din, *The Meaning and Purpose of Islamic Research* (Karachi, n.d. [1957]), pp. 1-2. The uneasiness felt by some Muslim circles "when observing non-Muslims who occupy themselves with Islam for purposes of study and observation" has been examined by C. A. O. van Nieuwenhuijze, "Frictions between Presuppositions," *Bulletin d'Informations*, Centre pour l'étude des problèmes du monde musulman contemporain, Bruxelles, V (March-April, 1958), 38-67, at pp. 39-47. To reserve Islam as a field of study to Muslims and thus to separate

The author divides Islamic (as all) research into (1) mechanical research and (2) original research. The function of "original Islamic research" is double. "(1) It refutes directly or indirectly the wrong philosophical ideas that have become prevalent at the time and have begun to have an adverse effect on the faith of the Muslims. (2) It affirms the truth of Islam and defends Islamic beliefs and ideas by making use of all the right philosophical ideas that are available at the time." [39] All research into matters connected with what we should call Islamic civilization which are not covered by the definition of Islamic research is merely "Oriental research," in which Westerners have been the pioneers; it "is entirely mechanical and concerns itself with translating, editing, annotating, summarizing, remodeling or indexing, ancient works of History, Philosophy, Religion, Lexicography, Science and Literature, written in the Oriental languages like Arabic, Persian, Sanskrit, Chinese, Indonesian and Turkish, etc." [40] Apart from missionary, administrative, and political motivations, Western scholars, in the pursuit of Oriental research, were doubtless actuated also by their desire "to satisfy their curiosity and to provide themselves with amusement by uncovering the hidden relics of an ancient civilization which according to them exists no longer and which has been superseded by a far superior civilization of which they are themselves the torchbearers. Their attitude is similar to ours in carrying out excavations at Taxila by means of which we lay bare to the world for their amusement or

---

a group of peoples, a set of beliefs, a civilization from the common concern of scholarship is, of course, a fundamentally antihumanist position. It is not necessarily but in actual fact accompanied by a lack of interest in the "other" faiths, civilizations, etc., unless their analysis seems indicated for apologetic purposes. If carried to its logical conclusion, that is, if it were adopted by (all) other societies as well, this position would spell the end of any kind of universal history, history of religion, cultural anthropology, and the like; needless to say, it carries political implications as well.

[39] *Ibid.*, pp. 2-3.

[40] *Ibid.*, p. 3.

for the satisfaction of their curiosity the buried signs of a civilization which has ceased to exist forever." [41]

Could the misapprehension of our cultural aspiration and the unproductivity in terms of historical research of another be stated more clearly? [42] The goal of the Muslim Orientalist is to reveal "the intellectual achievements of the ancient scholar of the East, which was the most cultured and civilized part of the globe till recently, and show their relation to the intellectual achievements of the present age." [43] Still, research in this direction would not be Islamic research. On the other hand, a "scientific interpretation of Islam . . . is a biological necessity for the Muslim community today and we can ignore it only at the penalty of death." [44] In order to survive, Islam must open an ideological offensive.[45]

The preoccupations directing Islamic (but also Oriental) research, as described and planned by Rafi-ud-Din, limit it to apologetics. They reflect the absence in contemporary Islam of a positive secularist ideology developed from the Muslim tradition itself which would parallel Western secularism as "a positive system of values, based ulti-

---

[41] *Ibid.*, p. 40.

[42] Cf. also *ibid.*, p. 5: "Since Oriental research is a mechanical process and has nothing original to give, it is characterized by its emphasis on petty things."

[43] *Ibid.*, pp. 5-6.

[44] *Ibid.*, p. 16.

[45] The philosophical basis of such an offensive, as of any valid scientific introduction to Islam, can only be Muḥammad Iqbāl's (d. 1938) philosophy of the self; cf. *ibid.*, pp. 22-23. The qualifications listed as essential for the Islamic research scholar (*ibid.*, pp. 24-25) remind one of those postulated by al-Māwardī for a candidate to the caliphate, or by Abul Ala Maudoodi (b. 1903) for the *mujtahid;* cf. Maudoodi's communication to the International Islamic Colloquium at Lahore (Dec. 29, 1957, to Jan. 8, 1958), "The Role of Ijtehad and the Scope of Legislation in Islam," pp. 5-6. Iqbāl would have supported Maudoodi only partially. For he insisted on the necessity of a "creative urge," *quwwat-i takhlīq*, to enrich humanity, and he admired the West for its willingness to accept spiritual risks; cf. the ref. in M. Siddiqi, *The Image of the West in Iqbāl* (Lahore, 1956), pp. 119-120 and 128-129.

mately on Greek ideas of justice, order, reason and humanity."[46] With the absence of self-understanding there comes almost of necessity a complementary absence of any understanding of the cultural differences between the Muslim and the Western worlds, a deficiency that is not even mitigated by an understanding of their religious components.

The intellectual situation from which Rafi-ud-Din speaks brings to mind the judgment pronounced by a young Arab intellectual on his own people who, in his view, have forgotten that

all the self-knowledge, the history, the culture, even the ambitions of the Arabs, have been defined and articulated in and by the West in the last two hundred years. Even now there is no denying the fact that the Arab intellectual understands himself and his situation best, not in Cairo, Damascus or Beirut, writing or speaking in Arabic, but rather in Paris or London or New York, writing or speaking in French or English. His real task in the present crisis, for the next 50 years, is to find a way out of the Arab's paralyzing solipsism, to come finally to understand the "other" instead of resting inertly in the "other's" understanding.[47]

The functional necessity for the great collectives to achieve self-interpretation through the understanding of the "other" could not have been brought out more forcefully. And one seems to feel that Sharabi realizes that a shift in aspiration will have to precede the shaping of a creatively effective self-image. Changes in aspiration are *Umbrüche*—in the last analysis to be accepted as discontinuous leaps from one kind of human self-realization to another; their nature is perhaps most readily discernible in certain reversals of artistic taste, such as the sudden breakthrough of classicism in the 1750's and 1760's.[48]

[46] W. C. Smith, *Islam in Modern History* (Princeton, 1957), p. 109. Smith goes on to observe that "the Turks, alone among the Muslim peoples, have acquired such a positive secularism."

[47] H. Sharabi, "The Crisis of the Intelligentsia in the Middle East," *The Muslim World*, XLVII (1957), 187-193, at p. 193.

[48] Cf. also Howald, *op. cit.*, p. 28.

V

The interdependence of self-image and subsequent historical action (and historiographical explanation) is of course confined to no particular period and to no particular civilization. It is the very universality of this connection which makes it important to retrace it. The ideological preparation for what was to become the Greco-Macedonian conquest of the East by Isocrates, but also by Aristotle, as upholders of the essential superiority of the Hellenes over the barbarians, consists characteristically in the sharpening and the inculcating of a self-view that would explain and justify the anticipated assumption of rulership. If the distance between Greek and barbarian was as great as that between man and beast, Greek domination of the barbarian was obviously called for. The elements that shape the self-image—for the Greeks they were climate, the city as contrasted with the shapeless monarchies of the East, but also *paideia* and *dianoia*—vary;[49] the functional relationship between image and action, between aspiration and image, is, however, constant.

Political pamphleteers, among whom Isocrates must be counted at certain stages of his development, frequently argue their point on the basis of what they wish to be accepted as the self-image of their own or another group. The interdependence of aspiration and image is almost amusingly illustrated by the great Jāḥiẓ (d. 869). When he desires to make a recognized and respected place for the Turks in the caliphate he blurs the ethnic distinctions between them and the Iranians, and, above all, he emphasizes the assimilative effect of *walāʾ*, or clientship, which attaches the Islamized foreigner to the Arab tribe to which

---

[49] For convenient reference cf., e.g., G. Glotz, *La cité grecque* (2d ed.; Paris, 1953), p. 414. Note the insistence of Isocrates on the superiority vouchsafed the Greeks by the central or intermediate position of their clime between the monarchies of the torrid zone, etc., and the tribal peoples of the polar regions; the central position of their land was to be a point of pride to the Sasanian Persian as well as the Muslim Iraqi.

he wins affiliation. History records events that are suggestive of what may become possible in the future. Did not Ismāʿīl, born of non-Arab parents, become an Arab by divine command? Clientship emerges as the social instrument of that leveling of separatisms which religion requires when it pronounces the equality of the believers before the throne of God. Jāḥiẓ' objective, the attainment of unity in obedience to the caliph, colors, if it does not determine, the self-image he persuades the community to accept.[50] On another occasion, however, when Jāḥiẓ wishes to safeguard the prerogatives of the Arabs against clients who claim equality with them on the basis of their *walāʾ* (and superiority as heirs of the cultural tradition of their Iranian ancestors, which constitutes them, as it were, *dhawū 'l-ḥaḍāratain*), he exclaims: "What is more irritating than to find your slave claiming to be more noble than yourself while he admits that he owes his nobility to the freedom you gave him!" [51]

[50] Cf. "Risāla fī manāqib at-Turk" in *Tria Opuscula*, ed. G. Van Vloten (Leiden, 1903), pp. 1-56, and the recent analysis by F. Gabrieli, "La Risāla di al-Ǧāḥiẓ sui Turchi," *Rivista degli Studi Orientali*, XXXII (1957), 477-483, esp. p. 480.

[51] "Risāla fī Banī Umayya," in *Rasāʾil al-Jāḥiẓ*, ed. Ḥ. as-Sandūbī (Cairo, 1352/1933), pp. 292-300, at p. 300^{4-5}; the *risāla* is better known as "Risāla fī 'n-Nābita," under which title it has been discussed and translated by C. Pellat in *Université d'Alger. Annales de l'Institut d'Études Orientales*, X (1952), 302-325. In our context the construction of Muslim history, and especially of the *rāshidūn* period, which Jāḥiẓ develops at the very beginning of his *Epistle*, could also be cited in evidence of the interaction between aspiration and image. For an example from a different historical context, see J. G. A. Pocock, *The Ancient Constitution and the Feudal Law. A Study of English Historical Thought in the Seventeenth Century* (Cambridge, 1957), pp. 16-17, who states: "By 1600 or thereabouts there was hardly any constitutional movement [in all Europe] without its accompanying historical myth. No man granted us this liberty, it was said; it has been ours from beyond the memory of man; and consequently none can take it from us. In reply, the kings and their partisans tried to show that, in the words of James VI (and I), 'kings were the authors and makers of the laws and not the laws of the kings.' " The purposeful romanticism with which the English of that period tended to envelop the common law as the

The criticism directed by Sāṭiʿ al-Ḥuṣrī against Ḥusain Muʾnis would on the surface seem to be provoked by Muʾnis' view of the discontinuousness of Arab history.[52] In contrast to European history which, since the early Middle Ages, has known no breaks, and where each phase has grown organically from the preceding with the result that the modern Englishman, for example, experiences clearly the connections of the institutions under which he lives with the Magna Charta, the major phases of Arab-Muslim history are discrete. The age of the Umayyads is totally different from that of the *rāshidūn*, and again from that of the Abbasids; the Abbasid caliph differs from the Umayyad caliph, and the society of Baghdad from that of Damascus. The changes are not developmental but *sprunghaft*, and resemble new starts. "So when today we aim to revive the past generations of Muslims, we actually aim to manufacture an unnatural phenomenon; we aim to shape our history on the European model. But while the contemporary Englishman feels that there exists a genuine connection between himself and the Magna Charta and the habeas corpus, we feel truly that there is no real tie that would link us with the Banū Umayya or the Banū ʿAbbās." "For this reason it is only natural that of all peoples the Arabs are least influenced by their past and least tied to it." [53] Sāṭiʿ al-Ḥuṣrī does not find it too diffi-

---

result of immemorial custom, and which dictated the reading of historical sources, presents an interesting analogy to some treatments of the prophetic *sunna*. If Europe since the Renaissance has been trying to understand itself in part through an understanding of its past, such an undertaking is possible only because it is generally agreed that this past somehow still survives and, in any event, is still meaningful. That the Muslim world, by and large, has not developed a comparable outlook on history for its classical period is, in large measure, because Muslim history is perceived as a self-sufficient whole to whose interpretation neither the religious and moral morass of the *jāhiliyya* nor the incidents that filled the annals of the peoples denied or failing revelation have anything significant to contribute.

[52] Sāṭiʿ al-Ḥuṣrī, "Ḥawla māḍī 'l-ʿArab," in his collection of essays *Difāʿ ʿan al-ʿurūba* (Beirut, 1956), pp. 93-105.

[53] *Ibid.*, p. 96.

cult to make his case for historical continuity in the Arab-Muslim world. In fact he finds support in another statement of his opponent, in which Muʾnis stressed the survival of what one may call the Abbasid style of administration in modern Egypt.

The significant aspect of this debate is, however, neither Muʾnis' overstatement nor al-Ḥuṣrī's *mise à point*. It is the irreconcilable conflict of the aspirations underlying the irreconcilable conflict of the self-views which Muʾnis and al-Ḥuṣrī reflect in their presentation of Arab-Muslim history. Muʾnis does not find a commitment in the Arab-Muslim past, as Arab history has always moved in unrelated phases; one may therefore conclude that the future of the Arabs may be a new start, inspired perhaps by Western ideas and social models, but in any event one that may be conceived of as detachable from a past that is clearly experienced as an inadequate inspiration in the present sitution. Quite different al-Ḥuṣrī! To him Arab-Muslim history is as naturally structured as any history could be, and the Arab is as committed to it as any European is to his. The shapers of the future, we may infer, must take the past into account; the Abbasids are as real to al-Ḥuṣrī as the Magna Charta is to Muʾnis' Englishman.[54]

But the past has more than one lesson to teach. The early disintegration of the Muslim empire, and the Muslims' lack of political unity for the last millennium or longer, prove that the road toward such unity must first lead toward the unity of Arabic-speaking peoples. Whether or not the political unity of the Muslims is an objective capable of realization, the political unification of the Arabs must be achieved before *al-waḥda 'l-islāmiyya* can seriously be attempted *bi-maʿnā-hā 's-siyāsī*. Those who put the

---

[54] The debate in 1952 between ʿAbdalʿazīz Sāmī and Sāṭiʿ al-Ḥuṣrī on the one hand, and Muḥammad ʿAbdallāh ʿInān on the other, as to whether the "Saracens" who entered Switzerland in the tenth century were "Arabs" or non-Arab "Muslims" again reflects a difference in self-view which, in turn, is mirrored in the interpretation of historical data (*ibid.*, pp. 106-113).

unity of the Muslims ahead of that of the Arabs, and those who go so far as to consider Arab unity a danger to Muslim unity, fail to distinguish between "brotherhood in the faith" (*al-ukhuwwa 'd-dīniyya*) and a "political tie" (*ar-rābiṭa 's-siyāsiyya*). Yet, although al-Ḥuṣrī is confirmed in his conviction by arguments drawn from history, geography, and logic, he realizes that he will not be able to shake the beliefs of the religionists who, in our terminology, do not feel bound by history and whose aspirations deprive the logic of facts of its conclusiveness.[55]

VI

History is the battleground of aspirations; the self-image suggests the image of the past. Hence, the historical touch of Muslim apologetics, and hence also the need to demonstrate the glories of a past of which only selected episodes are accepted as significant and symptomatic in terms of prognostication. As early as 1923 Ṭāhā Ḥusain spoke of "those who see in the study of history only an opportunity to glorify ancestors"; although he made it clear that he did not accept their approach, "he conceded that they represented an inevitable phase in the development of a country renascent but not yet great, attributing to its past the splendor that it lacked in the present." [56] In 1947 Ṭāhā Ḥusain completed his observation by noting, "Once the Modernists had gained a decisive victory over the Conservatives, they took to re-thinking Islamic history, and from 1933 onwards they produced a literature of religious inspiration which was avidly welcomed by the reading public." [57] It is in this movement that Taufīq al-Ḥakīm's

[55] Cf. S. al-Ḥuṣrī, "Bayn al-waḥdat al-islāmiyya wa'l-waḥdat al-ʿarabiyya," in *Ārāʾ wa-aḥādīth fī 'l-waṭaniyya wa'l-qaumiyya* (3d ed.; Beirut, 1957), pp. 94-105, esp. at pp. 95-98, 101; the book was first published in 1947.

[56] P. Cachia, *Ṭāhā Ḥusayn. His Place in the Egyptian Literary Renaissance* (London, 1956), p. 181, with reference to *Ḥadīth al-arbiʿāʾ*, II, 79-86.

[57] *Ibid.*, p. 197, with reference to Ṭāhā Ḥusain's study "Tendances religieuses de la littérature égyptienne," *L'Islam et l'Occident* (1947), pp. 239-241.

Ahl al-Kahf (1933) and the "hagiographic" [58] biographies of the Prophet by Muḥammad Husain Haikal (d. 1956)[59] and ʿAbbās Maḥmūd alʿAqqād (b. 1889),[60] and of course Ṭāhā Ḥusain's own series, the novelistic *ʿAlà hāmish as-Sīra* (1933; 1937; 1946)[61] and the more historiographical *al-Fitna 'l-kubrà* (1947; 1953) are to be placed.

In the introductory section of his *ʿUthmān*[62] Ṭāhā Ḥusain allows us to recognize his double objective: the removal of the history of the *fitna* and its antecedents from the area of religious partisanship, and the identification of impersonal circumstances rather than the weaknesses or evil intentions of certain personalities as the causes of the disturbances that led to the assassination of the Caliph ʿUthmān. It is a mistake to measure ʿUthmān by the aspirations of his two predecessors to establish political and social justice, aspirations that could not but fail, as Abū Bakr and ʿUmar were far in advance of their times. Ṭāhā Ḥusain acknowledges his awareness of the religious implications of the events of the period for most Muslims, even to this day. But he professes himself free from any bias of this kind. He insists upon the uniqueness of the Islamic political order,[63] yet feels that ʿUmar perhaps did not go far enough in developing "consultation." [64]

---

[58] The expression is M. Rodinson's in *Diogène*, no. 20 (1957), p. 46, n. 17.

[59] *Ḥayāt Muḥammad* (imp. and enl. 2d ed.; Cairo, 1935). On the book and its critics cf. C. Brockelmann, *Geschichte der arab. Litteratur. Supplement* (Leiden, 1937-1942), III, 208-210.

[60] *ʿAbqariyyat Muḥammad* (Cairo, n.d.); cf. also his parallel works *ʿAbqariyyat aṣ-Ṣiddīq* (Cairo, 1951), *ʿAbqariyyat ʿUmar* (5th ed.; Cairo, 1948), and *ʿAbqariyyat al-Imām* (i.e., ʿAlī (2d ed.; Cairo, 1947).

[61] Not 1946-47 as stated by Cachia, *op. cit.*, p. 254; Brockelmann, *op. cit.*, III, 299-301, offers an analysis of the first two volumes.

[62] The book forms the first part of *al-Fitna 'l-kubrā* (the Great Civil War).

[63] E.g., Ṭāhā Ḥusain, *ʿUthmān*, pp. 31-32.

[64] Cf. *ibid.*, pp. 48, 60-63. The appointment on his death-bed by the caliph ʿUmar of a "consultative committee," *shūrà*, of six from whom his successor was to be taken made a profound impression although the procedure was not to be repeated. It found

One wonders whether Ṭāhā Ḥusain is conscious of the typically Sunnite character of his attitude when, with a notable advance in the sophistication of historical analysis, he exculpates persons and blames conditions.[65] He draws a favorable portrait of ʿAlī[66] in which, however, he does not depart from tradition. Where Ṭāhā Ḥusain penetrates more deeply than his Muslim contemporaries into the course of events and the circumstances that brought them about, he does so because the scope of his psychological comprehension is wider, and because his objective of impersonalizing the tragic sequence of happenings provides him with cues that the conventional black-and-white narrative necessarily lacks. But his deepened understanding of the period is not due to improved technical handling of the sources, to stricter canons of criticism, to greater sensitivity to anachronisms, and the like. He does not hesitate to reject the testimony of all the historians concerning the reasons that led to the recall of Saʿd b. abī Waqqāṣ from the governorship of Kufa, on the simple ground that those reasons reflect unfavorably on the third oldest of the *ṣaḥāba* and therefore cannot have been true.[67] Nor does he hesitate to utilize anachronistic traditions where they suit his purpose.[68] Yet he criticizes the thoughtless idealization, on purely religious grounds, of the early decades of

---

its way into the moralistic *Tale of the Holy Man Anthony* (*Antūnis as-sāʾiḥ*) by Ibn abī 'd-Dunyā (d. 894), in which a dying Christian king appoints six men to execute his will. They are to choose one of their number to take over the rule of the realm. Cf. F. Rosenthal, "The Tale of Anthony," *Oriens*, XV (1962), 35-60, at pp. 44-45 (translation), and 39 (Rosenthal's comments).

[65] Cf. *ibid.*, p. 49.

[66] *Ibid.*, pp. 152-153.

[67] *Ibid.*, pp. 90-95. The observation of R. Brunel, *Le monachisme errant dans l'Islam. Sīdi Heddi et les Heddāwa* (Paris, 1955), p. 24, comes to mind: ". . . les biographes musulmans se soucient fort peu de la précision historique, leur objet principal étant trop apparemment de mettre leur sujet en concordance étroit avec l'orthodoxie, sans s'attacher à suivre la réalité et à la rendre fidèlement. Ils s'estiment en règle avec celle-ci lorsque l'épure répond à l'opinion personnelle qu'ils se font du sujet."

[68] *Ibid.*, pp. 157-158.

the caliphate, and he shrewdly analyzes the motivations of the different interpretations that different Muslims place on the historical reports regarding the involvement of the *ṣaḥāba* in the opposition and the revolt against ʿUthmān.[69] To remove the *fitna* from the causes of inter-Muslim cleavage, and to demonstrate the uniqueness of the ideal Islamic order—these are the leading aspirations of Ṭāhā Ḥusain's work. The desire to bring to life for his generation the tales of the past, and to suggest a more subtle and, we may add, a more modern analytical approach even to semisacred history, represents the other elements that have shaped and limited Ṭāhā Ḥusain's presentation of historical events.[70] Fact-finding as such is not among them. To reintegrate the *fitna* in the consciousness of the educated as an ever-meaningful chain of happenings is to Ṭāhā Ḥusain clearly more important than the elucidation of moot points in the *fitna* itself.

It is not quite easy to extract the guiding vision from Ṣubḥī Waḥīda's *Fī uṣūl al-masʾala ʾl-miṣriyya*.[71] For one thing, it is in some respects a learned book, or at least is meant to be such. It offers the complete skeleton of a history of Egypt, oriented to its economic and social aspects. The presentation is, for the most part, based on somewhat haphazardly garnered secondary evidence; yet it is careful and avoids the shrillness of tone which is so rarely absent even from semipolitical writing in the contemporary East. It is an apologetic book, but it lacks the aggressiveness that usually accompanies apologetics; it is also a constructive book even though it is difficult to see how the "practicing" statesman could utilize its insights. For the image that this Christian paints of his country's

[69] E.g., *ibid.*, pp. 170-171.

[70] The subtlety of Ṭāhā Ḥusain's approach to history is best appreciated when it is held against the conventional dullness of Aḥmad Amīn's accounting for the Muslim decline by reference to adverse external events that have befallen the Muslim world; cf. his *Zuʿamāʾ al-islām fī ʾl-ʿaṣr al-ḥadīth* (Cairo, 1948), pp. 5-6, where the author betrays no realization of the internal development that takes place within a political and cultural unit.

[71] Ṣubḥī Waḥīda, *Fī uṣūl al-masʾala ʾl-miṣriyya* (Cairo, 1950).

position in the world is too complex and too close to historical realities for simple conclusions to be gained from it.

The Muslim conquest of Egypt was, in its effect, first and foremost an Arab conquest. It is remarkable how soon the Arabization of the country was accomplished. The distinction between Christians and Muslims continues to this day, but Egyptian society of both religious camps has become irrevocably Arabized.[72] The differences between Egyptian and Syrian and between Syrian and Iraqi ways of thinking are not due to any differences in national consciousness. The Muslim empire was not structured by national entities. The very names of the ruling dynasties, and the ease with which the Umayyads removed from their native Mecca to Damascus, with which the Abbasids enlisted Persian support, and with which the Arab Fatimids founded their state in north Africa, transplanted it to Egypt, and would, under favorable circumstances, have transferred its capital to Iraq, are evidence that the basis of the political society was not the nation. On the other hand, the Arab foundation of the society was everywhere strong enough to carry a political superstructure of varying geographical extent.[73]

It is understandable, and very largely justified, that Waḥīda emphasizes the continuity of Egyptian administration rather than the innovations introduced by succeeding regimes, but it would be unfair to charge him with blindness to the changing characteristics of the major periods through which Egypt lived. Yet the sameness of an Egypt that experienced only one incisive transformation, namely, its Arabization, remains the dominant motif. The homogeneity of what we should wish to call the orbit of Muslim civilization—in preference to Waḥīda's concept of an area deriving its uniformity from its Arabization—militates in Waḥīda's vision against a strong sense of the "individuality" of Egypt. The underplaying of the Muslim factor

---

[72] *Ibid.*, pp. 39-40.
[73] Cf., e.g., *ibid.*, pp. 42-43.

affecting Egypt as the result of the Arab conquest may be connected with Waḥīda's tendency to resolve the Christian-Muslim conflict as merely a social differentiation within the Arabic civilization of his country; at the same time he tries to isolate Egypt by a lengthy discussion of its own particular history before and under Islam; and, simultaneously, a third outlook induces Waḥīda to oppose the views of those who explain the ills of present-day Egypt as deriving from the general situation of the world after the discovery of the Cape of Good Hope. This analysis, incidentally, leads him to reject the identification of individual powers as the culprits in the unsatisfactory state of Egyptian affairs.[74]

Waḥīda sees clearly the contradictory conclusions reached by his contemporaries in diagnosing Egypt's cultural position: one group led by Ṭāhā Ḥusain holds that the country's intellectual kinship with the West compels her, in the conflict between Eastern and Western civilization, to range herself with the West; the other, best represented by Taufīq al-Ḥakīm, believes that Egypt must adhere to the Eastern tradition as the one more closely in tune with what is best in mankind.[75] But the diversity of the aspirations that motivate Waḥīda and large sections of the society for which he speaks prevent him from subscribing to the objectives of either party. The outlook that appears to Waḥīda to be most readily compatible with those aspirations—even though, in the view of this writer at least, the tenet of Arabization as the only major break in Egypt's history has not been completely harmonized with it—is emphasis on the unity of the Mediterranean. Waḥīda insists on that he is aware of the differences among the peoples that inhabit the shores of the Mediterranean, and again of the differences between all of them and the Egyptians; yet he feels that the differences do not touch "the major lines" (*al-khuṭūṭ al-kubrà*) on which the lives of these societies are ordered. Those who desire to

[74] Cf., e.g., *ibid.*, pp. 2-3.
[75] *Ibid.*, p. 280.

take Egypt out of this Mediterranean context[76] are victims of a misunderstanding as serious as the misunderstanding of those who impute the unsatisfactory state of Egypt to innate defects in her population, and thus are led to despair of her future altogether.[77]

So Waḥīda's analysis ends by placing Egypt in a net of relations that justify the cultural tendencies of the Western-oriented and separate her from the Asiatic Muslim areas, while leaving her within a region of Arabization (rather than Islamization) which permits the merely Arabized Copt to identify in essentials with the Arabized Copt who has also been won over to Islam.

The future that Muḥammad ʿAbdalqādir al-ʿAmāwī[78] envisages for Islam—seen variously as a religion, a social order, a political system, a civilization—has very indistinct contours. The unlimited adaptability of the Koranic message makes it appear hazy. Its specific commitment to a program in history deprives it of its inspirational quality. In fact, we can reconstruct what al-ʿAmāwī believes the Islamic message is, almost exclusively by what he says it is not. As he expects and aggressively provokes opposition from "religious reactionaries," atheists, and those favoring an autocratic regime, we may assume that he stands for "true" democracy, that is to say, a democracy based not on the Western model,[79] but on what he apprehends as

[76] This context, we assume, accounts for the relatively minor effect of Greek rule which, to Waḥīda, actually was that of "foreign kinsmen" (to use an expression that goes beyond Waḥīda's position).

[77] Waḥīda, *op. cit.*, pp. 283-284.

[78] ʿAbdalqādir al-ʿAmāwī, *Mustaqbal al-islām* (2d ed.; Cairo, 1956).

[79] Western democracy is described with incredible superficiality in *ibid.*, pp. 193-199; for the kinship of Islamic principles and democracy, cf. pp. 204-205; see also (p. 206) the statement that in Islam *ḥukm* is based solely on *shūrà*. The Qurʾānic injunction *wa-shāwir-hum fī 'l-amri* (3:153), "And take counsel with them in the affair," has long been used in discussions of rulership. The Prophet's reliance on advice appears as an argument against unrestrained despotism in Niẓām al-Mulk's (d. 1092) *Siyāsat-Nāma*, ed. Ch. Schefer (Paris, 1891-1897), p. 85 (English

the progressive character of genuine Islam. The tendency that pervades all al-ʿAmāwī's thinking is to keep from Islam any particularization and limitation which the actual history of the Muslims (rather than Islam itself) may have imposed upon it. History has no force to bind the later generations. True Islam was realized only during the Prophet's lifetime, the reigns of the first two caliphs, and the episodic rule of the Umayyad ʿUmar II (717-720).[80] With the slate of memory wiped clean of historical (administrative, political) experiences, it is time for articulations of the faith. Admittedly, religious beliefs must be formulated; an *ʿaqīda* cannot be dispensed with;[81] but the *ʿaqāʾid* will come to be, or at least to contain, retarding elements that are as responsible for the decay of Islam as are colonization (*istiʿmār*) and the human inadequacy of

---

translation by H. Darke, *The Book of Government or Rules for Kings* [London, 1960], pp. 95-96; also by A. J. Arberry, *Classical Persian Literature* [London, 1958], pp. 75-76), and again in Saʿd ad-Dīn Warāwīnī's *Marzbān-Nāma* (written between 1210 and 1225), ed. M. M. Qazwīnī (Leiden and London, 1909), p. 176 (English translation by R. Levy, *The Tales of Marzuban* [London, 1959], pp. 174-175; Italian translation by F. Gabrieli in *RSO*, XIX [1941], 130).

[80] E.g., al-ʿAmāwī, *op. cit.*, p. 205. Al-ʿAmāwī's classical (non-Shīʿī) predecessors, such as, for instance, the Ibāḍī Abū Ḥamza ʿAbdallāh in his famous address of A.D. 747 (trans. G. Van Vloten, *Recherches sur la domination arabe* [Amsterdam, 1894], pp. 76-78, from Abū 'l-Faraj al-Iṣfahānī, *Kitāb al-Aghānī* [Būlaq, 1285], XX, 106-107) and Jāḥiẓ himself, *op. cit.*, p. 292^{5-6} (trans. Pellat, *op. cit.*, p. 310), extend the golden age through the first six years of ʿUthmān's rule. Jāḥiẓ does not mention ʿUmar II, but Abū Hamza gives that caliph credit for his good intentions but believes he failed to carry them out. Thābit b. Qurra (d. 901) held that the Arabs were to be envied for three personalities: ʿUmar b. al-Khaṭṭāb, Ḥasan al-Baṣrī, and al-Jāḥiẓ. His statement is quoted by Tauḥīdī (d. 1023), *al-Baṣāʾir wa'dh-Dhakhāʾir*, ed. A. Amīn and A. Ṣaqr (Cairo, 1373/1953), pp. 194^{11}-198^{6}. In Thābit's characterization of ʿUmar (pp. 195^{3}-196^{7}), there occurs (p. 195^{9}) the significant phrase: *wa mazaja 'd-dunyā bi'd-dīn wa-aʿāna 'd-dīn bi'd-dunyā*; this phrase is missing in the much shorter version of Thābit's discourse on ʿUmar in Yāqūt, *Dictionary of Learned Men*, ed. D. S. Margoliouth (2d ed.; London, 1923-1926), VI, 69^{10-19} (quoted from Tauḥīdī, *Taqrīẓ al-Jāḥiẓ*).

[81] Al-ʿAmāwī, *op. cit.*, p. 17.

the *rijāl ad-dīn* (and of those rulers who claimed to be God's representatives on earth).[82] The constrictive character of any definition of the nature of Islam implies a condemnation of sectarian movements. Al-ʿAmāwī turns against attempts such as those made by Goldziher or ʿA. M. al-ʿAqqād to explain the rise of the sects and the *fitna* in Islam as the result of large historical issues; he interprets those movements merely as the consequence

[82] *Ibid.*, pp. 14-16. The dislike for definition and explication of dogma is as old in Islam as doctrinal searching and dispute. The well-known *qāḍī* Abū Ḥāmid al-Marwarūdhī (d. 362/972-973), e.g., compares in a poem the situation of the *mutakallimūn* in their disputes with that of travelers through the desert who, under the direction of an incompetent guide, find themselves in the evening precisely where they were when they set out in the morning. Cf. Tauḥīdī, *op. cit.*, pp. 60-61. This attitude, coupled with skepticism regarding the ability of human reason to cope with theological problems, is frequently expressed in the first great theological debate of Islam. When asked his views on *qadar*, Ibn ʿAbbās is made to reply that this concept is like the sun: the longer you stare at it the more your eye will be blinded (*ibid.*, p. 40^{11-12}; cf. also p. 126). (The same impatience with rational probing of the mysteries of the faith has animated anti-scholastic movements in Christendom; the trial, in 1082, of the "consul of the philosophers," John Italos in Constantinople provides a famous example; cf. P. E. Stephanou, *Jean Italos, philosophe et humaniste* [Rome, 1949], esp. pp. 53-54.) The antitheoretical attitude and the horror of definition carries over into nationalistic writings of our times; cf., e.g., Michel ʿAflaq's view that nationalism should not be enclosed "in a framework of narrow definition," and that theory deadens and leads to inaccuracy, a position, incidentally, which makes his own efforts at circumscribing the nature of Arab nationalism look somewhat paradoxical (cf. Binder, *op. cit.*, pp. 12, 25). The Egyptian, Anwar as-Sādāt, *Revolt on the Nile* (London, 1957), p. 53, declares in a similar vein that he has always distrusted theories and purely rational systems. The intellectual vagueness of the conceptual framework of the aspirations voiced impressively in Anwar as-Sādāt's *Qiṣṣat al-waḥda 'l-ʿarabiyya* (Cairo, 1957; briefly discussed, together with a translation of the first chapter, by A. Miquel, "Patriotisme égyptien et nationalisme arabe," *Orient*, II/i [no. 5, 1958], 91-112) and the definition of Arab nationalism (*qaumiyya*) offered by the Third Congress of Arab Writers (Cairo, Dec. 9-15, 1957; French translation in *ibid.*, pp. 44-45) also reflect a state of mind for which *Gefühl ist alles* . . .

of oversubtlety and insincerity on the part of the newly converted, or of personal ambition of certain leaders, or the like.[83] Nor is there any conflict between reason and religion as such; where a conflict does obtain, it is between reason and the *ʿaqīda rijāl ad-dīn* and their personal *sulūk*.[84]

Al-ʿAmāwī insists that nothing in the nature of Islam would necessarily have led to the Sunnī-Shīʿī division, or to any other sectarian schism; the split between Sunna and Shīʿa was due exclusively to political circumstances.[85] As a matter of fact, the Shīʿī ideology is a "foreign body" introduced into Islam by people such as ʿAbdallāh b. Sabaʾ who had undergone but an outward conversion.[86] The contemporary Shīʿī cannot be accused of insincerity, remoteness from religion (*al-buʿd ʿan ad-dīn*), or the desire to destroy Islam; the instigators of Shiism, however, must be so charged.[87] The murder of Ḥusain is the blackest deed recorded by history;[88] as only the enemies of Islam stood to gain by it, they must be identified as its engineers.[89] All Muslim sects, the author insists time and again, owe their existence to extra-religious motivations, primarily to a desire to damage Islam.[90] The Islam al-ʿAmāwī has in mind is never clearly defined, but from his criticism of the sects and of the *Muʿtazila*, which is accused of removing the faith from the essentials by intro-

---

[83] Al-ʿAmāwī, *op. cit.*, pp. 131-135. Al-ʿAmāwī's attitude continues the irritation felt by classical orthodoxy with the attempts to conceptualize the idea of *qadar* and the like. Ibn Khaldūn, too, was sensitive to the socially disruptive effect of theological argumentation but found comfort in the conviction that the science of speculative theology was no longer needed since heretics and innovators had been eliminated and the orthodox leaders had built a fence around religion (cf. *Muqaddima,* ed. E. Quatremère [Paris, 1858], III, 36-43; trans. F. Rosenthal [New York, 1958], III, 44-54).

[84] Al-ʿAmāwī, *op. cit.*, p. 188.

[85] *Ibid.*, pp. 149-150.

[86] *Ibid.*, p. 154.

[87] *Ibid.*, pp. 156-157.

[88] *Ibid.*, p. 159 pult.

[89] *Ibid.*, pp. 158-161.

[90] E.g., *ibid.*, p. 185.

ducing the excessive refinements of philosophic reasoning,[91] there emerges an image of Islam as the smallest common denominator of what any Muslim community ever conceived Islam to be,[92] a set of attitudes justifiable from Koran and elements of the Sunna, elements that are selected so directly and naïvely in response to current objectives that the arbitrariness of the selection, in terms of both the Muslim *ʿilm al-ḥadīth* and Western critical scholarship, goes unnoticed. In the last analysis Islam is, to al-ʿAmāwī, what the "right-minded" people in any community want or experience it to be. More than anything else, it is an identification, a banner, a cause. It can be defined by negation rather than assertion, for al-ʿAmāwī has a horror of fixation, be it by theological definition, juridical stipulation, or the bare factuality of history. What all heretics have in common, in fact, the quality that makes them deviants and outsiders, is precisely the urge to define Islam, circumscribe doctrinal implications, and acknowledge historical precedent outside the timeless romanticism of that *rāshidūn* period which never was, but which represents the time when man was adjusted to the unseen order, in tune with the universe and fortified by the benedictions of the blessed origins.[93]

---

[91] *Ibid.*, pp. 180-181.

[92] The question as to whether ignorance of doctrine and aberrant practice exclude from the community, i.e., confer the status of *kāfir* on an individual or on a subcommunity, has been argued throughout the history of Islam. The latitudinarian view, which is also the only practicable one in backward and tribal areas with a strongly persisting *ʿurf*, holds that the profession of faith suffices to preserve the status of "believer." On this problem cf., e.g., L. Gardet and M.-M. Anawati, *Introduction à la théologie musulmane* (Paris, 1948), pp. 333, 340, 433-435.

[93] For this romanticism cf., e.g., al-ʿAmāwī, *op. cit.*, p. 122. Ibn al-Muqaffaʿ (d. 757), "Risāla fī 'ṣ-ṣaḥāba," in M. K. ʿAlī, *Rasāʾil al-bulaghāʾ* (4th ed.; Cairo, 1954), p. 126[14-15], designates the first four caliphs as *aʾimmat al-hudà*, a term that brings out their normative position very forcefully; cf. also the expression *sunan hādiya* used by Aḥmad b. Abī Ṭāhir in his famous letter to his son (written in the reign of Maʾmūn) and quoted by E. I. J. Rosenthal, *Political Thought in Medieval Islam* (Cambridge, 1958), p. 75.

There is a hint that the very universalism of the Islamic revelation carried with it the dangers of sectarian division, in view of the appeal of its message to peoples of different backgrounds.[94] There is, besides, a realization that Islam is "of one piece," that its bases support one another, that its religious and political aspects are inseparable.[95] But these insights are, as it were, not really understood. For al-ʿAmāwī brushes them aside to insist again and again that differences in religious views within Islam sprang from the hidden hostility to it on the part of Arabs and non-Arabs,[96] and the detrimental influences of the *mawālī* on Islamic life are dwelt upon at length.[97] Islam is a political system, but only three of those who ever held sway over the community were Islamic rulers; the others merely ruled in the name of Islam, but Islam cannot be held responsible for their administration.[98] Little wonder that al-ʿAmāwī's horror of history does not lead him to any comprehension of the past or of the historical process as such.

In his summary of pre-Islamic history,[99] which is offered to illustrate the degradation of the world before the coming of the Prophet, al-ʿAmāwī makes no effort whatever to provide accurate information.[100] What we may call deliberate ignorance continues into the presentation of the Muslim period; it is hardly conceivable that an educated Muslim could be so defectively informed on the history of his faith and the faithful as al-ʿAmāwī shows himself to be. Argument from psychological a priori is readily admitted: ʿAlī being what he was (the characterization is based on unsifted tradition), he could not have opposed

---

[94] Al-ʿAmāwī, *op. cit.*, pp. 127-128.

[95] *Ibid.*, pp. 52-55.

[96] Cf., e.g. *ibid.*, pp. 118-119.

[97] *Ibid.*, pp. 97-101; for the *mawālī* as forgers of *ḥadīth*, see p. 95.

[98] *Ibid.*, pp. 113-114.

[99] *Ibid.*, pp. 52-114.

[100] The materials used and the "facts" narrated are very similar to those presented by Abū 'l-Ḥasan ʿAlī al-Ḥasanī an-Nadwī, *Mā dhā khasara 'l-ʿālam bi'nḥiṭāṭ al muslimīn?* (2d ed.; Cairo, 1370/1951), pp. 21-64.

Abū Bakr's accession.[101] The report of ʿUthmān's death is taken indiscriminately from Ibn Saʿd and Ibn Khaldūn.[102] The events of the ninth century are stylized to bear out the prejudgment that the period was moving away from Islam.[103]

The reduction of Islam to an idea evasively located in the Holy Book and manifested for but a brief span in a human society eliminates any relation of this idea to history. Islam is described as capable of informing any historical situation,[104] but, strictly speaking, it has been realized only in two brief episodes. Al-ʿAmāwī's Islam could, but hardly ever did, validate history, nor did history ever validate Islam,[105] if al-ʿAmāwī's position is taken seriously. Al-ʿAmāwī's Islam—an extreme and, within the Muslim world, somewhat atypical instance of an aspiration to which history and hence historiography are valueless—empties history of any meaning to a believer and deprives him of any motivation to investigate its course. Divested of any function in the realization of al-ʿAmāwī's objective—the rebuilding of his society by means of an identification projecting past history onto a preëxisting revelation—history bows out. The vanishing of the life-giving context makes the data of the past sink below the threshold of distinctness. The Muslim reformer remains alone with a Book and the fiction of the short-lived blissful origins; he is free to remold his society in the name of an ideological entity that will shift its shape to accommodate his aspirations. But this freedom is gained by the sacrifice of history, that very history whose next phase al-ʿAmāwī intends to re-form.[106]

---

[101] Al-ʿAmāwī, *op. cit.*, pp. 119-122.

[102] *Ibid.*, p. 106.

[103] *Ibid.*, pp. 110-113.

[104] *Ibid.*, p. 92.

[105] To vary the expression used by Smith, *op. cit.*, p. 32.

[106] Max Scheler, "Reue und Wiedergeburt," in *Vom Ewigen im Menschen* (4th ed.; Bern, 1954), pp. 27-59, at pp. 33-35, derives the illimited interpretability of history from the illimited interpretability of the living individual's personal history. To the end of his life the individual is free to revise the meaning and

the valuation of his past—not of course what might be called its natural reality. Similarly, the historical fact is, so to speak, permanently unfinished and "gleichsam erlösbar." Through its power of reconsideration and revaluation history understood frees man from the power of history undergone. In contradistinction to the summation of past group experiences in so-called tradition, the science of history is above all the liberator from historical determination.

It may be that the refusal to "sacrifice" certain sections or aspects of history as realizations of mundane perfection has prevented Muslim apologetics from utilizing two lines of reasoning that have proven fairly effective in Christianity. Since the Italian Platonists of the fifteenth century, the concept of development has been serviceable in integrating the revealed religions in the history of thought. The absoluteness of essential content is safeguarded by consideration of the variables in the human or historical setting. Besides, the very omnipotence of the Lord makes his acts contingent from the point of view of the human observer and therefore recognizable only *ex eventu*. Hence the freedom of science as long as it does not aim beyond the heuristic or hypothetical character of its theoretical syntheses. This outlook which has been successful in the Roman Catholic milieu does not seem to have been adopted among Muslim theologians, possibly because of a sense of the aprioristic character of revealed knowledge which is experienced as having prestated all that man will ever be able to discover.

VI

The Intellectual Problem of Westernization in the Self-View of the Arab World

CULTURAL CHANGE means changing the purpose of life and the capacity for experience. The tension between the will and the power to perform, where a compromise may be reached only through a gradually attained understanding of the self, is felt as conflict between a comforting yet unsatisfying legacy and goals that are deemed to be necessary and yet are disquieting and hazardous; it provokes a battle within the heart of the individual culture participant and in the heart of the community as well. This spiritual conflict manifests itself as political agitation, whose feverish irrationality seems to free, indeed to calm, those possessed by it as it astounds, frightens, and disgusts an outside world implicated against its will.

The motivation for thus changing the purpose of experience is provided by the desire for self-assertion, by the fear of political subsidence and colonial subjugation, but also by the sheer attraction of another world, overwhelming in its self-assurance, and by lassitude and self-disappointment preceding political collapse, by boredom with a tradition that has become constricted, monotonous, and routine. It is not only that the legacy suddenly seems inadequate: the inherited problems that give rise to intellectual self-realization are felt to be irrelevant, and the sphere of intellectual activity cultivated by the community is seen to be divorced from real life; the intellectual legacy of the past tastes stale and loses its ability to energize, long before the traditional forms of life and structure inherent in the society at variance with itself begin to lose their pragmatic force. The fact that the form and the content of thought and of life, and the function and the organization of society, are not gripped by the need for change at the same time turns individual existence into an endless series of crises and conflicts; that the change in experiential capacity is expressed on different levels of society at different times and in varying degrees of intensity gives rise to collective tensions which make the troubles of individuals seem typical and therefore rather bearable, and yet, thanks to general insecurity and excitement, sharply intensify the poignancy of the personal dilemma.

Yet the discovery of new relationships, the acknowledgment of new values, the recapture of the seemingly familiar are fascinating, stimulating in the new field of vision, and conducive to action. When Ṭāhā Ḥusain (b. 1889), the great Egyptian writer and educator, suddenly comprehends as a student that his affliction with blindness in childhood and the death of his four-year-old sister were not physiological necessities but the product of the shoulder-shrugging resignation of his world and fate, due only to his milieu's careless ignorance,[1] this awakening to

[1] Cf. Ṭāhā Ḥusain's autobiography, *al-Ayyām* (Cairo, 1929), I, chap. 18. This was first published in the Cairo magazine *al-Hilāl* in 1926, and translated into English by E. H. Paxton as *An Egyptian Childhood* (London, 1932), of which see pp. 131-138. The second volume of the autobiography was published in Cairo in 1939.

the possibilities, long since realized elsewhere, of human self-help means recognizing a duty not to flinch before a radical transformation of the mentality and the organization of society and not to shrink from rethinking the most sacred beliefs and traditions.

Experiential change becomes an inner imperative; adoption of new human attributes which enable and require the ameliorative transformation of the milieu becomes a command for self-esteem; reform of education, of the state, of the social order becomes a sign of having proved one's mettle, of fruitful assimilation to an ideal of life—originally acknowledged to be heterogenetic but now thought to be orthogenetic—characterized by infinite, invigorating breadth of experience and action.

Nevertheless, the foreign origin of the ideal is not forgotten and remains as knowledge which troubles the spirit, threatens self-confidence, and serves as a weapon to those who are not receptive to the new life and are neither capable nor desirous of going beyond the traditional bounds of experience. For change not only enriches life; it blocks access to trusted spheres of experience, especially in the religious sphere where the ecstatic, like the quietism of mystical piety, falls into disrepute and gradually withdraws from the approved realm of experience.

The formulation utilized by the defenders of tradition and the interpretation given it, which is supposed to prove its adaptability, if not its conformity, to modern spiritual needs, show that in the Arab world cultural change, that is to say, Westernization as a psychological goal, as orientation to reality, is an accomplished though not a digested fact. If the statement[2] that at present the culture of the West represents the only productive culture, the only one that can actually be "lived," is somewhat exaggerated, it can scarcely be overlooked that, in spite of all the talk about Eastern spirituality and wisdom, the creativeness of the non-Western cultures is being completely absorbed in

[2] A. J. A. Mango, "Turkey and the Middle East," in *The Middle East in Transition*, ed. W. Z. Laqueur (London, 1958), p. 192.

our time by the task of integrating the foreign elements coming from the West while retaining, at the same time, a certain degree of autonomy. This is not to say that in the battle involving systems of value, canons of taste, social forms, and, above all, modes of thought, the old has succumbed to the new in all crucial points, and still less that the complexes of ideas adopted from the various phases and spheres of the West have been divested of their internal contradictions and have begun to function satisfactorily.[3] And yet our cultural aspiration has become the standard of valuation, and early habituation to our goals and methods has muddled the younger generation's perception of the actual nature of things past in the Arab world, and in what respects their world, in terms of its most private and intricate urges, could hardly have progressed without inspiration from the West. For collective bodies have always had difficulty in seeing themselves as evolved forms; that which was admitted only yesterday seems to have existed of old, and only where it touches on race and descent is memory long though not always reliable.

If the West—that is, North Atlantic Europe and North America—is regarded as a unity, it is equally justifiable to speak of an Arab world. Not that the West or the Arab world is culturally undifferentiated or seems so to the other; but the psychological problem of the Arab world is one, and, as far as endemic tradition is concerned, the otherwise clearly perceived distinctions between, say, French and English cultural concepts fade, because both impose upon the lands that come into contact with them almost identical problems of assimilation.

When contacts were first made, the basic concepts of both worlds were absolutely incompatible. Whereas in the East the individual was incorporated into and subor-

---

[3] For the neutralization of ideas by barring their extreme consequences and by not adopting the value judgments inherent in them, cf. F. Léger, *Les Influences occidentales dans la révolution de l'Orient. Inde, Malaisie, Chine,* 1850-1950 (Paris, 1955), I, v-vi.

dinated to family, clan, tribe, and ethnic-religious unity, with the state providing, as it were, only a modicum of outside coördination, the West represented the primacy of the human being and his integration at the same time into the "organic" state. The formal restraint of thought, in which the preservation of the known was at stake, collided with the West's passionate devotion to scientific progress, to domination of nature, to knowledge as an unending process. To the cult of the inherited, the West opposed active interference in social conditions and problems. Loyalty to persons was opposed by loyalty to an impersonal whole, to institutions. Whereas the Arab was prepared to satisfy himself with a suprarational interpretation of the real, the European insisted upon rationalistic criticism. As a corollary, the Arab was (and still is) inclined toward "personalization of problems"; he feels enemies, humiliations, triumphs where the Occidental makes allowances for material, objective, and, in any event, impersonal difficulties.[4] The eternal *provisorium* of European belief in progress, the willingness of the Occidental to approach along precarious paths in ceaseless advance and self-effacement a goal that is unattainable by his own definition, stood in sharpest contrast to the universe of the Arab East, transcendentally guided and at peace with itself, toward which the person had only the limited responsibility of obedience.[5]

---

[4] Cf. the splendid formulation by A. Franco Nogueira, *A luta pelo Oriente* (Lisbon, 1957), pp. 15-16. For the "personalization" of problems and its influence on psychology and politics, cf. H. E. Tütsch, *Vorderasien im Aufruhr* (Zürich, 1959), pp. 141-143.

[5] I have essayed a more thorough analysis of Western mentality in chapter v, "Self-Image and Approach to History." The refusal of Islam to accept *causae secundae, wasā'iṭ,* affects areas as seemingly remote from the religious aspiration as the theory of the trope; cf., e.g., Jurjānī, *Asrār,* pp. 338-351 (trans., pp. 394-409). The contrast between the Western and the Islamic outlook on man preëxists, as it were, the coming of the Prophet. Did not Polybius (d. *ca.* 120 B.C.) speak of man's natural love of innovation, *tò phýsei philókainon tōn anthrópōn,* which in

Comprehension of the fact that every cultural renovation, whether built on the native past or on foreign models, represents largely a psychological or, better, a human problem, did not fully enter into the consciousness of the Arab world until comparatively late. From the Saudi expatriate al-Qaṣīmī,[6] we hear the call, with an antireligious twist, to a new trust—indeed, a new belief—in man; in connection with an analysis of the "colonizable" Muslim of recent times the Algerian Malik Bennabi (b. 1905)

---

itself suffices to produce any kind of revolution (*Historiae*, xxxvi, 13, 3; trans. W. R. Paton, *Loeb Classical Library*, VI, 377).

To the documentation there cited, much can be added. For example, G. van der Leeuw, *L'Homme primitif et la religion, Étude anthropologique* (Paris, 1940), p. 169, says: "L'émergement de l'homme n'a aucun rapport avec l'évolution. C'est le chemin que tout homme, comme l'humanité toute entière doit parcourir tous les jours à nouveau, une route qui ne finit jamais et qui même n'est jamais commencée definitivement." The description may have general anthropological validity; nonetheless it reflects all too clearly the Western attitude toward life. One thinks also of Wilhelm von Humboldt's ideas on longing as the fundamental drive of all individuality. With this word, as P. B. Stadler, *Wilhelm v. Humboldts Bild der Antike* (Zürich and Stuttgart, 1959), p. 168, puts it, "is expressed at the same time the unattainability of that which is yearned for and the incomprehensibility of the origin of all longing." For the "primacy of the human being," cf. Humboldt's conviction that "the last goal of man" lies "in man" (*ibid.*, pp. 28-29), a conception that to Islamic thinking is just as absurd as it is blasphemous, and to which any intelligible meaning whatsoever is to be assigned only when the meaning is found in the glorification of the Creator through unquestioning submission of his commands. Here, too, may be recalled Husserl's genetic concept of truth as revision, improvement, and self-antiquation in the progress of the living present; cf., e.g., J.-F. Lyotard, *La Phénoménologie* (Paris, 1956), pp. 40-41.

[6] *Hādhī hiya 'l-aghlāl* (Cairo, 1946), pp. 25 ff., for example; cf. my analysis of this book in *Islam: Essays in the Nature and Growth of a Cultural Tradition* (2d ed.; London, 1961), pp. 216-223, and, in more detail, in "Attempts at Self-Interpretation in Contemporary Islam, II," in *Perspectives on a Troubled Decade. Tenth Symposium of the Conference on Science, Philosophy and Religion, 1949* (New York, 1950), pp. 135-184, on pp. 146-176.

speaks of the necessity of spiritual change as the prerequisite for political change.[7] One basis for this hesitation in bridging internal and external realities no doubt lies in the relatively narrow analytical interest that Muslim culture has traditionally brought to bear on self-dissection (outside the religious sphere of experience); still another lies in the impatience implicit in political impetuousness, which has whipped each andante into an allegro. The inevitability of a spiritual adaptation to new conditions was obvious in the extreme; yet, as experienced, it was predominantly negative; one understood that the changed course of events had made traditional values and goals obsolete but saw only infrequently a practicable alternative. The Berber soldiers who helped to quell the last rebellion against the Moroccan central authority said to their French officers: "This is the last battle. To reach this day, we have been fighting for twenty years. From now on life holds no interest for us. There is nothing to do but count sheep. Our children will no longer become men." [8] Family squabbles and village rivalries like those, for example, which used to animate Egyptian existence lose their capacity to fill the heart when one is made aware of world politics with its infinite contrasts.[9] Life takes on scope and new meaning for the one who acclimates himself successfully, whether as comrade in arms of the West

---

[7] See p. 232, below.

[8] R. Montagne, *Révolution au Maroc* (Paris, 1953), p. 60. A similar experience is reported by R. Maunier, *Sociologie coloniale* (2d ed.; Paris, 1949), II, 65-66, in order to illustrate the nostalgia for past times, which persists even when one is aware of the superiority of the present: "Voici bientôt vingt ans passés, lorsque j'allais en Kabylie de tribu en tribu, au dos de mon mulet, causant avec mon guide, je lui dis un jour: N'es-tu pas plus heureux maintenant qu'autrefois? Tu n'as plus besoin d'aller et venir avec ton fusil couché sur ta selle! Je vis alors briller un éclair dans ses yeux et il me dit: C'était bien mieux ainsi: en ce temps, on vivait! Vivre sans danger, pour ce vieux Berbère, ne valait donc pas!"

[9] Cf. J. Berque, *Histoire sociale d'un village égyptien au XXème siècle* (Paris and The Hague), pp. 15-16, with reference to Sirs al-Layyān, a large village north of Cairo.

or as its political opponent. The north African writer Mouloud Mammeri (b. 1917) puts this confession on the lips of one of his Berbers: " 'We must hope that they will win,' said Toudert. ('They' were the French.) 'Before they came here we had no doctors, no roads, no schools. We were like wild animals; the strong lived on the weak.' " But the author continues: "In the past, when Toudert was starving like everyone else, he was always mad to lead a riot; every day on the square he called on the Muslims to wage a holy war. No one took any notice, knowing it was senseless and that hunger made him behave as he did. But now that Toudert had become a rich man he supported the cause of those whom, formerly, he spurned every afternoon."[10] At this point it should be remarked that Toudert is depicted as an unsympathetic character and that in the end he perishes by violence in the traditional manner reserved for those of his ilk.

Westernization means, then, that the crucial realities of

[10] *The Sleep of the Just* (London, 1956), pp. 7-8. The reference to the strong who live on the weak is an allusion to the speech in which the Muslims, supposedly in the year 615, explained to the Negus of Abyssinia what Islam had afforded them. The account begins with a description of the barbaric conditions in Arabia before the advent of the Prophet. Cf. Ibn Hishām, *Sīra*, ed. F. Wüstenfeld (Göttingen, 1858-1860), I, 219-222; ed. Ibr. al-Ibyārī *et al.* (Cairo, 1356/1937), I, 358-359. Kara Ali, who stands economically and socially as *cultivateur* over the *fallāḥīn*, expresses himself in a similar vein; he too is a figure partially alienated from his people but is ethically more disreputable than Toudert. Mohammed Dib, *L'Incendie* (Paris, 1954), p. 69, has him admire the French for their economic ability. To them the population owes its opportunity to work: "Le Français est un grand homme, un sage; le Français est, on pourrait dire, un des Anciens. Il a fondé la première ferme et le premier vignoble. Il savait ce qu'il faisait!" In another section of this thoroughly anti-French book, an Arab woman says (p. 157): "Au temps où l'Arabe s'allongeait sur des coussins et sirotait du thé, les Français travaillaient, ils ne perdaient pas un instant. Ils prodigaient leur peine et leur force. Et voilà; à présent, les nôtres veulent reprendre cette terre, en disant: Elle est à nous; Ils n'auraient pas dû laisser le Français travailler à leur place: le Français ne leur aurait rien pris. Ils ont abandonné leur terre. Ils n'ont rien à réclamer aujourd'hui."

existence acquire a new meaning and that this meaning corresponds to a great extent to the Western conception of the spheres of life in question. This is true first of all for the external, legal circumscription of the individual. The intense sense of belonging to a kinship, certain noble families excepted, nowhere led to a legally regulated definition of the individual's identity, in the Roman manner, for example, with the assistance of a heritable gentile name. The idea of visualizing the population in terms of a census with a concomitant systematic registration of births, marriages, and deaths has never been autonomously developed in Islam and, when introduced into the Muslim community from the outside, has aroused disquiet and rebuff.[11] Not until the time of the anticlerical Shah Riza Pehlevi in Iran (1925), and of Atatürk in secularized Turkey (1934, with legal force from January 1, 1935), with the sharper focusing on the individual in the continuity of the family, was the enforced adoption of surnames implemented—a step that some of the Arabic-speaking lands have not yet taken and that even in French Morocco, for instance, was

[11] Sidi Keddour ben El-Khlifa, a comrade in arms of ʿAbd al-Qādir, in his long poem of social criticism, of the year [1277] 1861, explicitly condemns registering the child on the day of his birth and burying the dead only after certifying their death. A census encompassing women as well as men is also criticized. Cf. J. Desparmet, "Les Réactions nationalitaires en Algérie. IV. Élégies et satires politiques de 1830 à 1914," *Bulletin de la Société de Géographie d'Alger et de l'Afrique du Nord*, XXXIV (1933), 35-54, on pp. 45, 46. An example from another culture area of the antipathy toward a census is the comment of the Byzantine historian Theophanes (d. after 815), who reports *s.a.* 6224/732: "[Emperor Leo III ordered] . . . that all boys who were born be noted and recorded in lists as Pharaoh had once done with the children of the Jews. That not even his schoolmasters, the Arabs, had done with the Christians of the East" (*Chronographia*, ed. C. de Boor [Leipzig, 1883-1885], I, 410[14-17]; trans. L. Breyer, *Bilderstreit und Arabersturm in Byzanz* [Graz, Wien, Köln, 1957], p. 47). The Russian census of 1896 was considered a monstrous sin by the population (cf. M. Friedmann, *Ueber Wahnideen im Völkerleben* [Wiesbaden, 1901], p. 276 n. 1). It may be recalled in this connection that among Western nobility, family names began to gain currency in the first half of the eleventh century.

not attempted until 1951 because of its unpopularity. The frequently cited *Décret Crémieux* of October 24, 1870, which granted French civil rights to Algerians in exchange for their acceptance of the regulations governing French citizenship, found the Jews willing to relinquish their personal law based on religion.[12] A corresponding movement failed to materialize on the Muslim side. For the Muslim, his status as a believer was (and no doubt still is) the essential basis of his position in the world of men; membership in the Muslim community, *umma,* is for him —although I may be guilty of a slight exaggeration—the dominant feature of his individuality.

Can the relative fuzziness in the contours of identity be correlated with the relatively narrow interest, measured by our standards, which the Muslim traditionally brings to bear upon his own nature? Self-analysis, except when based on religious experience, is rare; in classical literature, even in biography and especially in autobiography, impenetrable discretion veils what seems to us the essential life of the spirit and emphasizes descriptive study. That which is nonrecurring and unique in inner experience is seldom described and, one suspects, seldom intentionally observed and comprehended. Because man, properly understood, is not a free agent, genuine significance accrues to his activity and movements only with regard to his relationship to God in his capacity as believer. The nature of man need be understood only in the light and according to the standard of the Koranic revelation.[13] The opening of the inner life as subject and problem of literary endeavor is one of the most significant results of contact with the West.

An admirable instrument of precise prose and refined poetry even before the time of Muḥammad, the Arabic

---

[12] The same offer had already been made to Jews and Muslims in a *sénatus-consulte* of July 14, 1865 (cf. H. Brunschwig, *La Colonisation française du pacte colonial à l'Union Française* [Paris, 1949], p. 35).

[13] Similar observations have been made by L. Gardet, *La Cité musulmane* (Paris, 1954), p. 67.

language during the first centuries of Islamic civilization, in a form dominated by the Koranic revelation, had to go through a process of assimilation of Iranian and, above all, Greek terminology and classification of thought before it could evolve into a vehicle of highly developed philosophy and science. The collision with the modern West has not only forced upon Arabic and neighboring languages an enrichment in present-day terminology; the traditional exposition of thought, held together in a series of associations by a meagerly developed system of hypotactic conjunctions and none too disciplined outside the field of theological-philosophical argumentation, desperately needed internal tightening and improved external period control in order to reflect the world of ideas of the modern West. The difficulties in translating, say, historical or sociological literature into Arabic have not yet been completely eliminated—for this the lexicographical gaps in idiom less than the propensity of the stylistic conventions of Western languages to elude Arabic syntax bear the blame.[14]

Invested with the shimmer of sanctity, the Arabic language, as the means of expression of the last and most complete message of God to an erring mankind—for the Koran is less a self-disclosure of the divinity than a proclamation and a command—was the most effective means and later the most effective symbol for awakening and preserving the believers' sense of cohesiveness. Studying and cultivating the language were to a certain extent religious

[14] In addition, cf. the detailed analyses of Persian modes of discourse, for which we are indebted to W. Lentz, "Der gedankliche Aufbau einiger zeitgenössischer persischer Prosastücke," *Der Islam,* XXX (1952), 166-208 (esp. the summaries on pp. 166-167, 203, 205, and a comparison, by concrete example, of European and Persian methods of exposition on pp. 189-193), and *Goethes Noten und Abhandlungen zum West-östlichen Divan* (Hamburg, n.d. [1958]), esp. pp. 35, 39-40, 86, 143-144. Lentz, "Yasna 28. Kommentierte Übersetzung und Kompositions-Analyse," *Mainzer Akad., Abh. geistes-u. sozialwiss. Kl.* (1954/16), pp. 28, 83, 85, adds that the associative technique of discourse and that of "thematic synchronism" are traceable from the time of the Gathas to the present.

necessities. The triumph over its senility (*shaikhūkha*) on the part of the great philologists—one cannot speak of language reformers in the true sense—of the nineteenth century, Christians in the main, begins scarcely a generation after the rise of nationalism in Europe and doubtlessly parallels the European movement. The secularization of the invigorated and enriched language has, of course, been only partially completed; the non-Muslim is still considered barred from deepest intimacy with Arabic, and in many places, as, for example, in Egypt, the right to teach his mother tongue in public schools is legally disallowed. Nevertheless, the joint ownership of the idiom and the love common to all for the "most beautiful of languages" provide probably the strongest and, at the same time, objectively the most demonstrable support for a Pan-Arab consciousness of unity, a duplication, if you like, of the cult of the mother tongue which was inherent in European nationalism and which led in Europe, as it has now led in the Arab national states, to opposition to competing languages.

The ambiguous status of Arabic as the sign of both religious and national unity reflects the dual character of Arab national feeling. The political unity of the Arab-dominated Islamic caliphate was shattered in the eighth century after barely a hundred years of existence. But the spread of doctrine was in no way obstructed by the political splintering, and the desire for cohesion, which makes itself felt in the tight emotional bond of heterogeneous believers locked together without formal organization in the Muslim *umma*, has proved to be a more widely effective means of growth and endurance than any political structure whatsoever. In the *umma* the Arabs, as tribesmen of the Prophet, had and still have a favored position in their own eyes and in those of non-Arab Muslims, whose number is approximately six times their own. The concept of the *umma* is universalistic, political only in the ideal-eschatological sense, exclusive vis-à-vis those of other faiths; the concept of a Pan-Arab community, as it today inspires a majority of the inhabitants of the Arabic-speaking lands (not to speak here of local concepts of nationality such as the Egyptian, Iraqi, or Tunisian), is a particularistic concept, which, to be sure, allows non-Muslim Arabs to coöperate with equal rights, but in principle releases the whole of Arabdom from the *umma* as the primary form of Muslim social solidarity. It almost goes without saying that the self-view of the Muslim Arab has remained bifurcated and that he, in his hopes, links more or less harmoniously the universalistic concept of the supranational *umma*, which is comparable to medieval *Christianitas*, with the particularistic, unilateral nationalism that has gradually come to prevail in the West.[15] The fact that the unity of the *umma* is ideological or, better, volitional, and that its foundation, constructed of memories of political grandeur, is dangerously reminiscent of myth-building, impairs the psychological efficacity of the idea just as little as in (and beyond) the Western Middle Ages the psychological-political efficacity of the "Rome concept" suffered from the lack of a real political foundation, though even the Gothic historian Jordanes already knew that the Roman Empire existed only in the imagination.[16]

The difficulty of accepting the modern Western concept of the state is intensified by the fact, for which the concept of the *umma* had to compensate, that classical Islam has developed an authentic concept of neither the state nor municipal law. The classical *umma* lives under a divine law whose protector is the *umma* itself; the ruler, on the other hand, is neither source nor guarantee of the law; his is only the executive power. Thus the state becomes a superstructure with which the population does not identify itself and whose territorial boundaries and other forms of structure are basically irrelevant so long as it guarantees the preservation and, if possible, the expan-

---

[15] Cf. the short but impressive formulation by Tütsch, *op. cit.*, pp. 125-126 n. 4.

[16] Jordanes, *Romana*, ed. Th. Mommsen (Berlin, 1882), c. 2 (p. 1), in *MGH. Auctores antiquissimi*, V/1.

sion of religion.[17] The opposition to Western national sentiment needs no elaboration. An integration of the two interpretations and aspirations is hardly to be expected. Thus the Arab Muslim has to make his choice even in this sphere of life. Indeed, it is precisely that incessant pressure to choose which condemns him to constant unrest and self-torture. What a contemporary Moroccan novelist has said of himself (in another context) describes only too well the over-all intellectual situation: "Choose? I have already chosen, but how very much I wish I no longer had to do so. For even though I have chosen to live in France and perhaps to die there—but this does not depend on me—I still keep my share in the world of my childhood and in that Islam in which I more and more believe." [18]

Such a contradiction can be resolved only in two very different ways. Either one draws conclusions from one's own endeavors, or one accepts their presuppositions. Self-knowledge and knowledge of one's goals provide the basis for a volitional decision to remove the intellectual impediments to a new orientation. Once having recognized herself as a part of Europe, Turkey was ready to take the steps that would confirm and prove such a relationship. When in 1924 Mustafa Kemal abolished the caliphate he also eliminated ideologically the political power of the Muslim *umma* as an instrument of solidarity. "The dream of the caliphate, cherished by the Muslims for hundreds of years, has never been able to achieve reality. Quite to the contrary, it has been a cause of disunity, anarchy, and war among the believers. Enlightened self-interest has now brought to light the truth that it is the duty of the Muslims to have separate governments. Their real intellectual bond is the conviction that all believers are brothers." [19]

---

[17] Cf. C. Cahen, "Mouvements populaires et autonomisme urbain dans l'Asie musulmane du moyen âge II," *Arabica*, VI (1959), 26.

[18] Driss Chraibi, *L'Âne* (Paris, 1956), p. 14.

[19] Quoted by R. Charles, *L'Âme musulmane* (Paris, 1956), p. 166, n. 1.

Of the Muslims of the Near East only the Turks have professed full allegiance to European civilization, although on a purely cultural level the Westernization of the ruling classes of Egypt has gone at least as far as that of comparable circles in Turkish society.[20] As an explanation the Arabs would probably allude to the peripheral position of the Turks in Islam, an explanation that certainly would not be easily accepted by the Turks, though its corollary—allusion to the central position of Arabism in Islam—seems to the Arab self-analyst to be sufficient ground for his lack of preparation to meet the challenge of the intellectual alternatives pressing him.

Just as the Hellenizing philosophers of the Islamic world from the ninth to the twelfth century accepted many of Plato's doctrines but none of his ontological premises, as a result of which the theorems based on them could not on the whole become operative within Islamic development, the Muslim modernist has exerted himself to adopt European practice without accepting the theory or the human presuppositions or the attitude toward the world lying at the basis of it. This frequently had the consequence that a thin layer of European theory and a reflection, as it were, of European practice found entrance into his society. The problem of the compatibility of Western institutions with the Near Eastern milieu was not defined in its essentials and, in any event, was not systematically explored. When, for example, the conflict in Egypt between parliament and the executive revealed the actual balance of power, instead of support being mustered for the reformatory zeal of a minority that was

[20] Only Turkey, as a member of the Council of Europe, has minted "Europa" stamps; of the Arab countries, to my knowledge, Tunisia alone has acknowledged symbolically the cultural possession shared in common with the West by a postage stamp depicting Vesalius with Avicenna. (The United Arab Republic has, in 1962, brought out a commemorative stamp for Dr. Theodor Bilharz.) M. Ferid Ghazi, "La littérature tunisienne contemporaine," *Orient*, XII (1959), 131-197, remarks (p. 131): "En fait—le Liban mis à part—nous avons en Tunisie un des exemples les plus réussis d'une synthèse Orient-Occident."

politically inflamed and intentionally blind to the progress achieved, word was given out that parliamentarism had failed, and the modernists found themselves allied with the orthodox in demanding the dissolution of parties and the creation of an integrated political front.[21] The fact remains unexplained that even today wide circles in Egypt, instead of being calmed and soothed by the elimination of an institution alleged to be inconsistent with tradition, hope for genuine popular representation.

What lies beneath this kind of conceptual smoke screen is not primarily political ambition and political disappointment, as the Arab world, like its Western counterpart, is fond of making itself believe for the sake of expediency, but the fact that the Arabs, and perhaps the Arabs of the East in particular, have no doubt reacted to Western culture and to their own Westernization, but without truly coming to terms with them. The Arabs do not really know what is wrong with them, and they are content to sketch the pattern, so frequently felt to be hostile, in broad strokes which do only scant justice to the singularity of the influence that they are undergoing.

On December 15, 1957, the Egyptian President Gamāl ʿAbd an-Nāṣir addressed the following words to the participants in the Third Congress of Arab Writers:

We need unanimity of thought in order to strengthen our solidarity and to shore up Arab national sentiment. Just as indispensable for us in this territory, in this arena of the cold war in which all weapons are employed, is intel-

[21] This was the first point of the reforms demanded in 1936 by Ḥasan al-Bannāʾ, founder and leader of the Muslim Brotherhood, who was murdered on February 12, 1949 (cf. *Orient*, IV [1957], 59). The almost exclusive concern with norms, at the expense of the actual social forms which the norms might reflect and the means by which those norms could be realized, has no doubt been particularly harmful in the case of the "experimental" parliamentary regime during the early phases of Egyptian independence. Much of the prestige of the *rāshidūn* period springs from an attitude that judges the qualities of a political system by its ideals rather than by its performance. Cf. Safran, *Egypt*, pp. 80-81.

lectual liberation; literature and ideas are the key weapons in this war. As leaders of thought you have a momentous duty to perform which consists of illuminating the facts and creating an Arabic literature which is liberated and autonomous, released from foreign domination and influence.[22]

What is such an appeal supposed to signify? If one bears in mind that the development of modern Arabic literature (Arabic prose in particular) has consisted almost exclusively of assimilating Western forms (novel, novella, short story, drama) and in presenting content that has become accessible through the newly acquired capacity for experience, one perceives not only the superficiality and the absurdity of such a demand, but also the evasion of analysis, from which political effects are feared—analysis that could entail intellectual decisions with social consequences. The order to withdraw into the self is a defense mechanism which is not, to be sure, being applied at the moment to the offerings of the communistic world.

The bankruptcy of the West is postulated—this at a time when the technical as well as the scientific-analytic superiority of the West, though veiled by political concessions, has become more overwhelming than ever before—and its soulless science and its unchristian materialism are stigmatized; the culture of the Islamic East directed toward a peaceful life common to all is contrasted with Western civilization with its monopoly on science. Political aspirations dictate antithesis upon antithesis:

The civilization of the West and its heritage, for which both Europe and America fear, lives only on the debris of the East and would not be flourishing had they not sucked its blood. . . . The East interprets civilization as based primarily on values rather than on matter. We affirm that the Chinese, Egyptian, and Indian civilizations have created morality and literature, sanctified the family, organized the relations among individuals and of individuals

[22] Quoted by J. Monset, "A propos du Congrès des Écrivains Arabes," *Orient*, V (1958), 41.

with society and the government. . . . But these civilizations have not had as their sole product the establishment of human values; they have also produced the awakening of the sciences and the arts, of geometry and architecture, which have endured for thousands of years as so many witnesses of the permanence and superiority of these civilizations.[23]

When the author indicts the West for the introduction of its style of life (with science, democracy, etc.), one is

[23] Anwar as-Sādāt (b. 1916), "Orient et Occident," in *Qiṣṣat al-waḥda 'l-ʿarabiyya* (Cairo, 1957), trans. A. Miquel in *Orient*, VI (1958), 152-154. J. Desparmet, "Les réactions nationalitaires I," *Bulletin de la Société de Géographie d'Alger*, XXXIII (1932), 178-179, reproduces the analysis to which Algerian Muslims subject their rejection of the West: "Si nous en croyons les écrivains actuels de l'Islam, elle [i.e., cette inimitié] s'expliquerait par l'intransigeance de la religion musulmane. Cela est vrai à leur point de vue, parce que sous le nom de religion ils embrassent l'ensemble de leurs disciplines, politique, morale, intellectuelle et qu'ils sentent en particulier leur personnalité religieuse en antagonisme avec la civilisation de leur vainqueur. Cependant, ils distinguent certaines parties de ce complexe psychique. De la ghira diniīa [*ghīra dīniyya*], qui est proprement le fanatisme, ils détachent la ghira islamiīa [*ghīra islāmiyya*], qui est le souvenir fidèle du passé de l'Islam et de sa culture traditionnelle, et la ghira arabiīa [*ghīra ʿarabiyya*] qui est l'attachement passionné à la langue arabe, en même temps qu'une aspiration plus ou moins vague vers un empire panarabe. A côté de ces sentiments généraux qui s'adressent à la communauté islamique, ils en notent la ghira outniīa [*ghīra waṭaniyya*], l'amour du pays natal, qui est en train de s'étendre aux limites du Maghreb, et la ghira djensiīa [*ghīra jinsiyya*], la solidarité de race, qui se dilate, aussi étrangement de nos jours jusqu'à englober tous les habitants du Nord de l'Afrique. Et ils retrouvent toujours un substratum commun, la passion de la liberté [*horrīa; ḥurriyya*], cette passion primordiale des nomades turbulents, gens nescia freni. C'est elle qui inspire, en réalité, les autres sentiments, qui en combine les éléments divers et les unifie dans la ghira goumiīa [*ghīra qaumiyya*] ou tendance nationalitaire, en leur proposant pour but l'istiqlāl, l'affranchissement final et l'autonomie. C'est ainsi du moins que l'on trouve la xenophobie actuelle analysée dans les articels des journalistes musulmans de l'Algérie."

reminded of the concept of "cultural aggression" developed by the Chinese Communists. This form of imperialistic stratagem, to cite a report dated December 29, 1950, by the writer Kuo Mo-Jo to his government, is implemented above all by American subsidies granted to Chinese religious, cultural, and medical enterprises as well as by American support of schools and welfare institutions. Two hundred hospitals, more than two hundred orphanages, approximately twenty leper sanitariums, thirty schools for the blind, and so on, are enumerated in order to corroborate the thesis: "It [this aggression] has enabled the American imperialists . . . to lead the Chinese people into error and to debase them with the intention of morally enslaving them." [24]

The relative haziness and immaturity of the self-view and of the insight into the nature and meaning of cultural change in the Arab world become evident by contrast with testimony from Japanese society, which has exposed itself with incomparably greater consciousness of implications and goals to a similar process of adaptation. Two documents may be adduced which express the same aspirations and themes which are of concern to the Arab. But how differently is the subject thought through; what a clear adjustment is made between perception of realities and consciousness of aims:

> With this strong will for vast, open seas of knowledge, the goal of which is truth, the narrow confines of the old police state were broken [in 1868] and the rigid despotism of the moral code was doomed to destruction. But hand in hand with the ideal of truth goes an inclination—not to be denied—toward power, toward imperialism. After half a millennium the modern Japanese empire again becomes imperialistic. . . . This time the foreign intellectual means which it appropriates and then applies is called American-European culture.
>
> Thereby, however, the ring of the destined course of the Japanese spirit is closed. Starting with the ideal of power,

[24] Léger, *op. cit.*, II, 213 n. 3.

it returns, beyond the ideals of beauty, sanctity, virtue, and truth, to power.[25]

The antithesis of Eastern spirituality and Western materialism also rings a bell with a Japanese critic—yet with what subtlety and resonance! And how clearly is the function of Westernization recognized and comprehended:

Scientific thought with its sanctity of the laws of number and substance confronts Japanese universality of thought with its organic, living reality. It seemed once as if the Shintoist spirit, with its gods and its religiosity of action, might be suppressed by the abstract law of general validity. Does the modern European spirit triumph in Japan because it is mightier and more progressive than the Japanese? It appeals to the Japanese mind at least in the sense that it operates more precisely on a rational level and is able to make things accessible, be they spiritual or material, insofar as things can be expressed in laws and numbers. The separation between the spiritual and the material was foreign to the Japanese people. . . . Nevertheless, because of political necessity, Japan had to come to terms with this new mode of thinking. . . . In order to defend itself against colonization by Occidental nations, the Japanese mind had to acquaint itself with their nature and essence and, if need be, learn to master their methods. This was the outer cause which was just as crucial as the inner.[26]

---

[25] R. Kanokogi, *Der Geist Japans* (Leipzig, 1930), quoted according to O. Benl and H. Hammitzsch, *Japanische Geisteswelt* (Baden-Baden, 1956), p. 313. Kanokogi was an ideologist of the extreme right who stood close to the militarists and died soon after the end of World War II.

[26] J. Kitayama, *Westöstliche Begegnung. Japanische Kultur und Tradition* (Berlin, 1941), quoted according to Benl and Hammitzsch, *op. cit.*, pp. 314-315 n. 24. The refinement of Japanese self-interpretation follows upon, and to some extent accompanies, a generous use of the cliché opposing "Eastern morality and Western techniques" in nineteenth- and even twentieth-century writings. The fact that Japanese modernization was directed primarily against the dominance of the Chinese tradition may have helped to take the edge off the fight against the Western model. Acceptance of essential parts of the Western world view was

If, in comparing the Japanese with the Arab view of the self, one finds oneself compelled to acknowledge the superiority of the Japanese analysis, it must in partial explanation be conceded that the Japanese had uniquely to reconcile the relation between native and foreign culture, but were never in doubt about their national identi-

---

rather rapid; thus, the Copernican theory took less than twenty years, between ca. 1793 and 1811, to displace earlier concepts. But in line with reactions familiar from other culture areas, a number of "scholars of native learning, equating the sun with the deity Ame-no-minaka-nushi no kami, 'the god who rules the centre of the heavens,' claimed that the Copernican theory was one of their most ancient beliefs." Cf. D. Keene, *The Japanese Discovery of Europe. Honda Toshiaki and Other Discoverers, 1720-1798* (London, 1952), pp. 36-37, 111-114, 156 n. 80. The following definition of the intention of the "morals course" for Japanese secondary schools released in 1958 will provide a more recent basis for comparison with official attitudes in some of the Arab countries. "While consistently inculcating a respect for human dignity, to show how that respect is expressed in practice within the family, the school and other groups to which the individual belongs, and to train Japanese who will strive for the creation of a rich and distinctive culture and the development of a democratic state and society, and to make a positive contribution to a peace-loving international society." The topics range from "developing a respect for life and health" and "learning that dress, speech and gesture should be appropriate to place and occasion" in the early elementary years, to a final section in the last middle-school year on patriotism, the short outline of which runs: "As citizens of our country it is natural for us to feel an affection for our land and our fellow-countrymen and to respect and admire our cultural traditions. We should foster this natural sentiment and strive to build an even better country. However, we should not forget that a spirit of patriotism can only too easily develop into racial prejudice and narrow self-sufficiency. We should be on our guard against this and strive to get a full appreciation of the national cultures of other countries and to develop a general love of humanity, while at the same time, each in our own country, trying to create a distinctive culture which can be a source of pride to us as members of international society." Cf. Teikoku Chiho Gyosei Gakkai, *Dotoku Kyoiku jisshi yoko* (1958), pp. 3, 4, and 30; as quoted by R. P. Dore, *Education and Politics in Japan: 1870-1960.* Unpublished paper prepared for the Seminar on the Political Modernization of Japan and Turkey, Gould House, Dobbs Ferry, New York, September 10-14, 1962, p. 50, n. 1.

fication. The interweaving and the reciprocal competition of a common Arab national sentiment with particularistic patriotisms on the one hand, and a religious affiliation extending beyond Arabism on the other, confronted the person of Arabic tongue with a problem of self-understanding. The solution of this problem, considered on a purely logical level, would have had to precede an interpretation of his future cultural position, but in fact the problem forced itself upon him through his position within Islam.

The observation of the non-Arab Muslim, Jamāl ad-Dīn al-Afghānī (d. 1897), one of the most influential leaders of an awakening Islam in the late nineteenth century, that there are only two elements—language and religion—which make it possible to link a large number of individuals to one another, and that nationality and national unity are reducible to mere linguistic unity, fails to correspond exactly to the complexity of the Arab situation. For with this equation the existence of an Egyptian, a Syrian, or a Moroccan nationality, and of a matching national character within a comprehensive linguistic unity, is not taken into account; and al-Afghānī's interpretation of the significance of religion, which is subordinate to language as a means of bestowing cohesiveness and permanence on the community (a nation has frequently changed its religion without losing the identity conferred by language), in so oversimplified a form is completely unacceptable to wide circles of the Arabic-speaking public.[27]

About half a century after al-Afghānī a traditionally educated Tunisian living in Algeria, Aḥmad Taufīq al-Madanī (b. 1899), found a formula that is more representative of the consciousness of the majority. "Remember and do not forget," he addresses the Algerian reader, "that Algeria can prosper only if you act within the spheres of its religion, its language, and its national sentiment.

[27] The critical passages from one of al-Afghānī's Persian articles have been translated by M. Hendessi in *Orient,* VI (1958), 125.

. . . Take these words as the motto for your life and your actions: Islam is my religion; Arabic, my language; Algeria, my fatherland." [28] Pan-Arabism, of course, would not be satisfied with such allegiance pledged to Algeria. Its attitude is expressed in words spoken in 1933, at almost the same time, by Aḥmad az-Zayyāt: "Islamic Egypt can be no more than one chapter in the book of Arab glory; for it finds the sources of its vitality, the sustenance of its power, the foundation of its culture solely in the mission of the Arabs." [29] One may approximate nationalism to religion, as the Turkish reformer Ziya Gök Alp (1875- or 1876-1924) has done, and may cite traditional pronouncements of the Prophet from which the new sentiment extracts a completely new meaning without altering a single word. One may divide the intellectual world into culture and civilization, adopt the civilization of the West, and still desire to preserve the culture of Islam.[30] With such formulas one does not get at the root of the problem of nationality on the one hand, or of the cultural problem of Westernization on the other.

[28] *Kitāb al-Jazāʾir* (Algiers, 1932), p. 4; quoted by S. Bencheneb, "Quelques historiens arabes modernes de l'Algérie," *Revue Africaine*, C (1956), 475-499, at p. 491. This declaration is also the motto of the Association des ʿUlamāʾ Réformistes d'Algérie, founded in 1930. Cf. also the assertion of the newspaper *Najāt* (Constantine) of May 28, 1930, that the rise of Algeria is possible only on the basis of the four principles of Islamic orthodoxy, the ancient Arabic language, the purest patriotism, and modern applied science (quoted by J. Desparmet, "La réaction linguistique en Algérie," *Bulletin de la Société de Géographie d'Alger et de l'Afrique du Nord*, XXXII [1931], 1-31, on pp. 23-24).

[29] Quoted in *Mélanges de l'Institut Dominicain d'Études Orientales* (MIDEO), IV (1958), 338.

[30] Cf. U. Heyd, *Foundations of Turkish Nationalism* (London, 1950), pp. 57, 78-81. Cf. also the quotation in N. Berkes' *Turkish Nationalism and Western Civilization. Selected Essays of Ziya Gökalp* (London, 1959), p. 101: "To share a common human life in a civilization-group is not detrimental to the existence of the family or state, nor to the integrity of religion or the nation. We Turks have to work to create a Turkish-Islamic culture by fully appropriating to ourselves the mentality of contemporary civilization and its sciences."

Probably the most serious attempts to explore the nature of *ʿurūba*, of Arabism, have been made by Christian Arabs, no doubt because the Christian-Arab intelligentsia saw in overcoming the primacy of religious adherence by a superimposed national sentiment the sole possibility of effectively securing equality of rights in the Arab lands of Islamic confession. The analysis offered in 1947 by Nabīh Amīn Fāris (b. 1906) is typical in essentials and valid, if you like, in general as an expression of a secularized view of the self, in which common historical experience replaces to a great extent the religious bond as the formative element of the community.[31]

Our creed is Arabism, *ʿaqīdatu-nā ʾl-ʿurūba*—a genuine, living, efficacious unity. . . .

What is this genuine unity? And on what pillars does it rest?

There are people who try to make racial origin, *ʿunṣuriyya*, one of the pillars of this unity—what is more, the only pillar. How can *ʿurūba* exist if it is built upon racial origin, at a time when miscegenation is rife, when the base is mixed with the noble? We live in an era in which no trace of racial purity remains. Where can we still find purity of descent, where an unadulterated house and lineage? Do you consider the British king to be English when his family is Germanic, of the house of Hanover, and changed its name to Windsor shortly after the beginning of the First World War? Shall we call Faiṣal b. Saʿūd an authentic Arab as to race when his mother is a Turk? Shall we accept ʿAbdallāh, who plays the king in Transjordan, as a noble Hāshimite when there is non-Arab blood in his veins? George VI is a pure Englishman if we make language and the educative power of history our criteria; Faiṣal b. Saʿūd and his rival ʿAbdallāh b. al-Ḥusain are Arabs to the core with regard to language and the educative power of history.

There are others who make geographical situation a basis of this unity. If we agreed to this, the foreigner who has lived among the Arabs for centuries or generations becomes an Arab. This contradicts both fact and truth.

---

[31] *al-ʿArab al-aḥyāʾ* (Beirut, 1947), pp. 102-107.

Still others make religion one of the pillars of this unity. And this, too, contradicts fact and historical truth. Al-Quṭāmī, al-Akhṭal, and Ḥunain b. Isḥāq were Christians; as-Samauʾal, Ibn Sahl al-Isrāʾīlī, and Ibn Maimūn were Jews; Thābit b. Qurra and al-Battānī were star-worshipers who, desirous of acquiring the rights of the protected religions, *ahl adh-dhimma,* claimed Sabianism as their faith during the reign of al-Maʾmūn. Yet all of them were true Arabs in whom today we take pride, whose sayings we quote, of whose deeds we boast. Religion is not a pillar of *ʿurūba* nor has it ever been. This I say knowing full well that the Arabs emerged in history only under the banner of Islam. But those who marched under that banner and raised it in three of the five continents of the earth were both Muslims and non-Muslims.

The pillars of this authentic unity rest upon two bases, beside which there is no third: language and the formative force of history [*at-tarbiya 't-taʾrīkhiyya*].

What, then, is language? Is it a chain of sounds which man utters to express his needs? Or is it a means of clarifying and strengthening ideas and of cloaking and obscuring them at times? Or is it a treasure hoard for the inheritance and the culture of the people? Or an archive for their poetry and literature [*ādāb*]? A mirror of their hopes and dreams? Or an inexpungeable, imperishable record of their civilization and their works? A key to their thoughts and deeds before ever they entered history? Language is all this and more. It is a part of the spiritual being of a people. It is the symbol of its spiritual unity and is its strongest pillar.

The tumult that has been raising its voice during the last three decades has taken various forms, among them "Phoenician" propaganda, propaganda for a Mediterranean or a Pharaonic culture, or for the substitution of the Latin for the Arabic script and the encouragement of the vernaculars. It probably goes back to the feeling that the enemies of *ʿurūba* harbor against it. They believe that the ideal way to destroy it is to destroy the symbol of its unity and its very essence—the Arabic language. If we try to investigate the character of the proponents of those propaganda slogans and movements, be they Phoenician or Pharaonic, or again of the advocates of a Mediterranean culture, we shall find them limited to two types:

The first are those ignorant of the Arabic language—the Europeanized [*al-mutafarnajūna*] who have adopted another language or other languages, have taken the culture inherent in these languages as their own, and have been chained to a new mode of thinking, as language is one of the chains and boundaries of thought. I say "those ignorant of Arabic" because most of the advocates of Phoenicianism, Pharaonism, and Mediterranean culture are not proficient in Arabic, do not use it for speech and writing, and would not, as a rule, write letters to their fathers and mothers in it. Many find Arabic difficult and are attracted by the foreign languages which they have been learning and upon which they have relied since youth. Among them are those who, though they earn their living with Arabic, deprecate it.

The second type see *ʿurūba* and Islam as synonymous, and the flames of religious fanaticism rage in their hearts; seeing no way to overcome Islam except by overcoming Arabic, the language of Islam, they advocate Phoenicianism, Pharaonism, or the like, raise the banner of the vernacular dialects, and call for substitution of the Latin alphabet for the Arabic.

For these destructive movements, this modern *Shuʿūbiyya,* there is another, historical cause, namely, the lack of full equality among the subjects of the caliph or sultan, depending on their sect or creed. The Muslim and the non-Muslim were not equal before the *sharīʿa* [canon law]: *zakāt* [welfare tax] was incumbent upon the former, *jizya* [poll tax], upon the latter; civil rights and duties differed according to religion. In short, the *dhimmī* [the adherent of a tolerated religion having a scripture] was never a citizen but a protected client.

What are Phoenicianism, Pharaonism, and the other fads of today but the *Shuʿūbiyya* movements of yesterday [which in the ninth century aimed at achieving a status for non-Arabs equal to that of Arabs], the efforts of those who despair of escaping the chains that burden them. Do not think that the Arabs are unique in possessing this kind of political organization. As late as yesterday, even in England, Catholics and Jews were deprived of enjoying the rights and fulfilling the obligations of subjects who adhered to the official church. But this situation has come to an end in England, and it must come to an end in all the

Arab countries if we want to erect the pillars of the edifice on a firm foundation. Separation of religion and state is therefore one of the first duties of the Arab if he really wants to establish unanimity, to align the ranks, to keep pace with the times. Our national, Arab dreams will never be realized so long as all individuals of the nation do not become fellow citizens, equal before the law, equal in rights, equal in obligations. . . .

The first of these two pillars of unity, then, is language —the Arabic language with its poetry, its other literature [*ādāb*], its terminology, its expressions, all its words and proverbs, its script, its grammar. . . .

The second pillar is formation through history—development through the history of the Arabs with its events, its great men, its heroes; with the victories and defeats of the nation, its joy and sadness, its happiness and sorrow; the good that was turned to advantage, the bad that was their common share; with its memories, traditions, customs, tales, stories, legends, fables; that which moved the hearts of the people to compassion, grief, delight, and sorrow; and that which awakened in them the spirit of initiative and drove them to the fore. This education through history must tend to prepare individuals, to assume, consciously or unconsciously, responsibility for this history, and to cultivate it.

The formulation of a concept of the nature of Arabism is a prerequisite to situating Arab (or Arab-Islamic) culture; in turn, the demarcation of this culture's nature and position is almost indispensable to the attainment of a pragmatic-functional self-understanding. This necessity Fāris has also understood and, to meet it, he has made his own the view that in the world of today there are primarily three living civilizations: the Chinese, the Indian, and a third to which the rest of the civilized world belongs and which can best be designated as the Mediterranean. It was born of the most diverse elements; the ancient Egyptians as well as the Sumerians, the Iranians and the Babylonians along with the Greeks and the Romans and the Arabs, have contributed to its development. For this reason it would be a mistake to envision it as Aryan or Semitic, as heathen, Jewish, Christian, or Islamic. In any event it is now obvious that the different parts of the Mediterranean cultural world are distinct from one another in essential aspects, but that what is common prevails.[32] The intellectual unity of this civilization is derived from three elements: Greek thought, Roman order, and Semitic religion. In the development of these elements many nations, of course, shared. Thus Greek thought, for example, had its roots in Crete, Egypt, Babylon, and Persia; yet only with the Greeks were these strands woven into a rich fabric. The Semitic religion (*ad-dīn as-sāmī*) shows traces of Indian, Persian, and Egyptian religious motifs; yet only with the Semitic peoples were they organized into a purer conception of God.[33] The concrete task of the Arab world as determined by its geographical position and cultural structure lies in transmitting Western *virtus* (*futuwwa*) and science to the East and the wisdom and the "soul" (*ḥikma* and *rūḥ*) of the East to the West.[34]

---

[32] *Ibid.*, pp. 23-24. Fāris follows G. Sarton, "The Unity and Diversity of the Mediterranean World," *Osiris*, II (1936), 406-463, esp. pp. 407-408.

[33] Fāris, *op. cit.*, pp. 25-26 n. 30.

[34] *Ibid.*, p. 35. A different reaction to Arabism accompanies the *personnalisme* of another Christian Arab writer, René Habachi. To many, Arab unity has taken the place of a philosophy. Its insufficiency as an ideology has left them without an armor. A spiritual, existential mode of thinking is needed to make Arabism more than "une grande colère politique insuffisante à nous proposer un nouvel ordre de civilisation" (*Une philosophie pour notre temps* [Beirut, 1960], pp. 3-4). The decolonized peoples desire to live by a new philosophy completely their own which makes them experience themselves fully as masters of their destiny (p. 24). Arab unity is not something already available as an essence; actually, it is a goal to which one must work one's way starting from the differences that do indeed exist between the several countries concerned (p. 41). The supreme importance of self-realization by work (pp. 65 ff., 101 ff.) for breaking out of the sclerosis of the present and the tearful resignation vis-à-vis the heritage of the past is stressed for both ethical rejuvenation and practical effect. The task for the Arab indelibly embedded in the Mediterranean world as he is, is to find, perhaps in personalism, a form of life adequate for an Oriental which does not compel him to lose the Occident (pp. 107-108). As now constituted Arabism will not do to extricate the Arabs from

This construction is not difficult to recognize as an adaptation of the doctrine of Paul Valéry (1871-1945), who saw in the European mind a synthesis of three elements: Greek culture with its endowments of science, art, and literature; Roman, with its state administration and political institutions; and Christianity. More subtly and cautiously than Fāris has Ṭāhā Ḥusain, in the direct line of the French thinker and writer, used this perspective in his programmatic analysis of Egypt's cultural position. The fundamental question as to whether the Egyptian

---

their present "impasse de civilisation." It does not offer a sufficiently complete philosophy to give them a vision of the world in which they could play a historical role commensurate to their vocation. The double "refus neutraliste," which is its political aspect, is not creative; Islam, while inseparable from it, is actually pushed aside because "par son progressisme désirable et cependant simpliste, il [l'arabisme] nous écarte des sources de la transcendance et par là nous renvoie à une nouvelle immanence." Identification with "socialisme unioniste" goes beyond the Arab nation (because of linking its essence with a particular economic doctrine) and toward discarding "l'homme arabe." Too narrow a definition of Arab culture and language as the basis of Arabism would prevent the needed self-transcendence by tying the Arab to a normative past and leaving him without a true spiritual task (pp. 121-133). But seen from the personalistic viewpoint the Arab past offers all the elements required for a creative Arab present. "Devenir. Personne humaine. Transcendance. Liberté. Démocratie. Travail. Sens de l'histoire." These values, however, were the product of the Mediterranean area as a whole. "Parler de valeurs arabes alors c'est parler avant tout d'une Méditerranée de langue arabe, comme évoquer une pensée grecque c'est rappeler l'une des facettes de la Méditerranée, comme faire état d'une civilisation occidentale c'est se souvenir d'une Méditerranée latine. Chaque direction de la Méditerranée a sa vocation originale, mais aucune ne se comprendrait sans ce fond commun qui les a toutes alimentées au long de l'histoire." Those who for political reasons feel uneasy in regard to a Mediterranean culture must not forget that it is the culture which holds the key to political solutions and not the reverse. There simply is no Arab culture (as it has been shaped by history) without the Mediterranean, a fact which in no sense detracts from the cultural originality of the Eastern bank of that sea. "Renoncer à la Méditerranée, pour nous, c'est tout simplement renoncer, en tant que peuple, en tant qu'histoire, à toutes nos raisons d'exister (pp. 137-38)."

mind with its special faculties of intellect, imagination, and judgment belongs to the East (i.e., to India and China) or to the West is to be answered, according to historical, pragmatic, cultural-analytical criteria, unequivocally in favor of Western affiliation. Historically, Egypt's relations with the East have always been of secondary importance; antipathy to the Persians made Greeks and Egyptians allies. Pragmatically, it is unmistakable that the Egyptian of today finds himself in intellectual agreement much more often with a Frenchman or an Englishman than with a Chinese or a Japanese. Cultural analysis shows not only that Egypt represented at various times a refuge for classical culture, but also, and above all, that Islamic Egypt as well as Islam in general shares the Greek and Roman legacy with the West and that the Islamic religion claims to be nothing more than a completed and perfected Christianity and Judaism. Egypt and the West are not only congenial; essentially they are one. "There is no basic distinction between Europeans and us . . . ; the spirit of both cultures is inseparably one and the same. . . ."[35] Worthy of note in this construction is the special position assigned to Egypt, justly, no doubt, within the Arab-Islamic world; from a Pan-Arab standpoint Ṭāhā Ḥusain's interpretation errs through particularism, as, *mutatis mutandis*, also does that of the so-called "Phoenicians" of Lebanon, who regard themselves linguistically as Arabs but ethnically as successors of the Phoenicians and intellectually as the eastern outpost of Europe.

President Gamāl ʿAbd an-Nāṣir has interpreted the cul-

---

[35] *Mustaqbal ath-thaqāfa fī Miṣr* (Cairo, 1938), I, 63, 28; trans. J. Kraemer, *Das Problem der islamischen Kulturgeschichte*, (Tübingen, 1959), p. 4. I have analyzed Ṭāhā Ḥusain's thoughts on this subject in greater detail in *Islam: Essays*, pp. 208-216; cf. also Kraemer, *op. cit.*, pp. 4-6. As a supplement, mention may be made of P. Cachia, *Ṭāhā Ḥusayn. His Place in the Egyptian Literary Renaissance* (London, 1956), pp. 86-103. I know full well that Ṭāhā Ḥusain no longer sees Egypt (and the Arab world) in so close a connection with the West, but what is important in our context is the mode of interpretation and not the progressive development of any particular author.

tural position of his Egyptian homeland in a somewhat different manner. He sees Egypt surrounded by a series of circles or spheres of life, construed as concentric, which dictate naturally, as it were, the affiliations and the political conduct of the land. The innermost of these circles is the Arab world, which is just as much "a part of us as we are a part of it." The next circle is Africa, into whose conflicts Egypt will be drawn whether it wishes to be or not. The outermost circle is the Islamic world, the widest context to which Egypt meaningfully belongs. To what extent the succession "Egypt—the Arab world—Africa—the Islamic world" is to be conceived on a geographical-logical or an emotional-intuitive basis Gamāl ʿAbd an-Nāṣir leaves open. If it were a matter of a self-view, then no doubt the African sphere of life would be glossed over. In any event, the contrast between the secularized-Egyptian or Pan-Arab nationalists and the conservative-religious orientation of, say, the Muslim Brotherhood can easily be portrayed by reversing the progression of circles, because, for the orthodox, loyalty to the Islamic world would take precedence over that due the Arab world and even that due the homeland.[36] From this perspective the relation to the West remains open; nevertheless, the diagram presupposes—if it lays claim to cultural conclusiveness—the autarchy, if not of the Arab world, at least of the Islamic.

As so often, here, too, neutrality presumably masks disciplined antipathy. Ambivalence toward Western culture as a possession both to be striven for and to be feared—probably the dominant attitude in governmental and in-

[36] Gamāl ʿAbd an-Nāṣir, *The Philosophy of the Revolution* (Cairo, 1954), esp. pp. 53-56; cf. also "Problems of Muslim Nationalism," chap. ix, below, pp. 285-287. G. Levi Della Vida, *Aneddoti e svaghi arabi e non arabi* (Milan and Naples, 1959), pp. 146-147, sees Gamāl ʿAbd an-Nāṣir's analysis of the Egyptian situation as a maximum imperialistic program at which one may smile in view of the industrial weakness of the country; the unpreparedness of Africans to let the Arabs lead them; and, last but not least, the already marked rivalry of Pakistan and Indonesia within the Islamic world. Still, the program is symptomatic and a dangerous dream.

tellectual circles—is replaced on a lower social level by an aversion difficult to mistake, which, moreover, probably can and often does go hand in hand with admiration and a certain willingness to learn. The popular literature of Algeria, for example, has frequently given expression to the deep aversion with which wide circles confront Western civilization and the seemingly inseparable hegemony of its Christian representatives. In vernacular verse accounts, Western civilization is personified as a *ghūl*. About 1900, in the eyes of the population of the Mitidja (the plain south of Algiers), this *ghūl* was prodigious in size and strength, exceedingly ugly, in no way stupid, and the master of all sorts of magical tricks, but he was at the same time bestial, unscrupulous, greedy for wealth, and, above all, an unbeliever. He violates the Islamic moral precepts but in the end is subdued and either converted or killed. The *chansons de geste* of wandering minstrels are attuned to keeping awake the memory of Islamic martial glory, to strengthening pride in the ancestral faith and the conviction of its intrinsic superiority, and to preventing the antipathy against the French masters and the culture they represent from slumbering.[37]

For the educated—meaning, if not the Western-educated, those who become at least indirectly familiar with the profile, the methodology, the challenge, and the aspirations of the Western mode of thought—choosing sides is not so easy. Wounded pride may be healed to a certain extent by deriving some of the Western achievements from medieval Islamic roots, by representing others as morally suspect or as deleterious in application to the colonial area. Bennabi claims scientific synthesis to be a process transmitted from Islam to the West, and, with an

[37] Cf. J. Desparmet, "Les Chansons de Geste de 1830 à 1914 dans la Mitidja," *Revue Africaine*, LXXXIII (1939), 192-226, esp. pp. 212-213, 225-226; Desparmet's previously mentioned series of studies, "Les réactions nationalitaires en Algérie"; and Desparmet's essays, "La vieille poésie nationale; la conquête racontée par les Indigènes," *Bulletin de la Société de Géographie d'Alger*, XXXIII (1932), 173-184, 436-456, and "Élégies et satires politiques de 1830 à 1914," *ibid.*, XXXIV (1933), 35-54.

extremely free interpretation of the facts, characterizes Muslim law as the first legal system to develop from philosophical principles, in contrast to Roman law, for example, which was nothing but an empirical compilation of "formulas." The humanism of Islamic civilization is evident from the generosity of Muslim science in offering itself "unconditionally" to the human spirit. As far as the intent of such assertions is concerned, a precise statement of the past is only secondary; of primary importance is establishing a contrast to the arrogance with which, as the author feels, Europe has brought its science to "backward [*arriéré*] lands, or, more exactly, lands that it has thrown back." [38] While Bennabi denies the West morality in the higher sense, and states that the Occident has lost the balance between the spiritual and the quantitative, between finality and causality (as also happened in Islam when knowledge and the known, material data and the spiritual order, broke asunder), he finds superhuman, providential wisdom in the fact that Tamerlane defeated the Golden Horde and the Turks and thereby inadvertently and unconsciously blocked the spread of Islam to Moscow and Warsaw, to Vienna and Berlin. For only in this way was Christian Europe put in a position to perpetuate the achievements of civilization, a task of which Islam, spent since the fourteenth century, was no longer capable.[39]

But the world of today, though in need of Western cultural achievements, is trapped in a vicious circle:

The civilized man is a colonizer. The man-to-be-civilized is automatically a man-to-be-colonized, a colonial product, who is called "the native" [*l'indigène*]. A civilizer there is

---

[38] Malik Bennabi, *Vocation de l'Islam* (Paris, 1954), pp. 16-17. Cf. also ʿU. A. Farrukh, *The Arab Genius in Science and Philosophy*, trans. into English by J. B. Hardie (Washington, D.C., 1954), p. 9. This cliché is attributed even to Ṭāhā Ḥusain by A. Bausani, "Il Processo dell'Islam alla civiltà occidentale," *Oriente moderno*, XXXV (1935), 394-404, on p. 398; F. Gabrieli protests it in *ibid.*, pp. 401-402.

[39] Bennabi, *op. cit.*, pp. 152, 159.

none. Herein lies the tragedy. The civilized man accuses "the others" of passing on his civilizations a judgment steeped in ingratitude and insufficient esteem. Worse yet, he attributes this loss of prestige to a weakening of his material power. So he brings to bear his own "power" [*force*], which intensifies the adverse judgment, and this, in turn, intensifies the deplored application of power. In Algeria the magnitude of modern civilization, along with the poverty, the disease, and the ignorance prevailing at the same time, injects into the hearts of those-to-be-civilized a dilemma of intense moral agony.[40]

In order to appreciate the criticism of Western culture, especially in its radical forms, as an intellectual (i.e., not primarily a political) phenomenon, one must bear in mind that self-criticism, so characteristic of the West and of the English-speaking West in particular, has led in certain intellectual and political quarters to an attitude that denies all merit to European achievement per se and above all to European achievement in lands outside Europe. This attitude, which in effect invites the East to use the Occident as an all-purpose scape goat, draws its strength from the postulate, transferred from liberal politics to cultural anthropology, of the equality of all men, from which has sprung the broader postulate of the equivalence of all cultures. That here obtains a confusion of historical uniqueness and functional values with the actual capacity for achievement in the sense of preserving and enhancing life, of mastering and broadening experience, is not taken into account.[41] A certain hostility toward power and the exercise of it, which as part of its Christian legacy is today peculiar to Western culture alone, supports the doctrine, which has its existential basis in an unwillingness to accept without apology the fact of superiority. The self-contradic-

[40] M. Bennabi, *Les conditions de la Renaissance Algérienne* (Algiers, 1949), pp. 99-100.

[41] In this context one may read, e.g., G. Fradier, *East and West. Towards Mutual Understanding* (UNESCO, 1959). *Mutatis mutandis* comparable to the Catholic Church, Islam visualizes itself as an absolute while utilizing simultaneously the values of Western cultural relativism.

tion inherent in non-Europeans' venturing all their energy to transfer Western civilization to their homelands, while simultaneously seeking to disparage it, is attributable to two facts: (1) though the manifold crises accompanying the transition, initiated often with great awkwardness and always with great impatience, must be laid at the door of "others," the process as a whole should not be wrecked; and (2) self-esteem, which might seem jeopardized by the enthusiastic surrender of inherited goals, is to be secured by stubborn insistence on the superiority of the native tradition of past achievement, which, however, is in fact treated like an enemy to be overcome.

The West promotes assertions of this order with naïve incomprehension, but, beyond that, with a peculiar "democratic-universalistic" impulse to decree the fundamental equality of all cultures, without once taking the trouble to think through (as the East has done so many times, even if with the help of a different terminology) the problems of what collective and individual possibilities various cultures actually afford their participants, and of how the statement of the fundamental equality of cultural presuppositions can be verified by given cultural phenomena. Moreover, the simplest ethnographic description demonstrates that cultures are differentiated according to their internal and external capacity for production or consolidation. That wide circles in the West are inclined, on thoroughly erroneous, largely socio-political grounds, and partly, too, on the basis of the exaggerated need of the West for self-knowledge through analytical ingestion of foreign cultures, to accept the relativity, zealously defended by non-Western assimilationists and conservatives, of cultural achievements, precisely at the time when the world is striving to appropriate Western culture (or its communistic offshoots) as quickly as possible, is one of those paradoxes in which Western intellectual life is so rich, but whose unthinking acceptance is nevertheless irresponsible from the standpoint of continuing Western progress.

Like Bennabi, other modern north Africans have turned away from Islam without desiring to dissociate themselves from it. Driss Chraibi (b. 1926) says of the hero of his book, *Le Passé simple:* "He, perhaps, is I. In any event his despair is mine. Despair of belief. This Islam in which he believes, which speaks of the equality with which God causes tolerance, freedom, and love to prevail in every created thing—this Islam he saw, as an ardent young man being educated in French schools, reduced to Pharisaism, to a social system and a weapon of propaganda. In short, he embarked for France: he needed someone or something to believe in, to love, to respect." [42] It is refreshing to encounter a construction of the self which declares integration, without self-betrayal and without fear of the foreign, to be possible and desirable as a collective program for the future. It is also characteristic that the voice of Maḥjūb b. Mīlād (b. 1916) comes out of the Islamic West—from Tunisia:

If we want to sum up the stand of "the new Tunisia" [*Tūnis al-jadīda*], vis-à-vis East and West, we should say:

If the essence of the East is reducible to the devotion of its immortals to the essence of truth, virtue, and beauty —to the devotion of Jāḥiẓ, Ibn al-Muqaffaʿ, al-Ashʿarī, al-Juwainī, Abū Ḥayyān at-Tauḥīdī, Abū Ḥāmid al-Ghazzālī, Ibn Rushd, Ibn Khaldūn, and their many peers—that devotion from which their writings and other works have sprung in vital interaction between eternal inherited Islamic values and individual spiritual motives, which is revealed in their works, and made effective through the concentration of their longings and the sincerity of their inspired spontaneity, then we are Easterners [*sharqiyyūn*] whose spirits, free and dedicated to the essence of things, roam in the "intellectual expanses" [*abʿād fikriyya*] of Arabism and Islam in the tradition of their creative, pioneering intellectual endeavors!

But this does not mean that we close the doors of our hearts to the thought of foreign immortals, whatever their nationality, just as they [i.e., our great forebears] have not

[42] *Op. cit.*, p. 13.

closed the doors of their hearts in bygone times to the best fruits of Greek philosophy, Persian thought, and Indian wisdom.

If, however, the East means that which we have inherited from the centuries of decay, namely, the stupidity of blind belief in authority, narrow horizons, shortsightedness, cowardice in confronting reality, neglect of the laws of reality, flight from assuming the responsibilities and the integrity of the intellectual life, then the "new Tunisia" is not of the East nor the East of it!

The new Tunisia is most eager to retain her devotion to her past and those precious deposits of that past which lie in the depths of her heart, but at the same time to devote herself to present realities and to the special demands of our time; she is eager, in other words, above all to provide herself in the "contemporary world" with an abundance of the constituents of power and strength and the means to a free, happy life!

Herein lies a precise definition of our position vis-à-vis the West! Insofar as the West looks into the face of reality and unveils its laws, adopts a strictly rational mode of thought in order to learn its secrets and how to control it, and has a sound system of organizing the chaotic elements of reality, the new Tunisia is of the West and to it directs its gaze!

But if the West means disbelief in man and his highest values, and arrogance in exploiting and controlling man even to the extent of destroying his rights and trampling morality under foot, and if the West is under the yoke of ambitious greed and the voracity of its instincts, then the new Tunisia is not of the West, nor does she desire to be; for the eons of decay and the follies of decay have not expunged from her memory the fact that the torch of the East, in the words of the great Mikhāʾil Nuʿaima, was borne "by a prophet with the resoluteness of the earth in his feet, the might of heaven in his arms, the brilliance of truth in his eyes, the meekness of knowledge on his tongue, and the sweetness of love in his heart."

In short, I believe that the new Tunisia has it within her power to rank in the vanguard of Islamic nations because she feels keenly the necessity to settle her "intellectual account" once and for all, and to lift the dust that has accumulated on the Islamic "intellectual edifice." . . .

If Tunisia enacts this "intellectual law," it is in the conviction that she is neither Eastern nor Western but combines in splendor the purest qualities and the loftiest values of East and West, yet is independent of both whenever she feels the necessity of adhering to her deepest sentiments, her freshest thoughts, and her purest intuitions.

Had I sufficient time, I would make it clear to you that there is neither inconsistency nor contradiction between the values of East and West when we adjust both balances correctly. By uniting Eastern and Western values we do not expose ourselves to the charge of cheap amalgamation or tawdry eclecticism, so long as the new Tunisia succeeds in uniting only those values that she can master with originality through energetic spiritual experience and in fusing them in the one caldron of her new, blazing intellectuality, intently aspiring to the service of reality and its laws and the noble ideals of mankind.

Had I enough time, I would make clear to you that it is the study of science and of contemporary streams of philosophy at Western universities which will enable the new Tunisia to immerse herself in the splendors of Islamic thought and philosophy. For this reason the representatives of the mentality of yesterday are least capable of understanding Islamic thought and Islamic intellectual tradition in their best manifestations, deepest significance, widest horizons; least capable, consequently, of defending them and of achieving the triumph of Islamic intellectual values.[43]

---

[43] Maḥjub b. Mīlād, *Tūnis bain ash-sharq wa'l gharb* (Tunis, 1956), pp. 22-25. Ben Mīlād's statement gains in weight when it is realized that his principal point is shared by many leading Tunisian intellectuals. An investigation organized by the important journal *al-Fikr*, in 1956, shows that a majority of those requested to state their views on Arab and Occidental culture are agreed that the cliché of a materialistic West and a spiritualistic East has no basis in reality. An awareness of the complexities of both Eastern and Western civilization permeates the replies to the rather sophisticated questionnaire which *al-Fikr* distributed. Equally important is the almost unanimously expressed readiness to maintain the cultural openness of Tunisia; a sense of the individuality of their homeland is paralleled by a sense of its natural and spiritual ties with both the Arab-Muslim and the Occidental worlds and, in some instances, of the kinship obtaining between those two worlds, at least in their Mediterranean set-

The situation out of which self-constructions grow and through which the political and cultural activity of the Arab-Muslim world is to be molded and guided has two basic trends, which generally one simply takes for granted as background material without making any special effort to include them in the construction or to base the construction on them. If one adopts the standpoint of classical, Sunnite Islam, the two phenomena immediately clash by virtue of their direction and operation. In practically all the Arabic-speaking countries the dissolution of Islamic law, this most powerful apparatus of unification and institutional cohesiveness of the Islamic world, is a *fait accompli;* where it is not, the state in question, such as Yemen or Saudi Arabia, either plays in the consciousness of the general public the role of a cultural "hick" who "doesn't count," or is in the process of shaking off the ties, apprehended as symptoms of backwardness, which bind it to the canon law by constantly reducing, like Egypt or Tunisia, the validity of the statutes of the *sharīʿa* and by removing it more and more from the legal spheres of everyday life, be it by public statutory measures or by administrative decrees. The reverence shown the canon law by conservative segments of the population frequently compels governments to apply methods anchored in the very law which they are designed to bypass in practice, or to confine themselves, as in Egypt, for example, to entrusting the regular courts with the application of a modified *sharīʿa* statute in the sphere of personal law (basically

---

ting or manifestations. For details cf. the analysis of the investigation by M. Lelong, "Culture arabe et culture occidentale dans la Tunisie d'aujourd'hui," *Revue de l'Institut des Belles Lettres Arabes, Tunis,* XIX (1956), 313-331, esp. at pp. 319 (Ahmed Ben Salah), 321 (Mohammed al-Halioui), 322 (Al-Hadi Hammou), 324 (Ahmed Abdeslam), 325-326 (Mohamed Farid Ghazi), 326-327 (Ameur Ghedira). Attention may be called in this connection to an earlier and perhaps less ambitious inquiry arranged by another Tunisian review, *An-Nadwa,* in 1954, whose results reflect the same mature and world-open spirit; cf. again M. Lelong's analysis, "L'Avenir de la culture nationale en Tunisie. Une enquête de la revue 'An-Nadwa,'" *IBLA,* XVIII (1955), 127-132.

the laws of marriage and of inheritance). Be that as it may in particulars, on the whole Western ideas and definitions of the law have to all practical purposes supplanted Islamic law, but this supplantation of a system of thought, regarded as obsolete and as a secondary phenomenon vis-à-vis the revelation, is not felt as irreligious, much less as a secession from the Islamic community. On the other hand, in Morocco, for example, the French protectorate, and the pacification and the centralization of the country which it has effected, have resulted in an extension of Sunnite, "standard" Islam to the popular, peripheral sphere of faith and law in rural, and especially mountain, populations of the Berber race. The Islam of the Arabized cities, long since won for Sunnite orthodoxy, has finally succeeded in bringing into view a mightily contested victory over local forms of belief and local religious usage, but this should certainly not leave the impression that the standardization of Moroccan Islam has been achieved under the hegemony of north Moroccan theologians, or will be so achieved during our lifetime. What has happened, rather, is a strengthening of orthodox practice under urban leadership and an extension of the effective competence of the urban *qāḍī*'s to outlying rural districts —the fruitful activation of a tendency which can assist the executive power rather more decisively than it could in the last two hundred years before the establishment of the French protectorate.

The same Western influence that has challenged Sunnite orthodoxy and, in areas south of the Sahara, for example, the application of canon law, has also fostered, no doubt out of the same need to stand by the regular, formally instituted order, the revival of classical Arabic in Algeria, where the local dialect was not far from becoming the literary language for certain genres. It is characteristic that it was a French civil servant and Orientalist, Octave Houdas (1860-1917), who made the use of classical Arabic mandatory in the madrasas, and that the French authorities prohibited in sharp language the use of the dialect, which was being backed by a few French professors, in the literary exercises of *lycées* and colleges. That the French authorities, in taking this step, were partly in accord with the sentiments of the nationalists should not conceal the fact that here too the West has been of decisive assistance in suppressing the popular, uncultivated, unclassical tendencies that contradicted its normative concept of what is Islamic or Arabic.[44]

Nevertheless, an outsider may conclude in summary that, apart from the strong bond with the religious community as such and with the political potential of the *umma* concept, the continuation of the old, traditional religious culture (outside Yemen, Saudi Arabia, and Morocco) is scarcely more than a working hypothesis. Those things that do continue are attitudes, reactive dispositions, that stem or seem to stem from the old culture, and memories that might serve as decorative motifs of an intellectual, artistic, and political program. Otherwise it is a matter of history, of past performance, which has the ability to bind the community almost as a body; which, being cherished, should maintain the self-confidence necessary for accepting the new; and which at the same time could give to the new that has already been accepted the cachet, thanks to which the renunciation of the traditional can be felt as indigenous and therefore tolerated. In the final analysis the life of a tradition depends on whether or not the questions that it was devised to answer are still critical.[45]

---

[44] As to the facts, cf. Desparmet, "La réaction linguistique en Algérie," pp. 3, 19-20.

[45] What the penetration of the West means *summa summarum*, Léger (*op. cit.*, II, 241 n. 3) has packed into an impressive paragraph of general descriptive validity, in which he has also done justice to the pain and irritation involved in this process: "Si leurs [i.e., the Westerners'] procédés individuels ont pu être irritants, si leurs comportement collectif a trop généralement manqué d'esprit de prévision, de vue à long terme, s'ils ont trop vécu dans un perpétuel présent, la somme de travail et le total de résultats effectifs qu'ils ont accumulés dans ce présent est un incomparable exploit: introduction et enseignment des sciences exactes, des techniques modernes, de l'organisation administrative, rythme nouveau imprimé à la vie, découpage plus

Interest in the West, in the form of effort to acquire historical-analytical understanding of its cultural aspirations and, in this sense, an end in itself, is slight in the Arab world. An Eastern Occidentalist as counterpart to the Western Orientalist has not come forward. What is lacking is not the study of the foreign culture, but self-construction, self-manipulation, in the light of the Western phenomenon that must be mastered, whether by partial assimilation or by purposive recourse to the past.[46]

---

strict du temps et accélération de l'emploi de celui-ci, révolution en matière d'hygiène, de médicine, d'alimentation, d'habitation, de mobilier, modification du canon de la beauté féminine, nouveau code de morale familiale, nouveaux goûts esthétiques et intellectuels, nouvelles lectures, nouvelles distractions, idée nouvelle du droit et de la justice, profonde impression spirituelle entraînant un complet réexamen des données religieuses et morales traditionnelles, perfectionnement et enrichissement des langages, révélations historiques et archéologiques, révélations des forces latentes de la nature, éveil de ses richesses endormies, apport de nouvelles sources de prospérité, révélation de l'individu à lui-même en tant que tel, révélation à l'individu de la collectivité à laquelle il appartient en tant que nation . . . ce bilan incomplet d'un court siècle de présence occidentale est suffisamment éloquent pour que l'Occident en conserve à jamais la fierté." In partial illustration of Léger's judgment we may quote from Salāma Mūsà's autobiography, *Tarbiyat Salāma Mūsà* (Cairo, 1948), p. 196; English translation by L. O. Schuman (Leiden, 1961), p. 139 (a bit periphrastic): "There were two subjects to which I gave a good deal of attention in my political struggle. One was the greatness of Egyptian civilization in Pharaonic times and the use a study of its history could have for stimulating national pride. *I became convinced of the propagandistic value of this historic approach by what I learned in Europe, and more particularly in Britain, about Egypt having sent the first waves of civilization to other parts of the world* . . ." (my italics).

46 The ideal seems to me to be expressed with extraordinary clarity in the following unsigned assessment (*Islamic Culture* [Hyderabad, Deccan], XI [1937], 3-4) of the achievement of the Indo-Muslim state of Hyderabad (absorbed by Bharat in 1948): "With all this modern progress Hyderabad remains an Oriental State, proud of its own culture, language, arts, and history. Hyderabad City has been described as the last great Oriental city left on earth. The Nizam and the Nizam's Government have shown that it is possible to modernize an Eastern State and still preserve its Eastern self-respect, the fervour of its

To my knowledge the Egyptian writer Muḥammad al-Muwailiḥī (1868-1930) was the first, in his book *The Story of ʿĪsà b. Hishām* (1906), to make a cultural-psychological sketch of the East-West antithesis and to seek an intellectual explanation for Eastern readiness to assimilate. In the course of time his train of thought has, depending on one's point of view, attained the authority of a classic or the glib rigidity of a cliché. In any event, his theory deserves careful attention because it reflects the evaluative conflict inherent in the assessing of native and Western cultural achievement.

The question of the Pasha, in al-Muwailiḥī's story, as to the cause of the ills observed on a trip through Egypt is answered thus:

> The Friend [*aṣ-Ṣadīq*]: "The true cause is the sudden intrusion of Western civilization [*al-madaniyya al-gharbiyya*] into the lands of the East and the Easterners' imitation of the Westerners in all phases of life. As if blind, they do not seek enlightenment in research, nor do they make comparisons or engage in circumspect reflection.

---

faith, the beauty of its outward seeming. The great traditions of the East are here intact. The religious tolerance which characterized the Mughal Empire—of which Hyderabad is the only portion which remains today—has been preserved most carefully, the Nizam's Government patronizing and assisting all religions in the State. So has the Mughal patronage of arts and learning. Every learned man in India, every author who has not means sufficient to produce his work, looks as a matter of course to the Nizam for a patronage which is given, without discrimination, to a very large number of institutions and persons irrespective of race and creed. Through this munificent patronage Hyderabad has become a centre of Islamic culture, second to Cairo as regards Arabic, second to none as regards Urdu and Persian; a centre, too, of Hindu culture where Sanskrit, Telagu, Marathi, Canarese and Tamil are taught in the schools and are producing literature." The use of history in the quest for prestige can be documented already in antiquity. T. S. Brown, for instance, has shown that Manetho's and Berossus' *Histories* were "a part of the contest for prestige" between Antiochus I (280-261) and Ptolemy II (285-246). Cf. his study "The Greek Sense of Time in History as Suggested by Their Accounts of Egypt," *Historia*, XI (1962), 257-270, at p. 268, n. 93.

They do not take into account the mutual antipathy of innate characteristics, differences in taste, variety of traditions and customs. They do not cull the true from the false, the good from the foul, but accept everything in one lump, thinking that therein lies happiness and well-being, under the delusion that thereby strength and victory will accrue to them. Therefore they foresake all their sound principles, their wholesome customs, their clean conduct. The truth of their forefathers they indifferently discard; thus foundations collapse, columns buckle, edifices tumble. Cut off from their spiritual sustenance, they grope about in darkness and dawdle with lies. With this thin coating of Western civilization they are content, and they acquiesce in foreign dominion, which they see as a *fait accompli* and a gratifying fate. Thus we destroy our homes with our own hands and live in the East as if we were Westerners, even though between their way of life and ours lies a distance as long as that between east and west."

The Pasha: "That may well be, but I know no reason for Easterners to adopt the worthless civilization of the West and to array themselves in its garments without considering for one moment a return to their former, true civilization and their authentic culture, for the Easterners are forerunners who have been studied and imitated in all that they have done in every time, at every place."

The Friend: "For this I know no other reason than the arrogance and the insolence which followed upon former glory and the prolonged vacillation, indifference, languor, and weakness by them engendered. They have ignored their past, disregarded their present, and failed to concern themselves for their future; their anxieties have made them shy away from the hardships of responsibility which their ancestors took pride in assuming and gloried in fulfilling. It delights them to take on this current gloss of the Westerners' civilization without discomfort or inconvenience, toil or trouble. The scope of the Westerners has thus assumed in their eyes vast dimensions, and under the delusion that Westerners occupy a level high above them, they bow and scrape while Westerners triumph and conquer."

The Pasha: "If only I knew how I could explore and examine the principles of Western civilization, both internally and externally, and how I could see for myself that which is both hidden and manifest on Western soil! But the distance is great; the quest, arduous!" [47]

If, with al-Muwailiḥī, the decline of Arab-Islamic civilization is attributed primarily to the spiritual weakness of its participants, the means to its salvation from his point of view must be of a cultural-psychological nature. A generation after Muwailiḥī the Syrian and Orthodox Christian, Qusṭanṭīn Zuraiq (b. 1909), who was educated in the United States and later became vice-president of the American University in Beirut and Syrian ambassador to Washington, attempted to specify the methods to be used in combating the internal weaknesses of Arab culture. In their way his statements are just as representative and, in this sense, just as classic as al-Muwailiḥī's diagnosis:

There is a difference of opinion as to the effective means of treating the sicknesses that afflict our Arab culture. Some among us believe that the seeds of these diseases are embedded in the Arab land [*fī 'l-bait al-ʿarabī*], and that it is incumbent upon us to nip them in the bud by raising the level of the mother soil [*mustawà'l-umm*], to enable her to perform her national duty so salubriously that the children of the nation [*abnā' al-umma*] will be instilled with love of their country and language, and national pride [*al-ibā' al-qaumī*] and patriotic self-esteem [*al-ʿizza al-waṭaniyya*] will be implanted in their souls. Others among us believe that the path to salvation is reform of the program of instruction and standardizing it in all Arab coun-

[47] *Ḥadīth ʿIsà b. Hishām* (3d ed.; Cairo, 1341/1923), pp. 457-459. For the history of this book cf. H. Pérès, "Essai sur les éditions successives du 'Ḥadīṯ ʿIsā ibn Hišām,'" in *Mélanges Louis Massignon* (Damascus, 1956-1957), III, 233-258. Worthy of comparison as a document of social criticism is Yūsuf as-Sibāʿī's book *Arḍ an-nifāq*, first published in 1949, which, though it can scarcely be spoken of as a work of art, expresses a certain originality and the courage of the author's convictions. Deserving special attention are the passages that deal with Palestine; the administration of Egyptian government offices; parliamentarism (included in a description of an election meeting), which is rejected by the author; and the population problem together with birth control (cf. pp. 57-67, 89-96, 96-100 [with 261-274], 161-166, a publication in the series *al-Kitāb al-fiḍḍī* [Cairo, n.d.]).

tries. A third group finds in the language the firm foundation of culture and directs its attention toward keeping it safe from harm and free of blemishes. Still others fear the effect of modern civilizational elements on our cultural inheritance and call for preservation of the old science, language, and *Bildung* [*ādāb*], and for protection of the inheritance from injury and deterioration. And still other ideas [*muqtaraḥāt;* literally, "proposals"] are brought forward. . . .

. . . A number of principles emerge which we should adopt as the basis for a successful battle for our culture. (1) The cultural battle cannot be isolated from the political battle to liberate the [Arab] countries and to strengthen their power [*sulṭān*]. For the governmental apparatus is one of the most strongly organized and most effective means of preserving and developing culture. If, then, the nation possesses complete freedom of action, the road lies straight in front of her to pursue a solution to this momentous problem. But if the opposite be true, the culture of the country remains exposed to danger, a balloon in the wind. In rising Western nations we see the government expanding its influence every day over the affairs of education and culture, intensifying its efforts to organize them and secure them in its grip, thereby to preserve their unity and to protect them from frivolous experimentation. We also see that those Arab countries that have taken the lead in the ascent to independence are able to make sacrifices to protect and revitalize Arab culture, sacrifices of which that part of the Arab fatherland which has not yet completely mastered its fate is incapable.

This link between the cultural and the political battle has become strong and prominent chiefly in the modern era. For those nations eager for expansion and predominance have devised effective means for destroying the culture of dominated peoples. They know that the culture of a nation is its central nervous system, its impregnable fortress, and that the surest way to subdue it is to dissipate its language, to squander its *Bildung* [*ādāb*], to sever the bonds that tie it to its legacy. . . .

These, then, are the five principles on which we must base our cultural war: autonomy in conducting our cultural affairs, clarity as to goals, fusion of consciousness and act, soundness of organization, and sincerity in carrying out the mission. All these are firmly linked with the national battle in the widest sense and are derived from it. Will our leaders of opinion and action be able to raise high the banner of this cultural battle and organize the factors it comprises? The warring powers of the modern era give no quarter to the nation that neglects its spirit and abandons its culture to the hand of destiny, exposing it to storms and gales. But perhaps we can take heed of these imminent dangers and strive to ward them off before these powers overwhelm and annihilate us in their disputes and conflicts while we slumber.[48]

But a cure for cultural ills, or even an assimilation that would not be tantamount to surrender, is to be expected only in conjunction with a decisive return to the legacy of the past. More than political subjugation, in the circles for which personages like al-Muwailiḥī and Zuraiq speak, obliteration of cultural identity is felt to be the real threat, the irreparable defeat. Under the date line of January 9, 1930, the Cairo newspaper *al-Fatḥ* writes:

Seen as a whole, the area dominated by foreign colonization is small; a day will come when the owner of the soil will find himself able to repossess what was stolen from him. But that the intruders may colonize the hearts of men and women—that is the ultimate loss, the final collapse. The real danger approaches us from the spiritual war that Europe is methodically conducting against the spirit of Orientals in general and of Muslims in particular, with the aid of its philosophical books, its novels, its theaters and films, and its language. The aim of this concerted action is of a psychological nature—to cut off the Oriental peoples from their past. What a conquering Europe fears more than anything else is this consciousness of the past which is beginning to awaken in the hearts of the Indians, the Chinese, and especially the Arabs. Once you have recognized that behind this spiritual awakening looms the practical wish to step out of a humiliating present to dash headlong toward a radiant future, you will

---

[48] Qusṭanṭīn Zuraiq, *al-Waʿy al-qaumī* (Beirut, 1939), pp. 184-185, 186-187, 195.

have understood the real reason that drives Europe to its intellectual crusade.[49]

To possess a past means to possess a history; to possess a history means to possess a nationality. And the possession of a national identity justifies and guarantees the possession of independence. "Remember [the past], for remembering [the past] is useful to Muslims." This fallacious interpretation of a Koranic verse[50] is used by Algerian politicians to explain their cultivation of the popular *ghazawāt* epic. Where a genuine national history does not exist, one is invented or discovered. Carthage is being built into the historical consciousness of the north African of today. Whereas the Romans were a colonial power, one might almost say that Carthage, following the French pattern, produced according to this interpretation a "regional culture," and that the Berbers stepped into the light of history in league with a cognate Semitic hegemony which meant cohesiveness, not dependence, and development, not self-deprivation.[51]

The relation between the indigenous Berber and the Arab conqueror is presented—in this instance with somewhat less vehemence though with remarkable stylization in details—in a way that declares and glorifies the community feeling of the races, the only feeling on which the political unity of an independent north Africa can be

[49] Quoted by Desparmet, "La Réaction linguistique," p. 13 n. 43.

[50] Sura 51:55: "dhakkir; fi-inna ʾdh-dhikrà tanfaʿu lil-muslimīna"; literally: "Warn; for verily warning benefits the Muslims." Desparmet, "Les Chansons de Geste," p. 194.

[51] This has become a commonplace of north African political thought; cf., e.g., A. T. al-Madanī, *Shamāl Ifrīqiya au Qarṭājinna fi arbaʿa ʿuṣūr* (Tunis, 1927), p. 32, al-Mubārak al-Mīlī (1880-1945), *Taʾrīkh al-Jazāʾir* (Constantine, 1929-1932), p. 93, and Bencheneb, *op. cit.*, pp. 489-490 n. 27. Bennabi, *Renaissance*, p. 90, amplifies the idea that Islam recognizes provinces, not, like Rome and Europe, colonies. Cf. further ʿAllāl al-Fāsī (b. 1906), *The Independence Movements in Arab North Africa* (Cairo, 1948), trans. into English by H. Z. Nuseibeh (Washington, 1954), pp. 1-8.

built.[52] The most important element in the retrospective and, as it were, retroactive identification of this kind is its psychological potential. The fact that young people with Berber names who grow up in a Berber-speaking home are able to learn the Arabic language as their own or, in any event, feel it as their own, and, in addition, that a whole people can convince itself that the history of another people, even in those initial phases of the process of interrelation, belongs to it as a source of pride and encouragement and as a rationale of its position in the world of history, throws a peculiar light on the human consciousness of reality in general and, to descend to a pragmatic level, on the almost unlimited possibilities of propaganda, or of self-propaganda.[53] It should be pointed out parenthetically that the transferability of a consciousness of tradition is by no means limited to north Africa, that the phenomenon quite obviously represents one of the elements that enabled the population of the United States, heterogeneous in origin, to develop the intense feeling of cohesiveness characteristic of it.

As far as the events to be interpreted are concerned, historical proximity stands just as little in the way of myth-building as does historical remoteness. One need only consider how the pacification, the centralization, and the economic strengthening of an inordinately misruled Morocco, accomplished through the offices of the French protectorate, are reflected in the doctrine of orthodox Moroccan nationalism. In an atmosphere in which historical consciousness, weak in and of itself, is inclined to confer absolute validity on the past in the service of not yet thoroughly secularized expectations for the future, it is not difficult to convince the youth that Morocco—for nearly two hundred years before the French arrived a unified state hardly in more than name—had been living in propitious circumstances before the French occupation.

---

[52] Cf., as one example among many, what Bencheneb, *op. cit.*, pp. 490-491, has to say about al-Madanī.

[53] On this point cf., e.g., Desparmet, "La Réaction linguistique," p. 13 n. 27.

The educational system, even for girls, had been flourishing. The sultan had been on the point of carrying out the boldest reforms of modernism when the foreigners pinned his arms. The evils of the land stem, if not from the friendly attitude toward the Berbers displayed by the French (whose invention the customary law of the Berbers is considered to be), from the religious backwardness of the population with its superstitious devotion to saints and heads of orders. The culture of Islam, oriented on the whole in intellectual opposition to that of the West, is in itself sufficient guarantee for the mutual understanding of the different segments of the population and for the safety of religious minorities (mainly Jews in Morocco), whose lot under the pre-French regime had been enviable, as is usual under a truly Islamic system of government.[54] Delight in the self knows no bounds. The Sunnite Lebanese ʿUmar Farrukh (b. 1906) assures his readers, to whom his thoughts should already have been familiar, in just as strident a form, from other therapeutic writings, that the Arabs, once having lifted from mankind the yoke of the antique cult of the emperor, led man out of the darkness of ignorance. He claims not only that without the Arabic translations of Greek thinkers the West would never have acquired knowledge of the Hellenistic achievement, but that without them it would have been altogether impossible for the Latin-Catholic West to have established a relationship with the Greek-Orthodox East. The magnanimity, the tolerance, and the compassion of the Arabs as reflected in Arab philosophy have no equal in the West. "The greatest glory of scholarship is absolute freedom of research, a blessing that only those who lived under the shadow of the Arab empire enjoyed." The anachronism of the idea, the distortion of the Greek attitude—"Did not the Greeks condemn Socrates because he had corrupted the

---

[54] Cf. Montagne, *op. cit.*, pp. 312-313. For verse accounts of particular events that were able to shake Algerian self-confidence, see Desparmet, "Les réactions nationalitaires," *Bulletin de la Société de Géographie*, XXXIII (1932), 444-456, where the popular tradition regarding the French conquest is examined.

youth by teaching them to think?"—and the free use of the concept of an "Arab empire" are bound up with a method of "morale-building" which utilizes the prestige of science while violating its principles.[55]

[55] Farrukh, *op. cit.*, pp. 6 n. 37, 8-10. The primitive simplification of the connection between Muslim and Christian eschatology and literary technique, as manifested in the assertion that Dante, who knew not a word of Arabic, borrowed directly from al-Maʿarrī's *Risālat al-Ghufrān* (p. 22) shows, in the light of the extraordinarily vast and easily accessible literature on the problem of penetration of the *Divine Comedy* with Eastern ideas, an indifference toward the most elementary principles of research, which is explicable only on political grounds. The hasty brushwork in the comparison of Greek, medieval Western, and Islamic thought (pp. 33-34), as well as the remarks concerning the breadth of interest of Islamic science and the "academic" character of its occupation with magic and witchcraft (p. 52), stands on the same level of methodologial carelessness. That this kind of therapeutic pedagogy does not always have to be so crude follows, for example, from L. Sédar Senghor's interpretation of Negro-African aesthetics; cf. his study, "Die negro-afrikanische Ästhetik," *Diogenes* (German ed.) IV (1957), no. 16, pp. 467-485. Sédar Senghor is by no means wanting in dubious "intuitive" generalizations (even his concept of a unified Negrodom [*négritude*] is obviously political); nevertheless, he strives for knowledge of essentials, whereas Farrukh is satisfied with incidental, half-remembered tidbits. Statements such as, "The European likes to recognize the world in the reproduction of the object, which he calls 'the *sujet*'; the African wants to know the world in patterns and rhythms, as it actually is" (*ibid.*, p. 475) and his effort to derive the west African's aesthetic from his ontology and to prove its general validity as a possible artistic view of the world, are certainly subservient in the final analysis to a "propagandistic" context, but at least they have an intrinsic heuristic value, whereas Farrukh's theses are interesting only to a certain degree as *corpora delicti*. It is, however, only fair to note that some of the more radical spokesmen for *négritude* have, if anything, exceeded the uninhibitedness of Arab *idéologues* such as Farrukh. Hallucinative self-reconstructions like that of Sheikh Anta Diop or Dika Akwa with their insistence on the priority in time and rank of African civilization—the ancient Egyptians were Negroes; it is they who have civilized the world; Moses and Buddha are such Egyptian Negroes; Christianity stems from a Sudanese people; Nietzsche and Marx reflect Bantu philosophy—sadly reflect on aspirations and level of those they

Such tactics give rise to the problem as to what internal limits are to be set to Westernization as a program. Science, as an end in itself at any rate, is sanctioned only outside the psychologically sensitive sphere of life. On science, ancillary no longer to theology but to the view of the self, obligations are imposed which, when given positive application, find expression in an opportunism that is all too narrow for Western taste. In the report of a Muslim participant concerning an international seminar on "Islam in the Modern World," which took place in Karachi (Pakistan) in January, 1959, we read this passage: "[Formerly Western scholarship] . . . made frontal attacks on Islam and the Prophet and drew confident comparisons with Christianity and Christ." (Unfortunately, this judgment on Western Oriental studies of the last century is still in vogue, though it actually fits but a small number of English and French representatives.) "Muslims have since learnt to repel these attacks. Their knowledge —English-educated Muslims' knowledge—of Islamic sources has much improved. They are able to expound Islamic theory and to attack Western theory in language which the West [alone] until now has spoken and understood. The new approach [of Western Orientalists] has completely dispensed with such direct attacks. Instead, [the West] . . . has adopted the approach of social science. The new approach is concerned not to criticise, confute or contradict, but only to understand. It seeks to relate social facts to their relevant social antecedents. But to some Pakistan participants, the result still smacked of

mean to carry away. For a concise survey of approaches to culture and religion in the new nationalisms cf. the dense pages of R. Emerson, *From Empire to Nation. The Rise to Self-Assertion of Asian and African Peoples* (Cambridge, Mass., 1962), pp. 149-169 and 378-396, esp. 153-158.

Some two years after this paragraph was written there appeared the comprehensive survey and analysis of French-African Negro writing by Lilyan Kesteloot, *Les écrivains noirs de langue française: naissance d'une littérature* (Brussels, 1963), a most informative introduction to mentality, ideology and achievement of *négritude*.

intellectual hostility." [56] In other words, orthodox circles primarily, but also modernistic circles, feel that the application of Western research methods is a misuse when the results contradict the view of the object which is, from their standpoint, psychologically necessary.[57] Where-

---

[56] *CCF* [*Congress for Cultural Freedom*] *Newsletter* (Paris), March 3, 1959, p. 2; the author is Professor Q. M. Aslam of Karachi University, Pakistan.

[57] In connection with a report on the International Islamic Colloquium of Lahore (Dec. 29, 1957-Jan. 8, 1958), C. A. O. van Nieuwenhuijze has probed deeply into the differences in assumptions with which Western and Muslim participants approach such a conference: "Frictions between Presuppositions in Cross Cultural Encounters," *Bulletin d'information*, Centre pour l'étude des problèmes du monde musulman contemporain, Bruxelles, V (1958), 38-67; the essay was published independently in *Publications on Social Change*, Institute of Social Studies, The Hague, XII (1958). Reports have also been made on the colloquium by, among others, R. Paret, "Das islamische Colloquium in Lahore (29. Dezember 1957 bis 8. Januar 1958)," *Die Welt des Islams*, n.s., V (1958), 228-234, and G. E. von Grunebaum, "Rückblick auf drei internationale islamische Tagungen," *Der Islam*, XXXIV (1959), 138-149 (English trans. in *Swiss Review of World Affairs*, VIII/2-3 [May-June, 1958]). The problem of communication between religious communities of different cultural backgrounds has been examined in some detail by W. C. Smith, "Comparative Religion: Whither—and Why?" in *The History of Religions. Essays in Methodology*, ed. M. Eliade and J. M. Kitagawa (Chicago, 1959), pp. 31-58. The difficulty of Muslims in making contact with non-Muslims has been almost too sharply characterized by C. Lévi-Strauss (*Tristes tropiques* [Paris, 1955], pp. 434-437), who speaks of the *équivoque* of the commended tolerance and of the inner drive toward polytheism. Contact with nonbelievers is somewhat disquieting for Muslims; to be endured, it requires continual self-restraint. Lévi-Strauss sees Islam as a "grande religion qui se fonde moins sur l'évidence d'une révélation que sur l'impuissance à nouer des liens au dehors. En face de la bienveillance universelle du bouddhisme, du désir chrétien de dialogue, l'intolérance musulmane adopte une forme inconsciente chez ceux qui s'en rendent coupable; car s'ils ne cherchent pas toujours, de façon brutale, à amener autrui à partager leur vérité, ils sont pourtant (et c'est plus grave) incapables de supporter l'existence d'autrui comme autrui. Le seul moyen pour eux de se mettre à l'abri du doute et de l'humiliation consiste dans une 'néantisation' d'autrui considéré comme témoin d'une autre foi et d'une autre conduite. La fraternité islamique

upon such "dialogues" in the East ultimately boil down simply to finding recognition "on its own terms" from the West.[58]

History is finding or giving meaning. For historical meaning to be intellectually and politically effective, an overt orientation must be recognized. The goal of this orientation is accepted as an article of faith. Self-exertion to reach the goal, though it may be expressed as nothing more than eager yet patient waiting, is obligatory for the believer. Whether the goal is to rebuild the blessed days of Islamic origins, or to achieve the ideal conditions of a perfection never yet attained, the nature of the goal and the justification for setting it represent the formulation of a hypothesis of the nature of man, of the world, or of God. Discovery of goals in the form of rediscovery, along

---

est la converse d'une exclusive contre les infidèles qui ne peut pas s'avouer, puisqu'en se reconnaissant comme telle équivaudrait à les reconnaître eux-mêmes comme existants." This analysis can be accepted as correct only if one concedes that the impermeability of the other "great religions"—which in Hinduism and Judaism is manifested chiefly as social exclusiveness—in spite of their ability to relate themselves to other faiths, is a problem yet to be solved.

[58] Cf. H. L. Mikoletzky in *Österreichische Hochschulzeitung*, X/17 (Nov. 1958), 1*a*: "Whenever there is talk among us of a better understanding of the East, it is probably a covert form of asking an existential acceptance of the East and its current political demands." The detailed study by Muḥammad al-Bahay on the connection between Muslim modernism and Western colonialism, *al-Fikr al-islāmī al-ḥadīth wa-ṣilatu-hu bi'l-istiʿmār al-gharbī* (Cairo, 1376/1957), is characteristic of the search for nefarious political backgrounds for each intellectual movement, which obsesses many Islamic circles, not only in Egypt. One notes further in this connection the observation of Jacques Berque, "L'Inquiétude arabe des temps modernes," *Revue des études islamiques*, 1958, I, 87-107, on p. 100: "La domination occidentale avait . . . tiré une sorte d'authenticité, et à coup sûr, son efficacité, d'une emprise scientifique sur ses 'champs d'action.' Aussi les sciences sociales participent-elles aux yeux d'un Oriental, d'une certaine compromission avec l'*Istiʿmār*. Il est vrai que les efforts sont prodigués par les responsables pour lutter contre ces assimilations ruineuses." Without question, however, recognition of the social sciences must precede recognition of the reality of the social milieu.

with innovation in the form of renovation, seems to be, in accordance with the structure of the human spirit, the most effective mode and interpretation of the purpose of collective action. It is to be understood in this sense when a mythical primary cause is exhibited in the basic themes of the Arab self-view, those assumptions decked out in the raiment of historical knowledge, with whose help the battle for Westernization is fought. Power that stirs the historical act through its ties with the past has been used by every culture; how far, in the long run, this power can be derived from a fictional past remains to be seen.

Whenever the Arab world chooses no longer to be satisfied with Islam as its great hope—and a nation cannot regenerate without hope—[59] it must reach back toward the past. And it must fashion the data of history on the basis of history's capacity to repeat itself in the service of present aspirations. When the data of history do not suffice, a history like that of Algeria, for example, must be created as the basis for and the projection of the national unity that is to be won. Muḥammad Ḥusain Haikal (1888-1956) has aptly said: "A nation lives only so long as it permits its past to live again." [60] That the possession of a history or, better, that the vitality of its history determines the vitality of a nation is a conviction generally accepted in the Arab domain. The 1938 Brussels congress of Arab students in Europe defined the "Arab movement" as "the new Arab renaissance which is always astir in the Arab nation; it is animated by the impulses of its glorious history, its unique vitality, and its legitimate interest in the present and the future." [61] The position of a cultural

[59] Cf. Ḥasan al-Bannāʾ in *Orient*, IV (1957), 45.

[60] Quoted by ʿAbd ar-Raḥmān al-Jīlālī (b. 1906), *Taʾrīkh al-Jazāʾir al-ʿāmm* (Algiers, 1373/1954), in Bencheneb, *op. cit.*, p. 496 n. 27.

[61] *Kitāb al-muʾtamar: al-Qaumiyya ʾl-ʿarabiyya: ḥaqīqatu-hā, ahdāfu-hā, masāʾilu-hā* (Beirut, 1939), pp. 13-14; the crucial passage is reproduced in C. Rabin, *Arabic Reader* (London, 1947), p. 144. Cf. further, e.g., Farrukh, *op. cit.*, p. vii n. 37, and the north African historians whose works Bencheneb has

phenomenon within the myth determines the originality that must be granted or denied it. When Muslim scholars resist acknowledging the survival of pre-Islamic (e.g., Byzantine or Roman) elements in the canon law,[62] their stand is just as deeply rooted in the dogma of the ultimate originality of Islam as is the assertion that the incisive reforms of our times mean essentially a reversion to the

---

analyzed. Attacks on Arab history, i.e., the belittling of its cultural achievement, are construed as an attempt to undermine the Arab nation; cf., e.g., Farrukh, *op. cit.*, pp. vii-viii. With reference to O. Hatzfeld's study, "Les peuples heureux ont une histoire. Étude malgache," *Cahiers du Monde non chrétien,* XVI (1950), 387-403, G. Balandier, "La Situation coloniale: approche théorique," *Cahiers internationaux de sociologie,* XI (1951), 44-79, has alluded, on pp. 60-61, to the fact that the colonizers' desire for self-assertion may utilize disparagement of the history of the native-born in order to prevent pride in being Malagasy, for example, and to the rise of nationalism based on this sentiment. Here, certainly, it may be pointed out that knowledge of the fact of a cultural lag vis-à-vis the West contributes to the eventual attempt of the native to deprecate his culture and is, at the very least, partly responsible for the cramped intensity of the revaluation. With regard to the Malagasy, Hatzfeld establishes further a lack of perspective in the linear-causal as well as the synchronous order of remembered events. What the Malagasy, like other people living outside the sphere of a clearly oriented consciousness of history, possess is less a history than a collective memory. According to Hatzfeld's distinction, history sticks essentially to events, that is, to changes, whereas collective thought concerns itself with intervals of stability: "Un groupe essaye de se rappeler plutôt ce qu'il a été que ce qu'il a fait, et surtout que ce qu'il a subi. Le groupe cherche à garder conscience de lui-même, de sa propre continuité, malgré les transformations apparentes et quelles que soient les circonstances" (p. 393; cf. further pp. 395-396). How differently the psychological role of history presents itself in a more stable cultural situation may be intimated with the words of Goethe (*Dichtung und Wahrheit,* Book 17; ed. Hanser p. 564): "Es entsteht ein allgemeines Behagen, wenn man einer Nation ihre Geschichte auf eine geistreiche Weise wieder zur Erinnerung bringt; sie erfreut sich der Tugenden ihrer Vorfahren und belächelt die Mängel derselben, welche sie längst überwunden zu haben glaubt."

[62] Cf. E. Tyan, "Méthodologie et sources du droit en Islam," *Studia Islamica,* X (1959), 79-109, on p. 81.

pristine era of Islam.[63] But Rabindranath Tagore's admonition remains unheard: "The educated Indian attempts to draw from history lessons for today which contradict the lessons of our ancestors. The East tries to appropriate a history that is not even the product of its own life." [64]

Arab nationalism is, as it were, divided between the champions of the primacy of politics and the champions of the primacy of culture. One could lay aside this division as simply a disagreement over the tactics to be employed, if it were not the symptom and the result of a process of intellectual development, and if it did not suggest a crisis in which only too many of the politically most important exponents of this nationalism have involved themselves. A further word of Tagore's may be cited as description and critique of this attitude, in which its very universality in the intellectual reaches of national movements is demonstrated: "The great majority of Indian nationalists of today is of the opinion . . . that we can apply all our creative energy in a political direction. We are not in the least aware that our present helplessness goes back to social inadequacies. . . . Therefore for all our misfortunes and inadequacies we assign the responsibility to those historical events which have suddenly broken in upon us from outside." Tagore has only contempt for "those among us who labor under the delusion that political freedom will make us free." [65]

The chimera of absolute independence, an independence that, it is true, seems unconcerned by the indispensability of foreign economic assistance, but resents each expression of the desire for discipline in international relations, screens, as it were, political demands from a consciousness

---

[63] For the concept of myths, cf., e.g., Van der Leeuw, *op. cit.*, pp. 133-134, 140, 143-144, 214-215, and F. Böhm, "Mythos, Philosophie, Wissenschaft," *Zeitschrift für deutsche Kulturphilosophie*, III (1937), 57-94, on p. 81.

[64] *Nationalismus* (München, 1921), pp. 132-133. The English original appeared in 1917.

[65] *Ibid.*, pp. 152-153.

of their insecure cultural substructure. First of all, only with full realization of nationalistic goals will a new and progressive philosophy be necessary.[66] Again and again "complete independence" is postulated as the prerequisite to serious intellectual endeavor. Only when no trace whatsoever of foreign influence remains on Arab soil can there be any real progress in matching the economic pace set by other nations. And only with the success of this endeavor will the Arabs be qualified to occupy an appropriate international position. This position once attained, the Arabs will be able to demonstrate the full measure of their capability and to contribute to the progress of mankind as they have done in days gone by.[67]

The concept that "liberation" will automatically release cultural creativeness has its parallel in the belief that the establishment of a Pan-Arab empire will in itself guarantee intellectual resurgence. The expansiveness of the political system becomes a stipulation to rivalry with the West and above all to intellectual penetration of the intrinsic and extrinsic uncertainties of Arabism.[68] The intellectual unproductivity of this attitude represents, in a certain sense, a counterpart to the philosophical unproductivity of Islamic reform movements. The perception that behind this gospel of the primacy of politics is concealed a feeling of weakness has caused N. A. Fāris, for example, to adopt a diametrically opposed position in which not only the priority assigned to cultural activity, but above all the

---

[66] Muḥammad Mandūr, editor of the Communist newspaper *ash-Sharq* in Cairo; cf. *MIDEO,* IV (1958), 348. The Greeks to whom this outlook brought political ruin would have sympathized. Polybius, *Historiae,* xviii, 41, 5, spoke representatively when he called "the attainment of sovereignty a thing than which nothing greater or more splendid can be named" (trans. W. R. Paton, *Loeb Classical Library,* V, 177).

[67] From an Arabic brochure by an anonymous author, published by the Société arabe in Cairo, and translated under the title "Que veulent les Arabes?" in *Orient,* V (1958), 171-180. The train of thought discussed in the text is found on p. 180. For the brochure, cf. M. Colombe, "Les fins économiques et sociales du nationalisme arabe d'aujourd'hui," *ibid.,* pp. 87-90.

[68] Cf. also Tütsch, *op. cit.,* p. 130 n. 4.

denial of the assertion that independence is a goal in itself, are noteworthy:

Now there are people who will say: "Gently, my friend. Before all these [social and cultural] reforms can be tackled, we must strive for political independence." As for me, I say that the political problem looms so large before us because it lies so close to our hearts, but that our economic, educational, and spiritual problems are of greater magnitude. So long as our minds have not been freed from the ignominy of spiritual slavery, such as that inherent in passive trust in God (*al-ittikāliyya*), intellectual independence will be inaccessible to us and the road to intellectual independence will stretch out unpaved before us. So long as our modern way of life is borrowed (*manqūl*), and our thoughts are those of others, the intellectual foundation of our political independence will be unsteady. To attack intellectual independence, we must secure our educational independence and fulfill our historical development, neither of which will be achieved without national, compulsory schools.

These then are the intellectual foundations of our political independence. Its material foundation is economic independence, without which political independence remains a figment of the imagination—a dream. . . .

I am not of the opinion that independence is an end in itself; rather, it is a means of attaining other goals, such as sharing freely in shaping history and creating a part of world civilization. What, then, is the goal to which *ʿurūba* aspires or must aspire?

The service that *ʿurūba* has performed for the world and the part that it has contributed to civilization lie in the realm of thought and the spirit. And I believe that the services of *ʿurūba* to the world of the future must not deviate from the realm of thought and the spirit, for therein the genius of the Arabs reveals itself and *ʿurūba* finds its ideal instrument. It is futile, then, to try to imitate the West in its material culture; failure is our lot if we do try. But in the realm of thought and the spirit there are at present, as there were in the past, wide horizons for us to explore and open skies through which we can soar like our ancestors of yore, illuminating with their light the paths of man, dispersing the shadows of the earth, as guidance for the world.[69]

With equal trenchancy Ben Mīlād rejects the view that the question of the future Arab culture and of the means of developing it is to be tackled only after settling the political problems. If he sees even more acutely than Fāris the connection between *thaqāfa* (culture) and *siyāsa* (politics), this connection is anything but a legitimate basis for deferring cultural endeavor.[70] When Bennabi chances to hear, in regard to his proposal for improving the lot of Muslim women in Algeria, the remark that political liberation of Algerian men is prerequisite to solving the question of women, he states laconically that this trend of thought "caractérise typiquement tout l'esprit politique algérien et toutes les erreurs que nous lui devons." It is clear, moreover, that the solution of England's political problems has not of itself brought the English problem of women closer to solution.[71]

Imperialism and/or colonialism as an alibi, the necessity of a humane revival as a preliminary stage of a political revival, and the primacy of civilization over politics, are the three points that one may perhaps lay down as the main ideas of Bennabi's analysis of the Islamic situation, mainly in north Africa. "Without civilization there is no history, for a people that no longer has its culture no longer has its history." "If one wants to define a culture pedagogically (i.e., nonhistorically), one must describe its goals and state its methods." Culture is not a science in and of itself, "but a theory of the common possessions of a nation in all its variety and its entire social stratification." Therefore, a productive culture must encompass four spheres of problems: "(*a*) A religious ethic for defining a common mode of conduct; (*b*) an aesthetic for defining common taste; (*c*) a system of logic for defining common

[69] *al-ʿArab al-aḥyāʾ*, pp. 110-111.
[70] *Op. cit.*, pp. 39, 43.
[71] Bennabi, *Renaissance*, pp. 70-71.

procedures; (*d*) a technique that is adapted to each of these categories." [72]

The lack of a culture of this kind is a mark of what Bennabi calls post-Almohade man ("l'homme post-almohadien"), who has not changed since the collapse of the Almohade dynasty of north Africa, to which Bennabi assigns the arbitrary date of 1369 (probably an error for 1269). Since the fourteenth century the Muslim has slumbered. Worse yet, he has reconciled himself to the dichotomy between thought and action; the confusion of seeming with being has become for him a custom, a necessity of life. Herein lies the reason that the north African imitates the European but does not try to understand him; takes his examinations in the West but does not study the West and returns home unchanged except in the most superficial way. From the perfection of Islam the perfection of the Muslim has been deduced; the assumed perfection of the Muslim order renders effort to improve it meaningless—one lives the evangel of stagnation. For hundreds of years the north African Muslim has made no invention, be it nothing more significant than the lengthening of the short stick by which the Algerian housewife is clamped to her broom in ceaseless toil. The blissfully accepted self-deceit of the poetry of words, of "*quantitisme*," and the readiness to transfer the spiritual-intellectual habits of Maraboutism, the cult of the saints, to politics still mark the north African Muslim as standing under the curse of the breach that has haunted the Muslim world since the Battle of Ṣiffīn (in the civil war between ʿAlī and Muʿāwiya in 657), and may perhaps be described as the substitution for an ever-deepening interiorization of the "thinning" effect of expansion. One must aver at present that those who achieved this expansion were the very ones who adhered to the pre-Islamic order in intellectual as well as social matters.

But one thing must be recognized above all. Colonialism is not a political whim but a historical necessity. One

---

[72] *Ibid.*, pp. 51-52.

succumbs to colonization only when one is colonizable. And one does not cease to be colonized before one ceases to be colonizable. Does not the Koran (sura 13:12) state that God changes the status of a nation only when it has changed its spiritual bearing? The Egyptians teach that rights are not given but wrested. Like so much else that comes out of Egypt and is ostensibly a cultural value, this conception proves to be wholly erroneous. Rights are neither gift nor plunder; they correspond directly to the obligation that a nation assumes. Not to be circumvented is the law that states: "Transforme ton âme et tu transformes ton histoire." In Europe, where man is established (*colon*), social maladies may be cured by modifying institutions; in Algeria, where man is colonizable, what matters is the curing of man. In the failure to recognize this state of affairs lies the weakness of Muslim reform movements in north Africa, which are all too readily satisfied by remolding *accidentia*.[73]

A similar state of uneasiness over the meaning and the content of allegiance to Arabism may be perceived, though none too frequently, in representatives of the Arab East. The entanglement of opinions and trends from which *ʿurūba* suffers is, of course, not at all surprising in the first phases of a newly evolving national consciousness. Still, the lack of restraint which characterizes the internal dispute is of significance. "There can be no room for doubt," declares the Syrian academician Ḥikmat Hāshim, "that this implacable furor attaches not the least significance to the elementary principles of logic and that it

[73] This summary applies on the whole to Bennabi's books, *Renaissance* and *Vocation,* in their entirety; in particular, quotations and allusions were gleaned from *Renaissance,* pp. 21-23, with *Vocation,* pp. 32-33, 82-86; *Renaissance,* p. 43, with *Vocation,* pp. 35-39; *Renaissance,* p. 35, with *Vocation,* pp. 23-24; and *Vocation,* pp. 75, 76-82. Bennabi's originality comes out particularly by comparison with religiously oriented authors who demand moral reversion to an "Islamic" state of mind; one thinks, e.g., of Sayed Kotb (Sayyid Quṭb), *Social Justice in Islam,* trans. by J. B. Hardie (Washington, D.C., 1953), p. 249. (The Arab edition first appeared in Cairo in 1945.)

declines to respect the ethical views of mankind." In order to purify and thereby to fructify *ʿurūba,* Hāshim seeks principles for a "coherent philosophical system" that will do equal justice to the thoughts, the beliefs, and the life of the nation. The five principles or, better, articles of belief or axioms which Hāshim adduces probably do not bear philosophical scrutiny, but they are important as concise statements of a controversial view of the self. The belief in the mind and in science, as well as the utility of productive work (principles 1 and 4), stands next to the assertion that the Arabs are "bearers of a message" (principle 5). More important, however, is the warning sounded in the discussion of the second principle, the "belief in a resolute *ʿurūba,*" that to be recognized as an Arab according to language, culture, and intellectual inheritance is meaningful in a deeper sense only if this knowledge of the self is felt to be an obligation. Arab nationalism "stands wide open" (principle 3); that is, it is a humanism of a liberal and universalistic stamp. This intrinsically somewhat imprecise conception of the essence of Arabism is interpreted as the obligation to strive for cultural and artistic achievements. It involves a process of exchange, of give and take, in which material desires are justified only on the basis of spiritual values.[74]

Far more explicitly has the eminent Lebanese writer Mikhāʾīl Nuʿaima (Naimy; b. 1889) dared to question Arab national sentiment as an end in itself. Of what avail is it for the Arabs to win back their homeland so long as it is threatened with collapse? "It would be a crime against the truth to ascribe all the ruin and misfortune which surround the Arab homeland to colonialism as one knows it today." "For standing at the side of foreign colonialism there is an internal colonialism" with which it is much more difficult to cope. "This colonialism has come to us neither from the West nor from the East. It springs from the depths of our existence. . . ." "*ʿUrūba* is no pana-

[74] H. Hachem, "Idées et croyances," trans. into French by A. Miquel from the monthly *al-ʿArabī,* II (Kuwait, 1958), in *Orient,* IX (1959), 93-97, esp. pp. 95-96.

cea." "It is not ʿ*urūba* that will give us health, or make the nomads sedentary; in short, it is not the key to all the problems confronting the Arab." It is a matter of concern that the irate answer that an unidentified nationalist has given Nuʿaima reflects the sentiment of the majority of leading political and journalistic circles. For these groups, self-criticism is intolerable. "We shall never cease to affirm that all our unhappiness, all our afflictions originate solely in colonialism." "We say to the professor [i.e., to Nuʿaima] that 'Arabism' is the panacea. . . . Arabism is the watchword of the Arabs who want to free themselves of Western colonialism; for Western colonialism is the single cause of ignorance, poverty, and sickness; Western colonialism alone is responsible for the diseases rampant in the Arab lands, and the bloody tragedy called Palestine." [75] The sterile passion of this self-view closes the circle with the vehement blindness of an Anwar as-Sādāt in confrontation with the West.

The word that arouses the most inflammatory passions in the Arab world, comparable to the electrifying effect of words like freedom and democracy in other cultural realms, is *qaumiyya*, a neologism coined about 1930. Derived from *qaum*—people, relatives, tribal or group associates, folk, nation—*qaumiyya* has no religious associations. Its meaning fluctuates and cannot be unequivocally defined. *Qaumiyya* may denote membership in a nation as well as the consciousness of such membership, but at the same time it may mean the national characteristics of a community living in a multiplicity of political unities and, finally, the nation organized as a state. Through its ambiguity the term reflects the plight of Arabism, which in the eyes of its leading advocates (though not, especially in the West, of all of them) represents a people whose homogeneity should find tangible expression in cohesiveness in state affairs. This unity of Arabism is based on the

[75] Mikhāʾīl Nuʿaima (Naīma), "L'arabisme, oui, mais . . . ," with the reply of an unknown author, "L'arabisme sans mais," trans. into French by J.-P. Pegairolles from *al-ʿArabī* II (1958), in *Orient*, IX (1959), 99-103, 105-108, esp. pp. 99-101, 106.

unity of its language, its historical experience, and its cultural life; on feelings of solidarity; and on the destiny of the community. Arab *qaumiyya* is directed toward battle, externally, in the service of liberation and unification of Arab lands and, internally, in the service of social justice and economic prosperity.[76]

Maḥmūd Taimūr (b. 1894), who has described Arab nationalism as the symbol both of the suffering that has made the Arab world vigilant and of the hope that inspires it to battle, has expressed the emotional-cognitional character of *qaumiyya* in the terse formula that, for Arabs, *qaumiyya* is "the prophecy of our era." [77] The older generation, and those young intellectuals for whom the primacy of politics is doubtful, are disturbed on the one hand by the aggressiveness and the exclusiveness of *qaumiyya* and, on the other, by the uncertainty of the relationship between it and the Islamic community, the *umma*. Thus Ṭāhā Ḥusain states that by turning against the Western tradition within which religious unity had given rise to national unity, "doubtless Islam gave birth to Arab nationalism; but Arab civilization was the product of genuine, loyal coöperation of Muslims and non-Muslims, whether they were Christians or Jews." [78] Suhair Qalamāwī, who in 1936 became the first female faculty member of Cairo University, has explained how Arab nationalism derived its unity from Islam, and therefore from religion, but how, in various phases, the concept later became bound up with the geographical homeland of the Arabs, the Islamic state, and Islamic culture. Since the close of the past century this nationalism has begun once more to come to terms with the Islamic religion, a process in which its frequent opposition to religion on the question of its original re-

---

[76] Cf. the remarks of J. Monset in *Orient*, V (1958), 44-45, where the definition and/or programmatic description of *qaumiyya* formulated by the Third Congress of Arab Writers is translated.

[77] *MIDEO*, IV, 339.

[78] *Ibid.*, p. 341.

ligious basis should not deceive us.[79] The effort of those interested in culture to defend the freedom of intellectual activity and of literature in particular against the onslaught of political pragmatism and its enslavement to trends of the moment (as is required in the communistic world especially), is unmistakable when Mme. Qalamāwī asserts: "Arab nationalism is a literary force and only then a weapon or a policy. It is a glorious reality and only then a means or a tool." [80] On the basis of the same attitude, the Tunisian Maḥmūd al-Masʿadī (Mahmoud Messadi, b. 1911; since May 1, 1958, secretary of state in the Tunisian Ministry of Education) demands for writers "freedom that is opposed to every surrender to 'guided' ideas, to every form of totalitarianism. The degree of his freedom determines the intensity of the relations that man maintains with his equals and with all others." [81] The attacks to which this position has been subjected show, of course, that in the narrowest sense "guided" cultural activity is more in conformity with the trend of the time in the Arab lands, at least in the East.

That the standard literary language represents the most powerful instrument of national development has been universally recognized for centuries. The fight against the vernacular, which both in Egypt and the Maghreb had the capacity almost to saturate the traditional literary language with local elements (in Algeria of the eighteenth and nineteenth centuries, just as in the time of Ibn Khaldūn, a popular literature was cultivated), is built, as it were, into Arab patriotism. The passion for "pure" Arabic is just as much a matter of religion as of national sentiment. "The *ʿarabiyya* and dogma are twins, Siamese twins. . . . Neither can survive without the other." [82] The

---

[79] "La critique littéraire et le nationalisme arabe," *MIDEO*, IV (1957), 262-268, on p. 264.

[80] *Ibid.*, p. 268 (concluding paragraph).

[81] *MIDEO*, IV, 349.

[82] *Balāgh* (Algiers), Oct. 21, 1930, in Desparmet, "La réaction linguistique," p. 12 n. 27.

special genius (*ʿabqariyya*), which every nation possesses,[83] has coined its own language and is encompassed by it. The insistence on language as a legitimate basis of Arab unity underscores the openness of Arab *qaumiyya*, which repudiates no one, whatever his belief, so long as he acknowledges speaking the mother tongue common to the Arabs. All the more surprising is the support of Communist intellectuals for the vernacular, a position which, if successful, would sacrifice Arab unity to the alleged interests of local substrata or, at best, to regional particularism, and then would find itself confronted with the task of developing the dialect of the country in question into a cultural language.[84]

From life to experience, from experience to reflection, from reflection to formulation—a long road, difficult to follow; doubly difficult when interpretation and form are not at one's disposal but must be worked out and are given neither goal nor tools in advance; frequently more difficult still when impatience and political passion tend to commit perception to partial truth. It is probably for this reason that Westernization, the battle of two cultures for the minds of individuals, has only recently become a literary problem. The Moroccan Driss Chraibi has described the flight of a young intellectual from his own milieu and the disintegration of a north African of constricted background who emigrated to France, has shown a son from a "traditional" home making his way in a European way of life and in European politics, and has sketched the mentality of the different generations (in a not too subtle antithesis). By means of the perhaps too transparent symbol of the physical drowsiness of his main figure, the Egyptian Albert Cossery of a Syrian-Christian family has tried to make credible the insurmountable in-

[83] Zuraiq, *op. cit.*, p. 189.

[84] Dr. Mandūr's position at the Cairo Writers' Congress is characteristic of the Communist attitude, and the unanimous opposition of even leftist writers attests to the dominant role of the standard language in general Arab consciousness; cf. *MIDEO*, IV, 342.

decisiveness and the fear both of fundamental change and of the full development of power inherent in an Egyptian milieu, though without finding from his observations a key to cultural change and cultural assimilation. The leftist Egyptian Muslim ʿAbd ar-Raḥmān ash-Sharqāwī has concerned himself with the problem of moral stagnation and inner vacuity, which, for individuals, are only too often the most palpable results of cultural schism. The hopelessness of a life between two worlds and the dependence of the success of acculturation on Western approval become extremely clear in the description sketched by the Tunisian Albert Memmi (b. 1920) of the breakdown of a young Tunisian Jew who cannot culminate his Westernization by being fully accepted by the French and who, in the end, turns his back on a career in the Western style and emigrates to South America. Where Memmi's fictional character Alexandre Mordecai Benillouche failed, the living Malik Bennabi seems to have succeeded; though acknowledging (occasionally misunderstood) Western values, realizing the necessity of renovating Muslim society, and even conceding a higher value to the European achievement of the last century as opposed to the achievement and the potential of contemporaneous Muslim society, Bennabi has been able to feel at one with his Muslim milieu. Even though one may be reminded occasionally of the doctrinaire and sentimental determination of the *narodnik*, even though in many respects Bennabi's Islam and his Europe border on fiction, he maintains his standpoint as an Algerian Muslim without—as the Frenchman in culture which he undoubtedly is—losing himself to and in France and her civilization.[85]

[85] Driss Chraibi, *Le Passé simple* (Paris, 1954), and *Les Boucs* (Paris, 1955); the rest is in his *De tous les horizons* (Paris, 1958), pp. 23-37, esp. pp. 32-33; A. Cossery, *The Lazy Ones* (Norfolk, Conn., n.d.); ʿAbd ar-Raḥmān ash-Sharqāwī, *Qulūb khāliya* (Cairo, 1957); A. Memmi, *La Statue de sel* (Paris, 1953). Mouloud Feraoun (1913-1962), in his novels *Le Fils du pauvre* (Paris, 1950) and *La Terre et le sang* (Paris, 1953), has succeeded in representing the contact and interpenetration between modern forms of development and life with Berber tribal

Roughly speaking, the tragedy of the person who has adopted Western culture is twofold. First, from the standpoint of the West: the greater the success of Westernization (unplanned, on the whole, before it gets under way),

---

life in the Haute-Kabylie, his home. For Bennabi's point of view, see his *Vocation*, pp. 70-74, 109-120, 127 ff., 151, 152-156, 158-159. His judgment of the weaknesses of the Islamic renaissance merits quoting: "L'aspect actuel de la renaissance musulmane est celui d'un mélange de goûts, de velléités, d'hésitations, voire d'attitudes pharisiennes. Actuellement elle est surtout marquée par le fait qu'elle a adopté des 'objets' et des 'besoins' au lieu de 'notions' et de 'moyens.'"

The closing scene of Chraibi, *Les Boucs* (pp. 193-194), contains a description, unsurpassable in its conciseness, of the breach between traditional and Western mentality; the tragic decrees of fate inherent in this breach become fully understandable when one focuses on the circumstances in which the north African heroes of this book live in Paris:

"Un petit Berbère cirait des souliers à Bône. Ils étaient noirs et appartenaient à un prêtre.

"Comment t'appelles-tu? lui demanda le prêtre.

"Yalann Waldik ('May your father be cursed'), dit le Berbère.

"Que fais-tu et quel âge as tu, mon enfant?

"Je suis cireur et j'ai dix ans.

"Le prêtre poussa un soupir.

"Dans dix ans, que seras-tu, je te le demande?

"Dans dix ans, je serai un cireur de vingt ans, si Dieu le veut.

"Le prêtre se mit en colère.

"Considère, mon enfant, dit-il. Si tu étais en France, tu apprendrais déjà le latin et le grec et dans dix ans tu serais un homme.

"Longtemps, le petit Berbère le regarda, stupéfait. Pour la première fois, il calcula, supputa, supposa. Puis il ferma sa boîte de cireur comme on ferme la porte d'un passé—et s'en alla. Il persuada son père de vendre son dernier bouc, lui expliquant qu'avec le prix de ce bouc il en pourrait acheter mille, dans dix ans. Et il s'embarqua vers la France.

"Et le prêtre dit à voix haute:

"J'ai sauvé une âme."

The traditional way of life, it may be remarked perhaps somewhat out of context, has found an extraordinarily precise presentation in a popular Algerian poem of the last part of the nineteenth century, which gives an explanation, uncommon for its pithiness, of what seems essential to the contemporary in his conduct of life; the poem has been translated by Desparmet, "Les réactions nationalitaires. IV," pp. 48-49. (That the works cited

the greater the political resistance to the West, but all the greater, too, the resistance to every feature of full Westernization, the political utility of which is not immediately discernible. The political retreat of the West makes Western civilization seem less satisfying; the turning back to the legacy of the past, especially the acceptance of traditional habits of thought and judgment, occurred a few decades too early to guarantee the protection of what had been achieved and what was needed to continue the political upsurge. The defense of the past, the frequently moribund habits of culture which could not die because they were not permitted to die, and the political character of this defense have led to rigidity in the view of the self as well as in the view of foreigners, rigidity that is any-

---

in the text represent only a selection of the books relevant here is self-evident, but is expressly mentioned by way of precaution.)

The tragedy of alienation and failure to reintegrate has been brushed in powerful strokes by Giuseppe Ungaretti, the great Italian poet who was born in Alexandria (1888), in his *In Memoriam*. The poem begins:

> His name
> was Mohammed Sheab
>
> Scion
> of emirs of nomads
> a suicide
> because he had
> no country
>
> He loved France
> and changed his name
> He became Marcel
> but he was not French
> and could no longer
> dwell
> in his people's tent
> where they listen
> to the Koran sing-song
> sipping coffee

Trans. Lowry Nelson, Jr., in C. L. Golino, ed., *Contemporary Italian Poetry* (Berkeley and Los Angeles, 1962), pp. 111-113.

thing but conducive to an adjustment of concurrent cultural tendencies. The individual ensnared in the process of Westernization is endangered on the one hand by the raising of the level of education in the Arab world, which, together with the freedom of political action already achieved, diminishes, paradoxically, his usefulness and especially his spiritual adjustment. On the other hand, there is not room enough in France or in America for the person who has adopted French or American culture, and when the individual does find shelter, unrestricted submission to the new spiritual-intellectual order is precluded for him through misunderstanding of the homeland, through disorder in the political sphere. It is doubtless incorrect for Arab propagandists to speak of the lack of generosity which inhibits the West from allowing Eastern peoples to share its cultural achievements, but it is true that it is difficult to draw political conclusions from a change that has taken place as a result of contact with us. The Arab, especially the Arab Muslim, finds himself in a modern house built with Western guidance in which he wants now to lead his own life without knowing exactly what is suitable for him.

Westernization is above all an act of the will. Its consummation is eminently adapted to increasing self-confidence once the justification for collective action is perceived (according, for example, to the Turkish model) in modernization as such and in the resultant participation in the Western cultural community. And yet this attitude presupposes the belief in the primacy of culture. The duality of the Arab world, which—as one feels tempted to formulate it—recoils before its intrinsic difficulties into politics, impedes that adjustment between a self-view and action, which, experienced as peace and composure, constituted the traditional Muslim mood of life.

In general, antitheses in historical life are not reconciled; they are lifted up in the agitation of events into new constellations of conflict and, from a spiritual point of view, become irrelevant. It may have been an insight of this sort which lay at the basis of Jamīl Ṣalībā's vision of a pluralistic world culture, within which the opposition of

Western and Eastern civilization loses its destructive force, and—what really counts for Ṣalībā—the conflict between the traditionalists and the advocates of radical Westernization in the Arab lands loses its emotional intensity. However superficial Ṣalībā's equating of Western and Eastern achievement, however careless his choice of historical facts, in his view the intention no doubt justifies the means. For without self-confidence sure of its possibilities, a quiet acceptance of the West on the Arabs' part is unthinkable. That Ṣalībā's warmhearted pluralism, which shows more similarity to a compromise with conflict than a triumph over it, will prove to be effective one may reasonably doubt. But as guideposts his thoughts should be very welcome indeed to an Arab world disenchanted with itself.[86]

---

[86] Jamīl Ṣalībā, "L'échange culturel entre l'Orient et l'Occident," *al-ʿArabī* (Kuwait, Dec., 1958), trans. into French by R. Jammes in *Orient*, IX (1959), 73-78, esp. pp. 75-76, 77-78. Ṣalībā, a member of the Syrian Academy, was first known through his Paris dissertation: *Études sur la métaphysique d'Avicenne* (Paris, 1926). Essentially, the debate is between those who feel that independence and political strength will, almost automatically, lead to cultural rejuvenation and hegemony, and those who have learnt from history that the durability of power not to speak of its meaning to the world as a whole is contingent on cultural preëminence already achieved or well on its way. From Athens to England, examples abound.

VII

Fall and Rise of Islam: a Self-View[1]

I

THE THEOLOGICAL CREATIVENESS of Islam is in abeyance and so, if to a less degree, is its political effectiveness (outside Pakistan). But Islam as a sense of community and as a system of values, and of mores to implement them, has remained intact, if subject to rearticulation, and active. Its self-assertion is more assured than its self-

[1] As-Sayyid Abū 'l-Ḥasan ʿAlī al-Ḥasanī an-Nadwī, *Mā dhā khasara 'l-ʿālam bi'nḥiṭāṭ al-muslimīn?* [*What Has the World Lost through the Decline of the Muslims?*] (2d ed.; Cairo 1370/1951), 255 pp. (A publication of the Jamāʿat al-Azhar li'n-nashr wa't-taʾlīf. Prefaces by Dr. Muḥammad Yūsuf Mūsà, Sayyid Quṭb, and Aḥmad ash-Sharabāṣī.) For the use of *inḥiṭāṭ* cf. Muḥassin at-Tanūkhī (d. 994), *Kitāb al-faraj baʿd ash-shidda* (Cairo, 1357/1938), II, 111$^{21-22}$, the phrase *nuqṣān al-ʿālam wa'nḥiṭāṭ al-buldān*, "the lessening of the world and the decline of the lands."

understanding. Although it seems to be groping for a self-interpretation apt to secure for it and to justify a role of leadership in our time, it does so on the basis of an image of itself as timelessly exemplary. Islam as it ought to have existed in the early days of its community life is envisaged as the leader of the world as it ought to exist tomorrow. Islam as the only definitive achievement, or gift, of history is to be the guide of a mankind that has become uncertain of itself—a metahistoric, divinely guaranteed, and hence normative core of whatever transient cultural forms it may be able to suggest to the civilized world as a means for survival and resurgence.

This faith in Islam, vague yet full of content, may not, again outside Pakistan, be subscribed to by the political and intellectual leaders of the countries commonly thought of as Muslim. But however oversimplifying or outright naïve such views may seem to them, however obnoxious their representatives will become to them in their opposition to "modernizing" reform, the mere existence of such a faith will be an encouragement and an inducement to a more positive attitude toward their nations' potentialities; in other words, it will be a temptation toward an alternative pride on which to draw when Westernization threatens to play havoc with direction and self-respect.

It is in this sense and no other that a book like Nadwī's (born in 1913) *What Has the World Lost through the Decline of the Muslims?* can be called a representative self-view of contemporary Islam. Neither its individual positions regarding the Muslim religion nor, perhaps, the almost deliberate inadequacy of the characterization of Islam's alleged antagonist, the West, will be too widely shared. But the unreflecting identification of Islam with changeless value, and the rationalization of what is not a sentiment but a knowledge of superiority, can hardly fail to meet with universal if private approval. The psychological effect on the average believer of an ultra-Muslim statement such as Nadwī's may be compared to the attitude of a moderate nationalist who will be unable completely to avoid a measure of identification with the claims and the actions of his extremist fellow national, whom yet he may in all sincerity disown or even combat.

II

The principal difference between Islam and Christianity as sociological entities is that Islam can, but Christianity can not, be viewed as a community of the "nation" type. A nationality has been defined as "a people who, because of their belief in their common descent and their mission in the world, by virtue of their common cultural heritage and historical career, aspire to sovereignty over a territory to seek to maintain or enlarge their political or cultural influence in the face of opposition." If the term "descent" be interpreted to include spiritual as well as physical kinship and the common heritage be designated as "religious and cultural," L. Wirth's definition of nationality would become a perfect description of Nadwī's concept of the nature of Islam.

The revival of Islamic power which the Indian Muslim hopes to stimulate is precisely in the nature of those "social movements, attitudes, and ideologies which characterize the behavior of nationalities engaged in the struggle to achieve, maintain, or enhance their position in the world," which are commonly known as nationalisms.[2] This self-view of Islam as a religious community that remains imperfectly realized unless it is also a political community, a view formulated some thirty years ago by Muḥammad Rashīd Riḍā (1865-1935),[3] to the effect that Islam is not

[2] L. Wirth, "Types of nationalism," *American Journal of Sociology*, XLI (1935-36), 723. (For this reference I am indebted to the late Professor J. S. Slotkin, University of Chicago.)

[3] Muḥammad Rashīd Riḍā, *Al-Khilāfa au al-imāma 'l-ʿuzmà* (Cairo, 1341/1922), p. 114$^{21-23}$; trans. H. Laoust, *Le Califat dans la doctrine de Rashīd Riḍā* (Beirut, 1938), p. 194: "Les musulmans, en effet, considèrent que leur religion n'existe véritablement que du jour où est établi un État musulman indépendant et fort, qui puisse, à l'abri de toute opposition et de toute domination étrangère, mettre en application les lois de l'Islam." Cf. also L. Gardet, *La Cité musulmane* (Paris, 1954), p. 22.

fully in being so long as it does not control politically some part of the world, is symptom and result of an unbroken continuity that connects, in fact as well as in the minds of the faithful of today, the ideology of the historical origins with that of the utopian future.

In a very profound sense the orthodox Muslim citizen of a modern state is binational. Not only is the conflict between the loyalties owed to his religious community and those owed to his nation-state potentially ever-present (to become actualized, e.g., in disputes such as that between the Egyptian government and the Muslim Brotherhood); but the rise of his nation-state is meaningful merely through the implied extension of the autonomous "domain of Islam" as an area within which the traditional law will direct and define the believer's personal life and status. The intransigence and the flexibility of Islam are those of a power system rather than of a religious movement. The *raison d'être* of the system is organization for the living out of certain spiritual injunctions, but the nature of the organization is part, or, at least, ineluctable consequence, of those injunctions themselves.

The Western world is apt to see Islam in the image of Christianity as it appears in the experience of the secular state, or again in the image of medieval Christianity which, although at certain points in control of the state, yet remained *ex professo* distinct from and superior to it. A book like Nadwī's remains largely unintelligible unless this vantage point is given up, even as the West, because of a corresponding misconception, has remained largely unintelligible to many a Muslim writer, not excluding Mr. Nadwī himself.

III

Nadwī's position may be summarized in the words of Dr. Muḥammad Yūsuf Mūsà, formerly of al-Azhar but at present a professor in the Faculty of Law of the University of Cairo, who restates in his preface the view of Sir Muḥammad Iqbāl (1876-1938) that "Islam was created to give direction to the world, human society [*al-mujtamaʿ*], and civilization." [4] The decline of Islam and its loss of world leadership were an unprecedented catastrophe not merely for the Muslims but for all the nations, for, in the author's own phrase, the Muslims were to humankind what health is to the human body.[5]

The darkness of the world into which Islam arose must be understood if its fundamental otherness is to be appreciated. Everywhere absolute rulers were exploiting the productive classes, with a materialistic upper class hoarding the treasures wrung from the poor. Christianity, either facing away from the world or losing itself in dogmatic quibbles, had become subservient to the powers of the day on which it had to rely to subdue dissenters. The Arabs themselves, though of noble disposition, were kept back by a decaying religion and a decayed morality.

The Prophet, who could have scored an easy success as a regional leader, refused to replace vanity by vanity. He did not allow himself to become a *zaʿīm waṭanī, a Führer* of the homeland. His mission was universal and it was total; that is to say, it concerned the whole world and it was meant to change human nature, not merely individual defects and abuses.[6] The effect of Islam was wondrous in that for the first time since man was created beliefs and actions no longer were divorced from each other. A puritan restraint controlled the collective as well as the individual life. The Muslim progressed from self-seeking (*anāniyya*) to service (*ʿubūdiyya*)[7] "This belief in Allah, the Messenger, and the Last Day, and this surrender to Allah and his religion, straightened the crookedness of life and put every individual in human society in his (proper) place." "Every single person in society became responsible for the whole flock." [8] Islam gave hope to man; it changed the mood of humanity into active optimism;

---

[4] Nadwī, *op. cit.*, p. 6^{4}.
[5] *Ibid.*, pp. 17-18.
[6] *Ibid.*, pp. 67-69.
[7] *Ibid.*, pp. 81-82.
[8] *Ibid.*, pp. 84^{4-5}, 85^{pult}.

it brought about, as it were, a rebirth or revival of mankind which affected individuals as it did social organisms. Under its impact the Arabs, who had lacked a constructive political tradition, were able to organize a state without any outside help. In fact, it was the world that needed them, not they who needed the world.[9]

These were the traits that qualified the Arab Muslims for universal leadership: (1) they possessed a revealed book and a divine law; (2) unlike most nations and individuals, they did not assume rulership without previous education of their character and previous cleansing of their souls; (3) they did not present themselves as executives for one particular race or country; and (4) they realized that man consists of soul and body, of reason and emotions, and thus were capable of developing a civilization in keeping with human nature.[10] In short, the companions of the Prophet were distinguished by the fact that they united "religion, morals, strength, and political ability."[11] Their victory ushered in the best period in history, that of the Rightly-Guided Caliphs, with its perfect balance of religious and political, practical and spiritual, aspirations and activities.[12] Much for the benefit of humankind Islam began to exercise a growing influence on the direction in which mankind was moving. Consciously and unconsciously the Islamic model formed views and attitudes in Christendom; standards of thought, law, the social order, and political organization were affected. In a sense, one could speak of a universal movement toward Islam. The world would have been fortunate had this tendency continued.[13]

---

[9] *Ibid.*, p. 95.

[10] *Ibid.*, pp. 96-100.

[11] *Ibid.*, p. 100$^{16-17}$.

[12] *Ibid.*, pp. 100-101. Cf. also W. C. Smith, *Pakistan as an Islamic State* (Lahore, 1951), p. 59, for the special position as Islam's most glorious period accorded to the era of the *rāshidūn* by wide circles, especially among the people in Pakistan; but see pp. 95-96 for evidence of Pakistani opposition to the *rāshidūn* myth. Gardet, *op. cit.*, p. 319 n. 2, remarks: "Très caractéristique est le culte fervent des premiers âges islamiques."

[13] Nadwī, *op. cit.*, pp. 105-109.

But with the transition from the *khilāfat ar-rāshidīn* to *al-mulūkiyya al-ᶜarabiyya*,[14] from the caliphate of the Rightly-Guided to the kingship of the Arabs, the decline set in. Deviations from Islamic fundamentals were permitted to occur which have failed of correction to this day, the most important of them the separation between faith and political conduct, *faṣl ad-dīn ᶜan as-siyāsa*,[15] which resulted in *siyāsa* becoming superior to *dīn*, and in the religious constituting themselves as a class apart from the generality of men. Pagan tendencies reappeared in government. When the rulers of Islam ceased to represent its spirit, Islam ceased to gain a hold on non-Muslim countries. In violation of the spirit of Islam, Muslim thinkers interested themselves more in metaphysics than in the useful sciences. Their accomplishments in the latter cannot compare with those of Europeans in the seventeenth and eighteenth centuries. Sects and innovations destroyed the uniqueness of true Islam. Still it must not be forgotten that throughout the Middle Ages the light of Islam continued to shine strongly: "The history of struggle (*jihād*) and renewal (*tajdīd*) in Islam is continuous with no break to cut it."[16] And despite the depth of their decline the Muslim nations have remained spiritually superior to the non-Muslim. It was the destruction of the caliphate by the Mongols which brought the decay of Islam to the notice of all. The rise of the Turks—with whose power during their heyday Nadwī is almost intoxicated—gave Islam another chance. The Turks could have surpassed Europe in the intellectual sphere but they soon fell into a state of torpor, in the sciences as well as in the arts of war. The decline of *ᶜilm* and *fikr* was not confined to the Turks but spread throughout the world of Islam. Actually, the ninth century was the last truly creative period.[17]

---

[14] Or: *mulūkiyyat al-muslimīn* (*ibid.*, p. 110).

[15] *Ibid.*, p. 114.

[16] *Ibid.*, p. 118^{8-9}.

[17] The exceptions adduced by Nadwī are to a man legists and theologians; cf. *ibid.*, p. 126.

From the sixteenth century onward Europe became stronger; but the Turks were strangely reluctant to take over the new sciences and skills, even those affecting the art of warfare. The characterization that Nadwī metes out to Europe is the conventional one of unadulterated materialism, which somewhat tiresomely has been repeated by one Muslim apologist after another;[18] and, as usual, it has been adorned with the same trappings of pseudoscientific quotations from European historians, largely obsolescent, and critics of contemporary civilization. Whether an Aḥmad Amīn (1886-1954) sees the strength of the West arising from the more adequate position accorded to women in its social arrangements,[19] or whether Nadwī sees Western ethics failing because they are confined to utilitarian or epicurean ideals,[20] or whether the defects of Western religiosity (in the Middle Ages and today) are pointed out, or the disintegrating influence on Muslim society of imported European nationalism—it is always the same mechanical concept of the West as an aggressive machinery, which at the same time is stimulated and hamstrung by its atheistic scientism, which may be coupled, as in Marxian communism, with a kind of social mysticism. The image of the West which Nadwī draws and assails is a close kin to that developed by Shaikh Ḥusain Qidwāʾī[21] and, in individual features, is a less sophisticated replica of certain ideas of Muḥammad Iqbāl's.[22] What makes Nadwī's presentation particularly distressing and even upsetting is the loss of insight which parallels the increase in apparatus and the scope of the analysis. Nadwī

[18] Cf. Gardet, *op. cit.* p. 319, on Muḥammad Iqbāl's and Muḥammad Ḥusain Haikal's condemnation of the Western world as materialist.

[19] Aḥmad Amīn, *Ḥayātī* (2d ed.; Cairo, 1952), pp. 252-253.

[20] Nadwī, *op. cit.*, p. 152.

[21] In T. Andrae, *Die letzten Dinge*, German trans. by H. H. Schaeder (2d ed.; Leipzig, 1941), pp. 116-118.

[22] On him cf. J. W. Fück, "Muḥammad Iqbāl und der indomuslimische Modernismus," in *Westöstliche Abhandlungen R. Tschudi zum 70. Geburtstag überreicht* (Wiesbaden, 1954), pp. 356-365; for our context, pp. 363-364 are particularly relevant.

confronts an Islam that is essentially outside and above history[23] with a West (or a Christianity) that exists only in history; he contrasts an idea with what to him are mere facts; and he apprehends those facts with a show of method that is vitiated by the obsoleteness of the tools as much as the lack of empathy for the structures which he undertakes to analyze.[24]

The Muslim remedy for the ills besetting the contemporary world, which, to Nadwī, are embodied in materialistic nationalism, is to unite against the real enemy, Satan. Once before in history, when the Arabs united under the impact of the message of Islam, did the fight against unbelief weld a disparate group together and made it desist from internecine struggles. Europe today is unsurpassed in inventions and discoveries. But these are not ends in themselves. They must be judged by their effect on mores and political conduct.[25] Nothing is wrong with technical progress as such. Islam sees man as "God's vicar on earth" (*khalīfat Allāh fī 'l-arḍ*); that is to say, man should make use of everything created, but he should do so in the interest of the faith.[26] The objects as such are neutral. By using them man makes them good or bad. In their irreligiousness the Europeans have nothing to guide their purpose, so they confuse means and ends (*wasāʾiṭ* and *ghāyāt*).[27] In Europe, therefore, power and science are

---

[23] Cf. the observations of J. Berque (*Annales: Économies, sociétés, civilisations*, VII [1952], 469-470) on the traditional attitude of Muslim jurisprudence: "Mais c'est qu'ils [les exposés musulmans du *fiqh*] procèdent d'une continuité dédaigneuse de toute prétention à l'exactitude locale et temporelle. Leur position se conçoit: c'est celle d'une tradition d'école, se justifiant par les grands ancêtres, mais, en fait, de ceux-ci ne prenant que son bien. Citations truquées ou déformées, jetées dans un fatras érudit, pêle-mêle d'époques et de pays: ce ne sont là que les matériaux d'un dogmatisme rétrospectif, produit de l'histoire sans doute, mais qui se sent et se veut hors de l'histoire."

[24] Cf. the particularly blatant instances, Nadwī, *op. cit.*, pp. 157-159, 163-165.

[25] *Ibid.*, p. 185.

[26] *Ibid.*, pp. 185-187.

[27] *Ibid.*, pp. 188-189.

ever growing while ethics and religion are ever declining.[28] This is why all its progress leads Europe nowhere but to suicide.[29] As European civilization is corrupt in its roots, no wholesome fruit can come of it.[30] Its dominant role is merely the consequence of the decline of Islam.[31] The spiritual damages sustained by man in the period of European colonization, and, we may add, by virtue of its power also in regions not under its direct control, are these: (1) the religious sense has become unavailing (*buṭlān al-ḥāssa 'd-dīniyya*);[32] (2) religious sentiment has declined (*zawāl al-ʿāṭifa 'd-dīniyya*);[33] (3) the rule of matter and stomach has become oppressive (*ṭughyān al-mādda wa'l-maʿida*);[34] and (4) a collapse in morals and social cohesion (*at-tadahwur fī 'l-akhlāq wa'l-mujtamaʿ*).[35]

Although the present moral decay has affected both East and West, the East has preserved its integrity better than the West.[36] Nevertheless, under the impact of Europe the whole world is moving toward another *jāhiliyya* (of materialism).[37] European ways of thinking, European philosophy, are paramount everywhere. The opponents of Europe agree with her aims and are merely waging a contest for leadership.[38] Strangely enough, many Muslims and even many Muslim states are only too eager to Europeanize in every respect. Yet the Muslim *umma* is the only power potentially capable of driving out the European spirit. The sole solution of the world crisis is thus the

[28] *Ibid.*, p. 189.
[29] *Ibid.*, p. 192.
[30] *Ibid.*, p. 199.
[31] *Ibid.*, p. 202^{9-10}.
[32] *Ibid.*, pp. 203-207.
[33] *Ibid.*, pp. 207-214.
[34] *Ibid.*, pp. 214-217.
[35] *Ibid.*, pp. 217 ff.
[36] *Ibid.*, pp. 217-218. Nadwī could still say, as did Abū ʿAbd ar-Raḥmān as-Sulamī (d. 1021) almost a thousand years ago, that "the Muslims are like one body" (*Ādāb aṣ-ṣuḥba*, ed. M. J. Kister [Jerusalem, 1954], p. 24^{1}).
[37] Nadwī, *op. cit.*, pp. 228-229.
[38] *Ibid.*, p. 229^{9-13}. The evaluation of the achievements of Asiatic nations on pp. 229-231 is rather interesting.

transfer of leadership to the Muslim world.[39] The message of Islam holds as good now as it did in the seventh century. In the words of one of ʿUmar's envoys to Yazdagird, the last Sasanian king of Iran: "God has sent us so we can lead out those he wishes from the service of the servants to the service of God alone, and from secular constraint into freedom and from the oppression of the [earlier] religions to the justice of Islam." [40] But before Islam can assume leadership once more a spiritual change must come over the Muslims, the primary symptom of which will be a resurrection of faith.[41] In addition, however, scientific leadership needs to be regained as well in this preparatory phase.[42] The Islamic world has to steep itself in the sciences, to gain mastery of technology and commerce, and also of the art of war.

In his final chapter[43] Nadwī calls on the Arab world to assume its traditional leadership (*ziʿāma*) of Islam. The religious importance of the Arabs is emphatically asserted. The present weaknesses of the Arab states do not affect the eternal function of the Arabs in the edifice of Islam. Faith will be the principal weapon of the Arab world in rebuilding itself and in readying its might. For it is the Arab world to which will fall the generalship in the final ejection of Europe; its faith, the power of its message, and divine help will assist it. "Behold the world of man looking with rapture at the world of Islam as its savior, and behold the world of Islam fixing its gaze on the Arab

---

[39] *Ibid.*, pp. 234, 232. Muḥammad Rashīd Riḍā, *Tafsīr al-Manār* (Cairo, 1346-1354/1926-1934, *IX*, 22-23, anticipated Nadwī in this regard; cf. J. Jomier, *Le Commentaire coranique du Manār* (Paris, 1954), pp. 262-264.

[40] Nadwī, *op. cit.*, p. 237$^{6-8}$; for the translation of *min ḍīq ad-dunyā ilà siʿati-hā*, cf. N. Abbott, *Perspectives on a Troubled Decade* (New York, 1950), p. 146 note *a*.

[41] Nadwī, *op. cit.*, pp. 240-241.

[42] *Ibid.*, p. 241$^{18-19}$. The observations on the "tornness" of the scientifically trained young Muslims, on pp. 243-244, are interesting.

[43] *Ibid.*, pp. 245-251. Nadwī's militancy is reminiscent of the Khāksār movement.

world as its secular and spiritual leader (*ka-zaʿīmi-hi wa-imāmi-hi*). Will the world of Islam realize the hope of the world of men (*al-ʿālam al-basharī*)? And will the Arab world realize the hope of the Muslim world?" [44]

IV

It is difficult not to be impressed with the enthusiasm that permeates Nadwī's presentation, with the drive of his unreflected conviction of the uniqueness of Islam as a religious civilization. But the admiration aroused by his *élan* soon shades off into wonderment, and thence into disappointment and a sense of futility, when one realizes that his prescription for the world is simply an injunction to return to, or, as he would say, to resurrect, a golden age that never existed.[45] Salvation by sameness, the implied belief that what worked once will always work, and the unconcerned readiness to forego the wider horizons that have been opened by man, and, for the most part, by Western man, during the last centuries—one cannot help feeling both frightened and depressed by the appeal that Nadwī's message appears to have for certain Muslim circles. The ultimate impenetrability of one civilization by another is demonstrated, unintentionally it is true, but, for that, all the more convincingly. Even as, in the late Middle Ages, orthodoxy in self-defense was prepared unhesitatingly to narrow down the scope of the Muslim experience by pushing Hellenizing philosophy and the natural sciences to the periphery, in precisely the same way, although perhaps

---

[44] *Ibid.*, p. 251[18-20] (the end of the book). On the concept of *jihād* in modern Egyptian writers, cf. Jomier, *op. cit.*, pp. 276, 279, 280-281. Recently, Nadwī has defined "the Jihad of today, the greatest need of the present hour," as the repelling of the "storm of atheism" which has set in as a consequence of certain thought tendencies set in motion by Western attitudes; cf. "Our Real Problem," *Al-Muslimoon* (Geneva), no. 5 (Jan., 1962), 1-3.

[45] This attitude must not be confused with the wistful longing for the past which we find, e.g., in Aḥmad Amīn, *op. cit.*, pp. 23-24.

with still greater radicalism, Nadwī is throwing overboard the Western concept of science—the objectivation of experience and its interpretation as a rational system—whose philosophical and operational meaningfulness he obviously never realized. The ample quotations from mostly outdated or otherwise questionable authorities do not serve the purposes of fact-finding, but serve rather as cumulative testimony in court. With the Western concept of science the Western urge to self-understanding through an analysis not only of one's own but of other civilizations is dismissed. It is a peculiar cultural provincialism to which Nadwī gives vent, peculiar in the sense that his Islam is located in a no-man's land outside history, even though he would have us discover it in the age of the first four successors to the Prophet. The stereotyped foils of Western, Indian, and Chinese civilizations which he introduces serve but to heighten our sense of the extramundaneness of his ideal. By refusing to face or merely to investigate the realities of the Islamic past, Nadwī seems to us to articulate the reluctance of many of our contemporaries, and especially of many non-Occidentals, to continue the effort of the subjugation of the outside world (including that of psychological phenomena) as something objective and independent of our volitional life. The kind of restorative Islam which Nadwī advocates—let it be stressed in this connection that there is not the slightest contribution to Islamic theology or law in his work, not even a restatement of the heritage—implies a certain relaxation of creative self-discipline in its directedness toward control of the external world. The loss in scope and depth is to be compensated for by the regained coziness of life in a universe that is thoroughly familiar and amenable to supposedly well-tried rules, which allow one to limit not only the strain of ever-widening and ever-intensifying human domination of the objective world, but the introspection of analytical (and therefore critical and disquieting) curiosity as well.[46]

[46] The psychological difficulties of passing from prescientific to scientific cognition, and the strain of self-discipline necessary to

Islam and the West share the tendency to integrate without a break in basic structure the revolutionary reformer and his contribution[47]—perhaps the most important prerequisite of an extended developmental continuity without loss of cultural and psychological identity. In this fundamental attitude of both civilizational areas there lie almost infinite possibilities of advance and rebirth. But Nadwī's Islam is a tired faith; the vividness of its self-confidence must not deceive us. Nadwī's Islam wishes to draw its solutions from what has been; it is willing to make one supreme effort to obtain the earthly paradise, that is to say, the relaxing beatitude of a static world whose problems are foreseen and taken care of in sacred precedent.

Needless to say, Nadwī shies away from any specific suggestion of how a victorious Islam would remove the illnesses that he diagnoses in our world. Rather, he does not shy away from the specific; it simply does not occur to him that the model of the golden age might not provide the required panaceas. Not a word, therefore, on the position envisaged for the minorities; not a word on how to prevent another fall from *khilāfa* into *mulūkiyya;* not a word about the reconciliation of conflicting power aspirations within a Muslim-controlled system of national states. You cannot learn from history when you derive your strength from what exists essentially only insofar as it can be protected or salvaged from history. But thus the inherent paradox of Islam as a power system of transcendental aspiration, of a timeless *civitas Dei* that to avail man must be made visible in this world and must therefore become subject to change and decay, is not attacked, let alone resolved. Let us hope that Islam will withstand the temptation that Nadwī has so persuasively formulated.

---

control the temptation to backslide, are well set out by G. Bachelard, *La Formation de l'esprit scientifique* (2d ed.; Paris, 1947).

[47] For the history of Western consciousness cf. E. Neumann, *Ursprungsgeschichte des Bewusstseins* (Zürich, 1949), esp. pp. 6-8, 406-407.

VIII

The Political Role of the University in the Near East as Illustrated by Egypt

NOT TOO INACCURATELY, the development of the European Middle Ages has been attributed to the interaction and the interpenetration of three elements: (in chronological order) classical antiquity, Christianity, and Teutonism. For medieval Islam the corresponding triad would be identified as Arabism (the pre-Islamic Arab legacy), Islam, and local cultural tradition existing at the time.

As the essence and the earthly embodiment of the last and richest revelation of the one God, and, accordingly, the legal basis and the goal of all social and political organization, and as the chief and probably only principle of a supranational consciousness of unity, Islam provides the impetus of development to this cultural process. Seen historically, Islam grew out of Arabism, which is now inextricably interwoven in Islamic civilization, and whose authority is guaranteed by the Prophet's Arab descent. Arabism is the legacy of the first Islamic ruling class, the linguistic bond at all times, molder of the literary, impediment to the artistic tradition, the source of the cultural lingua franca that was to become the treasure hoard of law, theology, and the sciences, flexible and ready to adapt but poor in the cultural experience of its (pre-Muḥammadan) origins and constricted by the short-windedness of the nomadic rhythm of life. Hence local cultures, especially those in urbanized areas, confront it with superiority and contempt; in such heartlands as Iraq and Iran they press their basic conceptions into the amalgam of Islamic life, and in outposts like north Africa they continue their own form of life alongside, or directly beneath, the official tradition. The diversity of actual life, therefore, is preserved to a great extent, fostered by early political disintegration but never endangering the will for Islamic unity. Such is the character of the basic elements in the building of Islamic culture.

Split more deeply by sectarian strife than the Christendom of the medieval West, interested only spasmodically and in certain places in the non-Islamic world, accustomed early to misrule and foreign domination, the Muslim complex of states, especially in the Near and Middle East, lost its cultural creativeness in the later Middle Ages, but not the power of assimilation and transmission, of expansion into less alert or less thoroughly organized territories. With the decline of Turkish might from the seventeenth century on, the balance of power shifted slowly in favor of the West. This was to lead to a more or less veiled European control, beginning approximately with the Napoleonic occupation of Egypt. The influence of the West, the great *novum* of modern time, presents itself to the Muslims as a lure as well as a menace, as a stimulus to self-renovation, and as the culmination of decline through colonization, protectorate, or direct assumption of power by the foreigner.

Political realities, among which orthodox tenacity holds

an important place, make reform indispensable but complicate every change even in practical, everyday matters by sharpening the desire first and foremost for securing psychological equality of status, overcoming inferiority feelings, and restoring self-esteem, even though this is to be accomplished for the present only by deferring a genuine amelioration of the general situation. Moreover, there is uncertainty wherein self-realization truly exists. The assumed inflexibility and proved inadequacy of Islamic tradition are corrected to some extent by recourse to an ideal and half-imaginary early history; nevertheless, national consciousness is not itself clear as to when recourse to the past degenerates into defection.

The goal of the modernizer, whose faith (but not his feeling of belonging to a Muslim or Islamic community) may already have begun to waver, is self-assertion, perhaps even self-expansion, in the present world. The orthodox wants above all to realize the possibility of the community's following the road to salvation prescribed by God and the tradition, and of establishing thereby the eternal validity of the divine message for mastering every present. In Arabic-speaking lands Arabism and Islam have ever been understood as a unity though not as an identity, and thus the transition to a nationalism that is basically secular in orientation but retains the religious bond was not too difficult, although here, too, the concrete form of the desired or already achieved national state remains hotly debated. But however the role of religion, whose elemental cohesiveness the Arab nationalist is at times inclined to rate too low, is conceived, it is nationalism that more and more proves to be the shield of the identity threatened by the West, and threatened also from within.

There can be no doubt that nationalism has penetrated the Eastern world from the West. Yet, in order to understand Arab or Egyptian nationalism at all, one must recognize—as one usually does not—that this is not the expansively cosmopolitan, recklessly optimistic nationalism of the French Revolution, nurtured in an age of reason, or that of the romantic neohumanism of Germany of the Humboldt era. It lacks, in spite of its occasional use as a catchword, the concept of the divine right of the nation; it lacks a formative ethic; it also lacks, it would seem, the later nineteenth-century belief in mechanistic progress; above all, it lacks the intellectual vigor of a primary phenomenon. Both power and the will to power are ends in themselves. The resentment of political slights engenders impatience and impedes long-range analysis and planning in the intellectual sphere.

The political-mindedness of the authorities entails a rash of precipitate gestures; the poverty of ideology is offset on the one hand by the intensity of the collective dream of power, and on the other by the knowledge of the superiority of the Muslim community. Technology, science, and public education are known to be in arrears. The cream of the youth is sent to Western universities. The cleft between those educated in Europe and those trained in the homeland proves to be wide and obstructs the foreign-educated from succeeding at home. The foreign university is the source of the foreigners' scientific power. What, then, takes priority over building up a university, as the university symbolizes all that is striven for—modernization, equality of rights, progress? Even under Lord Cromer's administration Egyptian nationalists advocate establishing a university in Cairo; the English High Commissioner is not very favorably impressed because he wants to see education built from the bottom up, starting with elementary school. But upper-class Egyptians, full of idealism, politically alert, and permeated by the emotional significance of founding a university, use private means to convert their plan into fact in 1908, soon after Cromer's departure from Egypt in May, 1907. In 1925, after the lifting of the English protectorate (1922), the Egyptian government assumes the costs and the administration of the institution, then called Egyptian University (renamed Fu'ād University in 1936 and Cairo University in July, 1953), and of its subsequently established sister institutes. In any event, only through nationalization was the university in Cairo given a truly meaningful place in Egyptian life. At the same time, however, the obvious difficulties of a young, immature university became national problems, and their solution, as well as the administration of the university itself, had to be attempted within the flux of political currents.

Until the 1952 revolution, these political currents found expression (so far as the university was concerned) mainly in three points of organization: Parliament, the royal court, and the orthodox Muslim circles who spoke through the al-Azhar mosque school. Possessing the right of budget approval, Parliament, in spite of relatively free elections, represented in its various parties chiefly those groups that were modernistic in religion, friendly on the whole to Westernization, radical in foreign policy (i.e., anti-English and striving for independence with every means), and rather cautious in internal policy. The monarchy (Fuʾād until 1936; Fārūq until 1952), granted by the constitution the right to dismiss the cabinet and disposed in general to be friendly toward the university, nevertheless took more heed of the wishes of Muslim circles insufficiently represented in Parliament. It was unsympathetic toward the turbulence, always latent and erupting all too often, of the nationalistic students; a seat of disorder, the university actually provoked police action, but the intervention of the authorities, until the very last years, failed to change decisively the course of events. The orthodox naturally regarded the university with distrust. In any event the political climate compelled the adoption of certain reforms in the "theological" curriculum;[1] for a short time (1929-

[1] Under the rectorship of Shaikh aẓ-Ẓawāhirī (1929-1935), the *Jāmiʿ al-Azhar*, the Azhar mosque school, became *Jāmiʿat al-Azhariyya* (Azhar University). It comprised three faculties (*kulliyyāt*): *kulliyyat uṣūl ad-dīn*, by which religious teachers were to be trained; *kulliyyat ash-sharīʿa*, Islamic legists and judges; and *kulliyyat al-lugha 'l-ʿarabiyya*, specialists in and teachers of the Arabic language. In each of the colleges there was a section (*qism*) in which the respective studies were to be pursued on a specialized and, as it were, scientific level. The right to appoint the rector (*shaikh al-Azhar*) was a point of dispute between government and king (cf. Fakhr ad-Dīn al-Aḥmadī aẓ-Ẓawāhirī,

1930) the government was even able to press upon al-Azhar, against the wish of the King, a "liberal" rector, al-Marāghī (who held the rectorship once more from 1935 until his death in 1945, this time in accordance with the Azharites' wishes). Yet it was in the nature of things that the Azhari theologians should keep a sharp eye on their "secular" colleagues, especially with regard to the handling of the state religion, which, with the wide ramifications of the data of Islamic dogma into all spheres of historical, humanistic, literary, and artistic opinion, meant in practice a substantial limitation of the theoretically guaranteed freedom of instruction.

The state university asserted its independence of conservative pressure with remarkable decisiveness; there were few *causes célèbres* like those of Ṭāhā Ḥusain and Khalafallāh, but with the increasingly grave situation of the country, the court became more and more favorable to the orthodox.[2] Although, technically, freedom of instruction and, *de facto*, the civil service status of professors were not violated,[3] the Azharites exercised a very obstructive, even a retarding, influence. It was only under Gamāl ʿAbd an-Nāṣir that the irremovability of professors for political reasons was disregarded in numerous cases. Hand in hand with this disciplining of the faculty from above—in Egypt as in other totalitarian states appointed deans have replaced the officials chosen under the monarchy, a development that set in as early as 1951; the rector and five members of the university council had always been appointed by the government—went the disciplining of

---

as-Siyāsa wa'l-Azhar [Cairo, 1364/1945], pp. 5-6, 8). The current pursuit of studies at al-Azhar has been concisely and suggestively described by J. Kraemer, "Tradition and Reform at al-Azhar University," *Middle Eastern Affairs*, VII (1956), 89-94 (also contains bibliographical data).

[2] That King Fuʾād had taken an active part in the founding of the university later named for him is by no means to be interpreted as lack of interest in al-Azhar. The King was a devout Muslim and deeply sympathetic toward al-Azhar.

[3] The professors were civil servants who, by disciplinary proceedings, could be suspended and relieved of their duties.

the students. In the past, of course, the government had from time to time made use of students in demonstrations. All the same, most of the student rallies and riots had either come out of opposition groups or had erupted spontaneously when students, without higher direction from party officials, used violence in trying to push through their standpoint on such questions as foreign policy issues and, well into the 'thirties, concrete problems of student life, like the regulations governing examinations. Student riots and strikes were the order of the day, and some conflicts among students were even settled by violence, such as those between the Azharis and their "secular" fellow students. Under the circumstances, the university's academic success fell far short of legitimate expectations. Here it may be pointed out that pupils in the secondary schools occasionally started rows long before the founding of the university; the first large riot of this sort of which I have knowledge was the demolishing of the building used by the editorial staff of the newspaper *al-Muqaṭṭam*, carried out by students under the direction of the nationalistic leader Muṣṭafà Kāmil (1874-1908) in 1893. Furthermore, even the Azhar students, although they did not on the whole go into the streets so readily as their secular fellow students, at least after the great crisis of 1934-35, organized some strikes and demonstrations of sympathy for the nationalistic students.

In order to understand their political significance, one must realize that the function of students, especially of those engaged in secular instruction, is quite different in Egypt—as in all underdeveloped countries—from the function of students in Germany or the United States, for instance. Not that the students in even the most advanced countries have failed to demand and receive the greatest attention and a certain consideration as the rising ruling class, but there they are no longer so definitely the shock troops upon which the future seems to hang. The strange paradox that for a long time Egypt, for instance, may not have a sufficient number of educated people to manage a completely modernized state with a completely modernized economy and system of education, and that a substantial percentage of those adequately educated cannot find appropriate employment in a society overtaken by its plans and dreams, burdens the students as a distressing expectation and heightens their instability. Subjectively, it makes little difference whether there actually is a lack of positions in all fields of work requiring a higher education, or whether social biases or simply lifelong habits hinder graduates from making use of existing opportunities for employment. Because life outside the capital—and, possibly, Alexandria—is felt to be exile, rural districts are often without necessary teachers and physicians; still the graduates prefer to vegetate in Cairo, and the government must snatch at all sorts of circuitous means in order to let the provinces share in the progress for which it strives.

The thinly veiled competition between those educated in Egypt and those educated in Western universities serves to intensify their predicament. Those who return with doctorates from England, France, the United States, or Germany form cliques whose unity is based on the country of education; their numerical weakness is compensated for to some extent by the greater prestige of foreign universities. The fact that independence as well as the cutting back of foreign economic influence means an increase in the posts open to university graduates is not wholly without effect on the students' supernationalism. But, however precarious their material outlook, students know themselves to be an elite, and it is difficult for the executive power to manhandle children of the ruling class and those who, because of their ability, enjoy an equal status.

The over-all situation of a country like Egypt makes the application of foreign basic research seem more urgent than the building up of its own. It must be recognized that the lack of elementary and secondary teachers actually turns the university in many a department into a teachers' college, although this holds true less for Cairo University than, perhaps, for the Syrian university in Damascus. The cited attitude toward basic research, together with the existing need for a livelihood, has the consequence of awakening a certain pragmatism in the students; it should be added here that the results of Western research are more easily transferable than its methods, and that the Western research mentality, as one of the most singular characteristics of our culture, can only very gradually be instilled into the thoughts and the feelings of the impatient young nationalists of the Near East.

The existence of institutions of higher learning built on Western principles is, like the introduction of parliamentary forms, in itself a contribution of the highest significance to the restoration of national self-esteem. In the long run, moreover, the founding of a university is also a step toward intellectual autarchy. That its ethos can be only that of radical nationalism is obvious: the homogeneity of this basic mentality is not affected by sharp differences among the students and the public opinion supporting them, whether it be a question of revolutionary social change; attempted political alliances; dictatorial, democratic, or communistic forms of government; or the right degree of secularization. So long, therefore, as the state has not yet achieved full independence, so long as the aspirations of foreign policy—even after the attainment of independence—require the intensification of an aggressive national feeling, the government will be in secret concord with the radical nationalistic movement, nourished, but not necessarily led, by university circles. One must not be unmindful that the ideology of Arab nationalism is extraordinarily simple and in no way has taken shape as a philosophy of history, social philosophy, or epistemology. Troublesome political consequences of nationalism are to be expected, therefore, only on the basis of demands for social reform aimed at strengthening the nation, and the university as such has not applied itself with particular assiduity to backing such demands.

The coöperation of Muslim and non-Muslim university students at school has probably helped to alloy these traditionally disparate elements, though they must be regarded as mixed rather than fused; closing the ranks against denominational tensions must seem extremely desirable to a government engaged in fighting the foreigner. But if the government is sure of its cause, and if it considers itself, with some justification, as the embodiment of the national idea, it feels obliged to place university students as well as faculty under strict supervision in order to maintain control and, above all, the initiative. The situation is analagous to that of the proletarian state which, by suppressing strikes, fomented before the seizing of power as a means of combating a hostile social order, but now considered inimical to society as a whole, considerably restricts the worker's freedom of movement. Thus the government of Gamāl ʿAbd an-Nāṣir has quite consistently (except on very special occasions) sent the students back to school from the streets, and, as already mentioned, has subjected the faculty to a sifting process and to control of instruction; professors who were too far to the left or who supported the Muslim Brotherhood too warmly were eliminated in 1954. It may be said that Egyptian intellectuals largely, but certainly not unanimously, opposed this step.

Backwardness as such, as soon as it is to be vanquished, heightens nationalistic sensitivity. The lack of a homegrown university tradition necessitates staffing a new university with foreign teachers. In the 1920's and the 1930's, this meant multilingual university instruction. But it also raised a question persistently repeated in every technical field: How long must we be educated by foreigners? It is not surprising that the opinion of the newly emerging graduates of Egyptian academies sounded more optimistic than that of foreign observers. In general, the observation seems to hold that intellectual (or academic) autonomy is claimed one scholarly generation, or perhaps fifteen years, too soon. Egypt was no exception. It is easy to understand that the permanent presence of foreign professors supplied a basis of irritation which was naturally intensified and exploited in the immediate interest of nationalism. The continual confrontation of native with foreign performance and efficiency in the academic world, painful enough in itself, was made more bitter by the political aspect, the acknowledgment of which had been made practically mandatory by certain concrete considerations: (1) the actual or imagined interference of foreign agencies in questions of appointment, and (2) political pressure, which was certainly manifest in the existence of graduates who lacked positions. On a higher level, if you like, the problem recurred in the question of the language of instruction.

From the earliest time imaginable, pride in the language has been the most basic component of Arab self-consciousness. Throughout the Middle Ages the formative power of Arabic had sufficed to accompany the assimilation of Greek science, the development of Islamic theology and law, and the evolution of a complicated governmental apparatus with a terminology very largely evolved from Arabic materials. Yet, in the nineteenth and twentieth centuries, when practically all fields of knowledge cultivated in the West had to be adopted with extreme speed, when foreign codifications of law were admitted on a selective basis, and when the government was transformed administratively according to European models, linguistic difficulties of a very appreciable order made their appearance. In many instances it was necessary to use foreign languages for research and instruction. And even today, to the best of my knowledge, medical study as well as instruction in some legal specialties is conducted in French in Syria and in English in Egypt. That tendencies to overcome this deficiency in vocabulary made themselves felt is scarcely to be wondered at. In 1932 King Fuʾād founded the Arabic Language Academy (*Majmaʿ al-lugha ʾl-ʿarabiyya*), whose chief task was the creation of an Arabic vocabulary equal to modern requirements. In Syria, where an Arabic academy had been established in 1919,[4] and in Iran and Turkey as well, equally energetic endeavors were initiated with official support. Hundreds, even thousands, of technical expressions were coined and traditional

[4] The informative and in many ways scientifically valuable *Majalla* of the academy has been published since 1922.

terms were adapted to new semantic needs, basically the same process of linguistic revival which Hungarian and Finnish, for example, had undergone in the nineteenth century. (The state of neo-Irish and neo-Hebrew is not really comparable, for Arabic had never ceased to be the living language of an educated stratum of society and of a national complex.) The technical difficulties of this enrichment of language are less important in our context than the obvious nationalistic aspect. Even though there were enough Egyptians to sneer at the artificiality of this afforestation of the language, all had to admit that such an undertaking, albeit a quixotism, represented a folly both necessary and noble. With the fruitful growth of technical Arabic, the education problem was alleviated, the position of foreign teachers weakened, and international scientific understanding perhaps somewhat slowed insofar as Greek and Latin terminology in the natural sciences and medicine, for instance, forms a convenient bridge among languages in the West.[5] The confusion of nationalistic with practical points of view in a work like that undertaken by the Cairo academy is probably unavoidable; one may even be surprised by the objectivity, the *détachement,* with which the academicians (among whom, moreover, there has been more than one European scholar) have tried to do justice to their task.

A problem that is less obvious to the nationalistic observer, but much more obstructive, has been the duality

[5] The Turks followed a somewhat different course. They endeavored to create new Turkish "elemental" terms in mathematics, for example, but left the technical language of higher mathematics international, i.e., European. A. Memmi, *Portrait du colonisé précédé du Portrait du colonisateur* (Paris, 1957), pp. 174-176, has given an excellent analysis of the psychological factors that lie at the basis of reverting to an ancestral literary language which has become (not indeed in theory but in actual fact) inaccessible to the people as a whole. In north Africa, the area of Memmi's special concern, classical Arabic is, by and large, further removed from the consciousness of the educated than is French; but a nostalgic self-restoration may work, even in Algeria, toward a reversal of the present linguistic and intellectual reality.

of the Egyptian system of education, ever present from its origin up to our day, reflecting the duality of Egyptian intellectual life. The modern educational system, initiated under the Khedive Muḥammad ʿAlī (d. 1848) as an instrument of military-political advancement, consists of a bewildering mass of foreign and native types of schools which in recent decades have gradually been standardized by insistence on a certain amount of specifically Arabic instruction and on the state certification of teachers.[6] All these schools, unequal in efficiency and a majority of them now supported by the government, are but a part of an educational cycle that leads from kindergarten through elementary and secondary school to application to the secular university. (That the French secondary schools also offer preparation for admission to French universities brings into even sharper relief the structure of this type of education.)

In recent decades the state has insisted to an increasing degree on Arabic and religious instruction, the principal motivation for which, besides national or nationalistic reasons, was provided in my opinion by the desire to build a bridge to the second course of instruction, which from the government's point of view had fallen into deplorable isolation. In this type of education the child was first

---

[6] Cf. Ẓawāhirī, *op. cit.*, p. 18[14–18]: the *Shaikh al-Azhar* is *al-imām al-aʿlà li-rijāl ad-dīn fī Miṣr* (roughly, the leading religious scholar in Egypt), which is not, of course, meant in the formal hierarchical sense; he is even *ar-raʾs ad-dīniyya ʾl-kubrà fī jamīʿ al-umam al-islāmiyya* (roughly, the highest religious authority in all Muslim nations), an expression that in any event is not intended to describe an organizational state of affairs.

It may be remarked parenthetically that the multiplicity of courses in the secular schools was felt to be excessive in many respects and disadvantageous from a national standpoint (cf., e.g., Ṭāhā Ḥusain, *Mustaqbal ath-thaqāfa fī Miṣr* [Cairo, 1938], pp. 62-65). Very much worth reading are the statements about Ṭāhā Ḥusain's pedagogical ideas and his concrete achievements as minister of education and dean of the Egyptian University in P. Cachia, *Ṭāhā Ḥusayn, His Place in the Egyptian Literary Renaissance* (London, 1956), esp. chap. ix, "Education," pp. 114-127.

instructed in the Koran at the so-called *kuttāb*, where he also learned reading, writing, and grammar; the *kuttāb* led to religiously oriented secondary schools and ultimately to al-Azhar, where religious jurists, theologians, judges of the canonical courts, *imām*'s, and the like were trained. Al-Azhar was (or is) no university in the Western sense but an institution to transmit Islamic learning; I hesitate to speak of a single theological faculty or college because the Islamic sciences embrace not only theology, tradition, and law, but also grammar, poetics, and rhetoric as well as mathematics, astronomy, and the like (to the extent needed for divine service). The range of instruction therefore goes beyond that of a Western theological faculty but, on the other hand, remains behind it because of the exclusion of church history and philological-critical disciplines. As al-Azhar also operates a *kuttāb* and a secondary school, the student may spend his entire time in school there.

The pressure of public opinion and the change of heart among influential faculty members led to slight adjustments in the Azhar curriculum between the two world wars, mainly in the lower grades. Natural sciences were offered, the demands in mathematics were intensified, and a foreign language was even made available to the students. But it is certainly no exaggeration to state that, seen as a whole, the Azhar of 1920 and the Azhar of 1950 pursued the same goal, and it is doubtless true that the official system of education made no provision to convert from a traditional to a secular curriculum. In the not too infrequent instances of defection by an Azhari from the religious course, all examinations had to be repeated, and under certain circumstances the student in question could lose years before he gained admission to Cairo University. The conservatism of al-Azhar is in part rooted in the intrinsic logic of the Islamic system and in the needs of religious practice and administration; conscious and irritated opposition to modernists of dubious religious loyalty is also involved. Still a third element is not to be underestimated. For hundreds of years al-Azhar has been the leading Islamic institution of its kind. The student body is international; the influence of Azhar instruction reaches the outermost limits of the Islamic world. It not only symbolizes, it embodies the cosmopolitan, international character of the Islamic system of thought and instruction and thus finds itself *eo ipso* in opposition to the narrow nationalistic mentality which has received its practical expression, together with the even less congenial tendency toward Westernization, in the secular course of studies. Even from the national standpoint, however, al-Azhar is a precious possession; only through this institution can Egyptian and Arabic influence penetrate certain parts or circles of the Islamic world.[7] Because Egypt is in many ways superior to the Islamic societies in Africa or on the Arabian Peninsula, and is also gripped by the spirit of the West more strongly than the native lands and the social classes of the majority of foreign Azhar students, radical modernization in all probability would loosen the bond of the university with other Islamic lands and substantially reduce its (and consequently Egyptian) influence.

The peculiar political-cultural constellation of our time which forces a country such as Egypt to represent itself to the West as more thoroughly modernized than it actually is compels it to act in a more orthodox way for the benefit of the south and the east than its actual functioning justifies. In fact, Egypt strives fairly consistently to limit the scope of public and private life ruled by Islam. Only recently were the courts of canonical jurisdiction abolished

[7] The donation of 3,000 copies of the Koran to Senegal, along with a number of scholarships for university students, as announced on June 14, 1961 (*Cahiers de l'Orient contemporain,* XLVI [1 May to 31 August 1961], p. 287), may be mentioned as one minor indication of a continued endeavor to establish a position of influence in Africa through the channel of Islam.

The Egyptianizing, or rather the closing, of foreign schools after the Suez intervention in late autumn, 1956, dealt a blow, which will be felt for a long time, not only to the advance of Western principles of education but also to the level of instruction. This is, of course, not the first time that the emotional needs of the moment have seriously interfered with the long-range objectives of a nationalistic movement.

(while the canon law was left in the hands of the regular courts, as authoritative for certain spheres of life). Nevertheless, religious instruction was intensified—anticommunistic considerations may have figured in finally securing a hearing for the frequently raised demands of religious circles—and, as already pointed out, this created points of transition between the two courses of education. Whether or not these possibilities of transfer will work to the advantage of "theological" education is questionable; to me the opposite effect seems more probable. Be that as it may, the two-facedness of Near Eastern nationalism as Arab-Egyptian, Arab-Syrian, and Muslim-Arab, Muslim-Egyptian, will compel the governments ever anew to interfere out of political considerations in the development of both types of universities; the same considerations will probably secure in the foreseeable future paramount governmental support for the modern university.[8] So long as the positions of the two universities assert their symbolic content as embodiments of extremely antithetical sociopolitical ideals, their political neutralization will remain absolutely impossible.

Herein lies one crux of the life of the Egyptian university. The second is found in the problematical character of all Westernization. The basic factor in modern Western mentality is the stress on science as the path to

---

[8] For a brief time in 1957 the development of the secular university—indeed, even the maintenance of the *status quo*—was imperiled by the nonpurchase of books published in England and France and by a regulation that made dealings of university lecturers with foreigners (even colleagues), except with those who are professionally indispensable (there are still a few non-Egyptian professors on the faculties of jurisprudence and medicine), contingent on the written permission of the duly authorized dean.

It is true that in Egypt the rift between the modern and the traditional type of education is especially pronounced. Yet this duality is also characteristic of other Islamic states or communities, as if inherent in the phase of development; for Pakistan (and the Muslim minority in India), for example, one may compare the remarks of Wilfred C. Smith, *Islam in Modern History* (Princeton, 1957), p. 224.

truth and consequently as the most powerful nonreligious means of ethical amelioration of man and community. This mentality implies the belief in the power of man to evolve by his own volition and to transcend his (apparently) natural measure and his current phase. It is essentially the Greek heritage.[9] And it is lacking in the East. But if this mentality is lacking, science, on which the West's power and attraction rest, loses its real significance and retains only a pragmatic value. Along with this loss of value, however, also ebbs the incomparable strength of

[9] So also believes E. Husserl. Cf. chap. v, above, pp. 138-140 and n. 18. It may be instructive to quote Max Scheler's formulation of the principal objectives that a "modern, civilized, occidental nation" sets for its institutions of higher learning: "(1) Möglichst gute und getreue Bewahrung und Überlieferung der von der gemeinsamen Geschichte der abendländischen Völker erarbeiteten höchsten Wissens- und Bildungsgüter. (2) Möglichst methodische, pädagogische und kraftsparende Lehre und Unterweisung zu Berufs- und Fachausbildung aller im Dienste des Staates, der Kirche und der Gesellschaft stehenden 'Fachleute,' Beamten aller Art, der freien Berufe, Kaufleute usw. (3) Methodische Fortführung der wissenschaftlichen Forschung. (4) Möglichst allseitige geistige Durchformung und Durchbildung der menschlichen Persönlichkeit (described on p. 394 as 'persönliche Gestaltgewinnung') durch Lösung der spezifischen 'allgemeinen Bildungsaufgaben'; schliesslich die höchste Beseelung dieser Bildungsaufgabe durch persönliche Vorbilder, an denen sich jeder Mensch ebensosehr ein Beispiel nimmt, als er sie als Mass über sich und seinem Verhalten empfindet. (5) Möglichst richtige, einfache und zweckentsprechende Vermittlung aller Wissens- und Bildungsgüter durch die verschiedenen Schichten und Klassen des Volkes hindurch; das heisst also auch durch die Vermittlung von Zwischeninstitutionen, die zwischen den höchsten Schulen, Forschungs- und Bildungsanstalten und dem, was jeder durch das Leben und die Volksschule lernt, in der Mitte stehen" ("Universität und Volkshochschule" [written in 1921], in *Gesammelte Werke* [Bern and München, 1951——], VIII, 383-420, at p. 387). A good part of the spiritual difficulties with which modernists as well as orthodox in the Middle East have to contend has been caught in the perceptive phrase which Memmi (*op. cit.*, p. 31) has coined for the *colonisateur qui se refuse*, but which possesses the widest applicability: "Il n'est pas si facile de s'évader, par l'esprit, d'une situation concrète, d'en refuser l'idéologie tout en continuant à en vivre les relations objectives."

the impulse that it has engendered in Western man. The energy of the Muslim is fed from other sources. It can easily be judged what difficulties must be fought in order to give a scientific character to a mode of thought and to a social order in a society that in the last analysis lacks faith in science. From this contradiction the tragedy of the educational conflict in Egypt, in the Arab world, and in the Islamic domain in general is to be derived and understood.[10]

[10] Since this passage was written the Egyptian government has practically eliminated foreign-controlled educational institutions on the primary and secondary levels, has succeeded in breaking through the walls between the two educational systems by securing possibilities of transfer, has substantially increased the number of schools on all levels, has consistently devoted a remarkably high proportion of its budget to education, and through its president has declared the necessity for a cultural nationalism.

Two important developments within al-Azhar need to be specifically registered. On June 5, 1961, the institution announced that it would henceforth accept qualified girl students from any part of the Muslim world; and the law of June 22, 1961, made al-Azhar officially the "highest Islamic scientific organism"; its rector becomes "the *imām* of the faithful" and the highest theological authority within Islam. Among the organizational innovations the most important is the creation, within the university proper—as contrasted with the preparatory and the secondary "cycle of instruction"—of six faculties: Islamic studies, Arabic studies, administration, technology, agriculture, and medicine, of which, however, only the first three were expected to function as of October 1, 1961. Holders of the Bachelor's degree from a "lay" school are admissible to the Azhar University after passing an examination. Cf. *Cahiers de l'Orient contemporain*, XLVI (1 May to 31 August 1961), pp. 285-286. (Reference owed to Dr. H. Haddad, University of California, Los Angeles.)

B. Dodge, *Al-Azhar. A Millennium of Muslim Learning* (Washington, D.C., 1961), was received after the present study had gone to press.

IX

Problems of Muslim Nationalism

I

"A NATIONALITY," in the words of Louis Wirth, "may be conceived of as a people who, because of the belief in their common descent and their mission in the world, by virtue of their common cultural heritage and historical career aspire to sovereignty over a territory or seek to maintain or enlarge their political or cultural influence in the face of opposition. Nationalism refers to the social movements, attitudes and ideologies which characterise the behavior of nationalities engaged in the struggle to achieve, maintain, or enhance their position in the world." [1]

To assess the potentialities and the function of nationalism in the contemporary Muslim world these fundamental facts must be taken into consideration:

1) The unity of the Muslim world, such as it is, has long

[1] *American Journal of Sociology,* XLI (1935-1936), 723. Cf. chap. vii, above, p. 181.

ceased to be political; it is based on the reality of a religious, and the conviction of a cultural, tie among the "believing" nations or groups.

2) In essence, this unity has always consisted in the successful superimposition by aristocracies of fighters and scholars (often at logger heads) of certain standards of belief and especially of conduct over a considerable number of highly diverse local traditions.

3) By modifying or broadening Wirth's definition of a nationality to include a community held together through "the belief in their common descent or their common faith"; the community of Islam, the *umma Muḥammadiyya,* could be subsumed under it, in contradistinction to Christianity but in analogy to Judaism.

4) Nationalistic movements have, at various times in the past, threatened or disrupted the political unity of Islam while leaving intact, in the minds of the Muslims, its religious and cultural oneness.

5) At other times, movements of a typically cultural nationalism have tried to pry loose large areas of the *dār al-Islām* from the supremacy of Arab culture which acted, as it were, as the representative of the prophetic tradition, or else to insert their ideas and their spokesmen into the framework of this culture and its bearers while leaving intact both its continuity and its sense of identity. In many instances the compromise of the local "nationalistic" with the universal "Islamic" tradition or movement was attained through the rebels' seeking leadership in a multinational state or a culturally pluralistic *umma* rather than political independence or cultural *apartheid.*

6) Finally, it must be remembered that the consensus of the pious of the last three or four generations seems agreed to consider nationalism within Islam a scourge unknown prior to Western expansion into and interference with the *dār al-Islām.* This idea, though in conflict with historical fact, is significant as a self-view that involves a program.

National states have been in existence within the domain of Islam for many a century; yet the canon law recognizes only the one and indivisible *umma Muḥammadiyya.* Intent upon maintaining the unity of the faith, which was seen to be contingent on the oneness of the religious community and made visible in the oneness of the law, the spiritual leadership of the believers has always been passionately interested in the integrity and the expansion of the Muslim territory as a whole, while exhibiting scant concern over its distribution among the competing princes of the day.

The problem of present-day nationalisms in Muslim-dominated countries therefore differs essentially from that of nationalisms in the West in three ways:

1) The Muslim nationalisms operate within a religious and cultural organism which itself shows certain characteristics of a nationality and with whose "supernationalism" it stands in competition.

2) Because of this situation, but also because of their immediate origin as hostile children of the West and their consequent current ideology, they are apt to be or to appear as anti-Islamic and, in any event, as secularizing movements.

3) Owing to the derivation from Western sources of much of their intellectual and emotional inspiration, they are in the ambiguous position of nativistic movements of foreign kindling, of apostles of the future greatness of their community which can be realized only by a curtailment of that community's most cherished institutional, intellectual, and even religious achievements—these very achievements appearing now at the same time as warranty and obstacle of glory to come.

II

Much of ancient philosophy is imbued with skepticism regarding the ultimate value of (political) power. Christianity has added the sentiment that it is more wholesome for the salvation-bent soul to avoid any contact with power; many a strict Muslim, especially if his piety shows an ascetic or a mystic hue, views power and its responsibilities as a foremost spiritual risk. It is these circles that circulated dicta like the answer allegedly given by ʿUmar, the second caliph, when asked why he did not spread administrative responsibilities among the most outstanding companions of the Prophet: "They are too eminent (*ajall*) to be soiled by administration (*al-ʿamal*)." [2]

This attitude is not, however, that of the consensus of the doctors. The Muslim theologian was not weighted down by that typically Christian feeling that power is sinful in itself and that its exercise calls not only for an explanation but for an apology. On the contrary, the community and its spokesmen realized from the very beginning that Islam could be perfected only within an Islamic political organization whose maintenance and advancement were, to say the least, a prerequisite to the service of God, if they did not in themselves constitute such service. Ibn Taimiyya (d. 1328), the great Hanbalite theologian whose influence has been growing for the last two hundred years, declares it a duty to consider the exercise of power as a form of religion, as one of the acts by which man draws nearer to God.[3] And in our own time Muḥammad Rashīd Riḍā (d. 1935) has reaffirmed the inseparability of Islam as a religion and Islam as a political entity by stating that Islam is not fully in being so long as there does not exist a strong and independent Muslim state that is able to put into operation the laws of Islam.[4]

---

[2] Ṭarṭūshī (d. 1126 or 1131), *Sirāj al-mulūk* (Cairo, 1306/1888), p. 116^{11-13}.

[3] *As-Siyāsa 'sh-sharʿiyya fī iṣlāh ar-rāʿī wa'r-raʿiyya*, ed. ʿAlī Sāmī an-Nashshār and Aḥmad Zakī ʿAṭiyya (2d ed.; Cairo, 1951 [?]; the foreword is dated May 24, 1952), p. 174^{7-8}: "faʾl-wājib ittikhādh al-imāra dīnan wa-qurbatan yataqarrabu bihā ilà 'llāh; fa-inna 't-taqarrub ilaihi fī-hā bi-ṭāʿati-hi wa-ṭāʿat rasūli-hi min *afḍal* al-qarabāt" (trans. H. Laoust, *Le Traité de droit public d'Ibn Taimīya* [Beirut, 1948], pp. 173-174; the translation is quoted in part by L. Gardet, *La Cité musulmane* [Paris, 1954], p. 107).

[4] See n. 3, p. 246, above. In his commentary on the Qurʾān (*Tafsīr al-Manār* [Cairo, 1927-1934], I, 11) Muḥammad Rashīd Riḍā reports that perusal of *al-ʿUrwa 'l-wuthqà*, the short-lived journal which, in 1884, Muḥammad ʿAbduh (d. 1905) and

The Muslim as nationalist is thus not impeded, as the Christian is, by an uneasy conscience when it comes to that glorification and potentially ruthless utilization of power which is, after all, one of the chief characteristics of a nationalistic movement.

To quote Wirth once more: "The personal feeling of expansion with which nationalism infuses a citizenry, and the collective force which such a movement generates, is not likely to halt abruptly after the formal goals of the movement have been attained. After a nationality has achieved political autonomy, it sometimes redefines its aims in terms of empire or degenerates into a state of national chauvinism." [5] The Islamic tradition as such will not prevent a government from making itself the tool and the promoter of a development that is best described in the words of Aldous Huxley: "Within five years of achieving its liberty every oppressed nationality takes to militarism, and within two or three generations, sometimes within a single generation, it becomes, if circumstances are propitious, an imperialist aggressor, eager to inflict upon its neighbors the oppression of which itself it was so recently the victim." [6]

Jamāl ad-Dīn al-Afghānī (d. 1897) published in Paris, impressed him above all in three respects: (1) He found there an exposition of the way in which God deals customarily with man and the societal order. (2) He obtained confirmation of the fact that Islam is a religion of political dominance and power uniting the happiness of both worlds. It is a religion at the same time spiritual, social, and military; its military strength is destined to protect the law as well as the vitality of the religious community but not to compel the conversion of the outsider. (3) He found it asserted that the Muslims had no nationality proper apart from their affiliation with their religious community; they are brothers who are not permitted to split for reasons of birth, language, or government. Rashīd Riḍā became acquainted with *al-ʿUrwa* as late as 1892-93 (cf. J. Jomier, *Le Commentaire coranique du Manār* [Paris, 1954], pp. 28-31).

[5] *Loc. cit.*, p. 726.

[6] *Themes and Variations* (London, 1950), p. 45. One feels reminded of G. Bachelard's observation: "En fait, penser à une puissance, c'est déjà, non seulement s'en servir, c'est surtout en abuser. Sans cette volonté d'abuser, la conscience de la puissance

National socialism in Germany had to hamstring the opposition of the churches; but the conflict in Egypt between the nationalistic government and the conservative Muslims is of a different order. It does not turn on the aversion of the religious to the consolidation of a power felt to be basically evil, but on the divergent aims of two rival totalitarianisms opposed not in their attitude to power and its utilization as such but to the ideology to which this power should be made serviceable; it is the conflict between an internationalist Pan-Islamic and a nationalist Egyptian (Pan-Arab or the like) expansionism. The advocacy by the Indian Muslim, ʿAlī al-Ḥasanī an-Nadwī (1913——), of the transfer of political leadership to the Muslim world is couched in the customary nationalistic terms, not excluding the readiness to use force against the West to make Islam prevail.[7]

Although the traditional Muslim thus will agree with the Muslim nationalist as regards his power concept, he will find himself in intense disagreement when it comes to the allocation of loyalties, and in intellectual as well as emotional difficulties when he is confronted with the nationalist's dynamic or operational (or pragmatic) ideas of law and the state.

Few culture areas have been subjected to so much and so violent change as that of Islam; none perhaps has so

---

ne serait pas claire" (*La Psychanalyse du feu* [9th ed.; Paris, 1949], pp. 157-158). The progress of science, first of geography, later of social psychology, and, besides, the lesson of immediate historical experience, have deprived mankind of both stage and actors in the tragicomedy of its self-idealization. The mythical lands of the North and the West had to be abandoned; the noble savage has disappeared and behind him in rapid succession the noble proletarian and the noble victim of imperialist oppression. The innocence of a human collective never outlasts its bondage. One wonders where a future utopianism will be able to locate its dreams to impregnate them with an illusion of reality; all considered, it is the imperial powers at their stage of saturation and incipient decline which show collective mankind at its best, that is in this context, at its politically most tolerant.

[7] ʿAlī al-Ḥasanī an-Nadwī, *Mā dhā khasara 'l-ʿālam biʾnḥiṭāṭ al-muslimīn?* (2d ed.; Cairo, 1370/1951), pp. 241-242, 247-248.

consistently refused to accept the ontological reality of change. The truth of Islam, as it has come to be held in some contrast to the more flexible outlook of its origins, is not only one and indivisible, it is also immutable; it is neither growing nor shrinking; its understanding may vary in adequacy but it has been changelessly available since it was vouchsafed mankind through the Seal of the Prophets. This goes for doctrine and conduct as well as for their institutionalization. When the social reality fails to come up to the ideal, human heedlessness is the cause; but the ideal needs no revision. Even though the consensus of the learned has in fact been developed into an instrument of legislative adjustment, and even though there exists a rather keen sense of the cleavage separating Islamic origins from the reality of contemporary Islam, development is still acceptable only as decline, that is, as the abandonment of divine precept, or as the remedying of some misunderstanding, as the uncovering of some implication of the revealed truth which had hitherto been missed.

It need scarcely be said that this outlook makes it none too easy to come to terms with historical development as such, with the particular phase one happens to find oneself in, and, above all, to arrive at a comprehensive overview of one's cultural milieu. It also tends to discourage the idea of legislation, especially of short-term legislation, as a suitable means of improving the state of society, which is rather to be ameliorated by the energy of a just and God-fearing executive. At this point the Muslim outlook comes very close to that of the Christian Middle Ages, of which it has been said, "Where a modern democrat is prepared to respect the law in so far as he can regard himself as its author, medieval obedience was founded on the opposite sentiment, that laws were respectable in so far as they were not made by man." Whereas modern thought (to quote another author) regards legislation as the highest activity of the state, to which judicial enforcement is logically subordinate, medieval (and Muslim) thought typically admitted legislation only as "a part of the judicial procedure—a more or less surreptitious incident of '*jus dicere.*' "[8] One need only think of the *maẓālim* jurisdiction and the court of the *muḥtasib* to admit the applicability of this observation to the Islamic world.

The traditional Muslim's first loyalty is to his faith and the community of the true believers; attachment to family or local group usually follows, with dedication to his prince (rather than his state) relegated to the third place. In accordance with this attitude the law considered any Muslim a full-fledged "citizen" of the Muslim-ruled state in which he happened to find himself. Hence the possibility of taking employment in distant countries under different princes; in one sense no Muslim could be an alien in any Muslim land. European control of Muslim countries caused the first break in this practice,[9] and local nationalism has by now almost abolished it. So nationalism with its limited notion of citizenship has undercut Muslim political mobility; and the modern nationality concept, together with the nationalism that developed it, has been under severe attack by conservative opinion as the very worst of the many fateful gifts that the West has induced the East to accept. The positive aspect of an Arab or Pakistani feeling that nationalism, even within the accidental limits of existing states, such as Iraq or Lebanon, represents a unifying element counteracting the separatism or at least the indifference to the larger unit of the local religious, tribal, and ethnic communities, which outside the protective shell of a territorial state would be neither economically nor politically viable entities, is apt to be overlooked by the traditional orthodox. The (relative) social isolation of the various subcom-

---

[8] Ewart Lewis, *Medieval Political Ideas* (New York, 1954), I, 2, quoting (in part) H. M. V. Reade, *Cambridge Mediaeval History*, VI, 616, and John Dickinson, *The Statesman's Book of John of Salisbury* (New York, 1927), introduction, p. liv n. 164.

[9] Cf. Gardet, *op. cit.*, p. 29 n. 1, on the case of ʿAbdalḥakīm, a Tunisian and therefore a *protégé français,* who, in 1905, was denied by a French court that Moroccan citizenship which, on the basis of traditional Muslim law, he had claimed as a resident of Morocco.

munities makes it possible for such unawareness to persist in comparatively wide circles, while at the same time the adjusting of parochialism to nationalism remains the most irksome problem of domestic politics.

It must be remembered in this connection that "secular" nationalism in the Arab-speaking areas is of two (not always neatly separated) kinds. It may be focused on the individual state or it may tend to include the *ʿarabiyya* as a whole. As a rough generalization the intelligentsia (and the non-Muslim intelligentsia even more than the Muslim) may be said to incline toward a Pan-Arab nationalism, and governmental circles toward a local nationalism, which is not to suggest that the Pan-Arab feeling is not being played for all it is worth whenever expedient (at present, for instance, in relation to the problem of north Africa).

The creed of Pan-Arab nationalism, genetically but not inherently connected with democratic aspirations, may be sketched somewhat as follows. The community of the Arabs, that is, the Arabic-speaking peoples, stretching from the Persian Gulf to the Atlantic inhabits regions that possess considerable geographical similarities and great economic potentialities. The population represents "a young race that has its origin in the harmonious fusion of various human strains which Islam has brought together in one crucible." Within this community there is no distinction of color or race. The blood mixture has resulted in a great similarity of intellectual and moral aptitudes even though the variety of physical types has been maintained. This Arab "race" is extremely "prolific, courageous, enthusiastic, enduring, patient, and guided by the spirit of fairness." The absolute superiority of Arabic over all other languages allows it a great civilizational role.[10] The

[10] The position of their language in the cultural self-view of the French comes to mind. It characterizes the different mentalities of the two areas of civilization that what to the Arabs is a signal reason of pride in their tongue, its wealth in synonyms, is considered by the French a dangerous weakness, for to them the ideal language has one word for each object and each concept; synonyms are but a complicating factor in the vocabulary en-

influence of Islam confers on "Arabism" a sense of spiritual values which sets it off against the materialism of the West. What internal divisions exist, such as sects or tribes, are but the result of ignorance or of foreign interference.[11] Add to this the claim, made with varying degrees of conviction, that the most outstanding features of modern civilization in the West have their origin in the Arab-Muslim tradition and the peculiar feeling of being a chosen people derived from their central position within Islam, and you have all the elements from which historical constructs are constantly being devised and revised, all designed to justify aspiration and hope for the future in terms of past achievement.

More important than to point out the factual or even the psychological weaknesses in the *soi-disant* historical ideology of Arab nationalism is the realization that this kind of defensive pseudo learning has been paralleled in other areas under comparable circumstances. Thus the rise of France and of French civilization in the Renaissance of the sixteenth century was accompanied by the "*légende gauloise.*" No less a thinker than Jean Bodin (d. 1596) has had his hand in the development of the myth, according to which there existed at a very early date in France a highly advanced civilization from which

---

dangering the clarity that is its true aim and glory (cf. H. Gillot, *La Querelle des anciens et des modernes en France* [Paris, 1914], p. 445, and the discussions extending throughout the seventeenth and eighteenth centuries on French as the *langue universelle*). The Arabic point of view is defended, as it were, by Théophile Gautier (1811-1872) who prefaces his appreciation of Balzac's style with this observation: "La langue française, épurée par les classiques du dix-septième siècle, n'est propre lorsqu'on veut s'y conformer qu'à rendre des idées générales, et qu'à peindre des figures conventionnelles dans un milieu vague" (quoted by E. R. Curtius, *Balzac* [Bonn, 1923], p. 435).

[11] R. Montagne, "La Crise politique de l'Arabisme (Juin 1937-Juin 1938)," *La France méditerranéenne et africaine*, I (1938), 19, summarizes an article by ʿAbdarraḥmān ʿAzzām, published in *al-ʿArab* (Jerusalem), Aug. 27, 1932 (not accessible to the writer). Cf. the position taken by al-Kawākibī (1849-1902) in his *Umm al-Qurà*, as summarized by S. G. Haim in *Oriento Moderno*, XXX (1955), 133-134.

the Greeks were to borrow the secret of their arts and sciences. Reviling the Greeks and the Romans as liars and charlatans because of their claim to cultural innovation, the French nationalist historians of the time try to see the rise of their country prefigured, as it were, in the perfection of Gaulish civilization, of which classical civilization was but an ungrateful beneficiary.[12] Measured by this cobweb of legends, the Pan-Arab myth surprises by its sanity and realism.

Myth or reality—the Arab finds himself entangled in a number of circles or life circles which he has to arrange and value in some orderly sequence. There is his nation (in the narrower sense), there is the *ʿarabiyya*, there is the world of Islam; there may be geopolitical units which invite identification; there is the relationship to the West which needs to be clarified, for to a certain extent the interpretation the Arab puts upon it provides the key to his self-interpretation.

Eight years ago Gamāl ʿAbd an-Nāṣir, then prime minister of Egypt, published a series of three magazine articles under the title *The Philosophy of the Revolution*.[13] In this highly informative booklet the concept of the life circles within which Egypt or any Egyptian has to move is set forth poignantly and in a manner to make it immediately evident how a different shade of nationalistic orientation would have to express itself.

After first observing that "the era of isolation is now gone," Gamāl ʿAbd an-Nāṣir states:

I survey our conditions and find out we are in a group of circles which should be the theatre of our activity and in which we try to move as much as we can. . . .

---

[12] Cf. Gillot, *op. cit.*, pp. 125-130. The devaluation of the Roman element in the Byzantine heritage by Theodoros Metochites (d. 1332) is another instance of a nationalistic movement striving for self-understanding at the expense of historical insight (cf. H.-G. Beck, *Theodoros Metochites. Die Krise des byzantinischen Weltbildes im vierzehnten Jahrhundert* [München, 1952], pp. 80-81).

[13] Cairo: Dar al-Maaref, 1954, 73 pp.; published also in Arabic and in French.

We cannot look stupidly at a map of the world not realising our place therein and the role determined to us [*sic*] by that place. Neither can we ignore that there is an Arab circle surrounding us and that this circle is as much a part of us as we are part of it, that our history has been mixed with it and that its interests are linked with ours. These are actual facts and not mere words.

Can we ignore that there is a continent of Africa in which fate has placed us and which is destined today to witness a terrible struggle on its future? This struggle will affect us whether we want it or not.

Can we ignore that there is a Moslem world with which we are tied by bonds which are not only forged by religious faith but also tightened by the facts of history. I said once that fate plays no jokes. It is not in vain that our country lies to the Southwest of Asia close to the Arab world, whose life is intermingled with ours. It is not in vain that our country lies in the North East of Africa, a position from which it gives upon the dark continent wherein rages today the most violent struggle between white colonisers and black natives for the possession of its inexhaustible resources. It is not in vain that Islamic civilisation and Islamic heritage, which the Mongols ravaged in their conquest of the old Islamic capitals, retreated and sought refuge in Egypt where they found shelter and safety as a result of the counterattack with which Egypt repelled the invasion of these Tartars at Ein Galout.[14]

As if the ranking of the circles had not been made sufficiently explicit, Gamāl ʿAbd an-Nāṣir continues:

There is no doubt that the Arab circle is the most important and the most closely connected with us. Its history merges with ours. We have suffered the same hardships, lived the same crises and when we fell prostrate under the spikes of the horses of conquerors they lay with us. . . .[15] If we direct our attention after that to the second circle, the circle of the continent of Africa, I would say, without exaggeration, that we cannot, in any way, stand aside, even if we wish to, away from the sanguinary and dreadful struggle now raging in the heart of Africa between five

[14] *Op. cit.*, pp. 53-55. The battle was fought in 1260.
[15] *Ibid.*, p. 56.

million whites and two hundred million Africans. . . . The third circle now remains; the circle that goes beyond continents and oceans and to which I referred, as the circle of our brethren in faith who turn with us, whatever part of the world they are in, towards the same Kibla in Mecca, and whose pious lips whisper reverently the same prayers.[16]

Touching upon the feelings aroused in him by a visit to the Kaᶜba in Mecca, Gamāl ᶜAbd an-Nāṣir concludes:

When my mind travelled to the eighty million Moslems in Indonesia, the fifty in China and the several other million in Malaya, Siam, and Burma, and the hundred million in Pakistan, the hundred million or more in the Middle East, and the forty in Russia, as well as the other millions in the distant parts of the world, when I visualise these millions united in one faith I have the great consciousness of the tremendous potentialities that cooperation amongst them all can achieve: a cooperation that does not deprive them of their loyalty to their countries but which guarantees for them and their brethren a limitless power.[17]

In this passage the intoxication with (generously exaggerated) numbers of Muslims is less significant than the anxiousness to forestall the accusation of wishing to weaken their "patriotic" loyalty in favor of their Islamic loyalty and the hierarchic arrangement of the circles themselves. Leaving aside the play given to the African circle, which at least at this moment reflects government policy rather than popular sentiment, it is Gamāl ᶜAbd an-Nāṣir's rating of Egypt, the Arab world, and then the Muslim world, faithful reflection of political realities though it is, which the Muslim Brotherhood would want to reverse and the Pan-Arab intellectual to modify.

While the facts of life are likely to sustain, at least for the time being, Gamāl ᶜAbd an-Nāṣir's outlook on the Arab nation-state within the Islamic world as a whole, conservative Islam has in every single Arabic state (apart from Lebanon) fought an ideological battle turning on the

[16] *Ibid.*, pp. 70-71.
[17] *Ibid.*, p. 73.

constitutional designation of Islam as the official religion of the particular state. The outcome varied; but only in Syria the question of being called an Islamic state (which in many a sense she obviously is) became a hotly debated issue. It has been indicated that the conservatives carried the day by obtaining the insertion in the constitutions of 1950 and 1953 of a compromise formulation of their viewpoint by means of the statements: "1. The religion of the President of the Republic is Islam. 2. Muslim Law (*fiqh*) is the principal source of legislation." (The second statement is of great programmatic significance but, outside the area of personal status, of scant accuracy.)

The Muslim conservative has never ceased to argue that in Islam political conduct and religion (*siyāsa* and *dīn*) are inseparable and that the decline of the Islamic state, often reckoned from the death of ʿAlī, the last of the *rāshidūn* caliphs, in 661, was primarily due to the breaking asunder of the life of the *umma* into a religious and a worldly segment. Western democracy has lent the conservative spokesmen an additional argument:

> The principle followed in the constitutions of the world, in the organization of parties, and in the procedures of representative assemblies, as acknowledged by the entire world, is that the opinion of the majority is to be followed and acted upon. If, therefore, we say that the religion of the state is Islam, it being the religion of nine-tenths of the Syrians and of ninety-eight per cent of the Arabs, will we have exceeded the truth or deviated from democracy? [Note in this connection that] the states which have specified a particular religion in their constitution have not only taken the religion of the majority as the official religion, but in many cases have even taken the sect of the majority as the official religious sect.[18]

It may be mentioned in passing that it will be the application of that very principle of democratic vote-count-

[18] Shaikh Muṣṭafà as-Sibāʿī (b. 1900), writing in the Syrian newspaper *al-Manār*, Feb., 1950; trans. R. B. Winder in *The Muslim World*, XLIV (1954), 217-226. The above passage is from p. 219.

ing, of which they have been fervent advocates, which will in a perfectly legitimate way continue the non-Muslim communities in their precarious position as semi-outsiders, as long as the citizen's place in society in even the most modernistically structured Near Eastern state is very largely determined by his religious affiliation. By indirection, Shaikh as-Sibāʿī's next paragraphs illuminate this situation:

We, the Syrians, advocates of Arab unity, consider ourselves to be a part of the Arab nation and consider our Syrian fatherland to be part of the greater Arab fatherland. Our republic is today a member of the Arab League and will tomorrow, by the grace of God, be part of a single Arab state. According to the lowest estimate the Arabs number seventy million, of whom sixty-eight are Muslims and two are Christians, and all the states of the Arab League (except for Lebanon which has a special position) either specify that the religion of the state is Islam in their constitutions, as is the case with Egypt, Iraq and Jordan; or else their existence is implicitly based on that fact, as is the case with Saudi Arabia and Yemen.

Thus the esablishment of Islam as the state religion will be a strong factor for unity between ourselves and our Arab brethren and a formal symbol of the *rapprochement* between the states of the Arab League. Why, therefore, should we neglect the strongest factor—popular and official—for Arab unity? Why should we refuse to face reality? [19]

It is easily seen that the Shaikh, although, not unlike Gamāl ʿAbd an-Nāṣir, he seems to ascend from Syria via the Arab nation to the unity of Islam, sees in Islam the true bond that holds together the individual states and almost their principal *raison d'être*. Besides, one cannot help noting that his Pan-Arab feeling is considerably warmer than that of the Egyptian president.

But the significance of Shaikh as-Sibāʿī's plea goes even further when, at a later point, he deals with the difference

[19] *Ibid.*, p. 220. In this connection the observations of A. J. Toynbee, "The Ineffectiveness of Panislamism," in A *Study of History* (London and New York, 1934-1954), VIII, 692-695, make interesting reading.

between Western (and Turkish) and Arab nationalism and by implication touches upon the current key problem of the Near East (and other large areas of the world), its cultural relationship to the West:

National unity among the Arabs will not be achieved by throwing away the sympathies of sixty millions and by neglecting the national religious tie between them. Although it is understood that the nationalism of Europe decrees as a fundamental tenet the expulsion of religion, that step is not incumbent on us, the Arabs. Nazi Germany may have found in Christianity a religion which was foreign to it. Turanian Turkey may find in Islam a religion foreign to it. But the Arabs will never find in Islam a religion foreign to them. In fact they believe that Arab nationalism was born only when they embraced Islam and that this nationalism would not be so vital as it obviously is were it not for Islam. Therefore, let the advocates of nationalism distinguish between Europe and the East, between the Christianity of the West and the Islam of the Arabs.[20]

---

[20] Winder, *op. cit.*, p. 223; cf. Nadwī's dictum, *op. cit.*, p. 247[9]: "fa'l-islām huwa qaumiyyat al-ʿālam al-ʿarabī." Similar is the integration of Arab nationalism and Islamic universalism attempted by the ʿIrāqī ʿAbdarraḥmān al-Bazzāz, who sees Islam as the expression of "Arabism"; he, too, contrasts Arab nationalism, which does not find itself in conflict with Islam, with Turkish nationalism, which does (cf. his *al-Islām waʾl-qaumiyya ʾl-ʿarabiyya* [Baghdad, 1952], trans. S. G. Haim in *Die Welt des Islams*, n.s., III [1954], 201-218). Here we meet with a "secularization," as it were, of that line of thought which inspired the observation of Muḥammad Rashīd Riḍā (in 1900) that countries conquered by the Arabs were lasting conquests of Islam, whereas the majority of the countries conquered by the Turks turned out to be a burden for Islam. The relevant passage from *al-Manār* was translated by Miss Haim in *Oriente Moderno*, XXXVI (1956), 415-416. It is worth recalling that from its very inception the theory of Arab nationalism was molded by the necessity to establish its compatibility with an Islamic outlook. The Christian treatment of the problem presented by a division of loyalties between religious and political affiliation provides an illuminating contrast. Cf., e.g., Fr. Anselm Stolz in *Benediktinische Monatsschrift*, XVII (1935), 132: ". . . [The Christian] würde das Wesen der Kirche als beginnendes Gottes-

Islam's cultural and religious affinities, as recognized by revelation itself, are with Christianity and Judaism, or, in modern terms, with the Western rather than the Asiatic world. Modernism has, if anything, emphasized this fact. It is the spectacle of Western scientific and social progress, brought home to the Muslim world through its political superiority, which in the last analysis constitutes the foremost inducement to Westernize. Westernization develops what secularizing tendencies there are in the Islamic heritage; it relegates the canon law, in a sense the greatest achievement of traditional Islam, to the background; and it assails the social basis of traditional society by changing the status of women, introducing democratic procedures, and establishing a new kind of education.

The radicalism of the change and perhaps even more its inevitability have aroused a widespread emotional resistance which finds expression on different levels. A conservative paper like *Al-Islam, An Independent Exponent of Orthodox Islam* (Karachi, Pakistan), may write editorially:

Our intelligentsia, utterly ignorant of the scientific implications of the progress made by the West, sing the praises of Western culture only because it gives them opportunities of indulging in frivolous and vulgar pursuits. They hate Religion because it bans all such harmful activities. They want the separation of Religion from political life because by doing so they have no moral scruples. Bribery and nepotism, blackmarketing and smuggling, prostitution and games of chance can only be tolerated in an irreligious society and that is what the Intelligentsia want. The only attribute the Intelligentsia have ingrained out of

reich verkennen . . . , wollte er Werte des Volkstums denen der Kirche ebenbürtig an die Seite stellen oder gar ihnen überordnen." Stolz goes on to quote from the *Letter to Diognetus* a passage to the effect that the Christians live as strangers in their own fatherland. In this context it may be pertinent to recall P. K. Hitti's observation that the Shīʿa authorities in Karbalāʾ and Najaf "still consider Islam supranational, demanding loyalty that is transcendent and providing laws as good for the twentieth as for the seventh century" (*Cahiers d'histoire mondiale,* II [1955], 630-631).

their contact with Western life is HYPOCRISY which leads them to attain power by appealing to the democratic and religious sentiments of the people and then to condemn both Democracy and Religion.[21]

But within the ranks of the modernizers themselves the resistance can be felt as well; there it takes the form of an intense uneasiness about the derivative character of much of the cultural and political advance achieved (or aimed at). This uneasiness leads in turn to a tendency to interpret the borrowing as indigenous growth; in other words, to let heterogenetic change be experienced as orthogenetic. We have seen, in another cultural context, an outgrowth of this same psychological need in the short-lived fashion of the *légende gauloise*.

Where does all this leave Near Eastern, Arab, Muslim nationalism? It will doubtless be compelled to continue Westernization; its self-realization, not to say its self-preservation, depends on increased admission of Western ideas and techniques—organizational, economic, cultural.[22] At the same time conservative pressure will force the concealment of the borrowing, whenever possible, behind the veil of the orthogenetic legend. Political stability, the most urgent short-range problem, is contingent upon the stabilization of self-respect, and self-esteem in turn depends on an amalgamation of prides: pride in the Muslim past and its assimilative powers, pride in the moral and intellectual courage to undertake an all but complete rebuilding of one's life structure and to embark on the most hazardous adventure open to man, the rethinking and redefining of his universe in range and kind, and of his own identity in it.

[21] Vol. III, no. 1 (Jan. 1, 1955), p. 1.

[22] Cf. Nadwī, *op. cit.*, pp. 229-231, on the acceptance of European aims by Europe's Asiatic opponents.

X

Nationalism and Cultural Trends in the Arab Near East

IT WOULD BE no more than a slight exaggeration to derive all the major problems that have been plaguing the Muslim-dominated Middle East and, more particularly, its Arabic-speaking sections for the last 150 years from the necessity to respond to the impact of the West. This is not to say that the Muslim world was not earlier aware of its progressive political disintegration and ineffectiveness. Reform programs had been submitted to the Ottoman sultans as early as 1630. Throughout the nineteenth century and as late as the First World War, European experts and statesmen disagreed with regard to the advisability of forcing reforms on the Ottoman Empire. The majority saw the only cure for its numerous weaknesses in limited Westernization, a view in which most spokesmen for the articulate intelligentsia, both Turkish and Arabic, would concur; a smaller group of Westerners, on the other hand, realized the debilitating effect of changes tending to equalize the position of all the sultan's subjects and to impose a centralized administration, for which no suitable staff was available, on a political structure that had been kept together by the self-interest of the Muslim Turkish ruling class and the sealing off of potentially disruptive national differences by the relative isolation of the several provinces. The verdict that neither action nor inaction could have preserved the Ottoman structure without outside help may be justified by the shrinking of the Porte's European possessions and, even more convincingly, by the rise of her Egyptian "vassal," Muḥammad ʿAlī.[1]

Whether unconsciously or by design, the West has been ever present in the minds of the Middle Easterners since Napoleon invaded and effortlessly conquered Egypt at the close of the eighteenth century. It has been present as a menace, as a helper, as a model; it has been admired and it has been hated, but it has never relinquished its function as the principal orientation point for Middle Eastern aspirations, cultural as well as political, and there is no indication that it will do so in the foreseeable future. The Arabic East has been, and still is, wavering between assimilation and rejection—both equally impossible as total objectives—and is groping toward a redefinition of its religious and social tradition. But, whereas in the early phases of this endeavor the strength of the Islamic tradition impeded creative absorption of the inevitable bor-

---

[1] H. W. V. Temperley, *England and the Near East. I. The Crimea* (London, New York, 1936), though confining himself largely to diplomatic history and Western source materials, offers a suggestive picture of the state of the Ottoman Empire in the first half of the nineteenth century.

To avoid creating a one-sided picture it must be recorded that some *ʿulamāʾ*, especially of the higher ranks, endorsed the modernization policies of Maḥmūd II, including his measures to combat plague and cholera; cf. U. Heyd, "The Ottoman ʿUlamā and Westernization in the Time of Selīm III and Maḥmūd II," in: *Studies in Islamic History and Civilization*, ed. U. Heyd (Jerusalem, 1961), pp. 63-96, at pp. 64-69.

rowings into the inherited framework, lately the weakening of this tradition has tended to promote a defensive extremism on the part of those still unreservedly dedicated to the inherited way of life. The modernizing patriot is therefore compelled to dissociate himself from the religious heritage more radically than he would actually have wished were it not that he felt his ideal of a modern national state endangered by what to him are outmoded ideals and methods of social organization. Conversely, the upholder of the primacy of Islam is forced to emphasize the nation-building effect of the Koranic revelation, at first within the warring Arab tribes and, after the conquests, down to our own day, in cementing believers of many races and languages into the community of the faithful, which is, in some way, perceived in the guise of a nation or a state.

In a recent expression of this outlook, al-Kharbuṭlī summarizes and makes his own the late Ṣādiq ar-Rāfiʿī's views on "the Arab nationality in the Koran": "Ce Coran conduit les hommes vers ce qu'il y a de plus droit et son plus grand miracle, c'est la notion que nous pouvons en tirer de la nationalité arabe qu'il a édifiée sur les diverses nations en les articulant politiquement." Al-Kharbuṭlī develops this idea further, laying special stress on the unifying power of language: "L'une des choses impossibles, et que réalisa cependant le Coran, fut d'unir ceux qui avaient traversé les siècles en restant divisés, par une sorte de lien racial dans lequel ne se trouve d'autre sectarisme que celui de l'esprit." Without a linguistic tie neither religion nor anything else can bind the nations together: "Le fait que le Coran ait conservé son aspect arabe fait que tous les Musulmans, à quelque race qu'ils appartiennent, deviennent, des rouges aux noirs, au regard de la société et à leurs propres yeux, comme formant un seul corps, s'exprimant, dans le langage de l'Histoire, en une langue unique. Dès lors, tout particularisme racial disparaît." [2]

---

[2] ʿAlī Ḥusnī al-Kharbuṭlī, *Muḥammad wa'l-qaumiyya 'l-ʿarabiyya* (Cairo, 1959), a section of which has been published in French translation in *Orient*, XV (1960), 161-166; see p. 165.

It is worthy of notice that Voltaire, *Mahomet*, Act II, Scene

To the Middle Easterner who is conscious of the precarious position of his society, its problems are apt to appear as those of national-building by means of a feeling of national unity, which needs correlation to the sentiment of religious affiliation which, for many centuries, had successfully been claiming the first loyalty of the people of the region, regardless of whether their particular denomination was Muslim, Jewish, or Christian (of various creeds and rites). The traditional hierarchy of loyalties has been expressed with unexcelled precision by Muḥammad Rashīd Riḍā (1865-1935) who states, after pointing out that in our age the political interest of the Arabs and that of the Muslims are in full agreement: "Were they in conflict I should place the obligations imposed on me by my religion ahead of those demanded by the interest of my people (*abnāʾ jins-ī*)." [3]

How the members of those diverse and frequently hostile religious groups would be able to unite under the banner of the nation-state is a problem that some of the theorists of nationalism have faced rather squarely. The solutions suggested differ sharply. Some have argued that integration into a nationality happens automatically. The mere sharing of the geographical environment sets in motion a biological process of assimilation. The individual is not confronted with a decision. He belongs to his fatherland because he resides in it permanently, and because his ancestors have been living in the same country. This is the viewpoint adopted, for example, by Muṣṭafà Kāmil, one of the early leaders of the Egyptian national movement (1874-1908).[4]

5, shows a remarkable awareness of the nation-building force of Muḥammad's message projecting as plan into the Prophet's mind what Islam actually was to achieve for the Arabs. Voltaire's distortion of the Prophet's motivation did not stand in the way of a correct sociopolitical diagnosis.

[3] Muḥammad Rashīd Riḍā, "Al-Masʾala 'l-ʿarabiyya" ("The Arab Question"), *al-Manār*, XX (1917-1919), 33-47; see p. 34^{20-21}.

[4] Cf. F. Steppat, "Nationalismus und Islam bei Mustafa Kamil," *Die Welt des Islams*, IV/4 (Leiden, 1956), 241-341,

It would be a distortion of known facts to present emotional allegiance to the individual state or the local dynasty as a negligible factor in the life of the Middle East prior to acquaintance with modern Europe; yet it remains true that the consciousness of belonging with, say, the Muslim community took precedence, in the Arabic-speaking world at least, over any other self-identification to such an extent that the question of an ideological and moral conflict between the totalitarian claims of religion and nation never arose.[5] On the other hand, it is the very conflict between those claims which for the last century has been shaping the domestic policies and the cultural movement of the Arab Middle East.

The facts determining the precise nature of the friction between the internationalism of the *umma* (or *jamāʿa,* to introduce a term frequently used in the Middle Ages, or again the *fikra islāmiyya,* which among contemporary intellectuals appears to evoke comparable associations)[6] and the separatist individualism of the several *shuʿūb,* or nations, of which the Muslim world is composed, have

---

esp. pp. 256-257. Others consider the transcending of group loyalty toward a national loyalty as an act of will, i.e., as a matter of personal decision. It is possible to adopt or to reject a past; how much more readily is it possible to identify with a living community (cf. my *Islam. Essays in the Nature and Growth of a Cultural Tradition* [2d ed.; London, 1961], p. 62). On the possibility of identifying with a past not one's own by genealogical heritage, cf. further H.-I. Marrou, *De la Conaissance historique* (Paris, 1955), pp. 212-213. From a practical point of view, however, the political realities of the Arab states tend to diminish the importance of the problem. The Muslim majority is so overwhelming that the democratic process guarantees Muslim sentiment a preponderance in government which makes the conveying of non-Muslim loyalties toward the national state a matter of minor importance, in terms of the stability of the individual state.

[5] A modern Egyptian writer, Ṣubḥī Waḥīda, *Fī uṣūl al-masʾala 'l-miṣriyya* (Cairo, 1950), pp. 39-46, deals with medieval Islamic and especially Egyptian history largely from this point of view.

[6] Waḥīda, *op. cit.,* pp. 113-114, speaks very suggestively of the *ʿālamiyya,* the international outlook of the nongovernmental classes in Egypt from the Mamluk period on.

been set forth at the beginning of the preceding chapter. The tension between the two concepts of organization must be accepted as a permanent formative factor; this may be the reason that a Muḥammad ʿAbduh attempted to define both the *umma* and the nation as normative ideas; it may also be the reason that his desire to retain the *umma* as the basic political unit was immediately and violently opposed by the nationalists.[7]

Only recently, Abul ʿAla Maudoodi (b. 1903), leader of the Jamaʿat-i Islami of Pakistan, has restated the incompatibility of nationalism and Islam: "What is selfishness in individual life is nationalism in social life. A nationalist is naturally narrow-minded and niggardly." [8] Besides, nationalism stands condemned as an imitation of the West, and Islam objects to imitation. It would nevertheless be erroneous to infer from the large number of often quoted antinationalistic statements of respected theological leaders that all conservative Muslims are animated by a sense of the incompatibility of allegiance to their religion and allegiance to their nation. In fact, many an Arab Muslim, while refraining from probing too deeply into the potentially conflicting demands of those loyalties, seems to derive from history a comforting feeling that his religion and his civilization are at one, or, better still, that they presuppose each other. It is much more difficult to identify the cause of Islam with any of the actually existing Arab states; and where Pan-Arabism and Islam may be considered complementary aspects of the same cultural and political manifestation, the local nationalism cannot so readily be reconciled with the Islamic aspiration.

Nationalism as a means of removing the political and cultural inferiority of the Arab-Muslim states has been

---

[7] Cf. also N. Safran, *Egypt in Search of Political Community* (Cambridge, Mass., 1961), p. 71.

[8] Cf. F. Abbott, "The Jamaʿat-i-Islami of Pakistan," *The Middle East Journal*, XI/1 (1957), 37-51, esp. pp. 39-40. Antinationalism as complement and reverse of Islamic internationalism (conceived as a dynamic characteristic) was an element of Iqbāl's thinking; cf. M. Siddiqi, *op. cit.*, pp. 19-23.

willing to do away with institutional and legal precepts of Islam, though less so to abolish its practices and social mores. Except for certain backward-looking reform movements, such as Wahhabism, theology as such had been barren for a number of centuries; metaphysical and purely creedal dissensions no longer readily evoke popular passions. It is, by and large, only the Holy Book, the person of the Prophet, and, to a lesser extent, the *aḥkām dīniyya,* which possess a strong emotional appeal. The "scientific" interpretation of the Koran remains a delicate enterprise; a Koranic criticism after the fashion of Western Biblical criticism is out of the question; even the purely literary or stylistic analysis of the Book is an explosive subject. A biography of Muḥammad on the model of Buhl or Andrae would hardly be countenanced by theological opinion, and would probably embarrass even the "secular" intelligentsia. But the removal of Koran and Prophet from scientific analysis must not be confused with responsiveness to theological issues as such. The ignorance of the secular intelligentsia with regard to the Muslim creed and the theological disputes and problems of the past can hardly be exaggerated. When the position of Islamic theology on a matter like predestination is discussed, positions are taken with a view to evidence the compatibility of the Muslim outlook with modernization and progress; what irritation is engendered is not *furor theologicus,* but sensitivity to the suspected implication that the Islamic ideology constitutes an impediment to national advancement. The true theological conflicts are confined to limited circles within the *ʿulamāʾ* when conservative learning objects to pragmatic restyling of the religious heritage. The Islamic fervor of the public stems from its passionate affirmation of its identification with Islam as the (in its true form) most perfect body social and politic, not from dedication to creedal statements so long as they do not concern Muḥammad and the Koran and so long as the practices of popular devotion are left alone.[9]

[9] This is not to say that these practices are necessarily a shibboleth. Ibn ar-Rūmī (d. 889 or 896) had already made fun of

But Islam as a basis of social and intellectual integration, and embodiment of the last and most perfect revelation, the rationale of a cohesiveness that tied together a multilingual and multinational body of believers which did not possess, as the Catholics do, a directing ecclesiastical organization—this aspect of Islam had remained intact as the most precious element in communal identification. This continuing strength of Islam as a factor of social and hence political cohesiveness bestows on the nationalism of the Arab-Muslim peoples its double profile. On the one hand, it presents itself as a nationalistic movement of the conventional European style, based on a sense of racial kinship and with certain geographical claims that are justified on historical grounds. On the other, it is a thinly disguised Mahdist movement aiming at a forcible purification of Islam and at the revival of the traditionally demanded imperialism of the *umma*. The interlocking of these two activistic drives gives Arab nationalism its strength and makes it proof against the hesitations of a purely secular *Realpolitik*. The thinness of its theoretical expressions, which has often been remarked upon, in

---

Ramadan and had complained of its hardships. One of his poems begins: "Those in error deem Ramadan to be blessed but they are right, indeed, [who say] that it is long" (Ibn abī ʿAun, *Kitāb at-tashbīhāt*, ed. M. ʿA. Khān [London, 1950], p. 330[4]); but semiserious complaints of this kind did and do not give offense. A similar humorous reference to the month of fasting from an epistle of the famous vizier Ibn al-ʿAmīd (d. 970), together with more objectionable passages in which poets of the ninth and tenth centuries use religious concepts in their imagery, will be found in ʿAbdalqāhir al-Jurjānī (d. 1078 or 1081), *Asrār al-balāgha*, ed. H. Ritter (Istanbul, 1954), pp. 210-215; German trans. by the same (Wiesbaden, 1959), pp. 249-255. On the other hand, for large sections of the Muslim public, the words addressed in 1909 by Jurjī Zaidān (d. 1914) to Salāma Mūsà (*ca.* 1887-1959) would still be true: "Never mind if we criticize the Christians, for they have themselves already written the critique of their religion. But the Muslims we must treat with circumspection. They have not yet produced any self-criticism [*lam yaʾlafū 'n-naqd*]." Cf. S. Mūsà, *Tarbiyat Salāma Mūsà* (Cairo, 1948), p. 213; English trans. by L. O. Schuman (Leiden, 1961), p. 153.

contrast to the almost excessive theorizing of European nationalism in the nineteenth century, may be traceable in part to this sometimes contested yet all-important link with the aspirations of the religious community, which a systematic analysis and theory of *qaumiyya* would be bound to isolate, thus weakening the support of political nationalism on the part of the masses.[10] The emotional force of the Arab identification derives less from its historical-sociological content than from a similarity of attitudes holding sway from Morocco to Iraq and an inclination to consider the similarities more essential than the equally patent contrasts. This approach allows non-Arab groups like the Sudanese to adopt an Arab self-identification. "Arabism is a myth, sustained by a civilization; its political expression is the insurrection against the *fait accompli.*" [11]

---

[10] For *qaumiyya* cf., e.g., the listing of definitions by J. Monsot, "À propos du Congrès des Écrivains Arabes," *Orient,* V (1958), 39-45, esp. pp. 44-45. R. Charles, *L'Évolution de l'Islam* (Paris, 1960), pp. 83-97, offers an interesting analysis of this double-edged nationalism of the Arab-Muslim world; note especially his observation, pp. 83-84, that the new doctrine reflects the attraction of both universality and individuality, which has always been characteristic for the Muslims of Arab origin. Cf. also p. 85 on the negativism of Arab nationalistic thinking which is the natural consequence of its antitheoretical bent.

[11] J. Berque, *Les Arabes* (Paris, 1959), pp. 13, 14. Cf. also "Les arabes et les autres," *ibid.*, pp. 101-105. The mythopoeic quality of nationalism has been traced in every culture area, although the divorcement of the national myth from historical fact is not everywhere equally profound. Cf. the informative chapter, "Theories and Myths" (in Negro Africa), in Th. Hodgkin, *Nationalism in Colonial Africa* (London, 1956), pp. 168-184, and chaps. V, VI, and XI of this book. For a general statement, cm. Eric Dardel, *L'Histoire, science du concret* (Paris, 1946), pp. 122-125, and E. Kedourie, *Nationalism* (London, 1960), *passim.* As early as 1947 Michel ʿAflaq insisted on the necessarily negative character of any liberation or renewal movement in an oppressed country; he added, however, that for lasting significance the "awakening," *yaqẓa,* must soon proclaim a positive content. This is the task faced by the Arabs and, it must be admitted, most successfully confronted in the East by the Baʿth. Cf. M. ʿAflaq, *Maʿrakat al-maṣīr al-wāḥid* (3rd ed.; Beirut, 1963), pp. 9-17.

The perfection of Islam guaranteed the perfection of the Muslim community and through it justified a sense of individual perfection, not as an absolute of moral blamelessness but as a latent feeling of the superiority that is conveyed by possession of the fullest measure of truth ever vouchsafed human beings by their merciful Lord.[12] This

---

[12] Charles, *op. cit.*, p. 73, quotes L. Gardet to the effect that Islam is no longer content to restore itself to political and cultural equality, and adds that "il est désormais sûr (à vrai dire, il n'a cessé d'être imbu d'une telle conviction profonde) qu'il est le seul capable de résoudre les problèmes cruciaux que l'humanité tout entière affronte aujourd'hui." The somewhat unfortunate tactics of having the superiority of Islam corroborated by Western testimonials to the scientific achievements of the Muslim Middle Ages and by noting preannouncements of recent scientific discoveries in the Koran has its counterparts in equally puerile efforts on the part of Christian and Jewish writers of the eighteenth and nineteenth centuries. Under the best of circumstances it is dangerous for religion to identify with a given state of science; the shifts in science cannot but affect the religious message which supposedly drew support from agreement with its last but one phase. Besides, if ablution, for example, is justified as a hygienic measure, it will not be long before one comes to feel that more effective hygienic techniques make it a questionable procedure. Cf. the reflections of P. Rondot, "Les Musulmans devant la technique," *Cahiers de l'I.S.É.A.*, CVI (1960), 37-62, at pp. 45-51, 60-61. The prevailing attitude among Muslims toward the historical examination of Islam as such and the personality of the Prophet corresponds closely to that observed by E. Troeltsch in 1901 among certain Christian theologians and Church historians who, in his words, would permit research into Christianity and the Christian origins on the condition that "das Christentum sei als individuell historische. Erscheinung im Licht seines Anspruchs auf absolute und einzigartige Wahrheit ausschliesslich zu betrachten, *womit das dogmatisch-apologetische Bild des Christentums ohne weiteres mit der Sache selbst identifiziert wird.*" Cf. Troeltsch, *Die Absolutheit des Christentums und die Religionsgeschichte* (2nd ed.; Tübingen, 1912), p. xxii. The characterization of Christian apologetics of the nineteenth century which Troeltsch offers, *ibid.*, pp. 1-25, proves highly instructive for current Muslim apologetics with the qualification, however, that among Muslim theologians the breakthrough toward a historic-universalistic concept of their faith which, in Troeltsch' time was impending in the theological faculties of Europe, is yet to come and not actually in sight.

sense of superiority was shaken but not destroyed, and was ultimately forced into uneasy coexistence with an equally keen sense of inferiority which stemmed from the reversal by the West of what the Muslim world had habitually considered the natural order of things.

The illusion of Muslim political grandeur, which circumstances allowed to continue long after its reality had ceased, was shattered during the nineteenth century, and nationalism, the dominant note of the contemporary West, came in as a reaction to defeat, as a tool, as it were, to grow into the overruling passion of the region. Its origin or, more precisely, the political situation of its adoption accounts for the fact that its concern is primarily with foreign policy (and not with domestic reform), a bias that is semiconsciously assisted by the feeling that independence and national prestige are more directly needed for the restoration of self-respect, collective as well as individual.[13] Besides, it is in domestic affairs that the clash between the more strictly Islamic and the more decidedly modernistic outlook will be least reconcilable, and where, moreover, the modernists themselves are apt to split over the nature of the reform that everybody seems agreed, on a verbal level, is necessary. Yet it must be recognized as an essential trait of Arab (as of all Asiatic) nationalism that "nationalism implies social action," and that a sharpened sense of collective dignity tends to intensify the drive for internal amelioration.[14]

---

[13] The craving for self-respect has been incisively stated by Habib Bourguiba, "Nationalism: Antidote to Communism," Foreign Affairs, XXXV/4 (July, 1957), 648: "Our young men are inspired, above all, by an immense need for personal dignity."

[14] Bourguiba, *op. cit.*, p. 647. It is in the context of a statement such as this that Bourguiba's views on Islam, communism, and nationalism must be appraised. Bourguiba's formulations are these: "Some people believe that Islam is responsible for [the Arabs'] . . . resistance to Communist penetration. Certainly our Moslem religion inculcates respect for the individual and his liberty, implants faith in the transcendence of moral laws and inculcates us against the fallacious logic of dialectical materialism. On the other hand, Communism has made a successful compromise with Islam in the Soviet Republics of the Caucasus

In examining the problem of reform, rather than that of particular reforms, one must not overlook the varying degree to which, within one and the same person and one and the same social group or coterie, the several aspects of the Islamic religion have lost their hold. Any person, even a graduate of a Western university, is apt to be more conservative in his home than at his work. Doctrine may have become meaningless yet reverence and admiration for the Koran as unique in its form as well as its content remain strong; the five daily prayers may be neglected but the fast of the month of Ramadan is likely to be kept; the intellectual advocates the elimination of canon law from as many areas of public and private life as expediency permits, and yet maintains a romantic sense of the insuperable perfection of those early days of the Muslim community when a supposedly untainted and wholly Islamic regime gave the world the only period of true happiness it ever knew.

Like classical Judaism, Islam is more than a religion in the current interpretation of the word. It wants to be more than an integrated system of beliefs and devotional practices. It constitutes itself as the community of true

---

and Central Asia. It has skillfully hidden its philosophical tenets behind the social and material benefits obtained through an authoritarian and collectivist regime and a rapid improvement of what was an abysmally low living standard. Ignorance and poverty are quite capable of weakening the armor of the Moslem faith. The Arab masses can be tempted by an apparently generous system which simultaneously promises them freedom from European domination, social equality and better economic conditions, while also appealing to their old instinct for community living. The spiritual ramparts of the Moslem faith must be defended against Communism's insidious aggression by men with something constructive to offer. And only a nationalism resolutely committed to the path of progress can fit this need" (*ibid.*, pp. 647-648). Bourguiba's sense of the necessary unity of all the expressions of the national life of a people is remarkably strong: "The life of a nation somehow hangs together; to split the allegiances of its culture and mores, its economy and defense, would mean inviting dissolution. . . . A unified philosophy and a unified way of life are essential conditions of national stability" (*ibid.*, p. 653).

believers, and it claims that this community must and can conduct its entire existence by the precepts that are, explicitly or more often implicitly, contained in revelation and prophetic tradition. In fact, the community (or its spokesmen, the jurist-theologians or *ʿulamāʾ*) has always defined by consensus (tacit or articulate) the indispensable properties of a Muslim and, more particularly, of a Muslim life. A certain contempt for mere history as a binding experience has made it possible for the community to reorient itself at various times by what the contemporaries, in their concept of the golden age, felt to be the most relevant elements and hence the most relevant injunctions inherent in their heritage. The absence of an ecclesiastical organization facilitated the adjustment of the Islamic ideal to local exigencies, which is another way of saying that the ideas of the Islamic life have been varying greatly over the centuries and, at any given time, in different parts of the Muslim world. In terms of the Muslim legal language one could propose the formulation that a consensus on the measure to which Westernization is necessary for survival, or desirable for the resurgence, of the community has not yet been reached. Nor does there exist a consensus throughout the Muslim world as to whether Islam is or is not "essentially a political expression. . . . Is it a relationship with God capable of survival in any culture under reasonable conditions, or is it inevitably a religio-political entity in which form is as vital as spirit?" [15]

---

[15] K. Cragg, "Religious Developments in the 20th Century," *Cahiers d'Histoire Mondiale,* III (1956), 514. In *MIDEO,* III (1956), 475, it is reported that the Islamic Congress (*al-muʾtamar al-islāmī*), founded in 1953 in Mecca by King Ibn Saʿūd, Gamāl ʿAbd an-Nāṣir, and Gholām Mohammed, then governor general of Pakistan, sponsored (*inter alia*) a publication on this subject: *L'Islam est à la fois religion et nation.* Its train of thought is outlined as follows: "L'Islam est une relation entre Dieu et la créature, il organise l'autorité politique, la propriété, les rapports sociaux, les problèmes de la vie. Il ne sépare pas l'activité pratique du mobile religieux. Il ne sépare pas la religion du monde, il ne connaît pas le sacerdoce considéré comme un intermédiaire entre Dieu et les hommes. La renaissance islamique est basée sur la religion."

The traditional position has been well formulated in its reaffirmation by the *ʿulamāʾ* of al-Azhar when, in 1925, they condemned certain of the views expressed by one of their number, ʿAlī b. ʿAbdarrāziq, in his book *Islam and the Foundations of Authority.* "The shaikh ʿAlī is of the opinion that Islam is essentially a spiritual institution without any tie to temporal authority. . . . This theory is absolutely false. Koran and Sunna contain numerous precepts of a temporal character. . . . According to the unanimous consensus of the Muslims, Islam is the totality of the precepts transmitted by the Prophet in regard to doctrine, cult, and legal relations among the people. These precepts form one whole and cannot be dissociated one from another." [16]

It may be useful to recall in this context that the community (*umma*) is held exempt from error in religious matter and that extreme upholders of its *ʿiṣma ʿan al-khaṭaʾ* interpret it to include its collective infallibility in nonreligious affairs as well. Ghazzālī lists as examples the declaring of a state of war or peace and the founding of a settlement (*ʿimāra baldatin*), but is careful to add that while the *ʿiṣma* of the *umma* in point of religion (*dīn*) is accepted without qualification (*maqṭūʿ bi-wujūb al-ʿiṣma fīhi*), its *ʿiṣma* with regard to nonreligious matters (*fī ghair ad-dīn*) has been subject to doubt (*mashkūk*).[17]

Everybody seems agreed that membership in the Muslim community forms the strongest link among the very

---

[16] As the Arabic original of the *fatwà* is not at my disposal, I am translating from the abridged French version by L. Bercher, *Revue des Études Islamiques,* IX (1935), 75-86, esp. pp. 77-78; a German translation of Bercher's version was made by E. Gräf, "Probleme der Todesstrafe im Islam," *Zeitschrift für vergleichende Rechtswissenschaft,* XVII (1957), 115. The idea that Islam is "of one piece," that its various bases hold one another in place, and that the political and the religious cannot therefore be separated has recently been restated, e.g., by M. ʿA. al-ʿAmāwī, *Mustaqbal al-islām* (2d ed.; Cairo, 1956), pp. 52 ff. The observations of H. Laoust, "Le Réformisme orthodoxe des 'Salafīya,'" *Revue des Études islamiques,* VI (1932), 175-224, at pp. 199-205, are very informative in this context.

[17] *Al-Mustaṣfà min ʿilm al-uṣūl* (Cairo, 1356/1937), I, 113^{9-11}.

heterogeneous populations of the several Islamic states, but the conclusions drawn from this observation differ widely and irreconcilably. When one excepts specifically the states of Saudi Arabia and the Yemen and the religio-political movement of the Muslim Brotherhood, it may be argued that the Arab states are inclined toward limiting the role of the Muslim tradition in their political organization. True, the Syrian Constitution of September 5, 1950, makes an oblique reference to its Islamic foundation, and other states, too, have inserted some mention of their Muslim character into their fundamental charters. Thus the Constitution of the Republic of Iraq (July 27, 1958) and the Egyptian constitutions of April 19, 1923 (Art. 149), and 1956 (not, however, the Provisional Constitution of the United Arab Republic of March, 1958) declare Islam the religion of the state; so does the Fundamental Law of Morocco (June 2, 1961) and the document proclaiming the integration of Syria and Iraq in the United Arab Republic (April 17, 1963); but all the Arab states tend to curtail the actual validity of canon law and to remove the operations of the government from religious control. Pakistan, on the other hand, after a period of deliberation lasting almost nine years, has defined itself as "The Islamic Republic of Pakistan." The preamble to her constitution (adopted on February 29, 1956, and suspended in October, 1958), reads in part:

> In the name of Allah, the Beneficent, the Merciful.
>
> Whereas sovereignty over the entire Universe belongs to Allah Almighty alone, and the authority to be exercised by the people of Pakistan within the limits prescribed by him is a sacred trust;
>
> Whereas the Founder of Pakistan, Quaid-i-Azam Mohamed Ali Jinnah, declared that Pakistan would be a democratic State based on Islamic principles of social justice;
>
> And whereas the Constituent Assembly, representing the people of Pakistan, have resolved to frame for the sovereign independent State of Pakistan a constitution;
>
> Wherein the State should exercise its powers and authority through the chosen representatives of the people;

Wherein the principles of democracy, freedom, equality, tolerance and social justice as enunciated by Islam, should be fully observed;

Wherein the Muslims of Pakistan should be enabled individually and collectively to order their lives in accordance with the teachings and requirements of Islam, as set out in the Holy Quran and Sunnah;

Wherein adequate provision should be made for the minorities freely to profess and practise their religion and develop their culture . . .

Now therefore, we the people of Pakistan in our Constituent Assembly this twenty-ninth day of February, 1956, and the seventeenth day of Rajab, 1375, do hereby adopt, enact and give to ourselves this Constitution.

Article 24 enjoins the state to endeavor "to strengthen the bonds of unity among Muslim countries"; Article 25 specifies that steps be taken "to enable the Muslims of Pakistan to order their lives in accordance with the Holy Quran and Sunnah," and outlines specific measures toward this object. Besides, Article 32/2 requires that the president of the Republic be a Muslim.

Article 18*a* contains a significant deviation from traditional Muslim legislation, which was bent not only upon preventing apostasy from Islam but also upon maintaining the relative strength of other recognized religious groups. In contrast, this section of the constitution provides that "Subject to law, public order and moraliy—(*a*) every citizen has the right to profess, practise and *propagate* [my italics] any religion." The constitution furthermore requires the president (in Art. 197) to "set up an organization for Islamic research and instruction in advanced studies to assist in the reconstruction of Muslim society on a truly Islamic basis." A special tax for the maintenance of this organization may be imposed by Parliament. Article 198/1 states explicitly, "No law shall be enacted which is repugnant to the Injunctions of Islam as laid down in the Holy Quran and Sunnah, hereinafter referred to as Injunctions of Islam, and existing law shall be brought into conformity with such Injunctions." It is interesting that the "explanation" at the end of Article 198 stipulates that "in the application of this Article to the personal law of any Muslim sect, the expression 'Quran and Sunnah' shall mean the Quran and Sunnah as interpreted by that sect." [18]

It would seem to me that, on the theoretical level at least, as good an integration of traditional and Western ideas has been reached in this document as one might reasonably expect. The identification of Western nineteenth-century ideas as Muslim, whatever the scientific justification, assures a degree of acceptance which otherwise could not have been hoped for; and the very vagueness that lingers about the concept of the Islamic state safeguards the necessary developmental flexibility. The practical effectiveness of the ideas underlying the short-lived constitution needs to be watched. In any event, the attempted bridging of the gap between the Muslim tradition and the Western-inspired idea of the nation-state deserves the greatest attention.

Nationalism in the Middle East is, as has often been noted, a gift of Europe. It has been condemned by many conservative Muslims as a solvent of the traditional "Pan-Islamic" unity; it has been exalted as the only effective means of self-realization; it has been construed as subservient, and more often as pragmatically superior to religion; the limitations it imposes on traditional religion have been felt rather than formulated. In any event, nationalism is the answer of the East to Europe, more truly than it is the gift of Europe to the East. The Middle East was overwhelmed by Europe; self-affirmation in nationalistic terms was part of its defense. Backwardness could be overcome by assimilation only; but assimila-

---

[18] Government of Pakistan, Ministry of Law, *The Constitution of the Republic of Pakistan* (Karachi, 1956). The achievement embodied in this constitution has to be measured in terms of its avoidance of a merely emotional commitment to a Muslim political system, as it tended to dominate large sections of the intelligentsia in Egypt and elsewhere in the years immediately before and after the Second World War.

tion would obliterate identity. Nationalism would provide the incentive to progress and would at the same time be a barrier against self-obliteration.[19]

The Muslim attitude to Western cultural gifts has changed over the last two or three generations from exclusion to emulation and thence to hostility. This is not to say that a hostile East is less anxious to Westernize. Not the process but the ultimate purpose has undergone change. We of the West need to cultivate an awareness that tendencies that appear to be assimilative and actually do reflect a profound interest in the Occidental achievement and its absorption are, in the last analysis, motivated by the wish to overcome the West by taking over its hidden sources of creativeness. Here lies the explanation for the attention paid the Greeks by certain strata of the Arab intelligentsia; and this is why such concern is significant in our context even though the influence of their somewhat uncertain outreach into the classical world has remained decidedly limited and even though, by and large, the Arabic-speaking world rediscovered the Greeks at second hand, that is to say, from French and English translations and studies.

The preoccupation with Hellenic culture which is characteristic of a small number of writers in the early part of our century is designed to undermine the axiom of contemporary European superiority by contrasting it, by implication, with the achievements of Greek antiquity. When Sulaimān al-Bustānī (1856-1925) was celebrated by the Arab nationalist intelligentsia of his time for his translation of the Iliad (Cairo, 1904) it was due less to the remarkable linguistic and literary accomplishment of the Syrian statesman than to the realization that he had

[19] In this context the observation of K. Cragg, *The Call of the Minaret* (New York, 1956), p. 194, may be cited: "It must not be thought that the adaptation of many Western forms of political and social life signified either a passive or a hospitable attitude toward the West itself. Rather the nationalism into which the West has educated the Muslim East means a sharpened quality in the sentiments of the newly independent peoples."

struck a blow against European intellectual dominance. The *Iliad* is the description of a war between the East and the West, with the Asiatic Trojans heroically attempting to hold their own against the aggression of the Occidental Greek intruders. They fight the West for survival, physical and spiritual.

The intellectual leader of the next generation, Ṭāhā Ḥusain (b. 1889), still feels that the lesson of the *Iliad* retains its applicability to the modern world. It is Greek thought that may help bridge the gap between indigenous and modern Occidental civilization. The secret of Western superiority lies in the Hellenic heritage. As recently as 1949 Taufīq al-Ḥakīm (b. 1898), the outstanding dramatist of the Arab world, expressed the view, in the preface to his version of the Sophoclean tragedy *Oedipus Rex*, that the human ideal of the Greeks would constitute a powerful weapon in the hands of the Arabs to conquer the destructive human concept of the West. He sees the Greek idea of the nature and the position of man as more closely related to that of the Arabs, with both Greek and Arab denying man that central position in the universe which the Occident concedes to him. Taufīq al-Ḥakīm invokes the aid of Greece against the atheistic materialism of the West. Even as in the Middle Ages the Aristotelian and Neo-Platonic heritage assisted the Arabs in reaching a balanced synthesis of faith and reason, it will again be Greek humanism that will instill into the Orient of today the strength that is required to overcome the West.[20]

[20] Cf. S. Bencheneb, "Les Humanités grecques et l'Orient arabe moderne," *Mélanges Louis Massignon,* I (Damascus, 1956), 173-198, esp. pp. 178-180, 189-190, 194-196. The Persian prose translation of the Iliad by Saʿīd Nafīsī (Teheran, 1334; copyright 1957) is not a nationalistic enterprise like Bustānī's. Nor are the translations from the Greek which are owed to Ṭāhā Ḥusain and Aḥmad Luṭfī as-Sayyid (b. 1870); they rather mean to make accessible to the Arab reader significant humanistic achievements, in the hope, of course, that contact with the classics would prove as life-giving in Muslim Egypt as it had in the Western Renaissance. It must be remembered that Ṭāhā Ḥusain, at least in the 1920's and 1930's, tended to rate the Greek com-

In Persia, too, fear of the West has proven itself a spur to humanistic studies. It is less remarkable, however, that, as in the Arab world and in Turkey, concern for one's country's past and the cultivation of the mother tongue should have

---

ponent of civilization higher than the Oriental, an outlook that did not go unopposed. P. Cachia, *Ṭāhā Ḥusayn. His Place in the Egyptian Literary Renaissance* (London, 1956), p. 152, analyzes Ṭāhā Ḥusain's motivation in this manner: "The ʿAbbasid age Ṭāhā Ḥusayn considers the first of the two great periods of 'renovation' in Arab literature, the second being the contemporary Renaissance. The parallelism between the two is brought out by showing how much the ʿAbbasids owed to foreign contacts, and particularly by magnifying the contribution of Greek, i.e., Western culture, and minimizing that of 'Oriental' culture" (cf. also *ibid.*, pp. 58-59, 78-79, 84-85). To appreciate the significance of this turning to the ancient Greeks, the utter incomprehension of Greek literature on the part of most spokesmen for the Islamic tradition must be considered. To a Ḍiyāʾ ad-Dīn Ibn al-Athīr (d. 1239), the outstanding literary critic and theorist of his time, the concept of the tragedy, for instance, as presented to him through Avicenna appeared unintelligible and, for a speaker of Arabic, perfectly useless (cf. *al-Mathal as-sāʾir* [Cairo, 1312], p. 120; trans. in M. Canard, "Deux chapitres inédits de l'oeuvre de Kratchkovsky sur Ibn al-Muʿtazz," *Annales de l'Institut des Études Orientales* [Algiers], XX [1962], 21-111, at p. 39 n. 10). J. Kraemer, "Die Bildungsideale des Islams und ihre gegenwärtige Problematik," in *Erziehung zur Menschlichkeit. Die Bildung im Umbruch der Zeit. Festschrift für Eduard Spranger zum 75. Geburtstag, 27. July 1957* (Tübingen, 1957), pp. 278-289, states correctly on p. 278 that in Islam there never occurred that "totale Lebensbeziehung zum Altertum" (an expression taken from Spranger, *Kultur und Erziehung* [2d ed.; Leipzig, 1923], p. 10) which alone is able "einer solchen Kulturbegegnung . . . wesenserhöhende und wesensverwandelnde Bildungsmächtigkeit zu verleihen." The anti-Hellenic neohumanism of an ʿAbdarraḥmān Badawī (b. 1917) deserves mention in this context. Badawī recognizes the close ties that exist between the Greek and the Arab-Muslim civilizations; but he views the strangle hold of the Hellenic heritage on the Muslim development as truly tragic and celebrates personalities like Jāḥiẓ, Tauḥīdī, or Shihāb ad-Din Suhrawardī as liberators or "humanistic" leaders of the Islamic world. The problem of the Muslims is not how to recall or to revive Greek civilization, but how to forget it. Cf. Badawī, "L'Humanisme dans la pensée arabe," *Studia Islamica,* VI (1956), 67-100, and the passages analyzed by J. Kraemer, *Das Problem der islam-*

been stimulated by the desire to preserve the national identification, than that Iranian leaders have come to realize the necessity of a more extensive and, above all, a more scientific knowledge of the West. The urge to acquaint

---

ischen Kulturgeschichte (Tübingen, 1959), pp. 37-38. (It should be noted that a Tauḥīdī can be seen in a different light as well. M. Arkoun, in his excellent study "L'Humanisme arabe au IVe/Xe siècle, d'après el Kitâb al-Hawâmil wal-Šawâmil," *Studia Islamica,* XIV [1961], 73-108, characterizes [on pp. 73-74] the researches of the fourth century as a philosophico-scientific movement with man at its center and hence a humanism. This humanism, which Arkoun evaluates as a great achievement, derives its true meaning and fruitfulness from the "irruption de valeurs rationelles et de traditions profanes étrangères dans une conscience émotive dominée par la vision eschatologique [p. 74 n. 1]. Tauḥīdī recognizes that man is a problem for man, *inna 'l-insān ashkala ʿalaihi 'l-insān* [*Hawāmil,* p. 180; Arkoun, p. 98], and is impelled to bold questioning by a recognition of the ambiguities of the human condition. Although certainly not an upholder of the Greek philosophical tradition, Tauḥīdī can hardly be considered a thinker in the line of Muslim orthodoxy from whose mythical experience of the world and its social implementation he lives in perpetual and irremediable exile [*ghurba*].)

The kindred yet unmistakably divergent outlook of Indonesia is brought out clearly at the beginning of an address delivered in 1952 by Mohammad Natsir, then chairman of the Masjumi party, before the Pakistan Institute of World Affairs in Karachi: "Pakistan is decidedly an Islamic country by population and by choice as it has declared Islam as the state religion. So is Indonesia an Islamic country by the fact that Islam is recognized as the religion of the Indonesian people, though no express mention is made in our constitution to make it the state's religion. But neither has Indonesia excluded religion from statehood. In fact, it has put the monotheistic belief in the one and only God, at the head of the Pantjasila—The Five Principles adopted as the spiritual, moral and ethical foundation of the state and the nation. Thus, for both our countries and peoples Islam has its very essential place in our lives. This does not mean, however, that our state organization is theocratic, as I hope to expound later on. . . ." In the course of his address Mohammad Natsir shows his understanding of the fact that in terms of the contemporary social order the truly revolutionary element in the Prophet's message, and more particularly in his organizing the Muslim community at Medina, was the fact that "he and his followers from the tribe of Quraish severed the bonds of blood-

oneself with cultural phenomena outside ones own civilization is, broadly speaking, a peculiarity of the post-Renaissance West. It is, on the whole, only ourselves who feel the need for a more intense self-understanding to be at-

---

relationship to form a community based on allegiance to authority under one law, the beginning of nationhood." (M. Natsir, *Some Observations Concerning the Role of Islam in National and International Affairs,* Southeast Asia Program, Data Paper 16 [Ithaca, N.Y., 1954], pp. 1, 9.) Of recent observers, W. Braune, *Der islamische Orient zwischen Vergangenheit und Zukunft* (Bern and München, 1960), p. 160, has been most sensitive to the estrangement from the West which seems to mark Arab sentiment more and more: "There is no one who would, or could, renounce elements of Occidental culture. But an alienation, intensified to hatred, will be concerned with this culture only insofar as it may become a tool for the fight against the Occident." Braune's psychological analysis of the Occidental *skandalon* and Arab hostility is unusually insightful (*cf. ibid.,* pp. 161-167).

So is the strikingly perceptive study by Ali Merad, "Origines et voies du réformisme en Islâm," *Annales de l'Institut d'Études Orientales* (*Université d'Alger*), XVIII-XIX (1960-1961), 359-403. The author portrays reformism as "une des constantes spécifiques" of Islamic history (p. 360). From the conflict between ʿAlī and Muʿāwiya, in which Merad discerns the antagonism between those willing to embark on independent development of religious data and those insisting on unconditional maintaining of received ideas, he traces the principal types of reform to which Islam has shown itself responsive. He notes that movements tending toward restoration of the norms of the first *umma* are more likely to grip the Muslim masses than movements that address themselves to the *bon sens* of the individual (pp. 388-389). There is little interest in theological reform; what is listened to are rules of action affecting social justice, the over-all standing of the community and the concern with humane issues. However critical of Europe reformism may appear it really accepts the fact that our age is that of Europe; no *repli sur soi-même* is intended even though the necessity to protect pride and to buttress self-defense frequently gives reformist statements an aggressive and condescending touch. The alleged—so the author —ethical and humanistic achievement of Islam needs to receive what to some may appear undue emphasis, as it seems to provide the sole manifest basis of a dialogue with the West (pp. 396-399). Tauḥīdī's outlook on man reminds one of St. Augustine, *Confessions* IV. iv. 9: Factus eram ipse mihi magna quaestio. (Passage identified by Professor P. Levine, University of California, Los Angeles.)

tained through the analysis of other possibilities of mastering the human universe, as these have been realized on very different levels by the many civilizations traceable in history or in the contemporary world. (Here, incidentally, is the root of the ever-increasing dedication to cultural anthropology.) Somewhat surprisingly to our point of view, the Muslim East has never developed anything comparable to Western "Orientalism"; thus it seems an important innovation and, if you wish, a significant symptom of acculturation when an Iranian scholar-politician like Dr. Fakhr ad-Dīn Shādmān (who in 1948 published a book with the characteristic title *The Subjection of Western Civilization* [*Taskhīr-i tamaddun-i firangī*]) calls for *firang-shināsī*, that is, for a study of Western civilization in all its aspects. As a matter of fact, Dr. Shādmān (b. 1908) himself makes the comparison between his *firang-shināsī* and our Oriental studies. He is careful to point out that the young Iranian should not be exposed to investigations of this order before he is fortified in his own identity, so to speak, by a thorough knowledge of his linguistic and cultural patrimony. It is interesting to hear Shādmān insist that the difficulties in the way of a Persian desirous of knowing the West surpass those besetting the Westerner in search of an understanding of the East.

Shādmān's sentiment corroborates the statement of Syed Badiuz Zaman:

> Islamic ideology is definite, concrete and clear-cut, whereas the ideology of the West is indefinite, is ever shifting; it is experimenting and groping. Islamic ideology is more or less absolute whereas the ideology of the West is mostly relative. Islamic ideology supports transcendental divine laws; but the ideology of the West is a revolt against all transcendental and divine laws. They bring such laws down and then analyze and criticize them like other mundane laws. After such test only, they accept any statements of divine laws. Islamic ideology is one in its fundamentals —with the change of time there may be variations in details only; whereas the thoughts of the rebels against divine laws are not unanimous. They are divided into

several schools of thought. So, the peoples of the West have not got one ideology but several ideologies. And since they are ever experimenting and shifting, so sometimes two or three ideologies submerge into one; and sometimes from one ideology two or three branches shoot off. Then is there a possibility of its identification with the single ideology of Islam in course of time? Yes, there is. On that day the "Islamic versus West" will end.[21]

Nadjm oud-Dine Bammate has stated in somewhat more sophisticated terms to what extent Occidental civilization, to the Oriental, means perpetual change, incessant search for the new and the different, constant doubting of inherited ideas, and how he is primarily impressed by what seems to him the movement, the creative unrest, of the West. But he is confused by the quickly passing "modernity" of the Western achievement, the readiness of the Occidental to forsake yesterday's modernity, the many "Wests" that seem to coexist and from which he finds

---

[21] Syed Badiuz Zaman, *Islamic Literature* (Lahore), VIII/12 (Dec., 1956), 700 (p. 32 of fasc.). This is said as if to bear out the remarks of W. Thompson in *Islam and the West*, ed. R. N. Frye (The Hague, 1957), p. 39. Dilthey's concept of the "anarchy of values" endangering nineteenth century Europe goes somewhat deeper but reflects kindred awareness. In his last study, Der islamische Modernismus und das griechische Erbe, *Islam*, XXXVIII (1962), 1-27, J. Kraemer examined the motives which led to translations from the Greek into Arabic, Persian and Turkish, such as were undertaken with particular skill by Suhail Afnān (Persian) and Azra Erhat (Turkish). Kraemer is well aware of the multiplicity of impulses: the Turks wish to demonstrate that they belong to Europe; Suhail Afnān appears inspired by the desire to enrich his nation; in the Arab world it is difficult to mistake a "pragmatic" attitude—in spite of "humanistic" objectives which occasionally come to the fore. The secret of European success is to be ferreted out not merely through an adoption of technology and kindred achievements but also from the inside, as it were, by speedy appropriation of Western intellectual accomplishments which are based on the Greek tradition. The problem of the transferability of cultural elements which has been troubling the West for the last half century has not been perceived or at least not been recognized as a crucial question. It is to be regretted that the untimely death of the author has prevented completion of his work.

it difficult to identify the valid one. "Le moderne, pour l'Orient, c'est aujourd'hui en 1956, plus 1356 à Florence, plus Paris 1789, plus Moscou 1917, plus tant d'autres moments étrangers qui lui posent des questions toutes actuelles. Est-il possible de dissocier les modernismes successifs de l'Europe, et lesquels préférer? Le moderne, ce n'est pas uniquement la civilisation occidentale vue au present, c'est aussi le passé de l'Occident sous des formes diverses." It is, then, "l'exotisme du moderne et sa multiplicité foisonnante" which aggravate, for the Muslim in particular, the dialogue with the West, considering that his is a tradition that "does not love what passes" (cf. Koran 6:76). It is in keeping with this attitude and the attachment of personality and behavior to sanctified models that "dans la vie courante, le type humain du Musulman présente une certaine monotonie. Le Musulman, quand il est véritablement rattaché à la tradition, a dans le caractère quelque chose d'indifférencié, sans aspérités, sans traits individuels bien marqués. . . . En comparaison avec cette neutralité, disons le mot, ce conformisme, l'individualité de l'Occidental paraît infiniment riche et variée. Mais elle semble parfois confuse, voire incohérente, à l'Oriental." As one of the tragic results of these factors, "le dialogue entre les deux mondes [i.e., Islam and the Occident] sur la nature et la portée du moderne apparaît 'déphasé.' Dans ce décalage gît en partie le malentendu." [22]

Be this as it may, closer scrutiny of Shādmān's ideas reveals that his *firang-shināsī* is a defensive measure rather than a means of enlarging the cultural horizon. For one thing, "Occidental studies" are confined to the contemporary scene; it is a pragmatic enterprise designed, not to uncover the driving motive forces of the West in their

[22] N. Bammate, "La Tradition musulmane devant le monde actuel," *Tradition et innovation. La Querelle des Anciens et des Modernes dans le monde actuel. Recontres internationales de Genève* [XI] (1956), 119-150, at pp. 121, 148. Solas García (*ibid.*, p. 355) sums up the Muslim position in these words: "à la base de toute la pensée musulmane, il y a l'idée de désintéressement de toute richesse extérieure. On ne veut pas le choix libre. L'Occident devient, pour le musulman, 'la confusion.' "

developmental structure, but to capture as many as possible of the achievements and the techniques of the West into the service of Iran. Shādmān appreciates the value of that spirit of criticism to which the progress of Western science is due. Accuracy must be inculcated into the young. But what matters in the last resort is not *firang-shināsī* as such, but the preservation (or the regaining?) of intellectual independence. "We must realize," Shādmān insists, "that the attainment of complete political independence is based on the possession of intellectual independence."[23]

It is as part of this intellectual independence that linguistic independence, which all the cultural communities of the Middle East are so anxious to attain, must be viewed. In the Arab countries as well as in Iran and in Turkey, under the sponsorship of academies or under gov-

---

[23] Cf. B. Nikitine, "*Firang-shināsī,* ou L'Europe vue de Téhéran," in *Charisteria Orientalia* (Prague, 1956), pp. 210-226, esp. pp. 210-214; the text of the translated passage is reproduced on p. 214. The recent translations of Aristotle's *Poetics* and *De Anima* and of Plato's *Symposium, Protagoras,* and some other dialogues into Persian should at least not go unnoticed in this context. It deserves mention here that the Algerian Malik Bennabi (b. 1905) criticizes the Muslims for studying the West merely under the aspect of immediate usefulness, and thus takes up a position markedly different from Dr. Shādmān's (cf. *Vocation de l'Islam* [Paris, 1954], pp. 58 ff.). One may note that the Hellenization of Etruscans and Carthaginians, for example, likewise stopped at the threshold of literature and thus remained ultimately of very limited creative effectiveness; the Romans offer a contrasting instance of cultural borrowing in going far beyond the immediately useful when choosing from the Greek tradition. Cf. H. E. Stier, *Grundlagen und Sinn der griechischen Geschichte* (Stuttgart, 1945), pp. 329-330.

One wonders whether the Bible commentary which Sir Sayyid Aḥmad Khān (1817-1898) published in 1862 under the title, *Tabyīn al-Kalām,* might have led to "Occidentalist" studies had it not been rejected by both Muslims and Christians because of its eclecticism. In any event, this first commentary on the Bible ever to be written by a Muslim deserves more attention than it has received. On the work and the milieu from which it issued, cf. A. Ahmad, "Sayyid Aḥmad K͟hān, Jamāl al-Dīn al-Afg͟hānī and Muslim India," *Studia Islamica,* XIII (1960), 55-78, at pp. 56-58.

ernmental direction, there have been concerted and consistent efforts to create from material germane to Arabic (or Persian or Turkish) those terms that are indispensable if the language is to qualify as a vehicle of modern technical and scientific thought. The elimination of foreign loan words (European in Arabic; European and Arabic in Persian; European, Arabic, and Persian in Turkish) has been one of the major aims of every national "renaissance" in the area. What could not be eliminated was to be Arabized (Persianized and especially Turkicized) within the limits of the possible; in this regard, Turkish holds the edge because of the potentialities of adjustment offered by the Romanization of the alphabet. From the point of view of the internationality of science, which such steps were intended to promote, the effect was hardly encouraging; from that of national self-respect and the nationalization of university faculties, it was inevitable and in large measure successful.[24]

[24] Problems and procedures of "language reform" have been developed with admirable clarity in the famous "Message" which Muḥammad ʿAlī Furūghī in 1937 addressed to the Iranian Academy which, in 1936, had been founded for the express purpose of protecting, expanding and stimulating the progress of the Persian tongue. The *Payām ba-Farhangistān* (together with the statutes of the Academy) is accessible in French translation in *Revue des Études Islamiques,* 1939, 15-74. On the problem of the creation of terminologies cf. J. Bielawski, "Deux Périodes dans la formation de la terminologie scientifique arabe (La Période classique et la période moderne)," *Rocznik Orientalistyczny,* XX (1956), 263-320. It is instructive to compare the similar problem that the West had to face with the growth of new sciences and a new approach in philosophy during the sixteenth and seventeenth centuries (cf., e.g., the suggestive remarks of L. Febvre, *Le Problème de l'incroyance au XVIe siècle. La religion de Rabelais* [2d ed.; Paris, 1947], pp. 385-388). Already in the fourth and third centuries B.C. did Attic philosophy and Hellenistic science confront the problem of creating an adequate terminology solving it, as Arabic aspires to in our time, practically exclusively from its own linguistic materials. Cf. H. E. Stier, *op. cit.*, p. 97. Lucretius (99-55 B.C.) self-consciously and successfully faced the difficulty "to make clear the dark discoveries of the Greeks in Latin verses, especially since we have often to employ new words because of the poverty of the language

The tendency to search for the sources of a new and redeeming humanism, not in the West, whose impact first created the psychological need for a rethinking of the Muslim identity, but in the Muslim past, selectively accepted and reinterpreted, is even closer to the surface when Malik Bennabi (b. 1905), an Algerian from Constantine, rejects, not without irritation, the suggestion that the humanist bent in Muslim modernism has been stimulated by acquaintance with Europe. "If one considers," Bennabi concludes his discussion of the problem, "the kind of haughty gift which the European civilization of today makes of its science to the 'retarded' countries—or rather, to the countries which it has retarded—it is difficult to forget that certain Muslim intellectuals have paid for it the price of years of forced labor. Why, under these conditions, should the Muslim world go out to seek the inspiration to its humanism elsewhere than in its own millenary tradition?" [25]

Our traditional sympathy for the underdog, for liberation irrespective of the ruler to be cast out, and for independence irrespective of the level of the society that is to be lifted into statehood, has crystallized of late in the emotional doctrine that an underdeveloped country can do no wrong. We may object to the more flagrant excesses of the younger nationalisms, but we seem to feel that if

---

and the novelty of the matters, *propter egestatem linguae et rerum novitatem; De rerum natura* i. 136-139. A. Chejne, "The Role of Arabic in Present-Day Arab Society," *The Islamic Literature*, X/4 (April, 1958), 195-234 (pp. 15-54 of issue), has collected a considerable amount of material on the position of the Arabic language in traditional and modernistic mentality. It is, however, not only vis-à-vis the West that the Arabic countries are to regain or maintain cultural independence. Sāṭiᶜ al-Ḥuṣrī, *Difāᶜ ᶜan al-ᶜurūba* (Beirut, 1956), p. 132, in opposing the proposal of a regional cultural organization for the Middle East within UNESCO, argues that the Arabic countries need to free themselves from the cultures of Iran and Turkey rather than merge their cultures with those. And he observes (p. 135): "From the cultural viewpoint, Syria is closer to Tunisia than to Turkey, and Iraq is a closer neighbor to Marrakash than to Iran."

[25] Bennabi, *op. cit.*, pp. 16-17.

we remove frustration from their path they will soon quiet down and be content to develop within their traditional territorial limits and, in any event, become as reasonable or as resigned as the maintenance of world peace will require. Whatever the merits of this expectation on a world scale, it must be realized that nothing in the history of the area under consideration would encourage so sanguine an outlook which, at bottom, is nothing but a reflection of our own unwillingness to see the peace disturbed or to revise some of the fundamental (implied) tenets of our political faith. In spite of a good many discouraging experiences, our policies still proceed on the assumption, which in Lord Balfour's words underlies the Covenant of the League of Nations, that "if we supply an aggregate of human beings, more or less homogeneous in language and religion, with a little assistance and a good deal of advice, if we protect them from external aggression and discourage internal violence, they will speedily and spontaneously organize themselves into a democratic state, on modern lines." [26]

At all times and everywhere nationalism has tended to develop into imperialism. The depreciation of power and conquest by religion and philosophy, and by the growth of a peculiar distaste to assume or accept the fact of a superiority which one actually possesses, is perhaps not confined to the recent West, but it certainly has no basis in the Islamic tradition as such or in the historic experiences of the Middle East. Nationalism is conservative in its ethics because it is loath to tamper with the sacred past and is expansive in its political aspirations. India in Kashmir, the Chinese in their relations with Burma, Egypt in its claims on the Sudan and on Eritrea—their behavior is symptomatic of political attitudes which we are at fault

---

[26] Quoted by E. Kedourie in *England and the Middle East. The Destruction of the Ottoman Empire, 1914-1921* (London, 1956), p. 41; cf. also Kedourie's remark (p. 88) on T. E. Lawrence as a romantic who believed that "political action is a passport to eternal salvation," an outlook that seems to be widely represented in the contemporary Middle East.

to condone merely because we have to some extent outgrown them and expect the same sobering to take place in other societies sooner or later. Economic pressures, social maladjustment, the political constellation of the day provide the immediate irritations; but the true focus of the unrest and instability in the nation-states of the Middle East is nationalism, with its compulsion to assert oneself in the comity of nations in an ever larger and ever more drastic measure, the craving for self-realization through the exercise of power, the achievement of international equality which is convincingly experienced only when it has been transcended into regional paramountcy.

The Muslim tradition, like most cultural traditions, regards the exercise of collective power as honorable per se. Rulership confers nobility; subjection, or mere passivity, invites contempt. And, as the fuller and less contaminated truth ranks higher than the less complete and less carefully preserved, so the Muslim community as the guardian of this fuller and, humanly speaking, final truth ranks intrinsically higher than other communities. It is therefore but natural, in the strictest sense of the word, that the Muslims should dominate—not to convert and certainly not to compel the acceptance of their truth, yet to organize mankind (or as much of it as possible) under the banner of their truth. This view is clearly stated by Maulana Maudoodi: "He [the Muslim] will always be dominant, ruling and governing, for no earthly power can subdue the qualities and the spirit which Islam inculcates in its adherents." [27] In like manner the right of the Safavid princes to rule was supported by the reflection that "if the Safavid ruler was not himself the perfect man he was as the representative of the Hidden Imam at least closer to the possession of absolute truth than any of his fellow men. As such he was entitled to absolute rule. Opposition and dissent were wickedness." [28] It is at this

[27] Cf. Abbott, *op. cit.*, p. 38.

[28] Thus Ann K. S. Lambton, "Quis custodiet custodes (II)," *Studia Islamica*, VI (1956), 129.

The attitude that is indicated toward the protected religious

point that the ethics of nationalism and of religion meet. The omitting from the sphere of practical politics, and even from long-range planning, of the idea of a unified Muslim empire under a caliph has left the nation-states the supreme tools for the realization of a Muslim society. The tension that this situation created between a more religious and a more nationalistic outlook in general is sharpened in parts of the Arabic-speaking world by divergent nationalistic emphases. The Egyptian who is most acutely subjected to alternate possibilities of identification has Arab loyalties to reconcile with Egyptian-"Pharaonic" loyalties and, in any event, feels the obligation to assert and assure his leadership within the Arab world on the political as well as the cultural level.[29] For thousands of years Iraq and Egypt have been rivals, as independent states under various names and as provinces within the empire of the caliphs. Identification of both countries with Arab nationalism is not likely to eliminate a contest for hegemony. One cannot perhaps speak of an Egyptian cultural imperialism, but one must take note of the per-

---

communities is one of polite aloofness, with emphasis on the superior status of the Muslims; any imitation of the customs of non-Muslims is to be avoided, not because those customs would necessarily be intrinsically objectionable, but because *at-tashabbuh bi'l-kuffār* (assimilation to the unbelievers) must be guarded against; cf. the poignant passage in Ibn Taimiyya (d. 1328), *Tafsīr Surat al-Ikhlāṣ* (Cairo, 1323/1905), pp. 132-133. Ghazzālī (d. 1111), *Iḥyāʾ ʿulūm ad-dīn* (Būlāq, 1289/1872), II, 189[19-20], records this alleged saying of the Prophet: "When you see me do not rise as the foreigners [*al-aʿājim*] do." In *ibid*., p. 188[21-22], there is another alleged direction of the Prophet: "Do not shake hands with the protected non-Muslims (*ahl adh-dhimma*), and do not greet them first."

[29] The first concrete proposal for the borders of an Arab empire which was developed by the Syrian Christian, Najīb ʿAzūrī (d. 1916), in 1905, leaves Egypt on the side, partly for geographical reasons and partly because the Egyptians are not of the Arab "race." It was only in 1939 that Egyptian government circles tried to establish a more intimate connection between Egyptian public opinion and Arab nationalism. Cf., e.g., S. G. Haim, "Intorno alle origini della teoria del panarabismo," *Oriente Moderno*, XXXVI (1956), 410, 412 n. 2.

vading influence of Egypt through her writers, her exported teachers and professors, her cultural and information agencies in the Arab countries, and again of the mixed admiration and resentment exhibited by the recipients of Egyptian culture; and thus one senses another potential cause of tension which before long must needs find its reflection in the political relationships of the states concerned.

There is, as a further irritant, the competition between Egypt and Pakistan for the intellectual leadership of the Muslim world as a whole. In terms of cultural productivity in the narrower sense, the outside observer cannot but concede to Egypt a rather safe margin; in terms of the realization of the ideal of a specifically Islamic society, the Pakistanis may have a better claim. Pan-Islamic sentiment is probably stronger in Pakistan; so may be a kind of religious alertness due in part to the proximity of India. In the long run, the political center of the Muslim world may move east into Pakistan (and Indonesia); at the moment Pakistani dedication to Islamic solidarity is not adequately reciprocated by the Arab-speaking world, absorbed as it is in its immediate political problems and handicapped, as it were, by the fundamental indifferentism of large sections of its education classes. It is noteworthy in this context, however, that a writer like Malik Bennabi views the displacement of the center of the Islamic world into Asia as an accomplished fact, and that, moreover, he appears to view this displacement as an encouraging fact as well. For agricultural Pakistan and Indonesia will instill more creative attitudes into a revitalized and historically younger Islam than could have been evolved by Mediterranean Islam, which has been lulled to sleep by its safe majority position and which is burdened by its dynastic, tribal-nomadic, and narrowly dogmatic habits of thinking and organization.[30]

[30] Bennabi, *op. cit.*, pp. 163-167. It would be difficult to overemphasize the revolutionary character of Bennabi's observation in terms of the Muslim tradition. This tradition, to quote one illustration for many, is well reflected in al-Muqaddasī's decision

Nationalism is impatient. It is therefore unjust in judging the progress it has forced. And disappointment over its limited success in turn increases its sensitivity and tenseness. It is characteristic that such utopian elements as Arab nationalism may have generated or adopted have little to do with the internal, but a great deal with the over-all, organization of the Arab-Muslim region. This is in harmony with the overriding interest in foreign affairs to which we have already referred, but in conflict with the general observation that social decomposition (as it undoubtedly obtains in the Middle East) is usually accompanied by utopian reconstructions of society. The explanation for their absence from the Arab intellectual scene may perhaps be sought in the persistent strength of the religious outlook, not so much in any creedal or dogmatic sense as in the acceptance of an eternal human ideal willed and shaped by the Lord himself in contradistinction to the concept of man as an evolving or, better, a self-shaping entity that puts itself through a sequence of phases, every one of which is experienced as a critique and a conquest of

---

to begin his geographical survey with the Arabian Peninsula because it harbors the House of God, the birthplace of the Prophet, the cradle of Islam, the residence of the Rightly Guided Caliphs, etc.; cf. *Aḥsan at-taqāsīm* (written in A.D. 985; revised by the author in 988), ed. M. J. de Goeje (Leiden, 1906), p. 67. (The passage is mentioned in H. Lammens, "Le Califat de Yazid Ier," *Bulletin de la Faculté Orientale de Beyrouth*, V [1911-12], 651 [p. 332 of book edition].) The traditional outlook is expressed with striking concision by ad-Damīrī (d. 1405) in his zoölogical dictionary, *Kitāb al-ḥayawān* (Cairo, 1278/1861), II, 542[17], where the Arabs are designated as the prime authorities on a question of ritual practice, "for the reason that the Faith is an Arab one" (*li-anna 'd-dīn ʿarabī*); cf. R. Levy, *The Social Structure of Islam* (Cambridge, 1957), p. 174. The non-Arab Muslims obtained social and "national" equality with the Arabs in a rather slow and somewhat painful process during the early centuries of Islamic development; for convenient reference, cf. I. Goldziher, *Muhammedanische Studien* (Halle a. S., 1888-1890), I 130-133. In certain milieus full equality never was attained; equality of non-Arabs with Arabs of the Quraish, the tribe of the Prophet, was, to my knowledge, never admitted by orthodox legal theory.

its predecessor.[31] It is not easy to combine a sense of life's alternatives with the apprehension of God's truth as a static norm.

Religious truth is manifested in history, but essentially transcends history. Nationalism seeks validation through history alone. It aims at influencing the future and draws its justification from the past. And because history, in one sense at least, "is true for all those who want it to be true, that is to say, who construct the facts in the same fashion and use the same concepts," [32] nationalism finds it easy to provide itself with the requisite, that is, the pragmatically effective, historical background. Extension into the past, preferably into the remote and scientifically unfathomable past of one's community, identification of one's nation with an earlier people of inspiring or glorious associations, an eclecticism that blurs the contours of what has been, and a refusal, naïve or deliberate, to see the past other than in present garb—these are the means by which the nation myth is most readily and most frequently projected into the times when the world was still young. It would not be fair to point out these characteristics in the mythopoeism of Arab nationalism without an express indication that the difference between its constructivism and that of comparable movements is at most one of degree, and that Turkish nationalist mythology, for instance, or the mythology presented by some French writers of the sixteenth century, is if anything more arbitrary and more recklessly dictated by contemporary aspirations and prejudices. As I have elsewhere examined the nationalistic versions of their early history by Iraqi and Egyptian authors,[33] I shall for exemplification turn to a north African writer, ʿAllāl al-Fāsī (b. 1906), a leader of the Moroccan independence movement.

---

[31] Cf. R. Ruyer, *L'Utopie et les utopies* (Paris, 1950), esp. pp. 6, 21, 285.

[32] R. Aron in a letter to H.-I. Marrou, dated June 5, 1954, from which Marrou quotes (*op. cit.*, p. 224).

[33] Cf. my *Islam. Essays*, pp. 185 ff. and *Classicisme et déclin culturel* (Paris, 1957), pp. 12-13. See also pp. 101-104, above.

"No nation has defied a conquering power or a surging alien immigration so steadfastly as the people of north Africa have done throughout their history," says al-Fāsī near the beginning of his book *The Independence Movements in Arab North Africa.*[34] "If on occasion the conquerors succeeded in establishing footholds . . . , their presence, no matter how long lived, has been but a passing phase that left no lasting mark or impact." Although this observation may hold good for Phoenician, Roman, and Vandalian conquests, it certainly is completely out of place in regard to the Arab occupation, which by now has lasted some twelve hundred years and whose impact continues to grow at the expense of the earlier Berber population. But as al-Fāsī very naturally identifies with the Arab element, he does not account for its arrival in his generalization. After presenting the internecine anarchy of tribal society in north Africa as "a perpetual struggle for self-defense and liberty," al-Fāsī, without previous warning, redefines the identity of his society by emphasizing its "sense of communion with the spirit that permeated our forefathers from time immemorial." Subsequently, the forefathers are identified as the Berbers. Their name is presently discovered in the ancient song of the Salian priests whose invocation to the god included the line: "Satur tu, fere Mars, limen sali! Sta! Berber!" [35] "Thus," al-Fāsī reasons,

---

[34] Cairo, 1948; trans. H. Z. Nuseibeh (Washington, D.C., 1954); the passages analyzed are on pp. 1-8. For other and, in part, more sophisticated interpretations of Morocco's past as phases of her struggle for a future, cf. E. Gellner, "The Struggle for Morocco's Past," *Middle East Journal,* XV (1961), 79-90, in which he reviews Bin Abdallah, *Les grands courants de la civilisation du Maghreb* (1958); A. Lahbabi, *Le gouvernment marocain à l'aube du XXe siècle* (Rabat, 1958); and the prefaces contributed to these works by ʿAllāl al-Fāsī and Mahdi Bin Barqa respectively.

[35] The passage actually forms part of the *Carmen Arvale,* whose third section consists of a threefold repetition of the words: "Satur tu, fere Mars, limen sali! Sta! Berber!" E. H. Warmington, *Remains of Old Latin,* IV, 253 (LCL), renders the line thus: "Be full satisfied, fierce Mars. Leap the threshold! Halt! Beat the ground!" This translation identifies *berber* with

"the word *berber* stood for speed and mobility. The ancient historians used it to describe the Berbers inhabiting the banks of the Nile. . . . It is known, further, that the Nile valley included what was called the Berber valley. Thus, the name had been used to designate this Berber-speaking people on account of their mobility and nomadism or because of their habitation along the fast moving waters of the Nile." There follows the nationalistic exploitation of this peculiar specimen of scientific insight. "The linguistic genealogy of the term has a deeper sig-

---

verbera; Warmington considers this etymological connection as a guess (cf. p. 252 n. 1) and observes that *berber* may be merely an ejaculation. The explanation proposed by al-Fāsī is completely without scientific justification.

A more graceful way of drawing encouragement from one's past was found in another nationalistic period by Claude Bellièvre, a magistrate of Lyons, when in 1529 he recommended the purchase by his town of the newly found *Tabula Claudiana.* "Ce sera grande consolation aux gens de la Ville, quand ils verront un certain témoignage de la dignité de leurs majeurs et servira d'éguillon à vertu pour imitation des dits majeurs." The passage is quoted in J. Carcopino, *Points de vue sur l'impérialisme romain* (Paris, 1934), p. 162.

It is not only at this point that ʿAllāl al-Fāsī molds history to his argument. In 1949, discussing the nature and the importance of Islamic law, he permitted himself this flight of fancy: "Let us take the French code, for instance. The historians who discuss it, never refer to Islamic law, never refer to its influence on its general principles. But history teaches us that the legal system of Mālik, in particular, was one of the sources which inspired the French code when it was elaborated, and even did not fail to influence it afterwards. . . . French customary law was codified in 711 [*sic!*], and Islam penetrated into Spain and into the South of France in the eighth century. [The Arab invasion of Spain began in 711; Mālik died in 795.] . . . Even after the defeat at Poitiers [733], Europe remained under Muslim domination until the end of the fifteenth century. . . ." The passage is taken from J. Schacht, "Problems of Modern Islamic Legislation," *Studia Islamica,* XII (1960), 99-129, at p. 127.

The *Fundamental Law of Morocco* of June 2, 1961, provides in art. 14: L'État doit dispenser l'instruction suivant une orientation nationale arabe et islamique et en fonction des besoins de la nation, sur le plan de la formation technique, professionnelle et scientifique. The full text of the *Law* was published in *Middle Eastern Journal,* 1961, 326-328.

nificance in that it illustrates the unity of the peoples who inhabit the area between the Mediterranean and the Red Sea and as far as Senegal and Nigeria. This African family has exhibited an unfailing attachment to freedom in its struggle to defend its honor and diginity." Parallel to ancient Egyptian civilization was the ancient north African civilization, which contributed to it. Carthage is represented as a Berber cultural center ruled by foreigners "by virtue of a dynamism greater than that of the indigenous population." But (and we may surmise this is owing to their Eastern origin) al-Fāsī does not consider the Phoenicians an imperialist power; in fact, Carthage symbolized the unity of the Maghrib. The Romans were ultimately ineffective in north Africa—which is correct. In the light of the sources it is, however, somewhat astonishing to read that "the people of al-Maghrib . . . enthusiastically embraced Islam because they found in it the avenue to national liberation and independence, in addition to intellectual and spiritual enhancement." And now, as a projection of the present into the past, al-Fāsī breaks out into this general statement:

> Thus, the ancient history of North Africa discloses a perpetual struggle for dominance between the Latin family on the one hand, and on the other, the family that is known in the contemporary period as Arab, whose intellectual heritage comprises Greek, Semitic and Maghrib civilization. But we also find that victory has always been on the side of this Arab civilization which forms the real cornerstone of Mediterranean civilization. It is [and here al-Fāsī takes up a favorite cliché of Arab writers] a foundation in which the material did not contribute so much as the spiritual elements. It is upon this basis that the people of al-Maghrib feel their profound affinity to the rest of the Arab world.

The Moroccan nationalists does not, however, desire submergence of his country in an Arab unitary state. So al-Fāsī continues: "The Maghrib, however, despite its acceptance of Islam as its religion and Arabic as its language[36] has always felt pride in its own entity. . . . National consciousness existed in al-Maghrib before and after the advent of Islam." And he concludes the chapter by designating the present-day struggle in north Africa as one "between the Arab East and the Latin West." [37]

Yet it is al-Fāsī's formulation of the conflict between the Arab East and the Latin West which describes most graphically the intercultural struggle of the Middle East as experienced by the Middle Easterners themselves. Westernization for liberation, and rejection of the West for self-preservation, are the conflicting possibilities. There is

---

[36] Naguib Baladi, "L'Occident et la culture arabe contemporaine," in *Les Mardis de Dar El-Salam, Sommaire, 1954* (Cairo, 1956), p. 101, speaks of the nostalgia for Arabic felt by those Algerian nationalists who are not born to this language; they long for it because it is the language of their faith.

[37] For contrast cf. the statements of the Tunisian leader Habib Bourguiba (*op. cit.*, pp. 649-650): "From the very first stirrings of their independence movements, North Africans have had a latent tradition of democratic liberalism which binds them to the nations of the free world," and, especially, "African nationalism has its place within the Western orbit." A statement of Berber nationalism which would conflict with al-Fāsī's integrative views on Arab-Berber relationships may be found in Lhaoussine Mtouggui, *Vue générale de l'histoire berbère* (Algiers, n.d. [*ca.* 1956]). For good measure the beginning of the lead article of *Liberté. Organe clandestine du Parti Communiste Algérien*, no. 23 (March, 1958), p. 1, with its blend of mythologies, may be quoted here: "Sous la conduite de jeunes chefs, l'ALN [Armée de la Libération Nationale], dirigée par le FLN, se couvre de gloire. Elle continue les traditions de JUGURTHA et d'ABDELKADER. Elle a adapté à notre pays et enrichi les enseignements de la guerre anti-impérialiste définis par MAO-TSE-TOUNG." Ch.-A. Julien had remarked in 1952: "If a book is written on Jugurtha, the reason is that he is considered the defender of Berber independence; by contrast, to describe Juba, the very terminology of the *Résistance* is taken up again: he is a 'vil collaborateur.' " In this vein, the sixteen-year-old Kateb Yacine (b. 1929) had exclaimed, inspired by Tacitus' description of the Roman occupation of the Bretons: "Voilà comment nous, descendants des Numides, subissons à présent la colonisation des Gaulois!" Cf. J. Dejeux, "Regards sur la littérature maghrébine d'expression française," *Études sociales nord-africaines*, no. 61 (Oct.-Nov., 1957), pp. 26 n. 1, 62.

no third choice. For affiliation with the Russian orbit would, in the cultural sphere, imply the same option for modernization which the call for Westernization bespeaks. The problem lies in the conciliation of the two forces, nationalism and religion, which make valuable allies only in checking the indispensable intruder, but everywhere else compete for the undivided allegiance of individual and community.

I do not think the psychological situation of the contemporary Arab East could be summed up better and more concisely than in the words of Sāṭiʿ al-Huṣrī, the Syrian statesman and educator, who a few years ago, thinking of his own people, wrote: "How unfortunate are nations who are far from having realized their national unity and from having perfected their political personality; for they cannot make their political borders correspond to their national borders." And so they do not know what their homeland is.[38]

Let us hope that, in their own interest and in the interest of the whole world, it will not be long before the Arabs

[38] Literally: "So the concept of the fatherland with these nations is not clearly delineated nor of firm shape" (*op. cit.*, p. 6). We may compare the statement of the Kabyle, Jean Amrouche (b. 1906), writing in *Le Monde* of Jan. 11, 1958 (as reported by R. Charles, *L'Evolution de l'Islam* [Paris, 1960], p. 163, n. 1): "Une part d'eux-mêmes [that is, the Algerians], la part relative et profonde, est refractaire à toute assimilation: s'ils sont Français par le langage et par l'outillage mental, voire par les moeurs et les conduites sociales, leur âme, en arrière-plan, demeure irréductible. L'orage les habite. Ils ne savent plus qui ils sont." The psychological situation as it affects political and social action has been well characterized by J. Berque, *Les Arabes d'hier à demain* (Paris, 1960), p. 45: "Le vouloir être l'emporte sur le vouloir faire. Il le précède en tout cas. De là le curieux spectacle d'une émancipation qui va de l'affirmation à la réalisation, des superstructures à la base. Elle s'affirme d'abord politique, puis cherche à se rendre économique et sociale, c'est-à-dire à se justifier, ou, en d'autres termes à se meriter." Cf. also the analysis (*ibid.*, p. 116) of the development of the Banque Miṣr (founded in 1920) and of the attitudes of its founder, Ṭalʿat Ḥarb: "l'affirmation culturelle" at the beginning; "la réalité matérielle" follows.

find themselves. A possible direction, compatible with the realities of the nation-state and its emotional hold on the Arab elite, may have been indicated by the Lebanese Muslim, Kamāl Yūsuf al-Ḥājj (b. 1917). Interpreting *qaumiyya* as the *wujūd* (mode of existential realization) of *insāniyya* (humanity) as the *jauhar* (essence), al-Ḥājj demonstrates that *qaumiyya* derives its value and ethical justification from the superordinated ontological category. As in the present phase of history (or perhaps even at all times, considering the ultimate unchangeability of the human psyche) *qaumiyya* and hence the nation-state is the adequate framework for individual and collective self-realization, provided it is not hypostatized into an ultimate, a *qaumiyya lā-insāniyya* is as destructive as an *insāniyya lā-qaumiyya*. The transcending of *qaumiyya* by developing it as the noblest *wāsiṭa* (means) toward the supreme *ghāya* (end) constituted by *insāniyya* is the great task that al-Ḥājj recognizes as confronting all nations and a fortiori the Arabs, whose present situation would seem to impose on them a double progression from the Syrian or Lebanese *qaumiyya* to an Arab *qaumiyya*, and, without relinquishing either, toward a firm integration of these identifications in the consciousness of their obligation to *insāniyya* in which those identifications are anchored and from which they derive their valorization.[39]

---

[39] Kamāl Yūsuf al-Ḥājj, *Fī 'l-Qaumiyya wa'l-insāniyya* (Beirut, 1957), *passim;* cf. especially pp. 27 ff., 56, 63 (behind the passing *qaumiyya* stands the lasting *insāniyya*, a fact to which the very perfection of *qaumiyya* as the current realization of *insāniyya* tends to blind us), 90 to end of book. For contrast compare the definition of the Arab proposed by C. Maqsoud, *The Arab Image* (New Delhi, 1963), pp. 12-14. The key paragraph reads:
"The Arab is the identity of those who are either
(a) citizens of an Arab State,
(b) the million Palestinian refugees,
(c) the inhabitants of an Arab territory not free from colonial or semi-colonial rule.
(d) those who opt by free choice to belong to an Arab State after normal conformity to the basic legal requirements of the State.
These four main categories exclude, of course, those of Arab

origin who chose to settle in foreign territories and freely chose to belong to those foreign States [this clause bears on the internal politics of Lebanon]; and includes many who do not belong racially to the Arab stock but who have chosen to identify themselves and their subsequent generation (*sic*) with the Arab destiny. . . . Also the Arab is not a term identical with a Moslem because the elementary reality is that not every Arab is a Moslem and the large majority of the Moslems in the world are not Arabs. This is repeated here because the secular and non-racist dimensions of the Arab image are repeatedly blurred and distorted." (Pp. 12-13.)

J. Berque sees behind the surface phenomena of demands, intransigence, and xenophobia, in *qaumiyya* at the same time an "élan vers l'efficacité" and "la nostalgie de soi-même." The adaptation of the Arab world to modern conditions is, to him, marred by a secret sadness: its victories are but "the heroic version of a world-wide movement toward uniformity." In this regard emancipation continues what colonialism has begun. Cf. "Expression et signification dans la vie arabe," *L'Homme,* I (1961), 50-67, et p. 64. Berque further refined his analyses in his paper Les Arabes et l'expression économique, *Studia Islamica,* XVI (1962), 95-120.

XI

Acculturation as a Theme in Contemporary Arab Literature

I

ACCULTURATION, or more precisely Westernization, in the Near and Middle East has gone through distinct typical phases. After the shock caused by the discovery of inadequacy, there followed an almost complete surrender to foreign values and (not infrequently misunderstood) aspirations; then, with Westernization partially realized, a recoiling set in from the alien, which however, continues to be absorbed greedily, and a falling back on the native tradition; this tradition is restyled and, in some instances, newly created with borrowed techniques of scholarship to give respectability to the results. Finally, with Westernization very largely completed in terms of governmental reforms, acceptance of the values of science, and adoption of Western literary and artistic forms, regained self-confidence expresses itself in hostility to the West and in insistence upon the native and original character of the borrowed product.

It is during this stage that a deliberate *prise de conscience* of one's cultural character and its relationship to the native past and the alien intruder is sought. This *prise de conscience* at first uses historical material projecting predetermined conclusions into a description of the nation's development designed to buttress its self-respect. As the second and, thus far, the last step, literature begins to describe or to dramatize the culture conflict to which the authors, or their fathers, have been exposed.

II

The process of acculturation, with its quest for a new identification, the awakening of a responsiveness to new or hitherto disregarded stimuli, the intoxication of discovery, the embarrassment felt at the continuing social and intellectual heritage, and the anxiety to encounter one's aspirations for the future in the very past one has been so eager to slough off—this process is one of simultaneous triumph and pain, of a sense of vigor and inferiority, curiously blended in despondency over the inherited setting and the arrogance of the self-asserting conquerer. The individual and his society are divided against themselves, suffering from attraction and repulsion at the same time when confronted with the nonchalant aggression of Western mentality.

To my knowledge it was Ibn Khaldūn, the great Tunisian statesman, historian, and jurist, who first presented a sociological analysis of the fascination that power holds for the overpowered. "The vanquished," he wrote in 1377,

> always want to imitate the victor in his distinctive mark(s), his dress, his occupation, and all his other conditions and customs. The reason for this is that the soul always sees perfection in the person who is superior to it and to whom it is subservient. It considers him perfect, either because the respect it has for him impresses it, or

because it erroneously assumes that its own subservience to him is not due to the nature of defeat but to the perfection of the victor. If that erroneous assumption fixes itself in the soul, it becomes a firm belief. The soul, then, adopts all the manners of the victor and assimilates itself to him. This, then, is imitation.

Or, the soul may possibly think that the superiority of the victor is not the result of his group feeling (*ʿaṣabiyya*), or great fortitude, but of his customs and manners. This also would be an erroneous concept of superiority, and (the consequence) would be the same as in the former case.

Therefore, the vanquished can always be observed to assimilate (*yatashabbahu*) themselves to the victor in the use and style of dress, mounts, and weapons, indeed, in everything.[1]

What Ibn Khaldūn had to say almost six hundred years ago about the imitation of the conqueror by the conquered applies without qualification to the relation of colonial to metropolitan culture in our age and, with only slight amplification, to the pull exerted by any superior civilization, even if its representatives are not possessed of any political control.

[This attraction] . . . goes so far [Ibn Khaldūn continues] that a nation dominated by another, neighboring nation will show a great deal of assimilation and imitation [*iqtidāʾ*]. At this time, this is the case in Spain [i.e., in Muslim Spain, *al-Andalus*]. The [Muslim] Spaniards are found to assimilate themselves to the Galician nations [*al-Jalāliqa;* i.e., the Christian Spaniards] in their dress, their emblems, and most of their customs and conditions. This goes so far that they even draw pictures on the walls and [have them] in buildings and houses. The intelligent observer will draw from this the conclusion that it is a sign of domination [by others].[2]

Ibn Khaldūn is not concerned, however, with the psy-

[1] Ibn Khaldūn, *Muqaddima* (Cairo, n.d.), p. 147; ed. E. Quatremère (Paris, 1858), I, 266-267; trans. F. Rosenthal (New York, 1958), I, 299.

[2] *Muqaddima* (Cairo), p. 147; ed. Quatremère, I, 267; trans. Rosenthal, I, 300.

chological aspects of imitation and assimilation. He appears unaware of the driving power of the need to belong with the superior group, of the urge to secure the self-respect, individual and collective, by an attempt at cultural, hence social, hence political adjustment, and he is completely oblivious of the hurtfulness inherent in the *tashabbuh* which he describes. He simply is not interested in what to us has become one of the most disconcerting features of acculturation: that only very rarely is the achievement of progress, even of ardently desired progress, accompanied by what a French sociologist has called "le confort dans le progrès." [3] Yet it is the near impossibility of painless accommodation to culture change which is causing much of the unrest that is today tormenting the world outside the core countries of Western civilization.

Western man has assigned to himself an infinite task in every sphere of life. The anticipation of obsolescence has become part of his triumphs. The conviction that his environment can and hence must be improved leads to rejoicing in the eternally provisional. Incessant striving for perfection gives him a sense of strength that is constantly renewed by the realization that the struggle will never end and that he may never release himself from his commitment.[4] Operationally, we have accepted psychological and

---

[3] R. Maunier, *Sociologie coloniale* (2d ed.; Paris, 1949), II, 372.

[4] See p. 140, above. This sense of obligation to improve an imperfect world is characteristic of the modern West only; it was absent as late as the fifteenth century (cf., e.g. J. Huizinga, *Herbst des Mittelalters* [7th ed.; Stuttgart, 1953], pp. 32-33). It will be remembered that this manipulability of the human situation, perceived by him as *perfectibilité*, appeared to Rousseau as the source of all man's misfortunes (cf. *Discours sur l'origine et les fondements de l'inégalité parmi les hommes*, in *Oeuvres complètes* [Paris, 1793], I, 73-74). It is this almost limitless potential that makes him at length "le tyran de lui-même et de la nature." Rifāʿa Rāfiʿ aṭ-Ṭahṭāwī (1216-1290/1801-1873) allows himself to be sent to Paris in 1826 and trained as a translator because in his activity as interpreter there would be an advantage for the homeland (*an-nafʿ lil-auṭān*); in selecting French books for translation he is guided by the consideration

partial truth in lieu of absolute and final truth; its deficiencies are bearable only because, with the advance of science and social organization, the most immediately unbalancing errors are directly discarded. The stability of our mental and social universe hinges, as it were, on its rapid change. Our morality is built on the demand that everyone be fit to master any situation that may confront him, and that he must never prove himself inferior to his self-image. We may be destroyed, but we may not give up.[5]

Acculturation to the Occident would, for full effectiveness, compel acceptance of its basic outlook and its basic personality traits. But when acculturation is begun, and even when it has developed to a point from which the acculturating civilization no longer is able to retreat, these ultimate implications are not realized. In his dreams of the future the reform-minded Middle Easterner sees himself not merely in a technologically and politically improved, "Westernized" society, but in a society of the same binding absoluteness as the one in which his ancestors grew up; he envisages himself as secure in a stable network of dependencies and protectively limited, that is, government-shouldered, responsibilities. The new truth, more effective

---

of general utility (*an-naf*ᶜ *al-*ᶜ*āmm*), and more particularly of usefulness for the people of his own country (cf. as-Sayyid Ṣāliḥ Majdī [d. 1881], *Ḥilyat az-zaman bi-manāqib Khādim al-waṭan*, ed. G. ash-Shayyāl [Cairo, 1958], pp. 31^{1}, 32^{9-10}). He feels superfluous when ᶜAbbās Pasha (1848-1854) closes the language academy (*ibid.*, p. 38).

[5] The attitude has been well expressed by W. Dilthey (1833-1911), *Gesammelte Schriften* (Stuttgart and Göttingen, 1957 ——), Vol. V, *Einleitung des Herausgebers*, p. xv: "Wir sind zufrieden, am Ende eines langen Lebens vielfache Gänge wissenschaftlicher Untersuchung angebohrt zu haben, die in die Tiefe der Dinge führen; wir sind zufrieden, auf der Wanderschaft zu sterben." The last phrase of this statement, which goes back to *ca.* 1865, appears in free translation in L. Díez del Corral, *The Rape of Europe* (London, 1959), p. 295. One is reminded of the dictum of Maine de Biran (d. 1824): "La vie, c'est l'effort," and of the ideas of Karl Jaspers (b. 1883) about the "Unabschliessbarkeit des Weltwissens" and "Wahrheit im Durchbruch" (cf. W. Stegmüller, *Hauptströmungen der Gegenwartsphilosophie* [2d. ed.; Stuttgart, 1960], pp. 216, 224-225, 228).

than the old but just as final, is not to throw him on the road to everlasting transformation but to shield him from being abandoned to the whims of the foreigner, the tortures of self-criticism, the unpredictable risks of an expanding universe. The longing for the dependable situation, the withdrawal from ultimate responsibility which used to be God's and has become the state's, constitutes the basis of that *colonisabilité* without which, in the view of the French colonial administrator Mannoni and the Algerian Muslim Malik Bennabi (b. 1905), colonization has never been possible.[6] Actually, however, colonization is bound to bring the experience of threatened dependence relationships to wider and wider circles of the colonized, in precise proportion to the degree of Westernization and the degree of self-government attained. One wonders sometimes whether the craving for liberation in dependent areas and the craving for "full" independence in many states outside the Western core zone is not also a craving for the restoration of the traditional dependence systems, an honorable means for a psychological return to the good old days that never were.[7]

The realization that directed change was possible, that improvements could be compelled and even planned; the malaise of the Middle Eastern intellectual who felt uncomfortable in his defeat-stained tradition and equally uncomfortable in his marginal status vis-à-vis the Occident, and who might feel superior to the Westerner in his religious status as a Muslim and inferior to him in the desired mastery of contemporary reality; the pent-up irritation with himself, with the state, with the foreigner, with his tradition, and with the frustrations of reform—these moods found their expression in a thirst for indiscriminate freedom, an active distrust of authority, and a turbulent zeal that as likely as not would lead into a cul-de-sac.

---

[6] O. Mannoni, *Psychologie de le colonisation* (Paris, 1950), p. 87; for Bennabi see pp. 151, 170-172, above.

[7] Mannoni, *op. cit.*, p. 136, seems to think so with regard to the Madagascans.

The Iranian writer Fereidoun Esfandiary (b. 1931) says in the foreword of a novel that depicts the political life of his country in the early years after the Second World War:

Never before [in Asia] had the clamor for change been more widespread or more determined. Men were no longer willing to accept blindly, as holy and irreversible, the institutions that had been conveyed from generation to generation through many dark, miasmic centuries.

Young men and women oppressed by domestic rigidities abandoned their ancestral hovels and travelled far away; women trapped in their impossible veils struggled in many diverse ways to throw off the bondage of fathers, brothers, and husbands; peasants, landless and forgotten, journeyed to the cities to join others in fighting the feudal systems that had stifled their initiative and prolonged their poverty; the religious, shackled by their amulets, fought religion in the name of religion.

Urgent cries for Freedom rang from one end of Asia to another.

It was, however, through politics that the people sought to fulfill their goals. Politics offered the most respectable and dramatic opportunity for the release of their hostilities and for the expression of their hopes and their ideals.[8]

In the Moroccan Driss Chraibi's (b. 1926) novel *Le Passé simple*, Haj Fatmi Ferdi berates his son for what he has become and for what he has done under the impact of French education. After pointing out that in Morocco the prospective reformer would find it easier to whiten the Negroes than to change existing conditions, Haj Fatmi breaks out:

And then there were you. You, the poison. And I should not think that the Residency would have endeavored to let its cultural contribution reach our sons in the form of poison; or if this was their intention, it constitutes violation of the soul; in any event, from the day that you entered a *lycée* you have been nothing but that: poison. Everywhere did you see social injustice and, as you said,

[8] *The Day of Sacrifice* (New York, 1959), pp. vii-viii.

in one and the same person, from one moment to the next, temporal injustices: who asked you to see them? who the hell taught you that they were injustices? embittered people whom you wanted to comfort—a knight-errant in the century of the black market!—oppressed people whom you waved like a banner; you sowed rebellion among your brothers. You emptied my supplies in my storehouse into the hands of jackals who immediately returned to their good old beggary; was one bag of barley or of oats enough to shake them up? You find this funny! The poison, you injected it even into the extreme resignation of your mother. The idea of a revolt would never have entered her mind. You stuffed her full of it. She died of it.

And then Haj Fatmi widens the accusation to embrace a whole generation:

I am going to tell you: you are not the only one. I do not know anyone of your generation who does not resemble you. . . . The young are insolent, charged (*voltés*) with complexes, proud of their complexes, thieves taking compound interest from their loot, cynics, and if by chance they enter a mosque it is to pray to God with a loud voice to make them orphans, the faster the better. This youth that preens itself with being nationalistic, the only elements of the population who are convinced that Atatürk guides them from beyond the grave. And they complain. . . .[9]

In defense of the viewpoint of the young speaks Leïla Baalbaki (Lailà Baʿlabakkī, b. 1936), a Lebanese Shiite *muslima* become famous almost overnight through her novel *Anā aḥyà* (*I Am Alive*):

The fight that we are leading within our narrow frontiers aims at loosening the grip of fiction on our history, our society, our state, our people. . . . Our life begins henceforth with the break [with the past] and rises up ever more violently, ever more savagely, ever more constructively. From our early youth, in our effort to emancipate ourselves from all the foreign elements that lay us waste, confident in ourselves alone, concentrated on ourselves to become better fit for liberation, by means of that irruption

[9] *Le Passé simple* (Paris, 1954), pp. 248-249, 251.

into the tumult of life which will make our potentialities explode, too long oppressed, we are giving and taking at the same time. . . . We reject everything that awakens in us the slightest sentiment of weakness and inferiority, even though we should not go so far as to deny that man is all the more miserable the more he is eminent, and all the more imposing the more he is low and impotent. What matters in every regard is that our experiences flow from a human reality sufficiently intense for us to accept it, and that they do not gather up the debris of external influences that decompose and annihilate it [i.e., this reality].[10]

---

[10] Leïla Baalbaki, "Nous sans masques" (lecture given on May 11, 1959); French trans. by M. Barbot, *Orient*, XI (1959), 147-163, at p. 156. *Anā aḥyà* was published in 1958. What Augustin Berque (1884-1946) said of the Algerian intellectual applies with equal force to the Arab, the Middle Eastern, intellectual in general, and perhaps to most of the Western-schooled elites of new or resurgent nations in Asia and Africa. Ideas upon which one discourses in the West become in the Maghrib "maîtresses tyranniques, impérieuses, [qui] s'emparent jalousement de l'esprit. Elles sont idées forces, mais aussi réflexes défensifs. On pense ici, non pour penser, mais contre quelqu'un . . ." ("Les intellectuels algériens," *Revues Africains*, XCI, no. 410-411 [1947], 123-151, at p. 138). As if to complete his father's observation, Jacques Berque (b. 1910), *Les Arabes d'hier à demain* (Paris, 1960), p. 255, explains that the characteristic "unrest, inquietude, of modern times is quick . . . to incriminate someone else. This is, in fact, its crudest form. But beyond this level, on which the denouncing of colonialism echoes the detesting of oneself, another equilibrium is working itself out among moral suffering, bitterness, and a sense of guilt." Another observation of A. Berque's deserves recording, as it describes to perfection an important aspect of the contact between the intellectual and his people, which compensates for the prevailing sense of mutual estrangement: ". . . l'excitation des instincts du peuple par une idéologie qui lui demeure inaccessible" (*ibid.*, p. 128). The attitude of that important sector of the Arabic speaking world which Miss Baalbaki represents emotionally (and not necessarily in the individual positions she adopts) is well summed up in a passage formulated without regard to those new nationalisms whose partial reaction it describes so clearly. "Der verdrängende Protest gegen die eigene Vergangenheit ist der Versuch, die durch die Vergangenheit der Freiheit gegebene Aufgabe durch Ablehnung der Aufgabe selbst zu lösen." (*Handbuch theologischer Grundbegriffe*, ed. H. Fries [Munich, 1962-1963], I, 494.

What means is there to pacify this turmoil? What is the therapy that will give direction to this irresistible if aimless passion? The answer is: self-understanding. But what is the nature of this self-understanding to be? And what is its formative purpose?

III

The objective is clear: a self-image apt to facilitate the realization of collective ambition and, more immediately, the reparation of collective pride must be perceived or, if need be, created. The sting must be taken out of the prevailing dissatisfaction with actual conditions, cultural and political, by placing the blame on circumstances, of which a specific and unessential segment of the heritage may be one, rather than on any of the more permanent and pervasive factors of history, such as geography or the natural endowment of the people themselves. History must furnish the evidence of the Messianic hope.

To this extent, scant disagreement would arise. There can be less certainty, however, when it comes to determining the pragmatically most effective measures that must be taken to remove that "tornness" of the Arab intelligentsia who, like the brilliant Tunisian poet Abū 'l-Qāsim ash-Shābbī (1909-1934), are fascinated by the "efficient and seductive" civilization of the West but feel obligated to their own "dusty or embryonic" culture, and who tend to reject their heritage for that of the Occident and to construct, in justification, a self-image of dismal poverty and sterility.[11]

It is not Westernization that is offensive but the rationale of the proposed acculturation. To be acceptable it must be aspired to in the service of a restoration of the *ʿurūba* to its pristine glory. Costi Zurayk (b. 1909) advocates an incisive reorganization on Western lines as the goal of that peaceful revolution toward progressiveness

---

[11] Cf. A. Ghedira, "Essai d'une biographie d'Abū l-Qāsim al-Šābbī," *Arabica*, VI (1959), 266-280, esp. pp. 280, 273-274.

which alone can attain for the Arabs their legitimate cultural aspirations. The separation of state and religious organization is demanded, "for nationalism is inconsistent with literal theocracy. The states of the West," Zurayk argues characteristically, "have only realized national strength to the extent that they have uprooted sectarianism and organized their life on the basis of the latest achievements of open-minded, cumulative thought." For a similar reason, the positive and empirical sciences of the West must be made to replace the bequest of the past, "benumbing fancy and insubstantial romanticism, the lost guides that lead" ever further astray.[12]

"Some of us still believe that the attacks of the Turks and the Mongols are what destroyed the Abbasid Caliphate and Arab power in general. But here also the fact is that the Arabs had been defeated internally before the Mongols defeated them and that, had those attacks been launched against them when they were in the period of growth and enlightenment, the Mongols would not have overcome them. On the contrary the attacks might have revitalized and re-energized them." [13] So the Arabs will have to acquire more of the drives and means of modern civilization. And when it is urged by some that such acquisition represents "departure from our history and loss of our national traditions," it must be conceded that "some of our traditions are unsound, and [that] these will be demolished and routed by the forces of modern civilization whether we desire it or not." What is more, "that which is lasting and sound, and suitable to this (or any) time, can only be discovered, separated from the temporary and the worthless, and vitally and completely assimilated into our present lives, by the action of that liberated, organized mind which we must acquire from modern civilization and on the foundation of which we must build our revolution." [14]

---

[12] *The Meaning of the Disaster* (originally published in 1948), trans. R. B. Winder (Beirut, 1956), p. 40.

[13] *Ibid.*, p. 48.

[14] *Ibid.*, p. 41.

Zurayk's views, formulated under the impact of the lost war against Israel in 1948, are but an extension, as it were, of ideas that, in regard to Egyptian (Arab) literature, had been formulated with remarkable precision by ʿĪsà ʿUbaid in 1921: "We feel aggrieved to state that modern Egyptian literature in our present time is neither independent nor marked by the seal of our personality. It is still subject to Arabic literature, frozen in its imitation of the ancient or influenced by the foreign literature we have had to study in order to learn the secrets of true and superior art and to borrow from it its rules, its laws, and its style." The difference between the two authors is that ʿĪsà ʿUbaid feels the time has come to free Egyptian writing from the foreign model (as well as the indigenous tradition), whereas Zurayk sees a period of further intensive adjustment to the West lying ahead. But is this difference really so great, considering ʿĪsà's repeated plea for a veristic art on the European pattern to give the *coup de grâce* to the ancient literature, which is characterized as "rigidly frozen, obscure, and banal"? [15]

The attitudes behind programs of this kind have their analogues among every intelligentsia hoping for a cultural revival that is, more often than not, intended as a steppingstone toward political reform, and for an increase in the international power of its society. The Slavophile, or more properly Russophile, Ivan Kireevskij (1806-1856), in discussing the nature of European civilization and its relation to Russia (in 1852), criticizes the prevailing opinion that in his country there used to be nothing but barbarism and that Russian *Bildung* began only when the Russians decided to imitate Europe, so far in advance of themselves in all intellectual pursuits. The Western Europeans are here conceived of as the teachers, the

[15] Preface to *Iḥsān Khānum,* trans. H. Pérès, "Préfaces des auteurs arabes à leurs romans ou à leurs recueils de contes et nouvelles," *Annales de l'Institut d'études orientales* (*Université d'Alger*), V (1939-1941), 137-195, at p. 159.

Russians as the eager students, so gifted that they were likely to outdo their masters before long.[16]

This relationship of voluntary and at times enthusiastic submission to the teacher and guide is the harder to sustain, the greater the advances that have been realized. The heart will not be at peace unless it has been assured that the existing differential in level is but momentary, and that essentially the student is the equal of his teacher, if not actually his superior. In other words, at a certain stage of the acculturation process, resituating oneself, or reëvaluating oneself through a reëvaluation of one's society and culture, imposes itself as a psychological obsession. As one might expect, it is the model civilization and its representatives, be they colonizers, "imperialists," or merely individual bearers of the foreign culture, who provide unwittingly a good many of the data and the viewpoints by means of which this self-interpretation becomes feasible and meaningful.

It is in terms of a Western philosophy of culture that Leïla Baalbaki, in a passionate and beautifully written paragraph, demands an end to the confusion between "the heritage" and "the past." This confusion has proved calamitous, she argues, for by castigating the Arab past the invaders cowed the spokesmen of the Arab heritage. With the specter of their own civilization, disguised as

---

[16] Ivan Kireevskij, "Über das Wesen der europäischen Kultur und ihr Verhältnis zur russischen," in D. Tschižewskij and D. Groh, *Europa und Russland. Texte zum Problem des westeuropäischen und russischen Selbstverständnisses* (Darmstadt, 1959), pp. 248-298, at p. 250. The awkward blend of assertiveness and lack of self-assurance combined with an ambivalent attitude to the cultural models, in this case the French and the English, weighed down the Germans before they had reached their measure. Roughly one century before the Slavophiles German literary critics either indulged in or cautioned against undue and, as it were, anticipated self-praise. Characteristic passages are readily accessible in G. F. Hering, *Meister der deutschen Kritik, 1730-1830* (Munich, 1961); e.g., pp. 45-46 (Joh. Elias Schlegel; 1745), 47 (C. F. W. Nicolai; 1755) and 90-91 (H. W. von Gerstenberg; 1768).

liberty, the foreign nations frightened the Arabs into losing their self-confidence and reduced them to a chain of stillborn generations. Never will the Arabs compel the respect of mankind unless they rip asunder the veils that now mask their history and expose the bricks laid by their ancestors in the great edifice of human solidarity. No foreign state must henceforth be allowed to render aid, even in the vital concerns of Arabs, so long as it brushes aside the fact that it is the Arabs "who have erected the temples of Baalbek, built the Pyramids [!], promulgated the charter for the service of humanity, known God, and cleft the waves to spread science to the four corners of the earth." [17]

The foreigner must be expelled; his spirit must be submerged in the resurgent genius of the Arab heritage. His intrusion has been a crime mainly because it imposed "inorganic" change on the structure of the glorious past. The colonizer and the conqueror have laid the groundwork of a renaissance by creating the nations that now may strive toward a rise which to them appears as a resurgence. The enforced stability of a common order, political unity, and internal security have made it possible to conceive of a policy of cultural renewal whose motivation has been characterized by a European observer with the telling phrase: "They want to be like us, but not with us." [18]

For a society that is proud of its past and basically convinced of the superiority of its traditional structure to be resentful of change, induced or imposed, is as natural as the tendency of a conquering society to introduce reforms in morally sensitive areas. Plutarch reports that Gelon of Syracuse (*ca.* 491-478 B.C.) wrote into a treaty with the Carthaginians a prohibition of their customary child sacrifices.[19] And in another work Plutarch raises the question whether or not in one's colonies one ought to abolish cruel and barbarous customs, especially as these relate to

[17] *Op. cit.*, pp. 160-161.
[18] Mannoni, *op. cit.*, p. 141.
[19] *Apophthegmata basileōn*, 175A (Bernardakis, II, 9).

sacrifices of women and children.[20] Needless to say, Islam has labored everywhere to make usage conform to its precepts; the history of Morocco, for example, is one long battle to Islamize the Berbers. As early as 1582 the Moghul Emperor Akbar (1556-1605) discouraged the self-immolation of the Hindu widow on her husband's pyre,[21] a measure that the British found it necessary to repeat in 1829 in the form of an absolute prohibition. The complaint that makes interference per se a grievance arises for the most part only when the idealization of the past has become an instrument for the shaping of the future.

This reaction, however, is conditioned by the fact that "civilizing," or, rather, assimilating to the civilization of the ruler, is more often than not one of the purposes, stated or unstated, of colonization or domination in general.[22] This is universally true, even as colonization as a culture contact through conquest, acquisition, or occupation (of empty land) is a universal and, for that matter, extremely ancient phenomenon of which, incidentally, the growth of the Arab empire and its aftermath provide a number of particularly striking instances.

Culturally speaking, the modern "conqueror" has given more than he has received. This observation is especially true in the context of acculturation leading to the revival of the indigenous society. Much more than individual actions, such as the codification of laws under the influence of, or in competition with, the Occident, or the reviewing of existing institutions, has the necessity of a general stocktaking of intellectual and organizational possessions enhanced the rise of self-consciousness and, not infrequently, the sense of pride in the heritage, if not in

---

[20] *Aetia Romana*, quest. 83, 283F-284C (Bernardakis, II, 300-302); cf. Maunier, *op. cit.*, II, 110-111, 117.

[21] Abū 'l-Faḍl ʿAllāmī, *Āʾīn-i Akbarī*, trans. H. S. Jarrett, ed. Sir Jadu-Nath Sarkar (2d ed. rev.; Calcutta, 1939-1949), II, 45 (cf. also I, 215); R. S. Sharma, *The Crescent in India* (rev. ed.; Poona, 1954), pp. 449, 469. Muḥammad b. Tughluq (1325-1351) had failed to make his prohibition of the *satī* be obeyed.

[22] Cf. R. Maunier, *Sociologie coloniale* (Paris, 1932), I, 68-72.

the past—to borrow Miss Baalbaki's distinction. Paradoxical though this may seem, it was the European scholar who revealed to the Indians their forgotten sacred books, to the Egyptians the glories of their pre-Islamic civilization, to the Arab world as a whole the beauties of its popular literature. It is hardly an overstatement to claim that Western concern for their history and Western appreciation of their past achievement won for this history and this achievement the prestige they needed to become levers in that revaluation of autochthonous civilizations whose frequent superficiality and clichélikeness in no way detracted from its psychological and political effectiveness. Occidental scholarship furnishes the arms to combat the West; when the West is combated, its scholarship is combated as well, and room is made for a *mystique* of the past (no longer endangered by criticism), a *mystique* of the kind that all nationalisms everywhere are yearning for, but which the rationalistic bent of scientific research has made it increasingly difficult for us to construct and to sustain.

The recourse to the indigenous past is, however, also a means of self-protection against possible rejection by the civilization to which assimilation is desired, and in large measure achieved. Chraibi has given expression to this aspect of the flight into the tradition that, in the last analysis, has long been abandoned:

> You have sprung from the Orient and by means of your painful past, your fancies, your education, you will triumph over the Orient. You have never believed in Allah, you know how to dissect the legends, you think in French, you read Voltaire and admire Kant. Only the Occidental world for which you are destined appears to you speckled with stupidities and blemishes, more or less the same stupidities and blemishes from which you are escaping. Moreover, you anticipate its hostility; it will not accept you at the first trial. And on the point of exchanging your box for a folding seat (*strapontin*), you beat a retreat (*tu as des reculs*).[23]

---

[23] *Le Passé simple*, p. 99.

The *recul* of the Westernized is likely to lead into active opposition, at times into a two-front war, against the indigenous tradition and against the civilization of the Occident, each battle conducted as a fight for the true against the distorted, for the blessed origins against the decay they suffered at the hand of the *ʿulamāʾ*, for the humanitarian ideals of the West against the politicians who are debasing them. It cannot possibly be overemphasized that the arms leveled at the West by its opponents in the Middle East and beyond, arms that a modern opponent would want to use on the international stage, have one and all been preshaped by the West itself. This is true for the ideologies of nationalism and the mythology of absolute sovereignty; but it is true as much for the depreciation of colonial rule, the theme of the equality of races and the potential equality of civilizations. This last doctrine must sound somewhat absurd in the ears of those who use it to remake their heritage on the Western model.

There is nothing astonishing in this situation. For the three principal motivations for acculturation in our time are in psychological and, to some extent, also in chronological order: admiration for the richer civilization of the West; the use of it as a means to attain and demonstrate social distinction within one's own group or people; and its adoption as a means of emancipation.[24]

[24] On this point cf. Maunier, *op. cit.*, I, 138 ff. The prestige-building effect of adopting Western mores is analogous to the prestige-building effect of conversion to Islam in Negro Africa; on this factor promoting the expansion of Islam in our time cf. the references in J. Henninger, "Über den Beitrag der Laien bei der Ausbreitung des Islams," *Der Laienapostolat in den Missionen. Festschrift Joh. Beckmann* (Schöneck-Beckenried, 1961), pp. 345-371, on pp. 368-369. That an attitude of total rejection or, more positively described, of self-sufficiency or, rather, of unlimited confidence in the proper past, has always been present simultaneously with acculturative tendencies of various hues may be illustrated by a dictum of Muḥammad ʿAbduh in one of the harsher pedagogical moods of his earlier period. In 1886, in warning against foreign and, specifically, missionary educational influences, he refers his audience to pure Islam. In order to rise, "it is

IV

It is in the realization of this last goal that a *prise de conscience* becomes imperative; that the "personality," as it were, of one's own society has to be pitted against the (usually freely stylized) "personality" of the West; and that the shaping of the "personality" image of one's people proves unavailing unless this "personality" is placed against, or allowed to arise from, the background of history. The need for recourse to history is a direct outgrowth of human insecurity. Precedent bolsters and facilitates decision. When the stars can no longer be invoked to illuminate the future, past achievement can.[25] Not only do

---

sufficient for us to return to what we have abandoned and to purify what we have corrupted. This [mistreated heritage] consists of our religious and humanistic books, which contain more than enough of what we seek, and there is nothing in books other than ours which adds anything to them except that which we do not need" (Muḥammad Rashīd Riḍā, *Taʾrīkh al-ustādh al-imām ash-Shaikh Muḥammad ʿAbduh* [2d ed.; Cairo, 1344/1925], II, 353[22-26]; trans. C. E. Dawn, "From Ottomanism to Arabism: the Origin of an Ideology," *Review of Politics*, XXIII [1961], 378-400, at p. 389). The argument is strangely reminiscent of the explanation attributed to the caliph ʿUmar in justification of the burning of the Library of Alexandria, an incident long relegated to the realm of the fable.

[25] A. G. Chejne, "The Use of History by Modern Arab Writers," *Middle East Journal* (1960), pp. 382-396, has brought together ample evidence for this fact from a large number of contemporary Arab historians and publicists. The quotations range from M. H. Haikal's observation that "the knowledge of the past alone can safeguard the nature of our future, and enable us to direct our efforts toward a goal benefitting humanity" (*aṣ-Ṣiddiq Abū Bakr* [Cairo, 1942], p. 10; Chejne, *op. cit.*, p. 388) to Sāṭiʿ al-Ḥuṣrī's question, "Is scholarship for its own sake, or for the sake of the homeland?" (*Ārāʾ wa-aḥādīth fī 'l-waṭaniyya wa'l-qaumiyya* [Cairo, 1944], p. 135; Chejne, *op. cit.*, p. 393) and the Syrian decree of May 30, 1947, which declares the purpose of the study of history in the schools to be the strengthening of "the nationalist and patriotic sentiments in the hearts of the people," and which is supplemented by another decree explaining that "the history of the Arab nation and Arab Homeland must aim, first and above all, at depicting the great role played by our venerable ancestors in the progress and evolution of

"happy nations have a history,"[26] but they are willing to accept their history as it is, with its weaknesses and its limitations. Does an Englishman or an American feel humiliated when, as so frequently happens, it is pointed out to him by an Arab interlocutor that his ancestors

---

civilization" (Chejne, *op. cit.*, pp. 392-393). To this valuable collection, whose importance is enhanced by quotations in a comparable vein from German historians of the early nineteenth century, should be added the study of two Moroccan historians of our day which E. Gellner recently published as "The Struggle for Morocco's Past," *Middle East Journal* (1961), pp. 79-90. J. Berque, *Les Arabes* (Paris, 1959), pp. 24-25, has made a brilliant attempt to abstract, as it were, from countless statements and their implications a definition of what an Arab is in the eyes of those who pronounce themselves such: "Est arabe . . . ce qui apparaît comme antique, comme authentique, comme antérieur à toutes les deformations, à toutes les adaptations: en un mot, un trésor soustrait à l'histoire, et que celle-ci n'a pu que dilapider ou aliéner, qu'il faut donc reconstituer, dès que faire se pourra, et rendre à sa première splendeur. Est arabe, en second lieu, ce qui est unitaire, ce qui se correspond d'un bout à l'autre de la rive sud [du Méditerranéen]. Cette unité n'est pas une constatation. Elle est un voeu, un postulat. Mais il faut reconnaître tout ce que la réalité peut lui prêter de captieuse vraisemblance." Less for its direct relevance to Arab self-construction than for the enlargement it allows of a people's extrapolation into history, attention may be called in this context to the remarkable study of Américo Castro, "Présence du sultan Saladin dans les littératures romanes," *Diogène*, no. 8 (1954), pp. 2-31. Castro has shown (p. 6) how Italians, Frenchmen, and Spaniards of the thirteenth and fourteenth centuries utilized the figure of Saladin to bring to life their several aspirations of the moment: "La figure de Saladin se dessine, en réalité, sur des situations préexistantes, que l'on souhaitait rendre manifestes et qui gagnaient en prestige à être présentées dans le cadre d'une figure illustre, lointaine et exemplaire."

[26] This is the suggestive title of a study by O. Hatzfeld in the *Cahiers du monde non chrétien*, XVI (1950), 387-403 (on which see p. 226 n. 61, above). Conversely, it is, in the words of the Turkish writer Abdülhakk Şinasi (b. 1888), "der gemeinste und teuflischste Anschlag auf eine Nation, die Vergangenheit aus ihrem nationalen Bewusstsein zu reissen und aus ihrem Gedächtnis zu tilgen" (quoted by O. Spies, "Die neue Türkei im Spiegel der modernen türkischen Literatur," in *Aus Politik und Zeitgeschichte. Beilage zur Wochenzeitung "Das Parlament,"* August 24, 1960, p. 568*a*).

were barbarians, or worse, at a time when the caliphate led the civilized world? In fact, his is likely to be a composite reaction—a faint suspicion that, for personal reasons, the Arab may be overstating his case, and a discreet pride, left inarticulate, in his own comparatively close involvement in a great human triumph. When Goethe[27] says that reminding a nation of its past in a perceptive manner creates a general sense of well-being, of being pleased with the ancestors' virtues and smilingly indulgent of their vices, which it deems to have long since been overcome; when Goethe envisages this peaceful satisfaction as the typical response to history, he is indeed describing the attitude of a happy, self-assured, and self-satisfied society, of a society that, in a sense, has little need of that consultation with history sought so desperately by nations faced with the psychological complexities of acculturation.[28]

Consultation with history presupposes a certain fa-

---

[27] *Dichtung und Wahrheit*, Buch 17 (Hanser-Ausgabe, p. 564).

[28] Nor is W. von Humboldt right when he speaks (*Werke*, I, 380) of the "universal need of mankind to account, from time to time, to themselves for the transformations of its character." This need is clearly bound to specific cultural settings. He anticipates the dominant motivation of Western historical scholarship in the nineteenth and twentieth centuries when he describes what appears to him as the new German approach (which he contrasts with the French approach of the eighteenth century): "Wir hingegen gewöhnen uns jetzt die Eigenthümlichkeiten jeder Zeit und jeder Nation zu studieren, so viel wie möglich in dieselben einzugehen, und diese Kenntnis zum Mittelpunkt unserer Beurtheilung zu machen" (*ibid.*, I, 456-457). The first step is taken on the road that will lead to the self-consciously adopted attitude that H. H. Schaeder (1896-1957), *Der Mensch in Orient und Okzident* (München, 1960) pp. 399-400, was to formulate by finding the meaning of Oriental studies in the self-understanding of the Occidental. Perhaps the first great statement of Western self-confidence and an incipient feeling of cultural superiority was made by Pope Pius II (Enea Silvio Piccolomini) in a letter which he addressed to the Turkish Sultan Mehmed II in 1460; the document has been analysed by R. W. Southern, *Western Views of Islam in the Middle Ages* (Cambridge, Mass., 1962), pp. 99-102.

miliarity with its essential facts, bare or stylized, on the part of a large section of any given society. To create this familiarity is, in the early phase of the search for identification, the function of the historical novel. In the Arabic-speaking world the taste for this genre, adopted from the West, dominated prose fiction between 1880 and 1904. Jurjī Zaidān (1861-1914), the leading exponent of the historical novel in Arabic, clearly states its function in the preface to his *Charlemagne and ʿAbdarraḥmān* (1904): ". . . the people have a lively desire to read Muslim history, that is to say, the history of the Orient, its literature, and its sciences after the Roman period." The novel gives the reader knowledge of historical data in a much more plastic and drastic manner than a history book, and at the same time succeeds in acquainting him with the mores of the period in a direct and persuasive fashion.[29] In fact, Jurjī Zaidān intended to present his public with a complete cursus in Middle Eastern history in novel form, from the pre-Islamic period to the days of the greatest splendor of the caliphate, a plan, incidentally, which he was able to carry out to a remarkable extent.

Once a certain measure of familiarity with the past is attained, and the habit of having recourse to it is established, it becomes possible to use it as the foundation and the proof of a political program and a political *mystique*. Perhaps the most brilliant example in the Arab world of this blending of past and future in a political vision is the article by ʿAbdarraḥmān ʿAzzām (who, born in 1893, was from 1945 to 1952 the first secretary general of the Arab League), "The Arabs, People of the Future," published in the Palestinian journal *al-ʿArab* in 1932. After pleading for Arab unification on the analogy of the unification of Italy and Germany in the nineteenth century, ʿAzzām describes the Arabs as a youthful people in

[29] Cf. Pérès, *op. cit.*, p. 142. Cf. also Jamīl al-Mudawwar, *Ḥaḍārat al-Islām fī Dār as-salām* (1888), for whose preface cf. Pérès, *op. cit.*, p. 140; a detailed study of Mudawwar has been prepared by Erika Köcher, *Untersuchungen zu Gamīl al-Mudauwars Ḥaḍārat al-Islām* . . . (Berlin, 1958).

spite of the fact that they are "one of the ancient races that have given the world great civilizations." Unification would permit the Arabs to show new forces and abilities over and above those they possessed at the time of their first successes against Romans and Persians, and ever since, throughout thirteen centuries, against the nations of East and West. The achievement of the past turns into the cornerstone of a mystical vision of what lies ahead: ". . . in saving the Arabs, [the people of Arab tongue] will save the universe, that universe whose civilization has become senile and whose culture is about to go bankrupt; that world over which materialism has spread its wing since the civilization of the Arabs has reached its dusk." [30]

"On the other hand, the war of the classes is on the point of breaking out. Now there does not exist in the universe a race professing faith in equality and placing itself far above matter like the Arabs. If the Arab race becomes predominant, their qualities will become dominant with them and the material life will decline so that the spiritual life may rise. And if the Arabs give their qualities to, and instill life into, the universe they will have saved it from the calamities with which it struggled and they will have created it anew." [31]

---

[30] The sense of the universal messianic significance of the development of one's own society recurs on all cultural levels; cf., e.g., the belief of the Papua in New Guinea who, on the defeat of the Japanese at the end of World War II, thought the *Manseren* (Messiah) was on his way to New Guinea "to herald the beginning of the Golden Era of the Papuans which at the same time is the golden era of the world" (C. A. D. van Nieuwenhuijze, *Aspects of Islam in Post-Colonial Indonesia* [The Hague and Bandung, 1958], p. 13 n. 1). This and similar movements are discussed and analyzed in the proper world-wide context in G. Guariglia's illuminating study, *Prophetismus und Heilserwartungs-Bewegungen als völkerkundliches und religionsgeschichtliches Problem* (Horn and Vienna, 1959), pp. 63-132.

[31] *Documents de la Revue des deux Mondes*, I (July, 1958), 43-44. This view, to be appreciated, must be held against another which, although pushed to the side lines by nationalism, is still effectively present in the hearts of large sections of the Arab community. Two passages, taken somewhat at random from the memoirs of King ʿAbdallāh (d. 1951), will suggest its character:

The activist intent of the vision imposes certain limitations. If the past is to be criticized, the criticism must not touch its essential grandeur. The past must be appreciated as glory and as burden, as incomparable yet capable of recovery; it must be preserved and shed at the same time. The confrontation may be superficial; it is never carefree. The task is lightened by a long habituation to accept the "ought" for the "is," the ideal for the real; but it is rendered more heavy by a certain lack of serenity in facing the future. Despair and literary tradition allow a measure of self-praise which the decline of European nationalism has eliminated from Western self-characterizations, but which is in line with Rashīd Riḍā's famous assertion in 1900 that the Arabs are "in truth the best nation born into the world." [32] Although apprehensiveness dictates

---

"Accordingly . . . the Arabs were unified, converted to a single faith, and turned in a single direction. . . . Thus, by the grace of God, the Creator prepared for this fortunate nation (*umma*) these advantages and honored it with the 'seal' of the prophets and messengers. . . . Then they became a compact building, strengthening each other, no censurer finding them at fault before God." "The Arab nation (*al-umma 'l-ʿarabiyya*), the possessor of history and the master of a noble past, to whose Prophet the Koran descended and which conquered the East and the West in less than a quarter century [!], which produced a religious and cultural renaissance and the requisites of human brotherhood, is a nation (*umma*) that cannot be a servile colony, but which is a free, independent, and leading nation. As to its remaining under the shadow of non-Arab, but Moslem, governments [the reference is to the Ottoman Turks], this resulted from the submission of those nations to Islamic teachings and the Muhammadan brotherhood." The outlook is summed up in the lapidary phrase: "The Arabs are nothing except Islam." Cf. *Mudhakkirātī* (1st ed.; Jerusalem, 1945), pp. 73-74 (Appendix), 237-238, 22; the translation is C. E. Dawn's in his study "Ideological Influences in the Arab Revolt," in *The World of Islam*, ed. J. Kritzeck and R. B. Winder (London & New York, 1959), pp. 233-248, at pp. 234, 235, 237.

[32] The rationale of Rashīd Riḍā's judgment is the Arab contribution to Islam, whose greatness waned with that of the Arab empire; for reference cf. S. G. Haim, "Intorno alle origini della teoria del panarabismo," *Oriente Moderno*. XXXVI (1956), 409-421, at pp. 415-416.

much of the political as of the intellectual behavior, the only true danger threatening the Arab world is never openly faced: the possibility that the lag between the leading and the developing countries will increase rather than shrink, in view of the greater rate of growth of the former and their scientific and economic initiative. The refusal to come to grips with this possibility, not to say probability, is as self-defeating as the tendency, which becomes more and more noticeable, to confine foreign influence to the narrow area for which it is sought. This trend is the child of the same illusion that, more than a hundred years ago, persuaded a number of Eastern rulers that military improvements could be introduced from the West and kept in quarantine. The political uneasiness that supports this illusion strengthens the sentiment that an alien technology can not only be put to work (which may be possible), but can be creatively continued in isolation from the moral and intellectual context in which it arose.[33] At this point the past holds no advice. But it can give strength to bolster a dream whose potency does not as yet suffer by its imprecision. There is, however, a means to make its message more conclusive and hence more effective.

The stylization of the past can and will be rendered more precise or more concrete through selection of one particular period as the *pièce justificative* of the future, as the model on which the future must be patterned. It is only natural that, next after the period of the greatest

[33] Similar ideas and impressions have been formulated by Berque, *Les Arabes*, p. 105*a*, and *Les Arabes d'hier à demain*, pp. 126-127, 135, 264-265. Those are still relatively few who, like Ṭāhā Ḥusain, *Mustaqbal ath-thaqāfa fī Miṣr* (Cairo, 1938), I, 57, comprehend the material civilization of the West as a "product" of its spirit (for the passage cf. P. Cachia, *Ṭāhā Ḥusain. His Place in the Egyptian Literary Renaissance* [London, 1956], p. 93). Even Ṭāhā Ḥusain, however, never developed this insight or attempted to convey its lesson. For the "fundamentalist" view of the Muslim ideal vs. the Muslim practice, cf. C. A. O. van Nieuwenhuijze, "Frictions between Presuppositions," *Centre pour l'étude des problèmes du monde musulman contemporain. Bulletin d'Information*, V (March-April, 1958), 38-67, at pp. 60-62.

splendor of Muslim civilization in the eighth, ninth, and tenth centuries, the period of Islamic origins should be most frequently singled out for this role and that, consequently, it has had to undergo a good deal of reconstructing in which it has been viewed, depending on the writer's outlook, as socialistic, religiously impeccable, simple, pure, ever-victorious. To many (but by no means to all), the brief period of the Rightly-Guided Caliphs (632-660) is the only period in which a truly Islamic state existed. Then and only then did the world in the Muslim domain enjoy a perfect balance of religious and political, practical and spiritual, aspirations and activities.[34]

Unlike most nations and individuals, the Arab-Muslim leaders of that time did not assume rulership without previous education of their characters and previous cleansing of their souls; realizing that man consists of body and soul, of reason and emotion, they were capable of developing a civilization in keeping with human nature.[35] So Islam was able to implement, if only for a brief span, the principles of a political liberty holding the mean between democracy and aristocracy.[36] In short, the period has been selected as one of political and, even more, of sociological excellence, or rather, uniqueness.

The pragmatically purposeful idealization of Muslim society in history has its parallels in the pragmatically purposeful idealization of Russian society (before its modernization was begun by Peter the Great), which is typical of Slavophiles. The following passage from Kireevskij is especially significant because its author, like the Arab writers of more recent days, is concerned with fight-

[34] See p. 248, above, with reference to ʿAlī al-Ḥasanī an-Nadwī, *Mā dhā khasara 'l-ʿālam bi'nḥiṭāṭ al-muslimīn?* (2d ed.; Cairo, 1370/1951), pp. 100-101. The selectivity extends to intellectual movements as well. The shifting appraisals of the Muʿtazila are a case in point. Cf. the informative study by R. Caspar, "Le renouveau du moʿtazilisme," *Mélanges de l'Institut dominicain d'études orientales du Caire* (MIDEO), IV (1957), 141-201.

[35] See pp. 248-249, above, with reference to Nadwī, *op. cit.*, pp. 96-100.

[36] See pp. 115-121, above.

ing Westernization by means of a self-image that is itself very largely a result of acculturation accomplished.

While the orthodox Church directed society in the same manner as the mind directs the body, it never endeavored to impose on secular institutions the spirit of an ecclesiastical institution as it was inherent in the monkish knightly orders, the courts of the inquisition, and other temporal-spiritual institutions of the West. . . . In Russia [unlike the West] there were neither conquerors nor conquered. The country did not know an ironbound separation of rigid estates, neither oppression for the one, nor privileges for the other; it did not know the resulting political and intellectual battles, nor the mutual contempt, hate, and envy of the estates. . . . In this guise, Russian society developed independently and naturally, borne ahead by a single inner conviction, the work of the Church and of popular tradition. Nevertheless, or, rather, precisely because of this situation, sentimental enthusiasm for equality was as foreign to it as oppressive privileges. . . . Because of the naturalness, the simplicity, and the harmony of prevailing conditions, the laws that expressed them were without any formal artificiality,

in contrast to the jurisprudence of the West, which identifies the law with its form and considers the letter of the law the embodiment of absolute reason.[37]

The need to come to terms with the present through an adjustment of the past appears to be universal and in large measure independent of the level of sophistication which the crisis-bound society has attained. The Madagascan *demi-évolué* who published, under the pseudonym of Dama Ntsoha, two tracts, *Les Temps nouveaux* (1945) and *La Démocratie malgache* (1948), both in his own

---

[37] *Op. cit.*, pp. 281-283. The same train of thought recurs in F. I. Tyuchev (1803-1875), who describes the Orthodox Church as "a society of the faithful freely united in the spirit and the truth under the law of Christ"; the Roman Church, on the other hand, was "a political power, a state in the state," addicted to wars and politics (cf. H. Kohn, ed., *The Mind of Modern Russia. Historical and Political Thought of Russia's Great Age* [New Brunswick, N.J., 1955], p. 92).

language and in French,[38] proposes a reorganization of his country on the basis of the *fokon'olona,* a kind of village council, whose origin he projects, not quite accurately, into the remote darknesses of the past. The government resumes the character of an assembly of notables who are to revive the paternalistic regime which the French superseded. This concept is widened in the second treatise, where the *fokon'olona* (whose administrative structure is no longer clearly recognizable) are identified wit with the collectivity as such, which in tune with the traditional, premodernist view of the people, includes the dead. The overcoming of the paternalistic village councils is buttressed by recourse to a more distant and hence more genuinely Malagasy past in which Buddhism was the religion of the island. By adopting an ancient though imaginary tradition, Dama Ntsoha finds the strength to abandon a more recent tradition of undisputable reality.[39]

---

[38] On these books cf. Mannoni, *op. cit.*, pp. 190-197.

[39] The extreme to which a new nationalism may resort in giving itself a history is strikingly illustrated by a series of postcards published by Ghana which depict Africans teaching the ancient Greeks the alphabet and mathematics and discovering medicine, chemistry, and shorthand; the postcards are reproduced in *Newsweek,* Oct. 31, 1960, p. 45. One is reminded of Václav Hanka's (1791-1861) forgery, in the interest of Czech nationalism, of the so-called *Königinhofer Handschrift* (1817), and of *Libuša's Judgment* (1818), as well as the reluctance with which the Czech nationalists (in the 1880's) accepted the evidence offered by Czech scholars for their falsehood. Cf. H. Kohn, *Pan-Slavism. Its History and Ideology* (Notre Dame, Ind., 1953), p. 257, who quotes in connection with this affair the comment of the French historian, Ernest Denis, dating back to 1902-1903, but still uncomfortably topical: "Generally it is infinitely better to have no history than to keep up in the people the inclination to falsehood. It is a wrong piety to wish to cover up the errors of our fathers; the only means of honoring the memory of our fathers consists of abandoning their mistakes." Pragmatically speaking, the true purpose of any effective reconstruction of Arab-Muslim history ought to be the dispelling of that attitude in Muslim civilization which R. Charles, *L'Evolution de l'Islam* (Paris, 1960), p. 23, calls "l'hypnotique aperception de sa propre stabilité." In his dissatisfaction with his present state the Muslim tends to forget the contingent element or elements in his civiliza-

The Arabs as well as other non-Western nations who fight free of the West while acculturating to it are taking the road the Russians took little more than a century ago. From unconditional admiration of the West they moved, in the work of figures like P. V. Chaadaev (born between 1793 and 1796; died during the Crimean War; his dates were 1794-1856, according to the *Bol'shaya Sovyetskaya Enziklopediya*), toward transcending the discomfort of an unsatisfactory past—unsatisfactory, that is, in terms of the desired self-image—by first revaluing their lack of a (suitable) history as an advantage; the embarrassing *tabula rasa* reveals itself suddenly as an unlimited opportunity for a young and vigorous people.[40] The contrast to the Arab approach could not be more striking as regards the manipulation of the actual past, but intent and technique are the same. The classical formulation appears in a letter that Alexander Herzen (1812-1870) wrote to the German revolutionary Georg Herwegh (1817-1875), under the impact of the failure of the French and German upheavals in 1848-49: "Russland erscheint als das letzte Volk noch voll von jugendlichen Forderungen an's Leben zu einer Zeit, wo die anderen Völker Ruhe wollen, es erscheint im Uebermuthe seiner wilden Kräfte zu einer Zeit, wo die Anderen sich müde und abgelebt fühlen. . . . Viele Völkerracen traten vom Schauplatz der Geschichte ab, ohne in ganzer Fülle gelebt zu haben; aber sie hatten nicht, wie Russland, solche kolossale Ansprüche auf die Zukunft. Sie wissen: in der Geschichte *tarde venientibus* nicht *ossa*, sondern die besten Früchte, wenn sie fähig sind, dieselben zu assimilieren." [41]

---

tion. Islam "érigea le miracle en dogme, et sur cette contemplation, s'assoupit." Reconstruction, then, must bear the Janus-faced character of preserving the stimulating prestige of the past and breaking the impermeability to an alien inspiration which is needed to recover its former creativity.

[40] "Erster philosophischer Brief" (written in 1829), *in* Tschiżewskij and Groh, *op. cit.*, pp. 73-93, at pp. 73 ff.; cf. also n. 1 on pp. 73-74.

[41] "Brief an G. Herwegh, 25 August 1849," in *ibid.*, pp. 202-220, at p. 218.

The next step, accompanied like the earlier ones by a systematic and almost contrapuntal deprecation of the Western model, consists in a transvaluation of the deficiencies of the living past. Once again an illuminating example is offered by Kireevskij, writing in 1852. He puts the lag in intellectual activity in Russia, in comparison with her Christian neighbors, to good account by arguing that the culture of antiquity did not affect the Russians as overwhelmingly as it affected the Europeans because they received it only through the intermediary of Christianity. Only when Russia had been fully Christianized did she appropriate the latest results of ancient civilization—at this point Providence was pleased (by means of the Mongol invasion and its consequences) to arrest her further intellectual development. "Thereby," Kireevskij continues, "she was preserved from that noxious one-sidedness that would have necessarily fallen to her lot, if she had dedicated herself to a rationalistic *Bildung*, before Europe had completed the cycle of its intellectual formation." [42]

---

[42] *Op. cit.*, p. 260. Be it noted, incidentally, that Kireevskij's letter contains, pp. 269-270, a characterization of Islamic civilization which does not of course transcend the knowledge of his period and is of purely historical interest. Fundamentally, most spokesmen for Arab nationalism are kinsmen of the romantic intellectuals who, throughout nineteenth-century Europe, discovered in their own people the universal savior, in their own past the heroic age, and in their own nation's future greatness the liberation of all mankind and the resuscitation of true civilization. They share with the Slavophile thinkers of that period the conviction that the West nurtures a deep and permanent enmity toward their nation, and the wish to believe with full assurance that the heyday of the West is a thing of the past. The Slavophiles may have been somewhat more self-conscious in regard to their intellectual ancestry. Their admiration for German philosophy and, in general, for "the land of holy miracles," to borrow once again A. S. Khomiakov's (1804-1860) much-quoted phrase, did not, however, prevent them from viewing the downfall of the Occident as anything but a necessary prelude to the impending redemptive supremacy of the Slav. The Arab can no longer claim, as the Slavophile did, that the West is unaware of its peril; but he is beset by the same dilemma that haunted the

V

Self-construction through history allows partial liberation from the realities of the present; but to achieve an assessment of one's situation and characteristics at a given moment, it requires complementation by direct description. An analytical appraisal of nature and state of the conflicting and blending cultures has to be resorted to, which marks, from a literary point of view, a further step in that *prise de conscience* which, in our time, seems to be inseparable from the process of acculturation.

The most obvious and hence, as far as I can see, the earliest technique of self-analysis is the comparison of Eastern and Western mentality by juxtaposition and contrast. Shiḥāta ʿUbaid says in the preface to his novel *Dars muʾlim* (*A Painful Lesson*; 1922):

> Which person, endowed with a shred of reason, *au courant* of the psychology of peoples, would not be saddened and feel aggrieved when drawing a parallel between Europe and the East? Does he not see how the Occidentals, serious and active even in their moments of pleasure and leisure, are always grasping for something that widens their knowledge and opens their intelligence? Whereas we have inclination only for what will augment our pleasure or will permit us to step outside the circle of our actual lives and to throw ourselves in the infinite field of the imagination. A single glance at the books that are printed and circulated among them and among ourselves suffices to show the difference between the mentalities. Some claim that we do not have any writers capable of rivaling those of the West. This cannot be denied. But we have

---

Slavophiles, to wit, whether to reject *in toto* or to accept in part (and if so, what parts) the achievement of the great antagonist. Arab and Slavophile (and countless other latter-day nationalists outside the Western orbit) also share the monologuish character of their assault as well as their defense. Response and refutation were not then and are not now a major concern of the West; and, for better or for worse, it could hardly be otherwise. (The reference to Khomiakov is taken from N. V. Riasanovsky, *Russia and the West in the Teaching of the Slavophiles. A Study of Romantic Ideology* [Cambridge, Mass., 1952], pp. 62, 117.)

seen more than one writer of the new generation in full development follow in the footsteps of the Western writers and make an attempt that, if assisted, would have permitted him after a short time to resemble those Occidentals.[43]

On a more popular level, the rivalry reappears in anecdotes that pit, for example, an Egyptian magician against a European one, and have the Egyptian defeat his opponent before the khedive.[44] In general, the "Old Believer" recognizes the material superiority of the European and the greater efficiency of his ways, but he sees this as the result of a division by which God gave the infidels a brief span of well-being on earth while reserving eternal felicity to his own, the Muslims: "God has accorded me that prodigious favor of letting me be born outside the ranks of his enemies, of those whom he created only to increase the bliss of the elect by the spectacle of their tortures. . . . I am a Muslim. Praise be to God." [45] "We shall have Paradise. They have this passing life. This is their share. God says: 'I have created man and *jinn* only so they will adore me.' [46] The highest purpose of life is therefore to dedicate oneself to God. The infidels think only of their well-being, their money. It is they who keep everything going down here. God has assigned them this role. In this they are already, without knowing it, our servants." [47]

But with progressive acculturation this resignation dies down; a troubled feeling of superiority remains, and the analysis by anecdote and religious solace no longer suffices.

---

[43] Pérès, *op. cit.*, pp. 164-165.

[44] F.-J. Bonjean and Ahmed Deif, *Mansour. Histoire d'un enfant du pays d'Egypte* (Paris, 1924), pp. 187-188. Reference to this story is especially appropriate in the light of the fact that, in 1858, Napoleon III sent the great prestidigitator, R. Houdin, to Algeria with a view to having him demonstrate to the Muslims that the alleged miracles of their saints are nothing but a sleight of hand.

[45] *Ibid.*, p. 272.

[46] Koran 51:56.

[47] Bonjean and Deif, *op. cit.*, p. 169.

A self-image that is more carefully reasoned emerges through the emergence of an articulate image of the West and its civilization. It is based on selective experience, and is perhaps not so obviously programmatic as was the self-portrayal by means of history.

An example of such an effort to draw the antithetical picture of East and West which has proven so satisfactory as an instrument of self-appeasement and pedagogy is provided by the booklet written by Aḥmad Amīn (1886-1954), in his day one of the leading figures on the Egyptian intellectual scene, as a result of a political visit to London in 1947. This visit greatly affected his attitude toward the West and led him "to doubt the soundness of the prevailing belief that, in point of civilization (*ḥaḍāra*) the West was ahead of the East."[48] With this sentence, in the first paragraph on the first page, the keynote of the essay is sounded. Aḥmad Amīn does not know much of the West, nor does he pretend to. He is aware of and, in fact, shares the principal motivation that inclines the East, the Arab East, that is, toward culture change, and, like many of his compatriots, he seems to believe in a kind of planned syncretism. Preserve religion, add science; leave the essential structure of Muslim society untouched, but introduce such and such features from Europe. Bring the material culture of Egypt up to the Western level but do not sacrifice the warmth of a preindustrial society. Aḥmad Amīn is gently diffident when it comes to positive proposals, but quite assertive when he contrasts the two civilizations.

The East-West antithesis which gave the title to his essay dominates the presentation. Yet, Aḥmad Amīn is at pains to demonstrate that what cultural divergences do exist are not in any sense predetermined, say, by geography or race. It is attitudes and aspirations, not unchangeable, impersonal forces that work the cleavage. Besides, it is erroneous to attribute universal validity to Western civilization. It has its particular place in the human development, and in some ways it may be superior to what came before

[48] *Ash-Sharq wa'l-Gharb* (Cairo, 1955), p. 1.

it, but it does not embody an absolute in value or achievement. Aḥmad Amīn's view could be stated in the words of Prince N. S. Trubetzkoj (1890-1938), a leading exponent of the so-called Eurasian concept of Russian history: "European culture is not a universal culture (*Menschheitskultur*). It is the result of the history of a certain ethnic group." [49]

---

[49] From *Europa und die Menschheit* (written in 1923), *in* Tschižewskij and Groh, *op. cit.*, p. 520; cf. also p. 521. From a (if not necessarily the) Communist viewpoint, generously enlivened with Russian patriotism, the limited validity of European culture is aggressively asserted in various "wissenschaftstheoretische" statements, of which the following brief selections constitute a fair sample:

> "Die einzig wirklich wissenschaftliche, die marxistisch-leninistische Methodologie hat den sowjetischen Geschichtswissenschaftlern die Möglichkeit gegeben, kühn die wichtigsten Probleme der byzantinischen Geschichte, die ja ausserhalb des Gesichtskreises der bürgerlichen Gelehrten geblieben waren oder die zu lösen sich die bürgerliche Wissenschaft als unfähig erwiesen hatte, aufzurollen und sie richtig zu lösen. Im Gegensatz zu den bürgerlichen Byzantinisten studieren die sowjetischen Historiker den Weisungen Stalins gemäss die byzantinische Geschichte als die Geschichte der werktätigen Massen, die Geschichte der Völker."
>
> "Die sowjetischen Byzantinisten und Slawisten führen einen entschlossenen Kampf gegen die reaktionären Konzeptionen ausländischer Historiker, die versuchen, die historische Rolle des Slawentums bei der Herausbildung der mittelalterlichen Gesellschaftsordnung herabzusetzen."
>
> "Die wichtigste Aufgabe, die vor den sowjetischen Byzantinisten steht, ist der unversöhnliche Kampf gegen die reaktionäre bürgerliche Ideologie der Byzantinisten Amerikas und Westeuropas."
>
> ". . . der erste Band des *Vizantijskij Vremennik*, der 1947 erschienen ist, liess diesen Geist unversöhnlichen Kampfes gegen die reaktionäre Byzantinistik des Auslandes noch vermissen. Statt scharfer, entlarvender Kritik wurden im ersten Bande der Zeitschrift kosmopolitische Ideen der friedlichen Zusammenarbeit mit den bürgerlichen Byzantinisten des Auslandes vertreten. Darüber hinaus wurde im Leitartikel der Redaktion die zutiefst falsche und zudem antipatriotische These von der Byzantinistik als einer 'weltweiten' Wissenschaft aufgestellt, wobei die sowjetischen Byzantinisten die Aufgabe

There is another factor that ought to make the East cautious when it seeks acculturation: the decline of the

---

hätten, in dieser 'weltweiten' Wissenschaft einen 'ehrenvollen Platz' einzunehmen."

"Indem der Materialist in der Wissenschaft den Standpunkt des Proletariats vertritt, vertritt er auch eine wirklich objektive Beurteilung der Ereignisse; denn die marxistisch-leninistische Wissenschaft ist als Wissenschaft der revolutionärsten Klasse die allein fortschrittliche, objektive Wissenschaft." (From M. W. Lewtschenko, "Gegen den bürgerlichen Kosmopolitismus in der sowjetischen Byzantinistik" [1949], trans. in Johs. Irmscher, ed., *Aus der Sowjetbyzantinistik. Eine Auswahl prinzipieller Beiträge* [Berlin, 1956], pp. 13-22, at pp. 13, 15, 16, 17, 19.)

By substituting, as one must, "Western" for "bürgerlich reaktionär," the denial of the claim to universal methodological validity of Occidental science comes out in bold relief. The political-psychological motivation of the statements is obvious; the patriotic *parti pris* places these expressions of Marxist-Leninist self-reconstructions unmistakably alongside the other nationalistic ones with which I am here concerned. That our examples could, in the nature of things, be drawn only from the literature of a very few national groups should not stand in the way of recognizing the phenomenon as universal within a certain political-psychological framework. It would be easy to add illustrations from the *indigenista* restyling of Mexican history, from what a number of African states are trying to do with their past, etc., etc. The pluralistic concept underlying such movements, as well as the outlook of Trubetzkoj, has been well expressed by Alioune Diop in *La conscience chrétienne et les nationalismes* (Paris, 1959), p. 227: "Les institutions politiques, les lois économiques, l'équilibre des cultures sur notre planète doivent conquérir leurs dimensions planétaires en se mettant au service du nombre et de la diversité des peuples. Le monde n'a pas vocation de vivre de la seule culture occidentale, sous la seule autorité de l'Occident. La diversité des génies et des initiatives servira la paix mieux que la seule puissance européenne." Mention must be made of the fully negative reaction to the West in the antiacculturation movements as represented, for example, in the so-called "Zionist" churches of the Bantu; as an isolated trait of this hue Nkwame Nkrumah's (the first prime minister of Ghana, born 1909) accusation of the anthropologist guilty of "scientific exploitation" of the native by means of applied anthropology is worth noting in a mentality not generally committed to an extreme "nativism." Cf. G. Balandier, "Contribution à une sociologie de la dépendance," *Cahiers internationaux de sociologie*, XII (1952), 37-69, at pp. 65, 67.

West has already begun. In support, there is the inevitable quotation from Spengler; there are references to the two world wars, to the Occident's worship of power, its pride, the excessive influence of women, and the imbalance that obtains between reason and heart, between the material and the spiritual.[50] The whole section sounds like a subdued echo of Herzen's passionate statement on the dying West when, in the wake of the failures of 1848, the Russian exile felt moved to exclaim: "What impotence to create, to organize! Everyone begins to realize the dull heaviness of life! All are tired, and everyone's life is deteriorating!" [51] This diagnosis of Europe, then at the height of a breath-taking rise, reflects the defensive yearnings of the Slavophile, even as Aḥmad Amīn's diagnosis, a century later, seems indicative of the condition of the physician rather than of the patient.

The great asset of the East, according to Aḥmad Amīn, and of Russia, according to the Slavophiles, is spirituality (*rūḥāniyya*), which is contrasted with the West's materialism—a traditional cliché which in Aḥmad Amīn may have received its special nuance from the distinction between *Kultur* and *Zivilisation* of which Spengler, with whom Amīn was acquainted, has made so much. If, however, we disregard this particular influence, we are back to Kireevskij and his criticism of European mentality, in which the analytic outlook and the scientific knowledge—which Kireevskij recognizes and admires precisely as do Amīn and his compatriots—fail to affect the inner man and which, with progress, has lost the essential meaning of life

---

[50] Amīn, *op. cit.*, pp. 35-44; on pp. 38-41 the author quotes from Maxim Gorki a list of scandalous *fait divers* which the Russian writer had culled from Western newspapers; this section is one of the few passages of Amīn's essay which are frankly propagandistic and almost touchingly naïve.

[51] From *Vom anderen Ufer* (1850) *in* Tschižewskij and Groh, *op. cit.*, p. 195. The complaint or diagnosis of the *Erschlaffung* of European political energy, and so forth, was already being heard in the Napoleonic period. Cf. W. von Humboldt (d. 1835), *Werke* (Darmstadt, 1960), I, 493-496, for discussion and refutation of this charge (written *ca.* 1800).

itself.[52] In any event, the Easterner is not to forget that only from the sixteenth century did the cleavage between the civilizational levels of Occident and Orient develop. The realization of this fact should remove any feeling of inferiority and, more important, should help the Easterner to understand that the truly great achievements of the West had been adumbrated in the East; thus, for instance, democracy had already been represented by political figures like the caliph ʿUmar II (717-720) or Nūr ad-Dīn Zangī (1146-1174).[53] Kireevskij is more cautious in making specific statements of this kind, which exhibit too clearly their arbitrary character; but he maintains emphatically the cultural equality between Russia and the West during

[52] In Tschiževskij and Groh, *op. cit.*, pp. 262, 252.

[53] Amīn, *op. cit.*, p. 55. The reference to Nūr ad-Dīn Zangī may be based on a passage like the following, which is taken from Abū Shāma (d. 1267), *Kitāb ar-rauḍatain*, ed. Barbier de Meynard (Paris, 1898-1906), I, 43. There Zangī is shown in 1159 soliciting the consent of the *ʿulamāʾ* for some legal action in these words: "wa-laisa al-ʿamal illā ʿalà tattafiquna ʿalaihi wa-tashhadūna bihi wa-ʿalà hādhā kāna ʾṣ-ṣaḥāba (riḍwān Allāh ʿalaihim) yajtamiʿūna wa-yatashāwarūna fī maṣāliḥ al-muslimīna" (i.e., no action will be taken unless you agree to it and bear witness to it; in this manner the Companions [of the Prophet] assembled and consulted on the concerns of the Muslims). The injunction to consult goes back to Koran 42:36, where God's reward is promised to "those who have responded to their Lord and established the prayer, their affair being matter of counsel amongst them (*wa-amru-hum shūrà baina-hum*), and from what We have provided them with, contribute." The phrase is often quoted, but its bearing is never precisely defined; at least one author, Qudāma b. Jaʿfar (d. *ca.* 948) cites Alexander the Great soliciting the advice of Aristotle in support of the scriptural command (cf. D. Sourdel, *Le Vizirat ʿabbāside de 749 à 936* [Damascus, 1959-1960], II, 712-713). In 128/745-746, an "arbitration court" decides to "depose Naṣr [b. Sayyār, the Umayyad governor of Khurāsān] *wa-yakūna ʾl-amr shūrà*," presumably to let future leadership be a matter of consultation, either in the sense of government by committee or of the next governor to be agreed upon in committee. The phrase as quoted from Ibn Kathīr, *al-Bidāya waʾn-nihāya* (Cairo, 1932-1939), X, 27[1], goes unmentioned in J. Wellhausen's presentation of the pertinent events, *The Arab Kingdom and Its Fall* (Calcutta, 1927), p. 486.

the first centuries of its history; afterward she was kept back by a number of secondary (*nebensächlich*) and accidental events which prevented her from transmitting to the present the fullness of her culture.[54]

Aḥmad Amīn's characterization of the East (and, by contrast, of the West as well)[55] perpetuates the peculiar romanticization of a painfully experienced backwardness which Kireevskij had used for the same purpose a century earlier. Thucydides knew that people would make their recollection fit in with their sufferings (ii, 54, 2-3). The similarity of the psychological situation accounts for parallelisms; the absence of any kind of literary contact need scarcely be emphasized. The East is the home of the great religions. The religious outlook prevents life and its content from being considered in terms of usefulness alone. The Easterner, in his actions, takes the next world into account. Owing to its more intense spirituality, the East has produced the greater saints. The West in its advances is solely motivated by the quest of profit. Were it otherwise, *rūḥāniyya* would make him forgo armaments.[56] Kireevskij is too subtle to allow himself naïve "party-line" statements of this kind. But the inspiration of the beautiful page on which he confronts Russian civilization with Western civilization is the same: "The theology in the West became abstract and rationalist; in the orthodox world it preserved its inner spiritual wholeness. There [i.e., in Europe] the split of the faculties of reason, here [i.e., in Russia] the striving after their living synthesis."[57]

---

[54] *Op. cit.*, p. 257. The whole passage, pp. 255-257, is very important in our context: revulsion from *Westlertum* and concentration on the study of Russian history into which the established principles of Russian life are read.

[55] *Op. cit.*, esp. pp. 157 ff.

[56] *Ibid.*, pp. 140-141.

[57] *Op. cit.*, pp. 293-294. K. Goldammer, *Der Mythus von Ost und West* (München and Basel, 1961), pp. 30-31 and 52-54, aptly speaks of a "negative myth" which in the East (Goldammer's illustrations are largely Japanese and Indian) "diffamiert denjenigen, von dem man entscheidende Anregungen für die

With all this, Aḥmad Amīn admits that Westernization is proceeding apace. Suddenly he reverses himself and expresses the hope that science and industry will rise in the East (but of course without the defects they exhibit in the West). He is at pains to refute those who claim that Western civilization is not transferable, and he encourages his people by insisting that their own heritage predisposes them to receive the new culture that the Occident has brought to them.[58]

---

eigene Kultur empfangen hat, ja ohne den das eigene staatliche, gesellschaftliche, wirtschaftliche und kulturelle Leben nicht mehr denkbar wäre. Es handelt sich hier allenthalben, wie einst bei Herodot, um *Bewusstseinsphänomene* [Goldammer's italics], die aus den geschichtlichen Gegebenheiten hervorgegangen sind und die dann irgendwie kolletiviert, zum Gemeinbesitz erhoben werden" (pp. 30-31).

[58] *Op. cit.*, pp. 156-164. The same demand for the restriction of borrowing to science and technology is voiced in Haikal, *Fī Manzal al-waḥy* (1936); an even more radical condemnation of the West was to be pronounced by Aḥmad Amīn in his *Yaum al-islām* (1952); cf. N. Safran, *Egypt in Search of Political Community* (Cambridge, Mass., 1961), pp. 226-228, for a brief analysis of this work. Even more radical and, in a sense, consistent, is the appeal of Frantz Fanon (d. 1961; a native of Martinique who identified with Algerian anticolonialism) to repudiate all cultural vestiges of a colonial legacy. The rejection of the West needs to be violent; only through revolution could the *colonisé* discover his identity. To reject the West implies rejection of the Western-educated élite. Cf. D. C. Gordon, *North Africa's French Legacy. 1954-1962* (Cambridge, Mass., 1962), p. 3 (summarizing Fanon, *Les damnés de la terre* [Paris, 1961]). What would appear to be a more realistic and consequently a more productive attitude has been formulated by Muḥammad an-Naqqāsh who, first of all, affirms his belief in the tendency to progress as a major characteristic of man and then finds the natural, the inevitable road of advancement in Occidentalization. Such Occidentalization is already very largely an accomplished fact. Western civilization, so called, is actually not a prerogative of a number of Occidental lands but a common possession of the European and the American continents (with some qualifications) and of a part of Asia. Now that the Arab has put behind him his national struggles, he is free to examine the various modes of life and make his choice. What this choice is to be cannot be in doubt. Besides, the leaven of Western civilization has long since penetrated Arab society; it is now a

The "tornness" of the Arab conservative could not have been exemplified more guilelessly.

---

matter of completing the work and of taking conscious stock of the process. "Les générations montantes ne croient pas aux demimesures; elles n'acceptent pas d'emprunter à la civilisation occidentale ce qui nous convient et de rejeter ce qui nous ne convient pas. Personnellement j'avoue n'éprouver aucune admiration pour le dicton japonais: 'Acquérir les sciences occidentales et les techniques occidentales, mais conserver le culte des ancêtres et les traditions des aïeux.' La civilisation est composée de matière et d'esprit: il faut que ces deux éléments s'unissent et marchent côte à côte. Si nous ne communions pas spirituellement et intellectuellement avec la civilisation occidentale, c'est-à-dire avec l'apogée de la civilisation humaine, dans laquelle nous avons, nous Arabes notre part: si nous nous contentons de lui emprunter ses réalisations matérielles, nous serons à l'image de l'âne chargé de livres . . . ; nous en resterons au stade de la copie et de l'imitation; nous ne le dépasserons pas pour atteindre les domaines de l'invention et de la découverte; nous ne rejoindrons pas le camp des créateurs" (translated from an article in *al-ᶜUlūm*, Feb., 1960, in *Orient*, XV [1960], 167-174; the quotation is taken from p. 174).

Readers of Ṭāhā Ḥusain's *Mustaqbal ath-thaqāfa* will find in Naqqāsh's statement not only the same commitment to Western Culture but also the same defensive note which today's atmosphere, even more unavoidably than that of the late 'thirties, would seem to impose on the "Westernizer." One wishes that Egypt would regain the assurance which animated a Luṭfī as-Sayyid that its spirit could never be lost through borrowing from the West, an assurance that need not necessarily lead back to the "Pharaonism" in vogue between *ca.* 1926 and 1936. For Luṭfī's position cf. Safran, *op. cit.*, pp. 95, 143-147, 177.

At one with an-Naqqāsh in his rejection of the "spiritualism vs. materialism" cliché is the Indonesian socialist Sjahrir (b. 1910), the first prime minister of the Republic of Indonesia. Sjahrir is also one of a group of "internationalist" Indonesians who have understood the essential characteristics and drives of the West without losing confidence in the cultural potential of their own background. The following statement by Sjahrir is taken from P. K. Auwjong, "Traditionalisten und Internationalisten unter den indonesischen Intellektuellen," *Saeculum*, X (1959), 329-359, on p. 351: "Der Westen bezeichnet für mich das brausende, vordringende Leben, das Dynamische. Er ist der 'Faust' den ich liebe, und ich bin überzeugt, dass nur der Westen, im Sinne dieser Dynamik, den Osten aus seiner Sklaverei befreien konnte. . . . Den Kampf lieben um des Kampfes willen, das hat Goethe uns gelehrt. . . . Wir wollen dieses

VI

It is perhaps to be regretted that Taufīq al-Ḥakīm (b. 1902)[59] chose to present his concept of the Occident and

---

Leben, dieses irdische Leben, zum höchsten und schönsten Zweck machen; das ist es, was der Westen uns gelehrt hat, und darum liebe ich den Westen, ungeachtet seiner Roheit, ungeachtet seiner Grobheit. . . . Selbst den Kapitalismus ziehe ich dabei jener hochgerühmten östlichen Weisheit und Religion vor. Denn gerade jene hochgerühmte östliche Weisheit und Religion versperrten uns die Einsicht, dass wir auf die niedrigste Stufe gesunken sind, wohin ein Mensch fallen kann: zur Sklaverei, zur ewigen Unterwerfung. Was wir am Westen bewundern und lieben, ist jene unzerstörbare Vitalität. . . . Es ist nicht so töricht, wenn man mich zuweilen einen halben Abendländer nennt und dass mir darum diejenigen, die von der östlichen Kultur schwärmen und den 'materialistischen' Westen ablehnen, misstrauen. Ich hasse in der Tat jenen Selbstbetrug, diese Feigheit, und statt dessen verlange ich die mutige Sehnsucht nach dem Leben, das der Westen geschaffen hat. Dies bedeutet keineswegs, dass ich den Westen idealisiere. Ich kenne seine ganze Fäulnis und Faulheit in der kapitalistischen Welt und auch in der Kultur. Aber trotzdem meine ich, die Vorzüge des Westens im Vergleich mit dem sogenannten 'Osten' würdigen zu können." Yet, the survey of Auwjong's leaves one with the impression that, as in China, a majority of Indonesian spokesmen prefer the flight into the vagueness and illusiveness of an indigenous tradition which receives body only from the political ambitions that it is to support and justify.

The receptivity to Western influences which goes hand in hand with defensive and chauvinistic rejection is not too remote from the attitudes dominating Germany in the eighteenth century. "The Germany of Goethe's age was open to every foreign idea, new or old, and interested itself in every accessible literature. . . . This open-mindedness was the obverse of the lack of a national style. It is not surprising that catholicity, inclusiveness, became an ideal and that the outstanding characteristic of Goethe himself is, to use the phrase of an English critic, quoted by Goethe with approval in his maxims, his 'panoramic ability.' It hardly needs to be stressed that this attitude did not stand in the way of the development of a German nation and a German national style, a fact which might recommend it to nations in search of themselves" (W. H. Bruford, *Germany in the Eighteenth Century: The Social Background of the Literary Revival* [Cambridge, Eng., 1935], pp. 304-305). If cosmopolitanism may be viewed, in part at least, as an escape from unsatisfactory poits influence on the East in the form of a novel. For even though *L'Oiseau d'Orient*[60] (written in 1937; published in Arabic in 1938) can hardly be considered a work of art, and merely provides the author with occasions for unrestrained speechmaking, the form of the novel relieves him of the obligation to adduce documentation. It is clear that Taufīq al-Ḥakīm is himself greatly affected by the West and, more particularly, by France. The area through which his hero, an Egyptian studying in Paris, specifically transcends his own background is music. Beethoven appears as the ultimate achievement, but Occidental music in general is something singular and unmatched in its sublimeness. The flimsy love story of the book is meant to parallel, through the unimaginative egotism of the girl, the thoughtless and egotistical self-assertiveness of Western civilization. By putting his critique of the West in the mouth of a self-exiled worker from Soviet Russia, the author suggests that he does not entirely identify with Ivanovitch's strictures of Europe nor with his dream image of the Orient. The underlying approach is that of a *philosophia perennis* finding expression through all prophets and all religions, yet distorted through ritualism and the formalistic mentality of all clergies. Faith is deplored as the lost paradise; the essential activism of Islam is stressed against the tempting confusion of otherworldliness with quietism.[61] There is no antagonism among the three great

---

litical conditions at home, its ultimate usefulness for purely national aims must yet be recognized.

[59] According to J. Landau, *Studies in the Arab Theater and Cinema* (Philadelphia, 1958), p. 138, Taufīq al-Ḥakīm was born in 1898.

[60] Tewfik el Hakim, *L'Oiseau d'Orient*, trans. from Arabic (Paris: Nouvelles éditions latines, 1960), 190 pp. The title in the original is *ʿUṣfūr min ash-sharq*.

[61] The theme of the activism of Islam in contrast to Christian quietism is frequently developed. Berque, *Les Arabes d'hier à demain*, p. 257, discusses the view of Dr. Kāmil Ḥusain that Christianity pays more attention to avoiding sin than to doing right, to fear of injustice than to love of justice, to forbidding evil than to commanding the good. In Islam, on the other hand, the fight against evil and the enjoining of positive action go to-

monotheistic religions; their differences are minor, not to say irrelevant: "Moses is the Ten Commandments; Jesus, idealism; Muḥammad, realism. . . . Nothing is total; everything completes everything else" (p. 164). Only the East has known pure science, that is, science for science's sake; the scientific gains of the West do not contribute to man's nobility and net him only illusory profits like speed and comfort, not to speak of their debauchment in the service of imperialism. Ivanovitch revels in man's inability to penetrate the ultimate secrets; he dies when trying to set out for the Orient and is thus spared, in the author's view, the final disappointment of having to realize that his Orient, land of faith and of the autonomy of the humane, does not exist. While the dying Russian submerges himself one last time in his dreams, for which the Orient serves as a stage, Mohsen silently comments on the degeneracy of the contemporary East and its irreversible commitment to Western ideas and ways. "Primary educa-

---

gether. Berque asks, pertinently, by what paradoxical reversal did Christianity lead its adherents to activism, expansion, and constructiveness, while Islam closed itself off through interiorization. The comparative characterization suggested by Nadjm oud-Dine Bammate would seem to come nearer to the Occidental as well as to the Oriental reality; it has the additional merit of making explicit not only the fact but the nature of that interiorization to which the Muslim aspires: "Le moi de l'Occidental est une arme qui lui assure une mainmise sur les choses. L'oriental traditionnel a la démarche inverse. Il abandonne les choses par un effort d'intériorisation du moi. Si l'aventure offerte à l'Occidental est celle du choix libre, créateur de formes et de faits, le destin à réaliser par l'Oriental est la libre consécration à l'Unique. Pour l'homme de la tradition, la personnalité vraie n'est pas un point de départ mais un point d'arrivée, qui s'atteint par une simplification de l'individu. Certes, il ne s'agit pas de faire de soi le plus irremplaçable des êtres, de sa vie une aventure originale, singulière. La grande entreprise est cette intériorisation qui dépouille l'homme de ses traits individuels, de ses tics, pour le rassembler sur sa réalité absolue qui est le réalité de son âme pour Dieu" (Nadjm oud-Dine Bammate, "La tradition musulmane devant le monde actuel," *Tradition et innovation. La querelle des Anciens et des Modernes dans le monde actuel. Rencontres Internationales de Genève,* XI [1956], 119-150, at pp. 126-127).

tion, universal suffrage, parliament, all the institutions of Europe appear today the summit of progress in the East, and the Orientals believe in this alleged civilization as in their own religion. . . . One could perhaps today tear from the mind of the East the idea of the greatness of heaven, but never would one succeed in taking from it the conviction of the greatness of the material forces of the modern world" (p. 187). The Oriental is more firmly convinced of the mission of European science than of that of the prophets; not even European self-criticism could shake this conviction. When they may choose between Gandhi and Mussolini, the youth of the East have no hesitation in opting for the dramatic virility of the dictator (an attitude that Taufīq al-Ḥakīm, profoundly hostile to oppression in any form, deeply deplores). But, in the last analysis, Mohsen dissociates himself from the Russian's desperate criticism. With all its defects, the Occident is not to be rejected, but is something to be added to the Oriental heritage. " 'Stripped of its arrogance and its manner of self-sufficiency and superiority, the civilization of the West will be the basis of what tomorrow will be called universal civilization; the civilization of man—without thought of our location on the globe—which will contain all that is beautiful, useful, and viable in East and West. For Orient and Occident are but two parts of one apple created to form a whole. Once united in this total civilization, man will see the day of definitive peace. But to arrive there the new civilization must neglect nothing, despise nothing. It must comprise all, develop all, understand all, learn all in a spirit of modesty, charity, and love.' It was with this hope that the young Oriental looked at the West and its future which, to him, represented at the same time the future of all mankind" (p. 189). If syncretism can ever be considered a constructive program, Taufīq al-Ḥakīm must be paid the tribute of having advocated it by way of a vision whose utopian blurredness is somewhat compensated by the factual perception of what Islam and Christianity do and ever did hold in common.

Superior to the *Bird of the East* as a work of literature,

Ṭāhā Ḥusain's *Adīb* has been translated into French under the expanded and somewhat misleading title, *Adib ou l'aventure occidentale*.[62] The hero, an official who obtains a fellowship to study at the Sorbonne, gifted, unstable, doomed to succumb to mental illness, is totally committed to the West long before he leaves Egypt. There is no analysis of the nature of that foreign civilization for which the hero (whose name, Adib, if indeed it is a name, meaning the cultured, represents a criticism as well as a proleptic characterization) so passionately yearns; it is presented in the richness of its learning, in the freedom of its atmosphere. Life in Egypt is likened to breathing the air in the innermost recesses of the Great Pyramid; life in the West, to inhaling the fresh air on returning to the outer world (p. 168). Civilization is French civilization; staying in Paris against the orders of the Egyptian University when the German attack threatens to engulf the city in the fall of 1914, our hero feels that the disaster of Paris and of France would be tantamount to the disaster of civilization itself (p. 173). At one point he blames some of his difficulties on the unmethodical character of Egyptian education (p. 186); but basically the nature of the West, its superior attraction, the necessity to appropriate its achievement, are taken for granted. What does give concern, primarily to the hero's family and, in fact, to his society as a whole, but to some extent to himself as well, is the conviction that the West represents a moral temptation to which the visitor from the East is bound to succumb. This temptation is seen as an undermining of faith and a destruction of the moral fiber. But in contrast to his parents, well-to-do landowners in Upper Egypt, our hero seems to welcome that temptation and prepares himself for yielding, an attitude that he justifies, or at least explains, in one of the best self-analytical passages of the book (pp. 111 ff.). The problem does not, however, seem to pertain to the West; it is seen as the personal and

[62] The Arabic original appeared in Cairo in 1938; the French translation, prepared by Amina and Moenis [sic] Taha-Hussein, was published in Cairo in 1960.

private concern of the Egyptian who exposes himself to that alien setting—"ce monde nouveau," to use the hero's phrase, "qui règne sans partage sur mon âme et mon coeur"—years before he is to set foot on French soil. This uncontrollable longing for what at times is described as physical and intellectual expatriation induces the hero to divorce his gentle but illiterate wife so as to meet the university regulation that bars the married from receiving the fellowship. His lack of discipline deprives him and his country of the fruits of his study; he fails his examination a short while before the conflicting inner pressures, combined with that complete physical exhaustion of which they are the ultimate cause, drive him from the world of the sane and into death in a welter of painful delusions. The reader learns next to nothing of Ṭāhā Ḥusain's vision of the West; but he is compensated by occasional psychological insights and the poignant beauty with which they are proffered.[63]

VII

In contrast to a writer like Aḥmad Amīn there are a few for whom acculturation, at least in a personal sense, does not exist as a problem because it has been accomplished without leaving a break, or even a sensitive spot, in their work.[64] The Egyptian (Copt) Bishr Farès (Fāris; b. 1906)

[63] Despairing of explaining to his wife the reasons that have led him to repudiate her, Adib exclaims: "Dieu a voulu que les hommes ne se comprennent pas et qu'entre eux se dressent des murs infranchissables. Ils vivent, agissent et sont persuadés qu'ils sont ensemble et qu'ils se prêtent mutuellement secours contre la vie; en fait, chacun de nous habite une tour d'ivoire, nous ne voyons personne et personne ne nous voit" (p. 120).

[64] A very dramatic description of the dual personality of the Iraqi, the *Zwiespältigkeit* of his assumptions, reactions, and aspirations, was presented in 1951 by ʿAlī Ḥasan al-Wardī (trans. in G. Krotkoff, "Die Persönlichkeit des Irakers. Ein Beitrag zur Sozialpsychologie," *Bustan*, no. 1 [1961], pp. 7-11). The most gripping expression of the dividedness, not of loyalty, but of being itself, is the Algerian Malek Haddad's poem "La longue

may be placed in this group, although his first book, *L'Honneur chez les Arabes avant l'Islam* (1932), still exhibits some traits of the apologia.[65] The classic representative, however, is the Tunisian Maḥmūd al-Masʿadī (Messadi; b. 1911), in whom the French (or perhaps the European) and the Arab tradition appear flawlessly blended. Not syncretism, not search for reconciliation and compromise, but a natural synthesis as convincing as life

---

marche," which begins with the words: "Je suis le point final d'un roman qui commence . . ." (cf. M. Haddad [b. 1927], *Le Malheur en danger* [Paris, 1956], pp. 25-28). At the Congress of Afro-Asian Writers in Tokyo, March 1961, and again in Beirut on June 16, 1961, M. Haddad attacked the French for not unsuccessfully attracting the Algerians to their culture. Falling in with what has been termed "oppression culturelle" he speaks of the Algerian situation as of "the most perfidious case of depersonalization in history." Cf. Gordon, *op. cit.*, pp. 36 and 103-104. The hero of Henri Kréa's (b. 1933) novel *Djamal* (Paris, 1961), like the author the offspring of a mixed Franco-Arab marriage, finds himself driven to identify with the Algerian revolutionaries, being unable to support any longer his position at the edge of "European" society. Is it to read too much into the (rather uneven) book if one senses that *Djamal* will be the victim of another kind of *aliénation* in an independent Algeria? M. Haddad's *L'élève et la leçon* (Paris, 1960), incidentally one of the best novels yet written by a Muslim North African, brings to life, on pp. 144-45, one of the standard complaints of the Algerian Muslim intelligentsia, the foistening on them of a totally French-oriented vision of history.

[65] We owe to Dr. Farès a very perceptive (though fortunately no longer so painfully correct) analysis, "Des difficultés d'ordre linguistique, culturel et social que rencontre un écrivain arabe moderne, spécialement en Égypte," *Revue des études musulmanes* (1936), pp. 221-246. In 1927 M. H. Haikal described with especial finesse the lag between the Arab writer's increase in differentiated sensibility and the availability of adequate means of articulating his experience in his mother tongue in a brief paragraph; the passage, to which Miss C. F. Audebert, research assistant in the Near Eastern Center, UCLA, has drawn my attention, is quoted in H. A. R. Gibb, "Studies in Contemporary Arabic Literature, Part III," *Bulletin of the School of Oriental and African Studies*, University of London, V (1928-1930), 445-466, at p. 451 n. 1.

itself. One may differ in the evaluation of his intricately symbolistic writings—the drama, *as-Sudd* (*The Dam*); the novel, *Maulid an-nisyān* (*The Birth of Forgetfulness,* 1944); the brief tales united under the title *al-Aḥādīth* (*Les Propos,* 1945)—but it remains indisputable that their spirit is a novel crystallization of the Arab and the Western literary and philosophical traditions, and that the Arab component, for its part, reflects the classical heritage in form without excluding ideas and motifs from the popular sphere.

The heroic failure of Ghailān, the dam builder, evokes the climate of Greek tragedy. In contrast with the Muslim religious tradition, man is sufficiently important to be shown in his fight against destiny. *Maulid an-nisyān* could not have been written without the French medieval epics, especially *Tristan et Yseult;* at the same time its principal theme, embracing Madian's search for forgetfulness, his obsession with death, and his strange relationship with Laila and her jealousy of the past, presupposes Rilke and Thomas Mann. The style of the book, however, is Arabic at its most classical; that is to say, it is not the terse Arabic of the pre-Islamic narrative but the more subtly inflected language of the tenth century. The magic and the marvel of medieval Baghdad blend with the magic of medieval Brittany. The existential anguish of a Sartre and a Camus, the aestheticism of Baudelaire and Valéry, Rilke's and Thomas Mann's concern for suffering and decomposition, come to life through a style, an imagery, an invention of detail which are purely Arab, not perhaps in the sense in which the writers of the "golden prime" would have understood it, but as a development of unused potentialities which, before Masʿadī, one should hardly have suspected were waiting in the prose of caliphal Baghdad. And then there is the effortless blending of the Hellenic and the French (as in Valéry) with the ancient Arabic anecdotes and *akhbār* in the *vignettes* of the *Aḥādīth,* which exhibit a mastery of phantasmagory not previously met with in Arab literature and yet displayed as if fantasy had always been securely located in the Arab tradition.[66]

VIII

The very ease and the very perfection with which acculturation has come to pass in Masᶜadī's development, and

[66] On M. Messadi cf. M. Ferid-Ghazi, "La littérature tunisienne contemporaine," *Orient,* XII (1959), 131-197, esp. pp. 134-143; on pp. 157-163 a few scenes from *as-Sudd* are given in translation. Selections from *as-Sudd* (written in 1940; published only in 1955) in text and translation have been included in V. Monteil, *Anthologie bilingue de la littérature arabe contemporaine* (Beirut, 1961), pp. 241-255, and, in translation alone, in W. Plum, *Algerische Dichtung der Gegenwart* (Nürnberg, 1959), pp. 32-36. In Masᶜadī's work certain sections of the Arab-Muslim background and the Western background have become united to the same extent as, in the literatures of western Europe, the heroes of Shakespeare and of Homer have, as it were, coalesced, that is to say, have become points of reference familiarity with which may be taken for granted. Giosuè Carducci (d. 1907), in his "Presso l'urna di Percy Bysshe Shelley," *Odi barbare,* XLVIII, 11-30, brings together in the land of the departed the great creations of Greek and English poetry which have become part and parcel of all western literary tooling. Sir H. J. C. Grierson, *The Background of English Literature* (London, 1960; first published in 1915), p. 29 n. 1, refers to the poem in describing "the most permanent literary vistas on which the windows of English literature look out." Another kind of integration through a particularism common to French and Arab writers in north Africa is suggested by a remark of Mouloud Feraoun's (born 1913): "Je ne songe nullement à un nationalisme ou à un régionalisme étroits; l'essentiel pour moi est de trouver dans les oeuvres de Nord-Africains des êtres de chair et de sang tels que je les vois autour de moi. Ils peuvent s'appeler Rieux ou Smaïl, cela me fait également plaisir parce qu'*ils sont de chez moi.* Et je me dis que les gens de chez nous ne sont plus absents de la littérature" (quoted by A. Dupuy, *L'Algérie dans les lettres d'expression française* [Paris, 1956], p. 157 n. 2). Gordon, *op. cit.,* p. 30, quotes from an interview with Camus (d. 1960) of November 28, 1957, an expression of the same attitude. "I would like to recall that there was once a community of Algerian writers, French and Arab. For the moment this community is cut in two. But men such as Feraoun, Mammeri, Chraibi, Dib, and so many others have taken their place among European writers. No matter what the future may be, no matter how hopeless it may look, I am sure that this will not be forgotten."

perhaps also the extreme individualism of his writings, have kept him from dealing with acculturation explicitly as a personal or a collective problem. In fact, the only "Arabic" *romancier* who has made acculturation the dominant theme of a major work is the French-writing Moroccan, Driss Chraibi (b. 1926).

The strength of *Le Passé simple* lies in the description of the Muslim milieu; the weakness, in the shadowy haze of the Occidental atmosphere. The latter seems to be taken for granted; it certainly is presupposed as known by the reader. When the hero, or rather the narrator and protagonist—for with all the shrewdness of his self-analysis and his drastic revolt against his father, Driss Ferdi is a somewhat sorry and unquestionably a sterile and petty specimen—is allowed to enter the *lycée*, Haj Fatmi realizes that he will henceforth have an enemy in his house. He accepts the situation, however, in the interest of perpetuating his own position in the Moroccan business (and political) community, which he is convinced will require bicultural, French-educated leadership.

Nothing is said to cast a light on the author's concept of the Occident. The rich French of the book, its unsought allusions to the French cultural background, and the obvious influence of the French existentialist novel of the 'forties bespeak the author's familiarity with the West as represented by France, and bear witness to the ease with which he moves in the French intellectual milieu. This habitus which his (we should hope somewhat distorted) mirror image, Driss Ferdi, shares without much reflection is not seen as a problem. When his French friends fail to give him support in a crisis, which, incidentally, is largely of his own making, they do so not because of any sense of national, racial, or cultural *apartheid*, but solely in response to pressure, not to say blackmail, on the part of his ruthlessly insistent father. Such *apartheid* may exist; in fact, the prejudice against the *bicot* makes its appearance every now and then, but it remains a very minor factor and contributes little to the formation or even the psychological discomfort of Driss.

His problem is the Muslim milieu: Muslim intellectuality, Muslim piety, and above all, the patriarchal Muslim family. His father's barbarous tyranny; the blending in Haj Fatmi of a religious behavior of extreme formal correctness with an equally extreme cruelty in his human relationships and amorality in his business relationships; the reactions to the exigencies of this setting on the part of his mother and his brothers, exacerbated by Driss's obtuseness with regard to his father's true aims—which are indeed merely facets of an uninhibited drive for self-aggrandizement, but a drive of which Driss is the intended beneficiary—these are the ingredients of his existence which drive him to rebellion and with which, in the last analysis, he can cope only through evasion: first, by leaving his home in an attempt to break away, which collapses, and then by allowing himself to be sent to Paris by his father where, at the end of the novel, he plans to "forge himself arms" for a more effective revolt, while Haj Fatmi expects him to complete his preparation to step into his own shoes when the time comes.

The father, strong, single-minded, invincible in his conviction that he leads and upholds the life that God has prescribed for the true believer, secure in the correctness of his formal relationship to the religious law, and untroubled by moral considerations; the father, whom his sons think and speak of as the Lord and whose remoteness tortures and crushes them, is the real hero of the book; and the book fails when the author exceeds the modern novel's requirement of individuation by lending Haj Fatmi a variety of vices and involving him in business intrigues which degrade him into a "case" and diminish the significance of the milieu portrayal. This effect is clearly contrary to Chraibi's intent, for he proposes to emphasize a necessary or, at least, an organic connection between the rigid legalism of the Haj and the unconcern with which he crosses the border line of dissipation and crookedness.

The immorality of the Haj is, for the reader, easier to bear than the fanatical egotism of the son. Driss exhibits the brutality of the weak, the apodictic views of those who are uncertain, the romantic's implicit approval of anything done on genuine impulse, the aimless sophistication of the "half-baked" genius. By portraying him in this fashion Chraibi has made it possible to put into his mouth an uninhibited, but for this not necessarily adequate, diagnosis of the kind of Islam within which he grew up. Writing in an examination paper, whose questions he has changed to suit his mood, Driss characterizes the five basic commandments of his religion. As regards the "profession of faith" (*shahāda*):

> . . . everyone believes in God even though the "average Moroccan" does not respect the corollaries: one may swear and perjure oneself, lie, commit adultery, drink. But the faith is safe and God is very powerful and very merciful. As regards the prayers, only the aged perform them. And even with them praying is mostly a habit or a show. So that anyone who believes in God, fasts during Ramadan, keeps away from wine and pork, prays five times a day, and is hard up is almost automatically labeled a saint, provided he is of a certain age, carries around his neck a sufficiently heavy rosary, and features a rich beard. My grandfather has posthumously become a saint because he was poor, pious, and deranged.

After a few pages in this style Driss concludes: "Man proposes and time disposes, but not a single shoeshine boy of the Medina [the Muslim quarter] would admit this; and here lies the strength of Islam." [67] Acculturation will remain the fate or the accomplishment of the few—the mass has not been touched by almost fifty years of *la présence française*—and what is more, the French attempt assimilation more out of a sense of duty than from faith. "An old bigwig from among my friends, Raymond Roche by name, told me last night, 'We French are in the process of civilizing you Arabs. Badly, in bad faith, and without any pleasure. If by chance you arrive at being our equals: in relation to whom or to what will *we* then be civilized?' " [68]

---

[67] *Le Passé simple*, pp. 198-201.
[68] *Ibid.*, p. 197.

Much more clearly and in fuller awareness of its ramifications, the acculturation problem has been seen (but not resolved) by a Tunisian writer, Albert Memmi (b. 1920), who does not, strictly speaking, qualify for consideration in our context because he is not an Arab, but a member of his country's Jewish community. Yet his two novels, *La statue de sel* (1953) and *Agar* (1955), must be mentioned. It is not their unusual literary qualities that necessitate their inclusion but the manner, unsurpassed to my knowledge, in which the three-pronged acculturation problem of the Tunisian *Israélite* has been understood and brought to life. Uneasy in his attitude toward his own community, fascinated by Western civilization, and confronted by Tunisian Islam, itself in the throes of an assimilative movement, Alexandre Mordekhai Benillouche, after finding a modus vivendi allowing him to "Occidentalize" while remaining actively loyal to the Jewish society around him, is confronted with the refusal of the French to accept him on equal terms. True, their refusal is in large measure dictated by the political circumstances of the Fascist-Nazi era and the German occupation; after the occupation ends Benillouche is in fact encouraged to resume his academic work, and he can be certain, on passing his *agrégation*, of obtaining a position in the French system. But he finds it impossible to agree to "limited acceptance," as impossible as returning to the cultural environment of his childhood, or as a utopian integration in the Arab-Muslim world. He evades the issue by deliberately failing his examination and emigrating to Argentina—a decision that can be viewed only as an awkward postponement of the great choice. For in Argentina Benillouche will no doubt find it even more difficult to realize his identification, and we are left with the impression that his departure from Tunis and the area of French civilization is nothing but a symbolic gesture of defiance and resignation. In real life, Memmi has carried "l'aventure de la connaissance occidentale" to a more consistent conclusion by completing his studies and accepting a position with the Centre National des Recherches Scientifiques.

Memmi's second "acculturation novel' is in a sense a reversal of the first. It describes the attempt of the French-Catholic wife of an acculturated Tunisian Jew to find her place in her husband's society. The attempt fails, and the reader is left with the painful impression that what Memmi describes is not a "case" but the ineluctable result of a social constellation. Memmi's artistry is apt to obscure this verdict because he succeeds in personalizing the problem to the extent that one is hardly aware of it in the abstract, but follows with ever-deepening participation the fate of the characters.[69]

La terre et le sang (1953) by the Algerian Mouloud

---

[69] On Memmi cf. A. Dupuy, *La Tunisie dans les lettres d'expression française* (Paris, 1956), pp. 101-103, 128-131. *Agar* was translated into English by B. Rhys under the title *Strangers* (New York, 1960). On the whole, the *nahḍa* among the North African Muslims has been more effective in their French than in their Arab production; consequently, their French contribution to world literature is more significant than what *maghribī* authors have accomplished in Arabic. This judgment is easily substantiated by contrasting the listings of Arabic works owed to north African Muslim authors in H. Pérès, "Quelques Aspects de la renaissance intellectuelle au XXᵉ siècle en Afrique du Nord," *La Table Ronde*, no. 126 (June, 1958), pp. 161-172 (where further bibliographical references regarding the period between the two world wars may be found), and in J. Dejeux, *Regards sur la littérature maghrébine d'expression française*, Études sociales nord-africaines, no. 61 (Oct.-Nov., 1957). In this instance the realization of a cultural individuality is stimulated rather than impeded by the adoption of a more suitably perfected tool, the French language, and the technical and intellectual association supporting it. François Bondy has raised the question whether the symbiosis between North African literature and French language is to be considered a survival or a promise. In Egypt, the decline of French influence was accompanied by a decline in local creative writing. It is difficult to foretell whether the North African states will go on to great national literatures or whether they are just now passing through their literary golden age. Cf. *Das Sandkorn und andere Erzählungen aus Nordafrika*, ed. F. Bondy (Zürich, 1962), pp. 23-24.

Feraoun (b. 1913) would tend to suggest the opposite lesson, as it depicts the process by which another French-Catholic woman manages to take root and to win acceptance in the Kabylian mountain village that is the home of her Berber *fellāḥ* husband. But the story of Marie in Ighil-Nezman is indeed a "case"; it is true, her problem is one of acculturation, but in terms of the concerns of the Arabic- or Berber-speaking world it is atypical.

IX

Acculturation, Westernization, the cultural identification of the Arab, and more particularly of the Muslim Arab, are only in the process of becoming topics for literary analysis. Only where Westernization has been largely experienced and reacted to can the Arabs reach the degree of self-consciousness which is the prerequisite for examining, in a work of art, the interplay of the contending and blending social "personalities." The artist need not necessarily give form to his insights through invented characters and invented occurrences. Thinly disguised self-images though they may be, Driss Ferdi and Benillouche yet have an existence other than and apart from that of their creators. It is worthy of notice, as an indication of the level of self-penetration to which, at this moment in their history, the Arab intelligentsia has fought through, that such memoirs or autobiographies as have been left by Muslim Arab writers—I am thinking, for example, of Aḥmad Amīn's *Ḥayātī* (1950) and Muḥammad Ḥusain Haikal's (1888-1956) *Mudhakkirāt* (1951-1953), to which the *Tarbiyat Salāma Mūsà* (1948) may be added as the statement of a Coptic writer—are not essentially concerned with the culture conflict springing from contact with the West. The dominant culture conflict of their lives is between traditional Islam and "modernism," as mirrored inimitably in Ṭāhā Ḥusain's *al-Ayyām* (1926 and 1939).[70]

[70] Comparable to *al-Ayyām* in interest and literary freshness, but inferior because of its all too obvious surrender to the exigencies of Soviet "socialist realism," is the Tajik Sadriddine

Is it a matter of phrasing, or of a permanently different orientation of the individual to himself and his society, which has so far deprived the Arab world of works like Nehru's *Autobiography* (1936) or, more characteristic still, the *Autobiography of an Unknown Indian* (1951) by the Bengali Nirad C. Chaudhuri (b. 1898)? Nehru, and especially Chaudhuri, who has no political public to hold, know who they are and how they have, as it were, acquired their present selves. Neither obscures his psychological finesse by literary mannerisms;[71] Chaudhuri refrains

---

Aïni's (1878-1953) *Boukhara* (French trans.; Paris, 1956). The weakness inherent in a *littérature engagée*, primarily the sacrifice of validity to the supposed political requirements of the moment, tending to transform, or degrade, the work of art, the human statement, to an Exhibit A, have been suggestively touched upon by Dejeux, *op. cit.*; see esp. pp. 21-23 (in connection with the polemic over Mouloud Mammeri's [b. 1917] *La Colline oubliée* [1952]), and pp. 89-92 (apropos of certain north African reactions to Chraibi's *Passé simple* and the novelist's "reintegration" in the front of the Algerian revolutionaries in France). Salāma Mūsà's statement on himself is interesting above all because it shows his development into "a European by thought and inclination," who feels that France is "the home of every civilized human being who has embraced her culture"; he rejects Arab literature and the Arab tradition as insufficient, useless, and shackling, but turns his own modernized self into a fighter against that Europe and its cultural forces which hold his homeland in subjection (cf. *Tarbiya, passim,* but esp. pp. 55-56, 78, 114-115, 173 ff., 242 ff.; trans. Schuman, pp. 39, 59, 80, 123 ff., 175 ff.). A number of autobiographical works have been listed and very briefly characterized by A. G. Chejne, "Autobiography and Memoirs in Modern Arab Historiography," *Muslim World,* LII (1962), 31-38 (where, incidentally, Haikal's *Memoirs* are not mentioned).

[71] This is not, of course, to overlook the presence of "self-stylization" in many statements made by Indian intellectuals about themselves; for examples see E. Shils, "The Culture of the Indian Intellectual," *The Sewanee Review* (April and July, 1959), reprinted as a brochure in the Reprint Series of the Committee on South Asian Studies, University of Chicago (1959; 46 pp.). (The fuller treatment in Shils's book, *The Intellectual between Tradition and Modernity: The Indian Situation* [The Hague, 1961] became available only after the present study had gone to the printer.) When the acculturation problem of Indian and Arab is considered, it must be remembered that

completely from pleading a cause or preaching a gospel. Both are aware that their society is in transition and that, in a sense, they are walking on quicksand. Yet they are certain of their identity, certain also of its elements, their origin and growth, and of the aspirations that give them cohesiveness and unity. Could it be that a touch of doubt about their cultural identity is still preventing the Arabs from realizing the collective self-perception, the analytical plausibility of the Indians, whose sensibilities, too, had been sharpened by a confrontation with the West?

---

actually the individual is faced with three "options": the indigenous tradition, the modernized indigenous tradition (in varying stages of modernization and Westernization), and the Western tradition (again in varying forms and types). Remarkable also, on the Indo-Muslim side, is the self-view or self-stylization of Sir Muḥammad Iqbāl (1876-1938) in his *Payām-i Mashriq* (first published in 1924); he sees himself in this work as the Oriental counterpart to Goethe and is able, altogether, to analyze and correlate personal and cultural traits and developments without, incidentally, forsaking the inherited symbolism of Persian mysticism. Cf. esp. the preface and the dedicatory poem to King Amānullāh of Afghanistan (1919-1933), now easily accessible in the translation by E. Meyerovitch and M. Achena, *Message de l'Orient* (Paris, 1956), pp. 19 ff., 31 ff.

INDEX

G. E. VON GRUNEBAUM, Professor of History and Director of the Near Eastern Center at the University of California, Los Angeles, has previously been with the University of Chicago and, as Visiting Professor, the University of Frankfurt. He has taken part in many, and presided over some international conferences in the field of Islamic Studies, and he headed the delegation of the University of California to the XXVth International Congress of Orientalists in Moscow. He is the general editor of an extensive series on the Near East (German and English), *Bibliothek des Morgenlandes*. His numerous books and articles—among them *Medieval Islam: A Study in Cultural Orientation* and *Islam: Essays in the Nature and Growth of a Cultural Tradition*—have been translated into languages as far apart as French and Bengali. He is a Fellow of the American Academy of Arts and Sciences; a Foreign Fellow of the Accademia Nazionale dei Lincei, Rome; and an Honorary Associate of the Islamic Research Association, Bombay.

THE TEXT of this book was set in *Electra*, a Linotype face designed by W. A. Dwiggins. This face cannot be classified as modern or oldstyle. It is not based on any historical model, nor does it echo any particular period or style. It avoids the extreme contrast between thick and thin elements that marks most modern faces, and attempts to give a feeling of fluidity, power, and speed. Composed, printed, and bound by THE COLONIAL PRESS INC., Clinton, Massachusetts.